Webster's Dictionary Game

Wilbur Webster

Meadowbrook
Distributed by Simon & Schuster
New York

Library of Congress Cataloging-in-Publication Data

Webster, Wilbur.
  Webster's dictionary game.

  1. Word games. 2. English language — Glossaries, vocabularies, etc.
I. Title. II. Title: Dictionary game.
GV1507.W8W43   1987   793.73   87-5727
ISBN 0-88166-091-4
ISBN 0-671-64172-7 (Simon & Schuster)

Published by Meadowbrook, Inc., 18318 Minnetonka Boulevard, Deephaven,
MN, 55391. Book Trade Distribution by Simon and Schuster, a division of
Simon & Schuster, Inc., 1230 Avenue of the Americas, New York, NY 10020.

S&S Ordering#: 0-671-64172-7

10 9 8 7 6 5 4 3 2 1

Printed in the United States of America.

Editor: Bruce Lansky
Copyeditor: Barbara K. Bergstrom
Writer/Researchers: Barbara K. Bergstrom, Lana Harris, Kate Ryan
Art Director: Mary Foster
Design: Jill Rogers
Cover Design: Mary Foster
Production: Nanci Stoddard

Introduction

As far as the Websters are concerned, I'm the black sheep of the family. It wasn't because I went to Yale instead of Harvard, or majored in drama instead of English literature. It goes way back to a vocabulary test I flunked in the ninth grade at Exeter. Instead of writing down the correct definitions, I made up my own, just for fun.

My family wasn't as shocked by my first "F" as they were by what happened next. Wishing to make an example of me, my English teacher, Mr. Ephraim Crane, read my definitions aloud. Instant bedlam! Some of my classmates laughed till they cried. Some fell out of their chairs. And little Billy Cantwell wet his pants and didn't move from behind his desk until everyone else had left the classroom.

At school I basked in the glow of my newfound reputation as a comic. My grandparents, Noah and Miriam, publishers of the original Webster's Dictionary, considered my behavior heretical. But that wasn't the reason they didn't invite me into the family publishing firm after I graduated from college.

The real reason was I invented a game that had its roots in my prep school vocabulary test fiasco. Armed with a Webster's Dictionary, pencils, paper, and enough wine to keep the proceedings properly lubricated, friends and I would play a game we called "The Dictionary Game" or "Dictionary" for short.

We'd take turns looking up obscure words whose definitions no one knew. Then the other players would make up definitions that sounded plausible, write them down on a piece of paper, and hand them to the player with the dictionary (who would also write down the correct definition on a piece of paper). He would read all the definitions, amid gales of laughter, and we'd try to guess the correct one. We'd give a point to anyone who guessed the correct definition and a point for every vote a made-up definition received. And, we'd give the player with the dictionary (whom we called "Webster") a point for every vote the real definition did not get, as a reward for finding a particularly difficult and deceptive word. Sometimes we'd even award a point for the funniest definition.

When we played Dictionary, the laughter could be heard all over the dorm. Pretty soon word got out that playing Dictionary was the most fun a group of people could have while sober. The game spread through the Ivy League and eventually became established as one of the most popular games on college campuses throughout the U.S., Canada, and Great Britain.

My family should have thanked me for inventing this game. I'd guess that over the years several million dictionaries have been purchased by Dictionary Game players.

But because they never thanked me, I decided to create a special dictionary for Dictionary Game players. One that would have thousands of weird and wonderful words whose definitions they couldn't recognize or guess. That way, it wouldn't take much time to find a stumper. (With a standard college dictionary, it can take five or ten minutes to find a suitably esoteric word.) And, of course, I included complete rules, etiquette, and scoring information . . . to make the game go a lot more smoothly. (One of the problems is that the game is so inherently funny, laughing at the wrong time can introduce an element of unfairness.)

I've created this book in the same spirit that I flunked that vocabulary test back in prep school: for fun! If you enjoy playing Dictionary, this book will make it a lot easier and a lot more fun. If you've never played Dictionary before, you're in for a treat. I bet you'll agree it's the most hilarious word game you've ever played. And, if you're fascinated by words, I think you'll find this to be one of the most interesting and entertaining collections of words ever assembled.

Wilbur Webster, April 1, 1895

Publisher's Note

Wilbur Webster's manuscript was completed in 1895 and submitted to a number of publishing houses in New York. Unfortunately for Wilbur, no publisher would even consider it. Apparently, no publisher wanted to risk offending the Webster family.

Wilbur gave up the project and pursued a career in advertising, much to the further chagrin of his family. He enjoyed a successful career as a copywriter for one of the most widely distributed books of all time: the Sears Catalog.

I acquired Webster's manuscript for publication by Meadowbrook Press last year. A man who claimed to be Wilbur Webster III contacted me with a "manuscript of great antiquity and great value." Young Wilbur, it seems, had inherited the manuscript from his grandfather's estate and was celebrating his grandfather's birthday by submitting it to another publisher.

Because Meadowbrook Press operates in Minneapolis, outside the orbit of New York publishers who might be concerned about any possible controversy surrounding the black sheep of the Webster family, I agreed to publish an updated version of the manuscript. Although I have never been able to authenticate the origin of the manuscript as described in the Introduction, it seemed to me that the story was quite fascinating, if not altogether true in every respect.

Bruce Lansky, January 19, 1987

Publisher, Meadowbrook, Inc.

Webster's Dictionary Game

Rules

Webster's Dictionary Game is a unique form of entertainment for family and friends because it stimulates both your gray matter and your funny bone. In the process of playing it, you'll exercise your creativity and, as a bonus, expand your knowledge of esoteric words that will astound your friends and confound your enemies.

Number of Players

Four to twenty people can play Webster's Dictionary Game at one time. Individual competition works best for four to nine players. Ten to twenty people can play by dividing into four or more small teams or two large teams that compete against each other.

Terms

Webster: A player who selects an unfamiliar word from Webster's Dictionary Game book in the hope that none of the other players will be able to guess the real definition. WEBSTER scores points when the other players cannot guess the real definition. WEBSTER is also responsible for keeping score. Each player serves as WEBSTER for one round.

Bluffer: A player who creates a fake, but believable, definition in the hope that other players will mistake it for the real definition. BLUFFERS also try to guess the real definition. BLUFFERS score points when other players "vote for" their definition as the real one and when they guess the real definition themselves.

Equipment

Webster's Dictionary Game Book: This unique book contains a dictionary with more than 5,000 unusual and unfamiliar words and their surprising definitions. This dictionary makes it easy to find difficult words quickly to enhance your enjoyment of Webster's Dictionary Game.

The Definition Sheet: BLUFFERS create a definition and write it on a Definition Sheet, initial it, and submit it to WEBSTER. Use the design (see page 217) to create your own Definition Sheets on 3" x 5" cards or small sheets of paper.

The Ballot: BLUFFERS use the Ballots to take notes on the definitions as they are read and to vote for the definition they believe to be the real one. Use the design (see page 217) to create your own Ballots on 3" x 5" cards or small sheets of paper.

The Score Sheet: WEBSTER counts points scored by the players and writes them on the Score Sheet. Use the design (see page 216) to create your own Score Sheet on a piece of paper.

Playing the Game
Individual Competition

1. Equip each player with a supply of Definition Sheets and Ballots and a pencil or pen.
2. Each player has one turn per round as WEBSTER. Choose one player to be the first WEBSTER.
3. Before the start of play, all competitors should decide whether they want to adopt recreational or tournament rules regarding WEBSTER'S selection of a word.
   a. Recreational Rule: If any BLUFFER knows the meaning of the word selected by WEBSTER, he should announce this fact immediately. WEBSTER will then select a new word.
   b. Tournament Rule: If any BLUFFER knows the meaning of the word selected by WEBSTER, that is to his or her advantage. There is no need to disclose one's familiarity with the word.
4. WEBSTER selects a word from the Webster's Dictionary Game book and reads it to the BLUFFERS. WEBSTER then writes the word's real definition on a Definition Sheet.
5. After hearing WEBSTER'S selected word, each BLUFFER creates a fake, but believable, definition for it and writes it on his or her Definition Sheet. BLUFFERS then initial their own Definition Sheets and pass them to WEBSTER.

6. WEBSTER makes sure that all the BLUFFERS' Definition Sheets are legible and identified by initials. WEBSTER numbers all the Definition Sheets, including the real one (prepared by WEBSTER), and shuffles them all together.
7. WEBSTER reads each definition aloud once, to familiarize the BLUFFERS with them all. WEBSTER then reads the definitions a second time in the same order and asks the BLUFFERS to guess the one they believe is the real definition.
8. BLUFFERS make notes on their Ballots as WEBSTER reads the definitions. When the BLUFFERS have heard all the definitions twice, they indicate their guess by "voting" for the real definition on their Ballots. They then initial their individual sheets, and submit the Ballots to WEBSTER. BLUFFERS may *not* vote for their own definitions.
9. When all votes have been collected, WEBSTER reads each fake definition, citing its author and the BLUFFERS who voted for it. WEBSTER then reveals the word's real definition and the BLUFFERS who chose it. (If the players have decided to award points for the funniest definitions, WEBSTER should poll all players at this time.)
10. After calculating the points scored and totaling each BLUFFER'S score on the Score Sheet, WEBSTER passes the Webster's Dictionary Game book and the Score Sheet to the player on the left, who becomes the new WEBSTER.
11. Play continues until each player has had a turn as WEBSTER (one round) or until an agreed-upon number of rounds have been played. A game should not end in the middle of a round.

Scoring

- A BLUFFER who votes for the real definition receives 1 point.
- A BLUFFER who writes a vote-winning definition receives 1 point for each vote his fake definition receives.
- WEBSTER receives 1 point for each BLUFFER who did *not* vote for the real definition, plus 1 bonus point if *no* BLUFFER voted for the real definition.
- Optional: An additional 1 point may be awarded to the BLUFFER who creates the funniest definition, as determined by a vote of all players.

Etiquette

1. WEBSTER must read all definitions in a consistent, unbiased style.
2. BLUFFERS must not interrupt WEBSTER with questions or speculation about the definitions being read or their authors.

Team Competition

1. **Four or More Teams:** Follow the same rules that apply in individual competition. Play begins with the selection of the WEBSTER TEAM, whose members together select a word from the dictionary. Each BLUFFER TEAM creates one fake definition, agreed upon by team members, and has one vote. This team competition uses the same scoring system outlined above.
2. **Two Teams:** By prior agreement, players should decide whether or not to allow consultation among team members. (Consultation tends to allow a few superior players to dominate the game.) One member of the DEFINING TEAM selects a word from Webster's Dictionary Game book. Each of the other DEFINING TEAM members creates a fake definition. The GUESSING TEAM tries to choose the real definition, with each team member getting one vote. The GUESSING TEAM gains a point for each vote they cast for the real definition. The DEFINING TEAM gains a point for each vote the GUESSING TEAM casts for a made-up definition, plus a bonus point if no one on the GUESSING TEAM votes for the real definition.

Now that you know the rules—have fun! Don't hestitate to try any variation on the rules or scoring that may enhance your enjoyment of the game.

Notes on Pronunciation

Pronunciation symbols for Webster's Dictionary Game have been simplified to provide the reader with a guide to each word's pronunciation without burdening him or her with obscure symbols.

Each entry is followed by its most common pronunciation(s) in parentheses and its part of speech in italics:

cos-tive (KAHS-tiv) or (KOHS-tiv) *adj.*,

Hyphens are used to divide the syllables in pronunciation. Capital letters indicate that a syllable is to be stressed. Pronunciation of words of one syllable is always indicated in capital letters.

spawl (SPAWL) *v.*,

The key below shows equivalent pronunciations for the letters and letter pairs used in pronunciation guides throughout the book. A condensed table of vowel sounds appears at the bottom of each page of definitions.

a	at, carry	**n**	no, one
ă	about, pizza	**ng**	wing, going
aa	fair, dare	**o**	boat, oboe
ah	bother, bomb	**ŏ**	offend, bacon
air	hair, care	**oh**	low, snow
aw	bought, hawk	**ohr**	form, bore
ay	gray, day	**oi**	coin, join
b	boy, sob	**oo**	loop, soon
ch	choice, catch	**ow**	cow, house
d	doll, shade	**p**	pill, hip
e	bet, check	**r**	rat, far
ě	letter, fallen	**s**	hiss, sip
ee	feet, seat	**sh**	shop, wash
f	fish, if	**t**	tall, set
g	good, leg	**th**	think, the
h	help, behind	**u**	sun, cup
i	ill, fist	**ŭ**	helpful, suggest
ĭ	facile, gravity	**uu**	foot, pull
ī	tie, high	**v**	very, wavy
j	jaw, hedge	**w**	when, how
k	kite, take	**y**	yet, hay
l	let, sell	**z**	zip, crazy
m	marry, came		

aal (AYL) *n.*, an east Indian shrub whose roots make a red dye

aa-lii (ah-LEE-ee) *n.*, a hardwood tree found in Hawaii

aas-vo-gel (AHS-foh-gĕl) *n.*, an African vulture

ab (AB) *n.*, wool from the edges of a fleece

a-ba (ă-BAH) or (ah-BAH) *n.*, 1. a loose Arab garment 2. a fabric made from wool or animal hair

a-ba-cin-ate (aw-BA-sin-ayt) *v.*, to blind a person by placing hot irons or metal plates in front of the eyes

a-bac-tion (aw-BAWK-shŏn) *n.*, an act of driving away something, such as cattle

a-bas-i-a (ă-BAYZH-ee-ă) *n.*, being unable to walk due to a muscular impairment

ab-a-tis or **ab-at-tis** (AB-ă-tee) or (AB-ăd-ĭs) *n.*, a structure built from downed trees with sharpened branches, used to repel an enemy

a-bat-voix (ah-bahv-WAH) *n.*, a mechanism that projects reflected sound

ab-di-tive (AB-di-tiv) *adj.*, concealing

ab-du-cent (ab-D(Y)OO-sĕnt) *adj.*, detaching; separating

a-be-ce-dar-i-an (ay-bee-see-DAR-ee-ăn) *n.*, a person who is learning the basic principles of something, such as the alphabet

a-bele (ă-BEEL) *n.*, a white poplar tree

a-bel-mosk (AY-băl-mahsk) or **a-bel-musk** (AY-băl-măsk) *n.*, a tropical herb whose seeds flavor coffee and go into perfumes

ab-far-ad (ab-FAR-ad) *n.*, an electromagnetic unit of storage capacity

a-blep-si-a (a-BLEP-see-ah) *n.*, a type of physical or psychological blindness

a-boi-deau (ahb-wah-DOH) or **a-boi-teau** (ah-bwah-TOH) *n.*, a dam or similar structure to prevent flooding

a-bol-la (ă-BŎL-lä) *n.*, a cloak worn in ancient Roman times

a-bo-ma (ă-BOH-mă) *n.*, a South American snake

a-brax-as (ă-BRAK-săs) *n.*, a word used as a charm until the 13th century

ab-re-ac-tion (ab-ree-AK-shŏn) *n.*, the release of emotional energy when a repressed idea or emotion is expressed, particularly in therapy

a-bri (ah-BREE) *n.*, a type of shelter, especially a hole in a hillside

ab-squat-u-late (abz-KWA-chŭ-layt) *v.*, a slang term meaning to depart suddenly

ab-sterge (abz-TURJ) *v.*, an archaic term meaning to wipe clean

\a\ bat \ā\ about \e\ or \è\ check \ĕ\ letter \é\ cafe \i\fish \ī\ tie \i\ limit \o\ boat \ŏ\ bacon \u\ sun \ŭ\ helpful \ü\ fool

a·bu·lic (ay-B(Y)OO-lik) *adj.*, being unusually ambivalent about acting on or making decisions

a·bu·ti·lon (ă-BYOOD-ĕl-ahn) *n.*, a tropical plant of the mallow family

a·cal·cu·li·a (ay-kal-KYOO-lee-ah) *n.*, the inability to do simple arithmetic

ac·an·thol·o·gy (a-kan-THAW-lŏ-jee) *n.*, the study of spines

ac·a·ro·pho·bi·a (ak-kă-ră-FOH-bee-ă) *n.*, an abnormal fear of being prey to skin-crawling organisms

a·car·pous (ay-KAHR-pŭs) *adj.*, without fruit; infertile

a·cat·a·lep·tic (ay-kad-ă-LEP-tik) *n.* a person who suspends judgment in the belief that certainty is impossible

ac·cep·ti·la·tion (ak-sep-ti-LAY-shŏn) *n.*, a verbal acknowledgment that a creditor's claim has been settled

ac·cis·mus (ăk-SIZ-mŭs) *n.*, a pretended refusal of something that actually is coveted

ac·co·lent (AK-koh-lĕnt) *adj.*, residing close by

a·ce·di·a (ă-SEE-dee-ă) *n.*, spiritual sluggishness or indifference

a·cel·da·ma (ă-SEL-dă-mă) *n.*, a place associated with bloodshed

ac·er·o·la (AS-ĕ-roh-lă) *n.*, a West Indian shrub that bears cherrylike fruit high in vitamin C

a·cer·vate (ă-SĔR-vĕt) *adj.*, developing in bunches

a·cer·vu·line (ă-SĔR-vyŭ-lĭn) *adj.*, piled

a·ces·cent (ă-SES-sĕnt) *adj.*, sour

ac·e·tar·i·ous (as-ĕ-TAR-ee-ŭs) *adj.*, used in salads

a·ce·tum (ă-SEED-ŭm) *n.*, vinegar

a·chae·tous (ay-KEED-ŭs) *adj.*, not having bristles

ach·er·on·tic (ak-ĕr-AHN-tik) *adj.*, cheerless; depressing

a·chi·o·te (ah-chee-OHD-ee) *n.*, the seed of the tropical American annatto tree

a·chlor·o·phyl·la·ceous (a-klŏr-ŏ-fil-AY-shŭs) *adj.*, colorless

a·cic·u·la (ă-SIK-yŭ-lă) *n.*, a spine or bristle shaped like a needle

a·cic·u·lar (ă-SIK-yŭ-lăr) *adj.*, needle-shaped

ac·i·na·ceous (as-ĭ-NAY-shŭs) *adj.*, a botanical term meaning having seeds

ac·i·nac·i·form (as-ĭ-NAS-ĭ-fohrm) *adj.*, pertaining to leaves shaped like a saber with a curved blade

a·cin·i·form (a-SIN-i-fohrm) *adj.*, clustered like grapes

a·crae·in (ă-KREE-ĭn) *n.*, a chemical secreted by some butterfies to repel predators

ac·ro·a·mat·ic (ak-roh-ă-MAD-ik) *adj.*, esoteric information passed on verbally

ac·tin (AK-tĭn) *n.*, a muscle protein activated during muscular contraction

ac·ti·nal (AK-tĭ-năl) *adj.*, belonging to the mouth section of a radiate animal such as a starfish, from which its arms symmetrically extend

ac-ti-noid (AK-tǐ-noid) *n.*, having similar parts regularly arranged around a central axis

a-cush-la (ă-KUUSH-lă) *n.*, an Irish term for sweetheart

ad-da (AD-dă) *n.*, an Egyptian lizard

a-deps (A-deps) *n.*, the fat of an animal

ad-i-aph-o-rous (ad-ee-AF-(ŏ)-rŭs) *adj.*, neither right nor wrong

ad-i-pose (AD-ǐ-pohs) *adj.*, made of animal fat

ad-it (AD-ǐt) *n.*, the tunnel opening to a mine shaft

ad-lit-to-ral (ad-LID-ŏ-răl) *adj.*, found in waters near the shore

ad-min-i-cle (ad-MIN-ǐ-kĕl) *n.*, an aid or a help

ad-nate (AD-nayt) *adj.*, joined to another part

ad-o-nize (AD-ŏn-īz) *v.*, to make beautiful

ad-os-cu-la-tion (ad-ahs-kŭ-LAY-shŏn) *n.*, pregnancy by external contact only

ad-ro-ga-tion (ad-roh-GAY-shŭn) *n.*, the act of claiming or seizing without justification

ad-sci-ti-tious (ad-sǐ-TI-shŭs) *adj.*, derived from something else

a-dul-ter-ine (ă-DŬL-tĕ-rīn) or (ă-dŭl-tĕ-REEN) *adj.*, 1. false or impure 2. illegal

ad-um-brate (AD-ŭm-brayt) *v.*, to intimate beforehand

a-dunc (ă-DUNGK) *adj.*, curled inward; hooked

ad-vene (ad-VEEN) *v.*, to be joined with something

ad-ve-nient (ad-VEEN-yĕnt) *adj.*, caused by something external

ad-ver-sar-i-a (ad-vĕr-SAR-ee-ă) *n.*, the memos or remarks written on a text or document

ad-y-tum (AD-ĕ-tŭm) *n.*, the inner sanctuary for priests in an ancient temple

ae-ci-um (EE-s(h)ee-ŭm) *n.*, a reproductive body in rust fungus

ae-dile or **e-dile** (EE-dīl) or (EED-ī(ĕ)l) *n.*, an ancient Roman civic officer

ae-gro-tat (ee-GROH-tat) *n.*, a British term for a doctor's statement excusing a student from classes or exams

ae-ne-ous or **ae-ne-us** (ay-EEN-ee-ŭs) *adj.*, the color of brass

ae-o-ni-an or **eo-ni-an** (ee-OHN-ee-ăn) *adj.*, continuing for an indeterminate length of time

aer-o-man-cy (AIR-ŏ-man(t)-see) *n.*, predicting the future by using weather conditions

ae-ru-go (ee-ROO-goh) *n.*, the rust of certain metals

aes-cu-la-pi-an (es-kyŭ-LAY-pee-ăn) *adj.*, relating to the practice of medicine

af-fiche (a-FEESH) *n.*, a poster

af-fla-tus (ă-FLAY-dŭs) *n.*, an inspiration; a divine transmission of knowledge

af·fy (AF-fee) *v.*, an archaic term meaning to fuse closely together

a·gal·loch (ă-GAL-ŏk) *n.*, the wood of an East Indian tree that Orientals burn as incense

a·gam·ic (ă-GAM-ik) *adj.* without sexual organs; asexual

ag·a·pem·o·ne (ag-ă-PEM-ŏ-nee) *n.*, an institution where free love is practiced

ag·a·thism (AG-ă-thizĕm) *n.*, the conviction that everything moves toward eventual good

ag·a·tho·kak·o·log·i·cal (ag-ă-thoh-kak-ŏ-LAHJ-ĭ-kăl) *adj.*, made up of both good and bad

a·gene (AY-jeen) *n.*, a chemical used to bleach and age flour

a·geu·si·a (ă-GYOO-zee-ă) *n.*, the loss or damaging of the sense of taste

ag·ger (AJ-ĕr) *n.*, a high tide in which the water crests, recedes, then rises again

ag·i·o (A-joh) or (A-jee-oh) *n.*, an allowance for the value difference between two currencies

ag·i·o·tage (AJ-ŏ-tij) *n.*, 1. speculation in the stock market 2. dealing in foreign currency

a·gist·ment (ă-JIST-mĕnt) *n.*, the feeding of livestock for a fee

ag·mi·nate (AG-mĭ-nĭt) *adj.*, clustered; combined

ag·noi·ol·o·gy (ag-noi-OL-ŏ-jee) *n.*, the philosophical study of human ignorance

a·gon (ah-GAHN) or (ah-GOHN) *n.*, an ancient Greek contest in athletics, chariot or horse racing, music, or literature

a·goua·ra (a-gwă-RAH) *n.*, a South American wild dog

a·graf or **a·graffe** (ă-GRAF) *n.*, a hook-and-loop clasp, often decorated, for clothing or armor

ag·ri·ol·o·gy (AG-ree-ol-ŏ-jee) *n.*, the study of customs among peoples who lack a written language

ag·ros·tol·o·gy (AG-rŏ-stol-ŏ-jee) *n.*, the study of grasses

a·gryp·ni·a (ă-GRIP-nee-ă) *n.*, rites before certain feast days of the Eastern church

a·gu·nah (AH-goo-nah) *n.*, a woman who, under Jewish law, cannot remarry until she proves her husband's death or obtains a divorce

a·him·sa (ă-HIM-sah) or (ă-HIN-sah) *n.*, the Hindu principle of nonviolence

ai or **aie** (Ī) or (Ī-ee) *n.*, a sloth found in South America

ai·guille (ay-GWEEL) *n.*, a needlelike pinnacle of rock

ai·lur·o·phile or **ae·lur·o·phile** (Ī-LOOR-ŏ-fīl) *n.*, a person who adores cats

ais·chro·la·trei·a (īs-kroh-lă-TRĪ-ă) *n.*, a cult that worships the obscene

ait (AYT) *n.*, a British term for a small island, especially one in a river

a-ji-va (ă-JEE-vă) *n.*, a term for inanimate matter in the religion of Jainism

aj-o-wan (AJ-ŏ-wahn) *n.*, the fruit of an herb related to the caraway plant, used as a medicine and a condiment

alb (ALB) *n.*, a linen garment worn mainly by priests

al-ba (AHL-bă) *n.*, a French song or love poem

al-be-do (al-BEE-doh) *n.*, the part of the rinds of citrus fruits that provides pectin for jams

al-bes-cent (al-BES-ĕnt) *adj.*, whitish

al-bur-num (al-BŬR-nŭm) *n.*, sapwood

al-cai-de or **al-cay-de** (ahl-KĪ-dee) *n.*, the leader of a Spanish fortress or castle

al-cal-de (ahl-KAHL-dee) *n.*, a Spanish official

al-ca-zar (al-KA-zăr) or (al-KAH-zăr) *n.*, a palatial residence or fortress in Spain

al-drin (AHL-drĭn) *n.*, a chemical used as an insecticide

a-le-thi-ol-o-gy (ă-lee-thee-OL-ŏ-jee) *n.*, the branch of logic dealing with truth and error

a-leu-ro-man-cy (ă-LUU-rŏ-man(t)-see) *n.*, predicting the future by using flour

al-e-vin (AL-ĕ-vĭn) *n.*, a hatchling fish, particularly a salmon

a-lex-i-phar-mic (ă-leks-ĭ-FAHR-mik) *n.*, an antidote

al-for-ja (al-FAWR-hă) *n.*, a western U.S. term for saddlebag

al-ge-do-nic (al-jĕ-DAHN-ik) *adj.*, having to do with pain, especially when related with pleasure

al-ge-rine (AL-jĕ-reen) *n.*, a pirate

al-gid (AL-jid) *adj.*, cold; chilly

al-go-lag-ni-a (al-goh-LAG-nee-ă) *n.*, the experience of sexual pleasure when causing or suffering pain

al-go-pho-bi-a (al-gŏ-FOH-bee-ă) *n.*, an abnormal fear of pain

al-i-ble (AL-ĭ-bĕl) *adj.*, an archaic term for nurturing

al-i-form (AL-ĭ-fohrm) or (AYL-ĭ-fohrm) *adj.*, shaped like wings

al-i-un-de (AL-ee-ŭn-dee) *adv.*, from a different source

al-ja-mi-a-do (AHL-hah-mĭ-ah-doh) *adj.*, written in Spanish using Arabic characters

al-ka-hest or **al-ca-hest** (AL-kă-hest) *n.*, a universal solvent sought by alchemists

al-lele (ă-LEEL) *n.*, a mutant gene that usually causes hereditary variation

al-li-a-ceous (al-lee-AY-shŭs) *adj.*, smelling of garlic or onions

al-li-sion (ă-LIZH-ŏn) *n.*, the striking of a stationary ship by one that is moving

al-loch-ro-ous (ă-LAHK-rŏ-wŏs) *adj.*, turning color

\a\ bat \ă\ about \e\ or \ĕ\ check \ē\ letter
\ē\ cafe \i\fish \ī\ tie \ĭ\ limit \o\ boat
\ō\ bacon \u\ sun \ŭ\ helpful \ü\ fool

al·loch·thon or **al·loch·thone** (a-LAHK-thŏn) or (a-LAHK-thohn) *n.*, a mass of rocks moved along a fault a great distance from the place of origin

al·lo·graph (AL-lŏ-graf) *n.*, 1. something written, such as a signature, by one person for another 2. the specific shape of a letter

al·lo·nym (AL-ŏ-nim) *n.*, a pen name taken from the name of another person

al·lo·the·ism (ĂL-lah-thee-izĕm) *n.*, the worship of gods not approved by religious authorities

al·ma·gest (AL-mă-jest) *n.*, an early medieval writing on a branch of knowledge, such as astronomy

al·mo·ner (AL-mŏ-ner) *n.*, a person who distributes charitable gifts, such as food or money

al·muce (AL-myoos) *n.*, a fur-lined hood formerly worn by clergymen

al·mug (AL-mŭg) *n.*, a biblical tree, possibly the red sandalwood

al·o·gism (AL-ŏ-jizĕm) *n.*, an unreasonable statement or thought

al·o·pe·ci·a (al-ŏ-PEE-shee-ă) *n.*, baldness

a·lop·e·coid (ă-LAHP-ĕ-koid) *adj.*, foxlike

al·ou·atte (al-ŏ-WAT) *n.*, a howler monkey

al·phit·o·man·cy (al-FIT-ŏ-man(t)-see) *n.*, predicting the future by using barley meal

al·sike (AL-sak) or (AL-sīk) *n.*, a European clover with whitish or pinkish flowers

al·tri·cial (al-TRI-shăl) *adj.*, referring to birds whose immature hatchlings require a period of parental care

al·tri·gen·der·ism (al-trī-JEN-dĕr-izĕm) *n.*, the stage at which one develops interest in the opposite sex

al·u·del (AL-yŭ-del) *n.*, a pot open at both ends for use in experiments

al·u·la (AL-yŭ-lă) *n.*, 1. the small, stiff feathers on a bird's wing 2. a small structure at the base of a fly's wing

a·ma (AH-mă) or (A-mă) or (AY-mă) *n.*, 1. a Pacific Island term for a candlenut 2. in Japan, a woman diver who works without diving gear

am·a·del·phous (am-ă-DEL-fŭs) *adj.*, talkative; sociable

am·a·dou (AM-ă-doo) *n.*, a spongy substance made from certain fungi and used in the fuses of firecrackers

a·man·u·en·sis (ă-man-yŭ-WEN-sĭs) *n.*, a clerk; a secretary

am·a·ranth (AM-ă-ranth) *n.*, 1. a mythical eternal flower 2. a type of plant whose pollen causes hay fever

a·ma·te (ah-MAHD-ee) *n.*, a fruit-bearing Central American tree with shiny leaves

am·a·tho·pho·bi·a (am-ă-thŏ-FOH-bee-ă) *n.*, an abnormal fear of dust or dirt

a·max·o·pho·bi·a (ă-maks-ŏ-FOH-bee-ă) *n.*, an abnormal fear of sitting or riding in a vehicle

am·ba·gious (am-BAY-jŭs) *adj.*, an archaic term for indirect; circuitous

am-ba-ri (am-BAHR-ee) *n.*, an East Indian hemp plant used to make canvas and ropes

am-bi-tus (AM-bĭ-tŭs) *n.*, 1. the exterior edge of an object, such as a leaf 2. the range of melody in a Gregorian chant

am-bo (AM-boh) *n.*, in early churches, a large pulpit or desk from which to read

am-boy-na or **am-boi-na** (am-BOI-nă) *n.*, an East Indian tree with mottled wood

am-bry (AM-bree) *n.*, British dialect for a storeroom, closet, or pantry

ambs-ace or **ames-ace** (AYM-zays) or (AM-zays) *n.*, 1. the lowest dice throw 2. something that has no luck

am-e-lus (AM-ĕ-lŭs) or (AY-mel-ŭs) *n.*, a fetus without limbs

a-merce-ment (ă-MĔRS-mĕnt) *n.*, a fine whose amount is determined at the discretion of the court

am-ice (AM-is) *n.*, an oblong liturgical vestment

am-phig-o-ny (am-FIG-ŏ-nee) *n.*, reproduction through sexual means

am-phi-go-ry (AM-fĭ-goh-ree) or (am-FIG-ŏ-ree) *n.*, a verse without sense or meaning

am-phis-ci-ans (am-FISH-(ee)-ăns) *n.*, an archaic term for tropical residents

am-phor-ic (am-FAWR-ik) *adj.*, like the sound produced by blowing across the tip of an empty bottle

am-plex-us (am-PLEKS-ŭs) *n.*, the mating embrace of frogs or toads

am-pul-la-ceous (am-pŭ-LAY-shŭs) *adj.*, shaped like a two-handled bottle

a-mur-ca (ă-MUR-kă) *n.*, the sediment of olive oil

am-u-sette (AM-yŭ-zet) *n.*, an obsolete type of cannon

a-myg-da-la (ă-MIG-dă-lă) *n.*, 1. a tonsil 2. a structure of the brain

am-y-la-ceous (am-ŭ-LAY-shŭs) *adj.*, starchy

a-na (AY-nă) or (AH-nă) *n.*, a collection of amusing or entertaining stories about a particular subject

an-a (AN-ă) *adv.*, in equal parts; specifically, in regard to ingredients in pharmaceutical prescriptions

a-nab-a-sis (ă-NAB-ă-sis) *n.*, military advance

an-a-bi-o-sis (an-ă-bī-OH-sis) *n.*, an apparent plant death that is caused by dehydration and reversed with moisture

an-a-bleps (AN-a-bleps) *n.*, a tropical American fish with four eyes

an-a-clit-ic (an-ă-KLID-ik) *adj.*, relating to the psychic energy that depends on nonsexual drives

an-a-coe-no-sis (an-ă-si-NOH-sis) *n.*, a figure of speech that requests audience opinions on the subject being discussed

a-nac-re-on-tic (ă-nak-ree-AHN-tik) *n.*, a drinking song

\a\ bat \ă\ about \e\ or \è\ check \ĕ\ letter \é\ cafe \i\ fish \ī\ tie \ĭ\ limit \o\ boat \ŏ\ bacon \u\ sun \ŭ\ helpful \ü\ fool

an·a·cri·sis (an-ă-KRĪ-sis) *n.*, an inquiry in a civil law case that often includes torture

an·a·dem (AN-ă-dem) or (AN-ă-dĕm) *n.*, a wreath worn on the head; a garland

an·a·glyph (AN-ă-glif) *n.*, an ornament sculptured or embossed in low relief

an·ag·no·ri·sis (a-nag-NOH-rĭ-sis) *n.*, in an ancient Greek tragedy, the critical moment of recognition, discovery, or insight

an·a·krou·sis (an-ă-KROO-sis) *n.*, in music, the note or notes coming before a downbeat

an·a·lects (AN-ă-lek(t)s) *n.*, 1. surplus food from a banquet 2. randomly picked written passages

an·a·lep·tic (an-ă-LEP-tik) *n.*, a drug that stimulates the central nervous system

an·a·mor·pho·sis (an-ă-MOHR-fŏ-sis) *n.*, an irregular or warped image made by a distorting device

an·an·thous (ă-NAN-thŭs) *adj.*, having no flowers

an·a·stat·ic (an-ă-STAD-ik) *adj.*, of a printing technique involving a zinc plate

an·a·tine (AN-ă-tīn) *adj.*, ducklike

an·co·nal (an-KOHN-ăl) *adj.*, associated with the elbow

an·de·site (AN-dĕ-zīt) *n.*, a dark, grayish volcanic rock

an·e·mol·o·gy (an-ĕ-MAHL-ŏ-jee) *n.*, the study of winds

an·ep·i·graph·ic (an-ep-ĭ-GRAF-ik) *adj.*, lacking an inscription

an·er·oid (AN-ĕ-roid) *adj.*, using no fluid

an·frac·tu·ous (an-FRAK-chŭ-ŭs) *adj.*, circuitous

an·ga (ANG-ă) *n.*, a branch of yoga

an·ga·ry (AN-gă-ree) *n.*, in international law, the right of a nation or state at war to take the property of neutral nations

an·guil·li·form (an-GWIL-ĭ-fohrm) *adj.*, eel-shaped; sinuous

an·guin·e·ous (an-GWIN-ee-ŭs) *adj.*, sinuous-looking; snakelike

an·gus·ti·ros·trate (an-gŭs-tĭ-RAHS-trayt) *adj.*, having a tapered snout

a·ni (ah-NEE) or (ă-NEE) *n.*, a black tropical American cuckoo bird with a flat, bladelike bill

an·id·i·an (a-NID-ee-ăn) *adj.*, formless

an·il (AN-il) *n.*, a West Indian shrub of the bean family that yields an indigo-blue dye

an·ile (AN-īl) or (AY-nīl) *adj.*, of or like a feeble old woman

an·kus (ANG-kŭs) or (ĂNG-kŭs) *n.*, an elephant prod used in India

an·lace (AN-lăs) or (AN-lays) *n.*, a dagger used in medieval times

an·la·ge (AHN-lah-gĕ) *n.*, the basis or foundation of growth

an·na or **a·na** (AH-nă) or (A-nă) *n.*, a coin formerly used in India and Pakistan

an·not·i·nous (ă-NAHT-ĭ-nŭs) *adj.*, alive for one year

a·no·a (ă-NOH-ă) *n.*, a small wild ox with nearly straight horns

a-no-ci-as-so-ci-a-tion (ă-noh-see-ă-soh-see-AY-shŏn) *n.*, a means of preventing shock during surgical operations

an-o-dyne (AN-ŏ-dīn) or (AN-oh-dīn) *adj.*, relieving pain

a-no-mi-a (ă-NOH-mee-ă) *n.*, a saddle oyster

an-o-pis-tho-graph-ic (an-ŏ-pis-thŏ-GRAF-ik) *adj.*, inscribed on one side

an-or-chism (ă-NAHR-kizĕm) *n.*, the lack of one or both testicles from birth

an-sa (AN-să) *n.*, an anatomical structure that is loop- or ring-shaped

an-sate (AN-sayt) *adj.*, having a handle or handlelike segment

an-ser-ine (AN-sĕ-rīn) or (AN-sĕ-rin) *adj.*, characteristic of a goose; silly

an-te-lu-can (an-tĕ-LOO-kăn) *adj.*, an archaic term meaning that which occurs before dawn

ant-he-li-on (ant-HEEL-yŏn) or (an-THEE-lyŏn) *n.*, a luminous, white spot sometimes seen opposite the sun

an-ti-grop-e-los (an-tĭ-GRAHP-ĕ-lŏs) or (an-tĭ-GRAHP-ĕ-lahs) *n.*, waterproofed legwear

an-ti-mo-ny (AN-tĭ-moh-nee) *n.*, a brittle, lustrous, white, metallic chemical element

an-ti-phlo-gis-tic (an-tĭ-flŏ-JIS-tik) *adj.*, acting against inflammation

an-ti-pru-rit-ic (an-tee-proo-RIT-ik) or (an-tī-proo-RIT-ik) *adj.*, relieving or preventing itching

an-tre (AN-tĕr) *n.*, a cavern or cave

an-u-rous (ă-N(Y)UR-ŭs) *adj.*, tailless

ap-a-go-ge (AP-ă-goh-jee) or (AP-ă-gah-jee) *n.*, an argument that disproves a proposition by reducing it to absurdity

ap-a-tet-ic (ap-ă-TED-ik) *adj.*, imitating the colors and shapes of other animal forms

a-per-i-ent (ă-PIR-ee-ĕnt) *adj.*, working as a laxative

a-phe-li-on (ă-FEE-lee-ŏn) *n.*, a planet's farthest position from the sun

aph-tha (AF-thă) or (AP-thă) *n.*, a particle or blemish that can appear somewhere in the digestive tract, especially the mouth

a-pish-a-more (ă-PISH-ă-mohr) *n.*, a blanket used under a saddle

ap-lite (A-plīt) *n.*, a type of granite composed of quartz and feldspar

ap-o-ca-tas-ta-sis or **ap-o-ka-tas-ta-sis** (ap-ŏ-kă-TAS-tă-sĭs) *n.*, the state of being restored or saved, as in religion

a-poc-o-pe (ă-POK-ŏ-pee) *n.*, the loss of a sound or letter at word endings

a-poc-y-na-ceous (ă-pahs-ĕ-NAY-shŭs) *adj.*, of the family of tropical herbs, shrubs, or trees that includes the oleander and periwinkle

ap-o-dic-tic (ap-ŏ-DIK-tik) *adj.*, totally certain

\a\ bat \ă\ about \e\ or \è\ check \ĕ\ letter \é\ cafe \i\fish \ī\ tie \ĭ\ limit \o\ boat \ŏ\ bacon \u\ sun \ŭ\ helpful \ü\ fool

ap·o·dy·te·ri·um (ap-ŏ-dī-TI-ree-ŭm) *n.*, in ancient Greek or Roman bath houses, a dressing room

a·pog·e·ny (ă-PAHJ-ĕ-nee) or (a-PAHJ-ĕ-nee) *n.*, the loss of the ability to reproduce

ap·o·graph (AP-ŏ-graf) *n.*, a transcript

ap·o·laus·tic (ap-ŏ-LAHS-tik) *adj.*, dedicated to pleasure

ap·o·pemp·tic (ap-ŏ-PEM-tik) *adj.*, an archaic term meaning sung as a farewell message

a·poph·a·sis (ă-POF-ă-sis) *n.*, the refusal to discuss further a subject already either verbalized or implied

ap·o·ret·ic (ap-ŏ-RED-ik) *adj.*, having doubts

a·po·ri·a (ă-POH-ree-ă) or (ă-PAH-ree-ă) *n.*, a difference of opinions that fosters doubt

ap·o·si·o·pe·sis (a-pŏ-sī-ŏ-PEE-sĭs) *n.*, the purposeful incompletion of a thought in writing or speech

a·pos·til or **a·pos·tille** (ă-PAHS-tĭl) *n.*, an archaic term for a note written in the margin

ap·o·tro·pa·ic (ap-ŏ-trŏ-PAY-ik) *adj.*, intended to ward off evil

ap·pa·nage or **ap·a·nage** (AP-ă-nij) *n.*, a grant of land or other resources for the maintenance of members of a royal family

ap·pel (ă-PEL) or (a-PEL) *n.*, an act of warning in fencing; specifically, a tap of the foot

ap·pe·tent (AP-i-tĕnt) *adj.*, marked by longing

ap·pla·nate (AP-plă-nayt) *adj.*, leveled or horizontally enlarged

ap·ple·squire (AP-ĕl-SKWĪ(Ĕ)R) *n.*, an obsolete term for a pimp

ap·pro·pin·quate (ap-prŏ-PING-kwayt) *v.*, an archaic term meaning to come near

a·pros·ex·i·a (ay-pro-SEK-see-ă) *n.*, the inability to remain mentally focused

ap·ty·a·lism (ay-TĪ-ă-lizĕm) *n.*, a lack or inadequacy of salivary secretions

ar·a·chide (AR-ă-kīd) *n.*, a peanut

ar·bus·cle (AHR-bŭs-sĕl) or **ar·bus·cu·la** (ahr-BŬS-kyŭ-lă) n., a small tree or shrub

ar·bu·tus (ahr-BYOOD-ŭs) *n.*, an evergreen shrub or tree with red berries found in Europe and North America

ar·chi·di·das·ca·los (ahr-kee-dĭ-DAS-kă-lahs) or (ahr-kee-dī-DAS-kă-lahs) *n.*, the head teacher of a school

ar·chi·mage (AHR-kĭ-mayj) *n.*, a magician or wizard

ar·chol·o·gy (ahr-KAHL-ŏ-jee) *n.*, the creed of origins

ar·chon (AHR-kahn) or (AHR-kŏn) *n.*, in ancient Athens, a supervising authority

ar·deb (AHR-deb) *n.*, an Egyptian unit of measure

ar·e·nose (AR-ĕ-nohs) *adj.*, having the qualities of grit or sand

ar·e·ol·o·gy (ar-ee-AHL-ŏ-jee) *n.*, the study of the planet Mars

ar·e·ta·ics (ar-ĕ-TAY-iks) *n.*, the science of goodness

ar·e·te (ar-ĕ-TAY) or (ar-ĕ-TEE) *n.*, the sum of qualities that contribute to good character

ar·e·thu·sa (ar-ĕ-TH(Y)OO-ză) *n.*, a bog orchid that blooms in late spring

argh (AHRF) or (AHRK) *adj.*, English dialect meaning shy or fearful

ar·gil·la·ceous (ahr-jĭ-LAY-shŭs) *adj.*, associated with or containing clay

ar·gol (AHR-gŏl) *n.*, dung used as fuel in certain parts of central Asia

ar·hat (AHR-hăt) *n.*, a Buddhist monk who has achieved enlightenment

ar·il (AR-ĭl) *n.*, the outer casing of some seeds

ar·is·tarch (AR-ĭ-stahrk) *n.*, a harsh critic

ar·ith·moc·ra·cy (a-rith-MAHK-ră-see) *n.*, government by majority

ar·mi·ger (AHR-mĭ-jĕr) *n.*, a knight's helper

ar·mil·la (ahr-MIL-ă) *n.*, a bracelet, particularly for royalty

ar·mo·man·cy (AWR-mŏ-man(t)-see) *n.*, predicting the future by using an animal's shoulders

ar·mo·zeen or **ar·mo·zine** (AHR-mŏ-zeen) *n.*, a black silk woven into robes for clerical duties and for mourning

ar·ras (AR-ăs) *n.*, a rich tapestry

ar·ras (AH-rahs) *n.*, in Spanish law, a husband's wedding gift to his wife

ar·rhe·not·o·ky or **ar·re·not·o·ky** (ar-ĕ-NAHD-ŏ-kee) *n.*, the reproduction without fertilization that results in male offspring

ar·ri·viste or **ar·ri·vist** (A-ree-veest) or (A-ree-vist) *n.*, a person who uses any means to become successful

ar·um (A-rŭm) *n.*, an herb found in Europe and Asia

a·sa·na (AH-să-nă) *n.*, a yoga position

as·cham (AS-kăm) *n.*, a container for storing bows and arrows

as·ci·an (ASH-(ee)-ăn) *n.*, a person who lives where the sun cannot cast a shadow

as·cus (AS-kŭs) *n.*, the spore sac in certain fungi, such as mildew and yeast

a·so·ma·tous (ay-SOH-mă-dŭs) *adj.*, having no material body

as·per·gil·lum (as-pĕr-JIL-ŭm) *n.*, a brush or instrument used to sprinkle holy water

as·sai (ah-SĪ) or (ah-sah-EE) *n.*, a South American palm tree

as·sev·er·ate (ă-SEV-ĕ-rayt) *v.*, to speak in earnest

as·soil (ă-SOI(ĕ)L) *v.*, an archaic term meaning to pardon

as·sue·tude (AS-wee-tood) *n.*, a habit

\a\ bat \ă\ about \e\ or \è\ check \ĕ\ letter \é\ cafe \i\ fish \ĭ\ tie \ĭ\ limit \o\ boat \ŏ\ bacon \u\ sun \ŭ\ helpful \ü\ fool

a-ster-e-og-no-sis (ă-ster-ee-og-NOH-sis) or (ay-ster-ee-og-NOH-sis) *n.*, the inability to determine the shape of an object by feeling it

as-the-ni-a (as-THEE-nee-ă) or (as-THE-nee-ă) *n.*, the lack or loss of strength

as-trag-a-lo-man-cy (AS-tră-gă-loh-man(t)-see) *n.*, predicting the future by using dice or small bones

a-syn-de-ton (ă-SIN-dĕ-tahn) or (ă-SIN-dĕ-tŏn) *n.*, the omission of conjunctions in a sentence

at-a-bal (AD-ă-bal) or (AD-ă-bahl) *n.*, 1. a kettledrum used by Arabs 2. a drum in South America

at-a-rax-i-a (at-ă-RAK-see-ă) *n.*, a state of serenity

ath-a-na-si-a (ath-ă-NAY-zhi-ă) or (ath-ă-NAY-zhă) *n.*, everlasting life

ath-e-nae-um or **ath-e-ne-um** (ath-ĕ-NEE-ŭm) *n.*, an institution that promotes literary or scientific learning

ath-e-tize (ATH-ĕ-tīz) *v.*, to veto or note as false a passage of text

at-latl (AT-latĕl) or (AHT-lahtĕl) *n.*, the ancient Mexican spear thrower

at-o-ny (AT-ĕ-nee) *n.*, lethargy

at-ra-bil-i-ous (a-tră-BIL-yŭs) or (a-tră-BIL-ee-ŭs) *adj.*, sad, dismal

at-ra-ment (A-tră-mĕnt) *n.*, a dark, liquid substance, such as that secreted by octopuses

a-trich-i-a (ay-TRIK-ee-ă) or (ă-TRIK-ee-ă) *n.*, baldness

at-ter-cop (AD-ĕr-kahp) *n.*, British dialect for a bad-tempered person; literally, a spider

at-torn (ă-TŎRN) *v.*, to acknowledge the relationship of tenancy to a new landlord

au-bade (oh-BAHD) or (oh-BAD) *n.*, a musical piece composed for a morning performance

au-lar-i-an (aw-LAR-ee-ăn) *adj.*, having membership in an English university hall

au-lic (AW-lik) *adj.*, pertaining to a royal court

au-re-us (AW-ree-ŭs) *n.*, a Roman coin made of gold

au-rochs (AW-roks) *n.*, an extinct German wild ox thought to be the precursor of today's domestic cattle

au-to-ceph-a-lous (aw-tŏ-SEF-ă-lŭs) *adj.*, independent; self-governing

au-to-pha-gous (aw-TAH-fă-gŭs) *adj.*, self-consuming

au-top-tic (aw-TAHP-tik) *adj.*, based on one's own perception

au-to-sche-di-as-tic (ah-toh-skee-dee-AS-tik) *adj.*, improvised

aux-e-sis (awg-ZEE-sĭs) or (awk-SEE-sĭs) *n.*, the growth of cells without dividing

av-e-na-ceous (av-ĕ-NAY-shŭs) *adj.*, oatlike

av-i-din (AV-ĭ-din) *n.*, the protein in egg whites

a-vun-cu-lo-cal (ă-VŬN-kyŭ-loh-căl) *adj.*, near the home of a husband's maternal uncle

ax-il-la (ak-SIL-ă) *n.*, the armpit

ax-i-ol-o-gy (ak-see-AHL-ŏ-jee) *n.*, the study of values

ax-unge (AK-sŭnj) *n.*, goose or pig fat, sometimes used for medicine

a-zan (ah-ZAHN) *n.*, the Muslim call to prayer that occurs five times a day

a-zo-ic (ay-ZOH-ik) or (ă-ZOH-ik) *adj.*, referring to a period of geologic time when there was no life

a-zon (AY-zohn) or (AY-zahn) *n.*, a radio-controlled aerial bomb

a-zyme (a-ZĪM) *n.*, bread that is unleavened

B

ba (BAH) *n.*, in Egyptian religion, the soul, which is depicted as a human-headed bird

ba-ba (BAH-bah) *n.*, a popular French sponge cake, usually containing raisins, served soaked in rum syrup

ba-bas-su (bah-bă-SOO) *n.*, a Brazilian palm bearing nuts that yield a valuable oil

ba-biche (bă-BEESH) *n.*, in the Pacific Northwest, a lacing made of gut or rawhide, used to sew snowshoes

bab-i-ru-sa (bab-ĭ-ROO-să) or (băb-ĭ-ROO-să) *n.*, an East Indian swine

back-ber-end or **back-ber-and** (BAK-ber-ĕnd) *adj.*, a legal term meaning having possession of, especially stolen property

bac-u-li-form (BAK-yŭ-lĭ-fohrm) or (bak-YOO-lĭ-fohrm) *adj.*, rod-shaped

bac-u-lus (BAK-yŭ-lŭs) *n.*, a staff, especially one that indicates authority

bae-tyl (BEED-ĕl) *n.*, an irregularly shaped stone, such as a meteorite, believed to be sacred

ba-gasse or **be-gasse** (bă-GAS) *n.*, the pressed, dry residue of milled sugar cane often used as fuel, fiber, or animal feed

bal-a-noid (BAL-ă-noid) *n.* an acorn barnacle

ba-la-ta (bă-LAHD-ă) *n.*, the rubberlike, water-resistant gum of the bully tree used in making golf balls and machinery belts

bal-brig-gan (bal-BRIG-ăn) *n.*, a plain-knit cotton fabric used for making undergarments or sweaters

bal-da-chin (BAWL-dă-kin) or (BAL-dă-kin) *n.*, 1. a silk fabric interwoven with gold or silver threads, used especially in church 2. a canopy over a throne

ball-hoot-er (BAWL-hoot-ĕr) *n.*, a logger who, by himself, rolls logs down slopes too steep for more than one man

bal-locks (BAHL-iks) or (BAHL-eeks) or (BAHL-ŏks) *n.*, a vulgar term for testicles

\a\ bat \ā\ about \e\ or \ė\ check \ē\ letter \é\ cafe \i\fish \ī\ tie \ĭ\ limit \o\ boat \ō\ bacon \u\ sun \ŭ\ helpful \ü\ fool

bal·ne·al (BAL-nee-ăl) *adj.*, associated with baths, bathing, or lavatories

bal·ne·ol·o·gy (bal-nee-OL-oh-jee) *n.*, the study and practice of using baths as therapy

ba·nau·sic (bă-NAH-sik) or (bă-NAH-zik) *adj.*, serving only utilitarian purposes; practical

ban·do·line (BAN-dŏ-leen) or (BAN-dŏ-lin) *n.*, a preparation of quince seeds that is used to style hair

ban·dore (BAN-dohr) *n.*, a bass stringed instrument, popular in the Renaissance, that is similar to a guitar

ban·ghy (BAN-jee) *n.*, an East Indian shoulder yoke used to carry loads

ban·nock (BAN-ŏk) or (BAN-ik) *n.*, a flat bread of oat or barley flour, usually baked on a griddle, popular in Scotland and Britain

bant·ling (BANT-ling) *n.*, a baby

ba·ra·ba·ra (bah-ră-BAH-ră) *n.*, in Alaska and northern Siberia, a hut made of sod or turf

bar·a·thrum (BAR-ă-thrŭm) *n.*, an abyss

bar·bel·late (BAHR-bĕ-layt) or (bahr-BEL-ăt) *adj.*, a biological term meaning having wirelike hairs or bristles

bar·bi·can (BAHR-bĭ-căn) *n.*, the outer part of a city or castle that serves for defense

bare·sark (BAIR-sahrk) *n.*, an ancient Scandinavian fighter of great strength and fierceness

barm (BAHRM) *n.*, a yeast that comes from fermenting alcoholic drinks

bar·me·ci·dal (BAHR-mĕ-sī-dăl) *adj.*, giving the illusion of abundance

ba·rouche (bă-ROOSH) *n.*, a four-wheeled carriage

bar·ran·ca (bă-RANG-kă) or **bar·ran·co** (bă-RANG-koh) *n.*, a deep gulch or ravine with steep sides

bar·ti·zan (BAHRD-ĭ-zăn) or (BAHRD-ĭ-zan) *n.*, a small structure, such as a turret, used for lookout or defense

bas·cule (BA-skyool) *n.*, a device, such as a movable bridge, that operates on the principle of counterbalancing weights

bash·i·ba·zouk (bash-ee-bă-ZOOK) *n.*, a disorderly, uncontrolled person

bash·lyk or **bash·lik** (bash-LIK) *n.*, a hood worn by Russian soldiers for protection

ba·so·phile (BAY-sŏ-fil) *adj.*, flourishing in alkaline soil

bas·ti·na·do (bas-tĭ-NAY-doh) *n.*, 1. a beating with a stick 2. an Oriental form of punishment consisting of blows with a stick on the soles of the feet or on the buttocks

ba·thyb·ic (bă-THIB-ik) *adj.*, relating to or living in the depths of the sea

bat·ra·choid (BA-tră-koid) *adj.*, froglike or toadlike

bat·tol·o·gy (bă-TOL-ŏ-jee) *n.*, an extreme repetition of words while speaking or writing

bat-tue (ba-TOO) or (ba-TYOO) *n.*, the flushing of game from ground cover toward hunters by making noise

bauch-le (BAHK-ĕl) *n.*, a Scottish term for a shoe worn down at the heel

bau-sond (BAH-sŏnd) *adj.*, British slang referring to animals that have a white spot or "blaze" on a dark face or brow

baw-cock (BAW-kok) *n.*, an archaic term for a fine, good fellow

baw-tie (BAH-tee) *n.*, a Scottish term for a big dog

bax-ter (BAK-stĕr) *n.*, a baker

ba-ya-mo (bă-YAH-moh) *n.*, a sudden thunderstorm off Cuba's southern coast

bdel-li-um (DEL-ee-ŭm) *n.*, a gum resin similar to myrrh

be-bee-ru (bĕ-BI-roo) or (bĕ-BEE-roo) *n.*, an evergreen tree found in South America

be-del or **be-dell** (bĕ-DEL) or (be-DEL) *n.*, an administrator who leads processions at English universities

be-di-zen (bi-DĪ-zĕn) or (bi-DIZ-ĕn) *v.*, to dress in a gaudy, showy manner

bees-wing (BEEZ-wing) *n.*, a light, flaky deposit found in port and other bottle-aged wines

bel-cher (BEL-chĕr) *n.*, a colorful handkerchief worn around the neck

bel-dam (BEL-dăm) *n.*, an old woman, especially an ugly one

bel-em-noid (BEL-ĕm-noid) *adj.*, dart-shaped

bel-o-man-cy (BEL-ŏ-man(t)-see) *n.*, predicting the future by drawing arrows at random

bel-swag-ger (BEL-swag-ĕr) *n.*, an obsolete term for a pimp

bel-ve-dere or **bel-vi-dere** (BEL-vĕ-dir) *n.*, a structure built to afford a good view

ben-e-dick (BEN-ĕ-dik) or **ben-e-dict** (BEN-ĕ-dict) *n.*, a long-time bachelor who is newly married

ben-i-son (BEN-ĭ-sŏn) or (BEN-ĭ-zŏn) *n.*, a blessing

ben-ne or **ben-ni** (BEN-ee) or (BEN-ni) *n.*, the sesame herb

ber-ceuse (ber-SĔ(R)Z) or (ber-SEEZ) *n.*, a lullaby

be-som (BEE-zŏm) or (BIZ-ŏm) *n.*, a broom, especially one made of twigs

be-sprent (bĕ-SPRENT) *adj.*, an archaic term meaning sprinkled over

be-zique (bĕ-ZEEK) *n.*, a card game, similar to pinochle, that uses a 64-card deck

be-zoar (BEE-zohr) *n.*, a mass sometimes found in the stomach or intestines of cud-chewing animals, once believed to have magical curative powers

be-zo-ni-an (bĕ-ZOH-nee-ăn) or (bee-ZOH-nee-ăn) *n.*, an archaic term for an unscrupulous person

---

\a\ bat \ă\ about \e\ or \ĕ\ check \ē\ letter
\é\ cafe \i\fish \ī\ tie \i\ limit \o\ boat
\ŏ\ bacon \u\ sun \ū\ helpful \ü\ fool

bez-zle (BEZ-ĕl) *v.*, British dialect meaning to drink or eat excessively

bhak-ti (BĂK-tee) *n.*, in Hinduism, devotion to a god

bhang or **bang** (BAHNG) or (BANG) *n.*, the leaves or flowering tops of the female marijuana plant

bhees-ty or **bhees-tie** (BEES-tee) *n.*, in India, one who carries water

bhut (BOOT) *n.*, an Indian term for a mean spirit or demon

bi-ba-cious (bĭ-BAY-shŭs) or (bī-BAY-shŭs) *adj.*, having an addiction to drinking liquids

bib-cock (BIB-kok) *n.*, a faucet whose nozzle points down

bib-li-op-e-gy (bib-lee-AHP-ĕ-jee) *n.*, the art of bookbinding

bib-li-o-taph (BIB-lee-ŏ-taf) or (BIB-lee-oh-taf) *n.*, a person who collects or hides books

bi-cau-date (bī-CAH-dayt) *adj.*, having two tails

bi-cip-i-tal (bī-SIP-ĭd-ăl) *adj.*, having two origins

bi-cru-ral (bi-KROO-răl) *adj.*, two-legged

bi-dar-ka or **bai-dar-ka** (bī-DAHR-kă) *n.*, a boat made of wood, covered with sealskins, and used by Alaskan natives

bield (BEELD) *v.*, a Scottish term meaning to guard or give refuge

bif-fin (BIF-ĭn) *n.*, an English variety of apple that is often dried before being sold

big-ar-reau (BIG-ă-roh) *n.*, a type of cherry with firm skin

big-gin (BI-gĭn) *n.*, 1. a close-fitting children's cap 2. a 19th-century coffee percolator

bil-bo (BIL-boh) *n.*, 1. a sword 2. an iron bar used to shackle prisoners' feet

bil-lings-gate (BIL-ingz-gayt) *n.*, British slang for rough and insulting language

bin-dle (BIN-dĕl) *n.*, 1. a slang term for a bedroll 2. a slang term for a small package or envelope that contains a narcotic

bine (BĪN) *n.*, a twisting plant stem

bi-o-mor-phic (bī-oh-MOHR-fik) *adj.*, related to the forms of living beings

bi-o-nom-ic (bī-oh-NAHM-ik) *adj.*, associated with ecology

bi-o-ta (bī-OHD-ă) or (bī-ŎD-ă) *n.*, a region's flora and fauna

bip-a-rous (BIP-ă-rŭs) *adj.*, a zoological term for bearing offspring in pairs

bi-ret-ta or **ber-ret-ta** (bĭ-RET-ă) *n.*, a stiff, square cap that has three or four projections above the crown, worn by Roman Catholic priests, bishops, and cardinals

birk-ie (BIRK-i) or (BĬRK-i) *n.*, a Scottish term for an aggressive, independent person

birl (BĬRL) *v.*, 1. a Scottish term meaning to pour 2. to supply with drink 3. to twirl or rotate

bise (BEEZ) *n.*, in southern Europe, a chilling dry wind

bis-sex-tile (bī-SEKS-til) or (bi-SEKS-til) *adj.*, relating to the extra day of leap year

bis-ter or **bis-tre** (BIS-tĕr) *n.*, a brown pigment made from the soot of wood and used in pen or brush drawings

bis-tort (BIS-tawrt) *n.*, a European herb occasionally used as astringent; also called snakeweed

bis-tou-ry (BIS-tŏ-ree) *n.*, a small, narrow surgical knife

blae (BLAY) *adj.*, 1. a Scottish term for bluish black or blue-gray 2. dismal; sunless

blain (BLAYN) *n.*, a sore that has become inflamed

blath-er-skite (BLA-thĕr-skīt) *n.*, a verbose, incompetent person

bleb (BLEB) *n.*, 1. a blister 2. a bubble trapped in water or glass

blende (BLEND) *n.*, ore composed primarily of zinc sulfide

blen-ny (BLEN-ee) *n.*, a fish with a long, scaleless body that lives among rocky shores worldwide

bleph-a-ro-spasm (BLEF-ă-roh-spazĕm) *n.*, the involuntary winking of the eyelid muscle

blis-som (BLIS-ŏm) *v.*, to be in mating heat; specifically, a ewe

blithe-meat (BLĪTH-meet) *n.*, a Scottish term for celebratory food eaten on the occasion of a child's birth

blunge (BLŬNJ) *v.*, to merge; combine

bock-ing (BAHK-ing) *n.*, a wool fabric generally used to cover floors

bode-wash (BOHD-wawsh) or (BOHD-wahsh) *n.*, buffalo chips; dried dung

bo-lide (BOH-līd) or (BOH-lĭd) *n.*, a meteor or meteorite that has burst

bol-lard (BAHL-ărd) *n.*, a metal or wood post on a pier to which mooring lines are attached

bol-son (bohl-SOHN) *n.*, a desert valley with a flat floor

bom-bi-la-tion (bahm-bĭ-LAY-shŏn) *n.*, a whirring, droning sound

bom-by-cid (BAHM-bĭ-sĭd) or (BAHM-bĭ-sid) *n.*, a silkworm

bom-byx (BAHM-biks) *n.*, a domestic silkworm moth

bo-na-ci (boh-nă-SEE) *n.*, a type of marine food fish

bon-grace (BAHN-grays) *n.*, an archaic term for a hat or bonnet with a wide front brim

bon-i-face (BAHN-ĭ-făs) or (BAHN-ĭ-fays) *n.*, the owner of an entertainment club, hotel, or restaurant

bon-ny-clab-ber (BAHN-ee-klab-ĕr) *n.*, sour, dense milk

boo-book (BOO-buuk) *n.*, a small owl found in Australia

boom-er (BOOM-ĕr) *n.*, a fully grown male kangaroo

bo-ra (BOH-ră) or (BAW-ră) *n.*, 1. a turbulent, dry, cold wind that blows north or northeasterly over the Adriatic coasts 2. an aboriginal initiation rite by which boys are accepted into the tribe as men

---

\a\ bat \ă\ about \e\ or \ĕ\ check \ĕ\ letter
\ê\ cafe \i\fish \ĭ\ tie \ĭ\ limit \o\ boat
\ŏ\ bacon \u\ sun \ŭ\ helpful \ü\ fool

bor·bo·ryg·mus (bawr-bŏ-RIG-mŭs) *n.*, the gurgling sound of gas moving in the intestines

bosk or **bosque** (BAHSK) *n.*, a small thicket of bushes

bos·ker (BAHS-kĕr) *adj.*, Australian slang for very good

bos·ket or **bos·quet** (BAHS-kĕt) *n.*, an archaic term for a grove or thicket

both·y (BAHTH-i) or (BOHTH-i) *n.*, a Scottish term for a small cottage or hut, generally used to house farm hands or workmen

bot·o·née or **bot·on·née** (BAHT-ŏ-nay) *adj.*, ending in a cluster of balls, as appear on the arms of a cross

bot·ry·oi·dal (baht-ree-OID-ăl) *adj.*, having the shape of a grape cluster

bot·tom·ry (BAHD-ŏm-ree) or (BAHT-ŏm-ree) *n.*, a contract, much like a mortgage, that enables a ship owner to finance a voyage by using his ship as collateral

bou·din (boo-DAN) *n.*, blood sausage

bou·gie (BOO-zhee) or (BOO-jee) *n.*, 1. a candle 2. a medical instrument used to dilate a body opening

bou·stro·phe·don (boo-strŏ-FEED-ŏn) *n.*, an ancient method of writing in which the lines run alternately from right to left and left to right

boy·la (BOI-lă) *n.*, in Australia, a sorcerer or witch doctor

boz·zet·to (bŏt-SED-oh) or (bŏ-ZE-oh) *n.*, a clay study for a sculpture

brach (BRACH) *n.*, an obsolete term for a bitch hound

bra·chyg·ra·phy (bra-KIG-ră-fee) *n.*, shorthand

bra·chyl·o·gy (bra-KIL-ŏ-jee) or (bră-KIL-ŏ-jee) *n.*, a terse expression

brad (BRAD) *n.*, a slender wire nail with either a small, deep head or a projection at one side of the head end

branks (BRANGKZ) *n.*, 1. a Scottish term for a bridle or halter 2. a torture instrument

bras·sard (BRĂS-sahrd) or (BRAS-sahrd) *n.*, a band worn around the arm to identify the wearer's membership in a group

brat·tice (BRAD-ĭs) or (BRAD-ish) *n.*, a partition used to form an air shaft in a mine

brat·tle (BRAT-tĕl) *v.*, a Scottish term meaning to make a rattling sound

braw (BRAW) or (BRAH) *adj.*, a Scottish term meaning excellent or magnificent

braws (BRAWZ) or (BRAHZ) *n.*, a Scottish term for finest clothing

brax·y (BRAK-see) *n.*, a bacterial disease of sheep that causes bowel inflammation

bray·er (BRAY-ĕr) *n.*, a small, hand-inking roller used by printers

breast·sum·mer (BRES-sŭm-ĕr) or (BREST-sŭm-ĕr) *n.*, a horizontal beam that supports an exterior wall over an opening

brec-ci-a (BRECH-(ee)-ă) or (BRESH-(ee)-ă) *n.*, a composite of fragmented rock cemented together with sand, clay, or lime

brech-am (BREK-ăm) *n.*, a Scottish and Irish term for a horse collar

breg-ma (BREG-mă) *n.*, a junction point of the skull

breme (BREEM) or (BRIM) *adj.*, an archaic term for very rough or ferocious; specifically, in regard to weather

breve (BREEV) or (BREV) *n.*, a U-shaped mark over a vowel to show that it is short

brew-is (BROOZ) or (BROO-ĭs) *n.*, 1. U.S. dialect for beef broth 2. U.S. dialect for bread soaked in broth, roast meat drippings, or milk

bri-ard (bree-AHRD) *n.*, an old French breed of black sheep-herding dogs

brill (BRIL) *n.*, a European flatfish used for food and related to the turbot

brin-dled (BRIN-dĕld) *adj.*, streaked with dark spots against a gray background

bri-sance (brĭ-ZAHNS) *n.*, the shattering power of high explosives

brit or **britt** (BRIT) *n.*, the offspring of the herring

brits-ka or **britz-ka** (BRICH-kă) or (BRIT-skä) *n.*, an open, horse-drawn carriage with facing seats

brock-age (BRAHK-ij) *n.*, a coin that is imperfectly minted

bro-mal (BROH-mal) *n.*, a clear, oily liquid used in medicines

bro-mi-dro-sis (broh-mĭ-DROH-sĭs) *n.*, sweat that smells bad

bron-to-pho-bi-a (brahn-tŏ-FOH-bee-ă) *n.*, a fear of thunder

brool (BROOL) *n.*, a low rumble

broose (BROOZ) *n.*, in Scotland, a race that follows a country wedding

brul-yie (BROOL-(y)ee) *n.*, a Scottish and Irish term for a scuffle or brawl

bru-mal (BROO-măl) *adj.*, an archaic term meaning pertaining to winter

brum-by (BRŬM-bee) *n.*, an Australian term for an untamed horse

brume (BROOM) *n.*, a fog or mist

brum-ma-gem (BRUM-ă-jĕm) *adj.*, showy, but inferior and worthless

brun-ne-ous (BRŬN-ee-ŭs) *adj.*, a scientific term meaning dark brown

bu-bing-a (boo-BING-ă) *n.*, a large, tropical West African tree whose wood resembles rosewood and is used for veneers

bu-bo (B(Y)OO-boh) *n.*, an inflammed swelling of a lymph node, particularly around the groin or armpit

bu-buk-le (B(Y)OO-bŭk-ĕl) *n.*, an archaic term for a pimple

buc-cal (BŬC-ăl) *adj.*, pertaining to cheeks

bu-cen-taur (byoo-SEN-tohr) *n.*, the official barge of Venice, Italy

\a\ bat \ă\ about \e\ or \è\ check \ĕ\ letter \é\ cafe \i\fish \ī\ tie \ĭ\ limit \o\ boat \ŏ\ bacon \u\ sun \ŭ\ helpful \ü\ fool

buck-een (bŭ-KEEN) *n.*, 1. an Irish term for a poor young man who tries to copy the habits and dress of the wealthy 2. in British Guiana, a native Indian woman

buck-ish (BUK-ish) *adj.*, impetuous; dashing

buf-fo (BOO-foh) *n.*, a male opera singer who specializes in comic parts

buhl (BOOL) *n.*, an elaborate inlaid pattern of metals and tortoise shell used to decorate cabinetwork

buird-ly (BOORD-lee) *adj.*, a Scottish term meaning stout; strong; well-built

bul-bul (BUUL-buul) *n.*, 1. a Persian bird, often mentioned in poems 2. a singer or composer of sweet songs

bul-la (BOOL-ă) or (BUL-ă) *n.*, 1. a seal attached to an official document 2. an ancient Roman pendant consisting of a rounded metal or leather box

bul-lace (BOOL-ăs) *n.*, a wild European plum

bulse (BŬLS) *n.*, a purse or sack used to transport jewels

bum-ble-pup-py (BŬM-bĕl-pŭp-ee) *n.*, the card game whist played incompetently

bu-ran (boo-RAHN) *n.*, in Russia and Siberia, a violent gale that brings sandstorms in summer and blizzards in winter

bur-ga (BOOR-gă) *n.*, in Alaska, a snow-and-wind storm

bur-go-net (BŬR-gŏ-nĕt) *n.*, an open armor helmet, usually with a peak and hinged cheek pieces

bu-rin (BYOOR-in) *n.*, a pointed engraver's tool of tempered steel

burke (BŬRKE) *v.*, 1. to suffocate a person in order to sell the body for dissection 2. to quiet; stifle

bur-si-form (BŬHR-sĭ-fohrm) *adj.*, pouch-shaped

bus-by (BŬS-bee) *n.*, in the military, a full-dress fur hat that has a baglike ornament on top

busk-er (BŬSK-ĕr) *n.*, a wandering entertainer

bu-te-o (BYOO-dee-oh) *n.*, a hawk with broad, round wings and a fan-shaped tail

bys-sus (BIS-ŭs) *n.*, in ancient times, a delicate cloth

C

ca-ba-lli-to (ka-bă-YEE-toh) *n.*, a fishing boat of reeds used in the coastal waters of Peru

cab-e-zon or **cab-e-zone** (KAB-ĕ-zohn) *n.*, a family of large-headed fish found off the Pacific coast of North America

cab-o-tage (KAB-ŏ-tahzh) or (KAB-ŏ-tij) *n.*, the trade or shipping along a coast

ca-bret-ta (kă-BRED-ă) *n.*, a leather made from the skins of haired sheep that is used for gloves, clothing, and shoes

ca-bril-la (kă-BREE-(y)ă) or (ka-BRIL-ă) *n.*, a type of sea bass found off the coast of California and in the Mediterranean

cab-ri-ole (KAB-ree-ohl) or (KAHB-ree-awl) *n.*, 1. a kind of furniture leg that looks like an animal's paw 2. a ballet leap in which one leg is raised in the air and the other leg is brought up against it

cac-a-fue-go (kak-ă-FYOO-goh) or (kak-ă-FWAY-goh) *n.*, a strutting braggart

cach-a-lot (KASH-ă-laht) or (KASH-ă-loh) *n.*, a sperm whale

ca-chex-i-a (ka-KEK-see-ă) *n.*, physical debilitation brought on by disease, such as cancer

cach-in-nate (KAK-ĭ-nayt) *v.*, to laugh noisily or excitedly

ca-cique or **cazique** (kă-SEEK) *n.*, 1. the chief of an Indian clan or tribe in Mexico and the West Indies 2. a tropical American oriole that builds long, hanging nests

cac-o-dox-y (KAK-ŏ-dahk-see) *n.*, teachings that are unorthodox

cac-o-ë-thes (kak-ŏ-wee-theez) *n.*, a habitual, irrepressible desire

cac-o-gen-e-sis (kak-ŏ-JEN-ĕ-sĕs) *n.*, the inability to produce fertile hybrids

ca-cog-ra-phy (ka-KAHG-ră-fee) *n.*, poor handwriting or spelling

ca-col-o-gy (ka-KAHL-ŏ-jee) *n.*, garbled diction or pronunciation

ca-cu-mi-nal (kă-KYOO-mĭ-năl) *adj.*, pronounced with the tongue touching the roof of the mouth

ca-das-tre (kă-DAS-tĕr) *n.*, an official record used for tax assessments

cade (KAYD) *n.*, 1. a barrel, bottle, or cask 2. a young animal, especially a lamb, left by its mother and raised by humans

ca-delle (kă-DEL) *n.*, a black beetle harmful to stored grain and other insects

ca-di (KAH-dee) or (KAY-dee) *n.* a Muslim judge whose decisions are based on religious law

ca-du-ci-ty (kă-D(Y)OO-si-dee) *n.*, the weakness or feebleness of old age

cag-mag (KAG-mag) *n.*, British dialect meaning inferior, as in meat or a person

ca-id or **qa-id** (kah-EETH) or (KĪTH) *n.*, a Muslim municipal official, judge, or tax collector in North Africa

cai-tiff (KAYD-ĭf) or (KAYT-ĭf) *adj.*, heartless; wicked

caj-e-put or **caj-u-put** (KAJ-ĕ-pŭt) or (KAJ-ĕ-puut) *n.*, an East Indian tree that yields an oil used to soothe skin problems, toothaches, and intestinal disorders

cal-a-thi-form (KAL-ă-thĭ-form) or (kă-LATH-ĭ-form) *adj.*, shaped like a cup

cal-a-thos or **cal-a-thus** (KAL-ă-thahs) or (KAL-ă-thŭs) *n.*, a fruit basket held on the head to symbolize fertility in Greek and Egyptian art

\a\ bat \ā\ about \e\ or \è\ check \ĕ\ letter \é\ cafe \i\fish \ī\ tie \ĭ\ limit \o\ boat \ŏ\ bacon \u\ sun \ū\ helpful \ü\ fool

cal-ce-i-form (KAL-see-ĭ-fohrm) or (kal-SEE-ĭ-fohrm) *adj.*, slipper-shaped

cal-ci-trate (KAL-sĭ-trayt) *v.*, to kick

cal-dar-i-um (kal-DAHR-ee-ŭm) *n.*, in ancient Roman bath houses, a room with a heated bath

cal-de-ra (kal-DER-ă) *n.*, a large, basinlike depression resulting from the explosion or collapse of the center of a volcano

cal-e-fa-cient (kal-ĕ-FAY-shĕnt) *adj.*, heated; warming

cal-e-fac-to-ry (kal-ĕ-FAK-tŏ-ree) *n.*, a heated sitting room in a monastery

ca-lem-bour (KA-lĕm-boor) *n.*, a pun

cal-en-ture (KAL-ĕn-choor) *n.*, 1. a fever caused by tropical heat that supposedly afflicted sailors with violent hallucinations 2. any feverish passion

ca-li-che (kă-LEE-chee) *n.*, the gravel or rock in sodium nitrate deposits in Chile or Peru

cal-i-cle (KAL-ĭ-kĕl) *n.*, a cuplike depression or formation, such as those found in coral

ca-lig-i-nous (kă-LIJ-ĭ-nŭs) *adj.*, dark; dim

cal-i-pash (KAL-ĭ-pash) *n.*, the greenish, jellylike substance under a turtle's upper shell that is considered a delicacy

cal-lid-i-ty (ka-LID-ĭd-ee) *n.*, slyness

ca-lip-pus (kă-LIP-ŭs) *n.*, a genus of dwarf horses from the Pliocene Age

ca-lir-o-a (kă-LIR-ŏ-wă) *n.*, a genus of sawflies

cal-li-pyg-i-an (kal-ĭ-PIJ-ee-ăn) *adj.*, having well-shaped buttocks

cal-li-thump or **cal-la-thump** (KAL-ĭ-thŭmp) *n.*, a loud, noisy parade

ca-lotte (kă-LAHT) *n.*, 1. a skullcap worn by Roman Catholic clergy 2. an architectural term for a small dome

cal-pac or **cal-pack** (KAL-pak) *n.*, a large, black sheepskin cap worn in Turkey, Iran, and nearby countries

cal-trop (KAL-trŏp) *n.*, a group of plants with spines on the fruit or flower heads

cal-u-met (KAL-yŭ-met) *n.*, a long, ornamented pipe used by North American Indians during ceremonies; a peace pipe

cal-var-i-um (kal-VAR-ee-ŭm) *n.*, an incomplete skull

ca-lyp-tra (kă-LIP-tră) *n.*, a hoodlike covering on a flower or fruit

ca-lyx (KAY-liks) or (KA-liks) *n.*, the external set of leaves on a flower

cam-a-ril-la (kam-ă-RIL-ă) or (kam-ă-REE-(y)ă) *n.*, a group of unscrupulous advisers to a person of authority

cam-bism (KAM-bizĕm) *n.*, the principle and practice of making exchanges in commerce

ca-mel-o-pard (kă-MEL-ŏ-pahrd) *n.*, a giraffe

cam·er·a·lis·tics (kam-ĕr-ă-LIS-tiks) *n.*, the science of public finance

ca·mor·ra (kă-MOR-ă) or (kă-MAHR-ă) *n.*, a group of people banded together for dishonorable purposes

cam·pa·nol·o·gy (kam-pă-NAHL-ŏ-jee) *n.*, 1. the study and practice of bell making 2. the art of bell ringing

cam·pan·u·late (kam-PAN-yŭ-lăt) or (kam-PAN-yŭ-layt) *adj.*, bell-shaped

ca·naille (kă-NAY(Ĭ)L) or (kă-NĪL) *n.*, riffraff; a mob

cangue or **cang** (KANG) or (KAING) *n.*, a wooden Oriental punishment device, three or four feet square, used to confine the neck and hands

ca·ni·ti·es (kă-ni-SHEE-eez) or (kă-NI-sheez) *n.*, a hair coloration that is gray or white

can·nu·lar (KAN-yŭ-lăr) *adj.*, tube-shaped

ca·noo·dle (kă-NOO-děl) *v.*, to stroke; to fondle

ca·no·rous (kă-NOH-rŭs) or (kă-NOR-ŭs) or (KAN-ŏ-rŭs) *adj.*, melodious

can·ta·bank (KANT-ă-bank) *n.*, a person who sings ballads from benches or platforms

can·tha·ris (KAN-thă-rĭs) *n.*, an aphrodisiac prepared from dried beetles; also called Spanish fly

can·zo·net (KAN-zŏ-net) *n.*, a light, gay song written in part harmony

cap·i·lo·tade (KAP-ĭ-loh-tahd) *n.*, a stew made of minced meats

cap·ric (KAP-rik) *adj.*, relating to a goat

cap·ri·ole (KAP-ree-ohl) *n.*, 1. a leaping dance motion 2. a vertical leap and back kick performed by a trained horse

ca·pryl·ic (kă-PRIL-ik) *adj.*, having a rancid animal odor

cap·ta·tion (kap-TAY-shŏn) *n.*, an attempt to earn favorable attention or applause

ca·puche (kă-POOCH) or (kă-POOSH) *n.*, a hood, especially one worn by a Capuchin friar

cap·y·ba·ra or **cap·i·ba·ra** (kap-ĭ-BAR-ă) or (kap-ĭ-BAHR-ă) *n.*, the world's largest rodent, native to South America, that resembles a guinea pig

car·a·ba·o (kar-ă-BAH-oh) *n.*, a domesticated work buffalo in the Philippines

car·a·bid (KAR-ă-bĭd) *n.*, a ground beetle

car·a·cal (KAR-ă-kal) or (kar-ă-KAL) *n.*, an African and Asian cat, larger than a fox, with reddish brown fur, black ears, and long ear tufts

car·a·ga·na (kar-ă-GAH-nă) or (kar-ă-GAN-ă) or (kar-ă-GAY-nă) *n.*, a type of Asiatic shrub used for hedges in areas of the central U.S.

\a\ bat \ā\ about \e\ or \ė\ check \ē\ letter
\é\ cafe \i\fish \ī\ tie \i\ limit \o\ boat
\ŏ\ bacon \u\ sun \ŭ\ helpful \ü\ fool

car-a-geen or **car-ra-geen** (KAR-ă-geen) *n.*, a dark purple seaweed found on the coasts of northern Europe and North America

car-a-pace (KAR-ă-pays) *n.*, a shield or shell covering all or part of the backs of certain animals, such as the turtle

ca-ra-te (kă-RAHD-ee) *n.*, a tropical American skin disease characterized by white, brown, blue, red, or violet spots

car-bo-na-do (kahr-bŏ-NAY-doh) *n.*, meat or fish scored before being broiled

car-ca-net (KAHR-kă-nĕt) or (KAHR-kă-net) *n.*, an ornamental chain or piece of jewelry

car-cer (KAHR-kĕr) or (KAHR-sĕr) *n.*, a stall where racecourses began in Roman circuses

car-ci-no-mor-phic (kahr-sĭ-noh-MOHR-fik) *adj.*, crablike

car-doon (kahr-DOON) *n.*, a thistlelike, perennial Mediterranean plant with edible leaves and stalks

car-fax (KAHR-faks) *n.*, a British term for a junction where four or more roads converge

car-i-ta-tive (KAR-ĭ-tayd-iv) or (KAR-ĭ-tă-tiv) *adj.*, generous

car-min-a-tive (kahr-MIN-ăd-iv) or (kahr-mĭ-NAYD-iv) *adj.*, expelling gas from the digestive system

car-ni-fex (KAHR-nĭ-feks) *n.*, an executioner in ancient Rome

car-ni-fi-cial (kahr-nĭ-FISH-ăl) *adj.*, associated with an executioner or butcher

ca-roche (kă-ROHCH) or (kă-ROHSH) *n.*, an elegant 17th-centutry coach or carriage

car-phol-o-gy (kahr-FOL-ŏ-jee) *n.*, a delirious picking or pulling at bedclothes by exhausted, stuporous, or feverish people

car-pog-e-nous (kahr-PŎJ-ĕ-nŭs) *adj.*, producing fruit in red algae

carse (KAHRS) *n.*, a Scottish term for low, fertile lands, particularly along rivers

car-un-cle (KA-rŭng-kĕl) or (kĕ-RŬNG-kĕl) *n.*, a fleshy protrusion or outgrowth, such as a bird's comb

car-y-at-id (kar-ee-AD-ĭd) or (CAR-ee-ăt-id) *n.*, a draped female figure used as a column in a building

cas-ca-ron (kas-kă-ROHN) *n.*, in the southwestern U.S., eggshells stuffed with confetti and tossed during parties or festivals

ca-se-ous (KAY-see-ŏs) *adj.*, of or like the texture of cheese

ca-sern or **ca-serne** (kă-ZĔRN) *n.*, the barracks in a military garrison

casque (KASK) *n.*, 1. head armor 2. a hat shaped like a helmet

cas-sa-tion (ka-SAY-shŏn) or (kă-SAY-shŏn) *n.*, 1. an annulment or cancellation 2. an 18th-century musical composition, similar to a serenade, that is often performed outdoors

cas-tra-me-ta-tion (kas-tră-mĕ-TAY-shŏn) *n.*, the making of a military camp

ca-su-ist-ry (KA-zhŭ-wĭst-ree) *n.*, the study of cases of conscience or conduct

cat-a-bap-tist (kad-ă-BAP-tist) *n.*, a person who opposes baptism

cat-a-lo or **cat-ta-lo** (KAD-ă-loh) *n.*, the offspring of American bison and domestic cattle

cat-a-mite (KAD-ă-mīt) or (KAT-ă-mīt) *n.*, a boy held for sexually perverse purposes

cat-a-mount (KAT-ă-mount) *n.*, a wildcat such as a cougar or lynx

cat-a-pha-si-a (kad-ă-FAY-zhee-ă) *n.*, a speech disorder characterized by the meaningless repetition of a word or phrase

ca-tas-ta-sis (kă-TAS-tă-sĭs) *n.*, a play's climax

catch-pole or **catch-poll** (KACH-pohl) or (KECH-pohl) *n.*, a deputy who arrests people for debts

cate (KAYT) *n.*, an archaic term for store-bought food; a delicacy

cat-e-chin (KAD-ĕ-chĭn) or (KAT-ĕ-kin) *n.*, a chemical compound used for tanning and dyeing

ca-te-na (kă-TEE-nă) or (kă-TAY-nă) *n.*, a sequence of related things, especially the writings of the Fathers of the Church

cat-er-an (KAD-ĕr-ăn) *n.*, a military reservist in the Scottish Highlands

ca-thex-is (kă-THEKS-ĭs) or (ka-THEKS-ĭs) *n.*, the investment of emotional energy in an activity, object, or idea

ca-thol-i-con (kă-THAHL-ĭ-kahn) *n.*, a cure-all or universal remedy

cat-i-on (KAD-ī-ŏn) *n.*, a positively charged ion

cat-lap (KAT-lap) *n.*, a Scottish term for a very weak beverage, so called because only a cat would drink it

cat-mal-i-son (KAT-mal-ĭ-sŏn) *n.*, English dialect for a cupboard near or in the ceiling

ca-top-tro-man-cy (kă-TAHP-trŏ-man(t)-see) *n.*, predicting the future by using a mirror or crystal

catt-le-ya (KAT-lee-ă) or (kat-LEE-ă) or (kat-LAY-ă) *n.*, a showy tropical American orchid named after William Cattley, an English botanist

cau-dad (KAW-dad) *adj.*, toward the tail or end of the body

cau-dex (KAW-deks) *n.*, the central axis of a plant, including stem and root

cau-dle (KAW-dĕl) *n.*, a warm drink, usually made of wine or ale mixed with eggs, bread, sugar, and spices and served to the sick

cau-line (KAW-līn) *adj.*, growing on a stem, especially on the upper part

cau-se-rie (koh-zĕ-REE) or (KOH-zĕ-ree) *n.*, 1. an informal talk 2. a short, informal essay or article

cau-seuse (koh-ZĔ(R)Z) or (koh-ZEEZ) *n.*, a small, two-person sofa

cav-a-ti-na (ka-vă-TEE-nă) or (kah-vă-TEE-nă) *n.*, an operatic song or melody, shorter than an aria

---

\a\ bat \ă\ about \e\ or \ĕ\ check \ĕ\ letter \é\ cafe \i\fish \ĭ\ tie \ĭ\ limit \o\ boat \ŏ\ bacon \u\ sun \ŭ\ helpful \ü\ fool

ca·vie or **ca·vey** (KAY-vee) *n.*, a
Scottish term for a coop or cage for
fowl

caw·quaw (KAW-kwaw) *n.*, the
Canadian porcupine

cay·use (KĪ-(y)oos) or (kī-YOOS)
n., a western U.S. term for an
Indian pony

ce·ci·ty (SEE-sĭ-dee) *n.*, blindness

ce·la·tion (sĕ-LAY-shŏn) or (see-
LAY-shŏn) *n.*, the hiding of
something, especially pregnancy or
childbirth

cen·o·taph (SEN-ŏ-taf) or (sen-ŏ-
TAHF) *n.*, a tomb or monument
erected in memory of a person
buried elsewhere

cen·to (SEN-toh) *n.*, a poetic or
literary piece composed of passages
from other writings

ceph·a·lom·e·try (sef-ă-LOM-ĭ-
tree) *n.*, the science of measuring
the size of the human head

ce·rau·no·graph (sĕ-RAWN-ŏ-
graf) *n.*, a device that
chronologically records the
incidence of thunder and lightning

cere·ment (SEER-mĕnt) *n.*, a
usually waxed cloth used for
wrapping the dead

cer·e·ous (SEER-ee-ŭs) *adj.*, an
obsolete term meaning waxen

cer·met (SĔR-met) *n.*, a durable,
heat-resistant alloy

ce·ro (SER-oh) *n.*, a large game
fish, similar to a mackerel, found in
the warmer parts of the western
Atlantic

ce·ro·ma (sĕ-ROH-mă) *n.*, 1. the
swollen nostril area on the bill of a
bird 2. a room for oil and wax
anointment in ancient Roman
baths

ce·ru·men (sĕ-ROO-mĕn) *n.*,
earwax

cer·vi·corn (SĔR-vĭ-kohrn) *adj.*,
having antlers

cer·vine (SĔR-vīn) or (SĔR-vin)
adj., relating to or resembling a
deer

ces·pi·tose or **caes·pi·tose** (SES-
pĭ-tohs) *adj.*, a botanical term for
matted together or growing in
dense tufts

ces·tode (SES-tohd) *n.*, a parasitic
worm

ces·tus (SES-tŭs) *n.*, a belt worn
by a woman, especially a symbolic
one worn by a bride

ce·tol·o·gy (see-TAHL-ŏ-jee) *n.*, the
study of whales

chac·ma (CHAK-mă) *n.*, a large
African baboon

chae·tig·er·ous (kee-TIJ-(ĕ)-rŭs)
adj., having bristles

chafe·wax (CHAYF-waks) *n.*, a
former official at the English
chancery who made wax for
sealing documents

chal·one (KA-lohn) *n.*, a bodily
secretion that, when released,
depresses activity

cha·lyb·e·ous (ka-LĔB-ee-ŭs) *adj.*,
having a lustrous, bluish black color

cha·made (shă-MAHD) *n.*, a drum
or trumpet signal for a conference
with an enemy

cham-fer (CHAM-fĕr) *v.*, to cut a groove or furrow in

cham-fron (CHAM-frŏn) *n.*, the headpiece of a horse's armor

cham-paign (CHAM-payn) or (SHAM-payn) *n.*, 1. a spread of flat, open country 2. an archaic term for a battleground

chan-da-la (chăn-DAH-lă) *n.*, an East Indian of low caste; an untouchable

chank-ings (chang-kĕnz) *n.*, U.S. dialect for discarded bits of fruit or nuts

chan-tage (shahn-TAHZH) *n.*, extortion; blackmail

chan-te-relle or **chan-ta-relle** (shan-tĕ-REL) or (shahn-tă-REL) *n.*, 1. an edible, yellow mushroom that smells like an apricot 2. the highest string of certain stringed instruments such as the banjo or violin

cha-que-ta (chah-KE-tah) *n.*, a Spanish term for a heavy jacket, especially a cowboy's leather jacket

char-a-cin (KAR-ă-cĭn) *n.*, 1. a white, moldy-smelling substance found in some types of fatty algae 2. a bright-colored tropical fish often obtained for aquariums

cha-rette or **char-rette** (shă-RET) *n.*, a final, intensive effort to finish an architectural design project before a deadline

char-ka or **char-kha** (CHĂR-kă) or (CHAHR-kă) *n.*, in India and the East Indies, a spinning wheel

char-ta-ceous (kahr-TAY-shŭs) *adj.*, like or composed of paper

chas-mo-phyte (KAZ-mŏ-fīt) *n.*, a plant that grows in rock crevices

cha-toy-ant (shă-TOI-ănt) *adj.*, changing in luster or color, such as fabric

chee-cha-ko or **chee-cha-co** or **che-cha-ko** (chee-CHAH-koh) *n.*, a newcomer to the Pacific Northwest

cheese-par-ing (CHEEZ-pair-ing) *n.*, a worthless object hoarded by a miserly or poor person

che-lo-ni-an (ke-LOH-nee-ăn) *adj.*, like a tortoise or turtle

chev-a-line (SHEV-ă-leen) *adj.*, associated with horses

che-wink or **chee-wink** (chĭ-WINGK) or (chee-WINGK) *n.*, in eastern North America, a common finch

chi-a (CHEE-ă) *n.*, a plant found in Mexico and the southwestern U.S. whose seeds are used in making a native beverage

chiaus (CHOWS) or (CHOWSH) *n.*, 1. a Turkish messenger 2. a swindler

chig-e-tai (CHIG-ĕ-tī) *n.*, a Mongolian wild ass

chil-i-ad (KIL-ee-ad) *n.*, 1. a group of 1,000 2. 1,000 years; a millennium

chi-mo-pel-a-gic (kī-moh-PĔL-ă-jik) *adj.*, associated with marine organisms that usually live in the depths of the sea, but rise to the surface in winter

chinch (CHINCH) *n.*, a bed bug; a bug known to destroy grain crops

\a\ bat \ă\ about \e\ or \ĕ\ check \ĕ\ letter \ĕ\ cafe \i\fish \ī\ tie \ĭ\ limit \o\ boat \ŏ\ bacon \u\ sun \ŭ\ helpful \ü\ fool

chi·rog·no·my (kī-RAHG-nŏ-mee) *n.*, palmistry

chi·ro·meg·a·ly (kī-rŏ-MEG-ă-lee) *n.*, unusual growth of the hands

chi·ro·spasm (KĪ-rŏ-spaz(ĕ)m) *n.*, writer's cramp

chi·ro·to·ny (kī-RAHT-ŏ-nee) *n.*, the extension of the hands in bestowing a blessing during a religious ceremony

chirr (CHĬR) *n.*, the short, trilling sound made by some birds, animals, and insects such as the grasshopper

chiv·y or **chevy** (CHIV-ee) or (CHEV-ee) *v.*, 1. to pursue 2. to irritate persistently or badger

chla·mys (KLAY-mis) or (KLAM-is) *n.*, a short, woolen cloak worn by young men in ancient Greece

chon (CHOHN) *n.*, 1. A Korean monetary unit 2. a language spoken by the Tehuelche and Ona people of southern Argentina and Tierra del Fuego

chop·in (CHAHP-ĭn) *n.*, a Scottish liquid unit of measure approximately an English quart

cho·ral·ce·lo (koh-răl-CHE-loh) *n.*, a keyboard instrument that produces an organlike sound

cho·rog·ra·phy (kŏ-RAHG-ră-fee) *n.*, a systematic, detailed description of a region or district, sometimes using charts or graphs

chott or **shott** (SHAHT) *n.*, in northern Africa, a term for a shallow salt-water lake or its dried bed

chough (CHŎF) *n.*, a small Old World bird with red legs and glossy red plumage

chouse (CHOWS) *v.*, 1. to swindle 2. in western United States, a term meaning to herd cattle roughly

chow·rie or **cau·ri** or **chau·ri** (CHOW-ree) *n.*, a whisk used in Asia to shoo flies, especially away from people of rank

chrem·a·tis·tic (krem-ă-TIS-tik) or (kreem-ă-TIS-tik) *adj.*, associated with the acquisition of wealth

chres·tom·a·thy (kre-STAHM-ă-thee) *n.*, a compilation of writings by different authors, used as a language-learning aid

chris·om or **chrys·om** (KRIZ-ŏm) *n.*, 1. consecrated oil used in administering some church sacraments 2. a white cloth or robe worn as a sign of innocence at baptism

chrys·el·e·phan·tine (kris-el-ĕ-FAN-teen) *adj.*, made of or overlaid with gold and ivory

chry·soph·i·list (krĭ-SAHF-ĭ-lĭst) *n.*, a person who loves gold

chtho·ni·an (THOH-nee-ăn) *adj.*, inhabiting the underworld; ghostly

chu·fa (CHOO-fă) *n.*, a European plant with an edible, tuberous root

chum·mage (CHŬM-ij) *n.*, the housing of people in the same room in a college dormitory

chu·ri·gue·resque (chuur-ree-gĕ-RESK) *adj.*, associated with a Spanish baroque architectural style noted for its embellished decoration

chyme (KĪM) *n.*, in the stomach, partially digested food

ci-bar-i-ous (si-BAIR-ee-ŏs) *adj.*, an archaic term relating to food

cib-ol or **cib-oul** or **cib-oule** (SI-bŏl) *n.*, a Welsh onion or shallot

ci-cis-be-o (chee-chiz-BAY-oh) *n.*, an escort or lover of a married woman, particularly in 18th-century Italy

cic-o-nine (SIK-ŏ-nīn) or (SIK-ŏ-nīn) *adj.*, associated with storks

ci-cur-ate (SIK-yŭ-rayt) *v.*, to domesticate

cil-ice (SIL-ĭs) *n.*, a garment made of haircloth, formerly worn by monks

ci-mex (SĪ-meks) *n.*, a bed bug

cin-gu-lar (SING-yŭ-lăr) *adj.*, shaped like a ring

cin-gu-lum (SING-yŭ-lŭm) *n.*, on the crown of a tooth, a ridge around its base

cip-o-lin (SIP-ŏ-lĭn) or (seep-ŏ-LAN) *n.*, an impure type of marble with alternating green and white layers

cir-cum-fo-ra-ne-ous (sĭr-kŭm-fŏ-RAY-nee-ŭs) *adj.*, wandering from place to place

cir-ri-ped (SIR-ĭ-ped) *n.*, a crustacean that is free swimming as larva but becomes permanently attached as an adult

cis-co (SIS-koh) *n.*, a Great Lakes whitefish caught for food

cist (SIST) or (KIST) *n.*, 1. a box or chest originally made of wicker and used for carrying sacred utensils in ancient Roman processions 2. a prehistoric tomb

cith-a-ra (SITH-ă-ră) or (ki-THAH-ră) *n.*, 1. an ancient Greek musical instrument like a lyre 2. a medieval instrument that looked like a harp

cit-tern or **cith-ern** (SID-ĕrn) or (SITH-ĕrn) *n.*, a wire-stringed guitar popular in Renaissance England

cix-i-id (SIK-see-ĭd) *n.*, an insect related to the lantern fly that has a small, elongated body

cla-chan (KLA-kăn) *n.*, the Scottish and Irish term for a hamlet

clad-ode (KLA-dohd) *n.*, a leaflike branch

clam-jam-fry or **clam-jam-frey** (klam-JAM-fri) *n.*, 1. a Scottish term for a disorderly mob 2. a Scottish term for garbage; throwaways

clap-per-dud-geon (KLAP-ĕr-dŭ-jĕn) *n.*, a person who begs

clar-ence (KLAR-ĕn(t)s) *n.*, a closed carriage that seats four

clark-i-a (KLAHR-kee-ă) *n.*, an herb found in the western U.S. with narrow leaves and ornamental purple or rose-colored flowers

cla-ro (KLAH-roh) *n.*, a light-colored, mild cigar

clar-y (KLA-ree) *n.*, 1. a drink of wine, honey, and spices that is strained until clear 2. an ornamental aromatic herb found in southern Europe

clau-di-ca-tion (claw-dĭ-KAY-shŏn) *n.*, the act of limping

\a\ bat \ā\ about \e\ or \ė\ check \ē\ letter \é\ cafe \i\fish \ī\ tie \ī\ limit \o\ boat \ŏ\ bacon \u\ sun \ŭ\ helpful \ü\ fool

cla-ver (KLAY-vĕr) or (KLA-vĕr) *v.*, British dialect meaning to climb

clav-i-cy-the-ri-um (klav-ĭ-sĭ-THEER-ee-ŭm) *n.*, an early upright harpsichord

cla-vis (KLAY-vĭs) or (KLAH-vĭs) *n.*, a glossary that aids interpretation

clay-more (KLAY-mohr) *n.*, a large, double-edged broadsword used by Scottish Highlanders

clepe (KLEEP) *v.*, an archaic term meaning to summon by name

clep-sy-dra (KLEP-sĭ-dră) *n.*, a water clock

cler-i-hew (KLER-ĭ-hyoo) *n.*, a light verse, usually consisting of two couplets, that comments about a person whose name is included in the rhyme

cle-ro-man-cy (KLEER-ŏ-man(t)-see) or (KLER-ŏ-man(t)-see) *n.*, predicting the future by casting lots such as straws or pebbles

clev-is (KLEV-ĭs) *n.*, a U-shaped metal fitting with holes drilled at the ends to accommodate a pin or bolt

cli-nom-e-ter (klĭ-NAHM-ĕ-dĕr) or (klĭ-NAHM-ĕ-dĕr) *n.*, an instrument used to measure angles

clish-ma-cla-ver (klish-mă-KLAY-vĕr) or (kleesh-mă-KLAY-vĕr) *n.*, a Scottish term for gossip or idle talk

clo-a-ca (kloh-AY-kă) *n.*, an underground pipe for removing water and waste

clod-poll (KLAHD-pohl) *n.*, a stupid person

clo-nus (KLOH-nŭs) *n.*, a series of muscle spasms that usually indicates brain or spinal cord damage

cloot (KLOOT) *n.*, a Scottish term for a cloven hoof

clough (KLŎF) or (KLOW) *n.*, a narrow valley or ravine

cly-ster (KLIS-tĕr) *n.*, an enema

cne-mi-al (NEE-mee-ăl) *adj.*, associated with the shin or shinbone

co-ac-er-vate (koh-AS-ĕr-vayt) or (koh-ă-SĔR-vayt) *v.*, to gather together in a heap or group

co-ad-u-nate (koh-AJ-ŭ-nayt) *v.*, to combine

co-ap-ta-tion (koh-ap-TAY-shŏn) *n.*, a joining of separated parts, as in a broken bone

co-a-ti (kă-WAHD-ee) *n.*, a tropical American mammal related to the raccoon that has an elongated body, a long, ringed tail, and a slender, flexible snout

cob-bing (KOB-ing) *n.*, old brick material removed from furnaces

cock-a-lo-rum (kahk-ă-LOH-rŭm) *n.*, 1. a self-important, pretentious little man 2. the children's game of leapfrog

cock-a-rouse or **cock-e-rouse** (KAHK-ă-rauus) *n.*, an important person in the early American colonies

cock-shy (KAHK-shī) *n.*, 1. an object or person set up for ridicule 2. a British term for a balanced construction that serves as a target for tossed balls or sticks

coc·tile (KAHK-tĭl) or (KAHK-tīl) *adj.*, made by baking, such as a brick

cog·i·ta·bund (KAHJ-ĭd-ă-bŭnd) *adj.*, an archaic term meaning pensive

co·gon (koh-GOHN) *n.*, a tall, coarse grass found in the tropics and used for thatching

co·hosh (KOH-hahsh) or (koh-HAHSH) *n.*, a perennial herb used medicinally

co·hune (koh-HOON) *n.*, a Central and South American palm whose fruit yields a valuable oil similar to coconut oil

coign (KOIN) *n.*, a cornerstone or a corner

cois·trel (KOIS-trĕl) *n.*, an archaic term for a servant in charge of a knight's horses

col (KAHL) *n.*, a pass across a mountain range

col·li·gate (KAHL-ĭ-gayt) *v.*, to group together according to an underlying principle

col·li·mate (KAHL-ĭ-mayt) *v.*, 1. to make parallel 2. to adjust a telescope's line of sight

col·lo·cate (KAHL-ŏ-kayt) *v.*, to line up side by side

col·lop (KAHL-ŏp) *n.*, a portion of meat

col·luc·ta·tion (kahl-ŭk-TAY-shŏn) *n.*, a fight

col·ly (KAHL-ee) *n.*, British dialect for soot or grime

col·ly·wob·bles (KAHL-ee-wahb-ĕlz) *n.*, a stomachache

col·pi·tis (kahl-PĪ-dĭs) *n.*, an infection of the vagina

col·por·teur or **col·por·ter** (KAHL-pohr-dĕr) or (KAHL-pawr-dĕr) *n.*, a book peddler, especially a retailer of books of a religious nature

col·ter or **coul·ter** (KOHL-tĕr) *n.*, a blade or wheel attached to the beam of a plow, used to cut the ground ahead of the plowshare

co·ly (KOH-lee) *n.*, a fruit-eating African bird with soft, grayish-brown plumage and a long, pointed tail

col·za (KAHL-ză) *n.*, an annual herb used in the U.S. as forage for hogs and sheep, as a cover crop for orchards, and as birdseed

co·mate (KOH-mayt) *adj.*, hairy; shaggy

com·e·do (KAHM-ĕ-doh) *n.*, a blackhead

come·ling (KŎM-ling) *n.*, an archaic term for a newly arrived foreigner

com·men·sal (kŏ-MEN(T)-săl) *n.* a person who customarily takes meals with other people

com·men·ti·tious (kah-mĕn-TI-shŭs) *adj.*, an archaic term for imaginary or fabricated

com·mi·nate (KAHM-ĭ-nayt) *v.*, to threaten with punishment from God

com·mi·nute (KAH-mĭ-n(y)oot) *v.*, to crush into small pieces

---

\a\ bat \ā\ about \e\ or \ĕ\ check \ē\ letter \é\ cafe \i\ fish \ī\ tie \ĭ\ limit \o\ boat \ŏ\ bacon \u\ sun \ŭ\ helpful \ü\ fool

com·mis·sure (KAHM-i-shoor) *n.*, a joint

com·mo·rant (KAH-mŏ-rănt) *adj.*, residing

com·mo·ri·ent (kŏ-MOHR-ee-ĕnt) *n.*, a person killed in a disaster that claimed other lives

co·mose (KOH-mohs) *adj.*, having tufted hair

com·pesce (kŏm-PES) *v.*, an archaic Scottish term meaning to restrain

com·po·ta·tor (KAHM-poh-taydŏr) *n.*, a person who drinks with a companion

com·pre·ca·tion (kahm-prĕ-KAYshŏn) *n.*, an archaic term for communal worship

com·pur·ga·tor (KAHM-pŭr-gaydŏr) *n.*, a person who testifies favorably for another

con·cam·er·at·ed (kahn-KAM-ĕrayd-ĕd) *adj.*, an archaic term meaning vaulted

con·chol·o·gy (kahn-KAHL-ŏ-jee) *n.*, the study of shells

con·cil·i·a·bule (kŏn-SIL-ee-ăbyool) *n.*, a secret meeting, especially of rebels against church or state authority

con·cin·ni·ty (kŏn-SIN-ĭd-ee) *n.*, the harmony in the adaptation of parts to a whole or each other, especially literature

con·ci·ta·tion (kahn(t)-sĭ-TAYshŏn) *n.*, the act of creating agitation

con·dign (kŏn-DĪN) *adj.*, justified or deserved; specifically used in regard to punishment since the 17th century

con·dyle (KAHN-dīl) or (KAHNdĕl) *n.*, the rounded bulge on bones that occur in pairs such as those in a knuckle

con·gee (kohn-ZHAY) or (KAHNjay) *n.*, 1. leave taking; farewell 2. permission to leave

con·ger (KAHNG-gĕr) *n.*, a large eel used for food in Europe

con·gi·ar·y (KAHN-jee-ăr-ee) *n.*, a present, such as corn, wine, or oil, made to the soldiers or people of ancient Rome

con·gi·us (KAHN-jee-ŭs) *n.*, 1. a pharmaceutical term for a gallon 2. an ancient Roman unit of liquid measure

con·gou (KAHNG-goh) or (KAHNgoo) *n.*, a type of black tea from China

con·nate (kahn-AYT) *adj.*, existing from birth or origin; congenital

co·no·dont (KOH-nŏ-dahnt) or (KAHN-ŏ-dahnt) *n.*, a prehistoric fossil thought to be the teeth of extinct animals

con·qui·an (KAHNG-kee-ăn) *n.*, a two-handed card game using 40 cards that preceded forms of rummy

con·spue (kŏnz-PYOO) or (konSPYOO) *v.*, to spurn contemptuously

con·sue·tude (KAHN-swĕ-t(y)ood) *n.*, a habit or custom, especially one backed by law

conte (KOHNT) *n.*, a short tale with an adventurous theme

con·ti·cent (KAHN-tĭ-sĕnt) *adj.*, silent

con·to (KAHN-toh) *n.*, a unit of money in Portugal and Brazil

con·trec·ta·tion (kahn-trek-TAY-shŏn) *n.*, foreplay prior to sexual intercourse

con·trit·u·rate (kŏn-TRICH-ŭ-rayt) *v.*, to crush

con·tu·ber·nal (kŏn-T(Y)OO-bĕr-năl) *adj.*, cohabitating

con·vert·ite (KON-vĕr-tīt) *n.*, a prostitute who has reformed

coon·tie or (KOON-tee) *n.*, a type of tough, woody plant found in Florida that yields arrowroot

co·par·ce·ner (koh-PAHR-sĕ-nĕr) *n.*, a joint heir

co·pi·hue (kŏ-PEE-way) *n.*, a vine that has yellowish, edible fruit; also called chile-bells

cop·ro·la·li·a (kahp-rŏ-LAY-lee-ă) *n.*, the uncontrollable use of obscene language

co·prol·o·gy (kŏ-PRAHL-ŏ-jee) *n.*, the study of or preoccupation with excrement or obscenity

cop·ro·phil·i·a (kahp-rŏ-FIL-ee-ă) *n.*, an extreme interest in feces, especially in connection with sexual excitement

co·qui·na (koh-KEE-nă) *n.*, 1. a soft, whitish rock made up of pieces of shells and coral and used as building material 2. a clam used for broth or chowder

cor·a·cle (KAWR-ă-kĕl) *n.*, a small, wicker-framed boat covered with hide or leather and used in ancient Britain

cor·ban or **kor·ban** (KAWR-ban) or (KAWR-bahn) *n.*, an offering or sacrifice made to God by ancient Hebrews, especially in fulfillment of a vow

cor·beil or **cor·beille** (KAWR-bĕl) *n.*, a sculptured basket used for architectural decoration

cor·bi·na (kaw(r)-BEE-nă) *n.*, a game fish of the whiting family found along the Pacific coast of North America

cor·date (KAWR-dăt) or (KAWR-dayt) *adj.*, heart-shaped

cor·dil·le·ra (kawr-dĭl-ER-ă) or (kawr-DIL-ĕr-ă) *n.*, a chain of mountain ranges that extends for a great length

cord·wain·er (KAWRD-wayn-ĕr) *n.*, a shoemaker

corf (KAWRF) *n.*, a British term for a small wagon used for carrying coal, ore, etc., out of a mine

co·ri·a·ceous (koh-ree-AY-shŭs) *adj.*, of or like leather

corm (KOHRM) *n.*, the short, fleshy underground stem of a plant such as a crocus

cor·nu (KOHR-n(y)oo) *n.*, a bodily structure shaped like or resembling a 1081

cor·o·dy or **cor·ro·dy** (KOHR-ŏ-dee) *n.*, food or other goods given by a religious house to a king and then assigned to one of his subjects

cor·o·nach (KOHR-ŏ-năk) *n.*, in Scotland and Ireland, a dirge played on bagpipes or sung

cor·reg·i·dor (kŏ-REG-ĭ-dohr) *n.*, the chief official in a Spanish town or colony

cor·ri·gent (KOHR-ĭ-jĕnt) *n.*, a substance added to a medicine to counteract undesirable side effects

cor·rob·o·ree (kŏ-RAHB-ŏ-ree) *n.*, a sacred, festive, or warlike nocturnal gathering of Australian aborigines

cor·sac or **cor·sak** (KOHR-sak) *n.*, a small fox found in central Asia; also called an Afghan fox

cor·us·cate (KOHR-ŭ-skayt) or (KAHR-ŭ-skayt) *v.*, to sparkle or gleam

cor·vine (KOHR-vīn) *adj.*, associated with a crow

cor·y·ban·tic (kohr-ĕ-BAN-tik) *adj.*, wild; agitated

cor·y·phae·us (kohr-ĕ-FEE-ŭs) *n.*, 1. the head of a chorus 2. the leader of a group

cor·y·phée (kohr-ĕ-FAY) *n.*, a ballet dancer in a small group, instead of the corps de ballet or a soloist

co·ry·za (kŏ-RĪ-ză) *n.*, a medical term for the common cold, especially one centered in the upper respiratory system

cos·ci·no·man·cy (KAHS-ĭ-noh-mant-see) *n.*, predicting the future by using shears and sieves

cosh·er (KASH-ĕr) or (KOHSH-ĕr) *v.*, an Irish term meaning to live off others' generosity

cos·mo·tel·lur·i·an (kahz-moh-tel-LUR-ee-ăn) *adj.*, associated with the heavens and the earth or affecting both

cos·set (KAHS-ĕt) *v.*, to fondle or pamper; to treat as a pet

cos·tal (KAHS-tăl) *adj.*, of or relating to a rib

cos·tate (KAHS-tayt) or (KAH-stăt) *adj.*, having ribs

cos·ter·mon·ger (KAHS-tĕr-mŏng-ger) *n.*, a British term for a street vendor who sells fruits or vegetables

cos·tive (KAHS-tiv) or (KOHS-tiv) *adj.*, 1. constipated 2. slow

cos·tum·bris·ta (kohs-tŭm-BRIS-tă) or (kahs-tŭm-BRIS-tă) *n.*, a Spanish or Latin American writer whose writings realistically depict local or regional customs

co·teau (kaw-TOH) or (koh-TOH) *n.*, 1. a hilly, upland region 2. a valley's side

co·thur·nus (koh-THŬR-nŭs) or (kŏ-THŬR-nŭs) *n.*, a laced, thick-soled boot worn by actors in Greek and Roman tragedies

cou·ma·rou (KYOO-mă-roo) *n.*, the tonka-bean tree

cou·vade (koo-VAHD) *n.*, a primitive custom in which a man takes to his bed as if for childbearing while his wife is having a baby

cow·an (KAUJ-ăn) *n.*, a person who is not a Freemason, especially one who poses as a Freemason

coy·pu or **coy·pou** (KOI-poo) *n.*, a large, aquatic South American rodent valued for its fur; also called the nutria

cram·be (KRAM-bee) *n.*, an annual herb of the Old World; also called the sea kale

cram·bo (KRAM-boh) *n.*, a game in which one person or side must find a rhyme to a word or a line of verse given by the other

cramp·it (KRAMP-ĭt) *n.*, a term in the sport of curling for a sheet of iron a player stands on

cran·nog (KRAN-ŏg) *n.*, a man-made, fortified island in a lake or marsh of prehistoric Ireland or Scotland

crap·u·lous (KRAP-yŭ-lŭs) *adj.*, 1. given to excess in drinking or eating 2. suffering a hangover

cre·ance (KREE-ăn(t)s) *n.*, a cord attached to the leg of a hawk to prevent escape during training

creb·ri·ty (KREB-rĭ-dee) *n.*, frequency

crep·i·tate (KREP-ĭ-tayt) *v.*, to make a crackling sound

crib·ri·form (KRIB-rĭ-fohrm) *adj.*, sievelike; pierced with small holes

cri·nal (KRĪ-năl) *adj.*, associated with the hair

crine (KRĪN) *v.*, a Scottish term meaning to shrink or wizen

cri·noid (KRĪ-noid) or (KRI-noid) *adj.*, of or relating to the sea lily

cri·num (KRĪ-nŭm) *n.*, a bulbous herb cultivated for its fragrant, showy flowers, which are usually white and tinged with red

crith (KRITH) *n.*, a liter of hydrogen's weight at 0° C and 760 millimeter pressure

croft·er (KRAWF-tĕr) *n.*, a British term for a person who rents and works a small farm

crom·lech (KRAHM-lek) *n.*, 1. a prehistoric tomb or monument 2. a circle of upright stones surrounding a mound

cronk (KRAHNK) or (KRAWNK) *adj.*, Australian slang meaning ill or ailing

croo·dle (KROO-dĕl) *n.*, British dialect meaning to murmur

cro·qui·gnole (KROH-kĭ-nohl) *n.*, a method of giving a permanent wave to hair

cro·quis (kroh-KEE) *n.*, a sketch for a work of art

crore (KROH(Ĕ)R) *n.*, an Indian monetary unit equal to 10 million rupees

cro·sier or **cro·zier** (KROH-zhĕr) *n.*, the staff of a bishop or abbot that is similar to a shepherd's

cro·tal·i·form (kroh-TAL-ĭ-fohrm) *adj.*, resembling a rattlesnake

cru·or (KROO-ohr) *n.*, an obsolete term for clotted blood

crwth or **cruth** (KROOTH) *n.*, an ancient Celtic musical instrument whose strings are plucked or played by a short bow

cte·niz·i·dae (tĕ-NIZ-ĭ-dee) *n.*, a burrowing spider like the trap door spider

cte·tol·o·gy (tĕ-TAHL-ŏ-jee) *n.*, the study of the origin and development of acquired traits

\a\ bat \ä\ about \e\ or \ė\ check \ĕ\ letter
\é\ cafe \i\fish \ī\ tie \ĭ\ limit \o\ boat
\ŏ\ bacon \u\ sun \ŭ\ helpful \ü\ fool

cu-beb (KYOO-beb) *n.*, the spicy, unripe fruit of the Java pepper that is dried, crushed, and then smoked to relieve nasal congestion

cu-cu-line (K(Y)OO-k(y)ŭ-lĭn) *adj.*, associated with cuckoos

cues-ta (KWES-tă) or (KWAYS-tă) *n.*, a hill or ridge that is steep on one side and gently sloping on the other

cui-rass (kwee-RAS) *n.*, a piece of armor for the torso, originally of leather, that consists of a breastplate and a backpiece

culch or **cultch** (KŬLCH) *n.*, the stones and old shells that form a spawning bed for oysters

cu-let (KYOO-lĕt) *n.*, 1. a small face that forms the bottom of the facet of a stone 2. armor that covers the buttocks

cu-li-cide (KYOO-lĭ-sīd) *n.*, a poison that kills mosquitoes

cul-lion (KŬL-yŏn) *n.*, an archaic term for a vile fellow

cunc-ta-tion (kŭnk-TAY-shŏn) *n.*, delay; postponement

cu-nic-u-lus (kyoo-NIK-(y)ŭ-lŭs) *n.*, an underground passage or drain in ancient Rome

cup-ping (KUP-ping) *n.*, a process, formerly used for drawing blood to the skin surface, that creates a partial vacuum

cu-ri-o-log-ic (kyoo-ree-ŏ-LAHJ-ik) *adj.*, depicting things by their images instead of symbolically

cur-ple (KŬR-pĕl) *n.*, a Scottish term for the buttocks; rump

cur-rack or **cur-rach** (KŬR-ăk) *n.*, a Scottish term for a wicker basket carried on the back of a horse or donkey or on the shoulders of a person

cur-ti-lage (KŬRD-ĭ-lij) *n.*, a fenced-in yard that surrounds a house

cush-la-mo-chree (kŭsh-lă-mŏ-KREE) *n.*, an Irish term for sweetheart

cu-tin (KYOO-tin) *n.*, the transparent, waxy substance that, with cellulose, forms the surface layer of plants

cut-tle (KŬD-ĕl) *v.*, to fold cloth in pleats

cwm (KOOM) *n.*, a deep, steep-walled basin on a mountain that was probably formed by glacial erosion

cy-an-e-ous (sī-AN-ee-ŭs) *adj.*, deep blue; azure

cy-ath-i-form (sī-ATH-ĭ-fohrm) *adj.*, cup-shaped

cy-cas (SĪ-kas) or (SĪ-kăs) *n.*, a sago palm tree

cy-clos-to-mate (sī-KLAHS-tŏ-măt) *adj.*, having a spherical mouth

cy-e-sis (sī-EE-sis) *n.*, pregnancy

cym-ling (SIM-ling) or **cymb-ling** (SIMB-ling) *n.*, a summer squash with a ribbed edge

cy-mo-gene (SĪ-mŏ-jeen) *n.*, a flammable, gaseous petroleum product consisting mainly of butane

cy-mot-ri-chous (sī-MAH-trĭ-kŭs) *adj.*, having wavy hair

cyn·e·get·ic (sin-ĕ-JED-ik) *adj.*, associated with hunting

cyng·ha·nedd (kĭng-HAH-neth) *n.*, a system of rhyme and alliteration in Welsh poetry

cy·nol·o·gist (sī-NAHL-ŏ-jĭst) or (sī-NAHL-ŏ-jĭst) *n.*, a dog trainer

cyw·ydd (KĬ-with) *n.*, a Welsh verse formed in couplets or triplets

D

dab·chick (DAB-chik) *n.*, a type of water bird related to the loon; also called a grebe

dack·er (DAK-ĕr) *v.*, a Scottish and Northern British term meaning to stagger, shake, or waver

da·coit (dă-KOIT) *n.*, a member of a gang of Indian or Burmese robbers and killers

dac·ry·a·gogue (DAK-ree-ă-gawg) *adj.*, stimulating the shedding of tears

dac·tyl·o·gram (dak-TIL-ŏ-gram) *n.*, a fingerprint

dac·ty·lol·o·gy (dak-tĕ-LAHL-ŏ-jee) *n.*, the technique of communicating by making signs with the fingers; sign language

dae·dal (DEE-dăl) *adj.*, 1. skillful; artistic 2. intricate

da·ga·me or **de·ga·me** (dĕ-GAY-may) *n.*, a tropical American timber tree whose wood is used for building and making tools

dag·gle (DAG-ĕl) *v.*, an archaic term meaning to wet and soil by dragging through mire

da·go·ba or **da·ga·ba** (DAH-gŏ-bă) *n.*, a Far Eastern term for a shrine or altar for sacred objects

da·ha·be·ah (dah-(h)ă-BEE-ă) *n.*, a long houseboat used on the Nile River, often propelled by engines

dalles (DALZ) *n.*, the rapids of a river running through a canyon or gorge

dal·ton·ism (DAWL-tŏn-izĕm) *n.*, color blindness, especially the inability to distinguish red from green

dan·di·prat (DAN-dee-prat) *n.*, a 16th-century English coin worth about twopence

da·ni·o (DAY-nee-oh) *n.*, a brightly colored fish native to India and Ceylon and often kept in aquariums

dap (DAP) *v.*, 1. to fish by letting the bait fall gently into the water 2. to skip or bounce, as a stone on the surface of a lake

daph·ne·an (DAF-nee-ăn) *adj.*, timid; bashful

dar·bies (DAHR-beez) *n.*, a British slang term for handcuffs

---

\a\ bat \ă\ about \e\ or \è\ check \ĕ\ letter
\é\ cafe \i\fish \ī\ tie \ĭ\ limit \o\ boat
\ŏ\ bacon \u\ sun \ŭ\ helpful \ü\ fool

dar·i·ole (DAR-ee-ohl) *n.*, a pastry shell or aspic mold filled with sweet or appetizing food

dar·rein (dă-RAYN) *adj.*, a legal term meaning last or final

das·y·phyl·lous (das-ĭ-FIL-ŏs) *adj.*, having thick or thickly set leaves

das·y·proc·ta (das-ĭ-PRAHK-tă) *n.*, a type of rodent with long legs and three toes on each hind foot

dauw (DAUU) *n.*, a zebra found on the plains of central or eastern Africa with a striped belly and unstriped legs; also called Burchell's zebra

de·al·bate (dee-AL-bayt) *adj.*, a botanical term meaning covered with a filmy white powder

de·bye (dĕ-BĪ) *n.*, a unit of electrical measurement

de·cad·ic (de-KAD-ik) or (dĕ-KAD-ik) *adj.*, associated with the decimal system of counting

de·col·la·tion (dee-kah-LAY-shŏn) *n.*, beheading

de·cor·ti·cate (dee-KOHRD-ĭ-kayt) or (dĕ-KOHRD-ĭ-kayt) *v.*, to shell, peel, skin, or strip

de·crep·i·ta·tion (dĕ-krep-ĭ-TAY-shŏn) *n.*, the fracturing or crackling of some crystals upon being heated

de·cu·bi·tus (dĕ-KYOO-bĕd-ŭs) or (dĕ-KYOO-bĕ-tŭs) *n.*, 1. the position assumed when lying in bed 2. a bedsore

dec·us·sate (DEK-ŭ-sayt) or (dee-KŬ-sayt) *v.*, to make in the form of an X

de·dans (dĕ-DAHN) *n.*, spectators at a tennis game

de·di·tion (dĕ-DI-shŏn) *n.*, the act of surrendering

ded·o·lent (DED-ŏ-lĕnt) *adj.*, an archaic term meaning callous; feeling no grief

de·fal·cate (dĕ-FAL-kayt) or (dee-FAL-kayt) *v.*, an archaic term meaning to appropriate money entrusted to one's care; to embezzle

def·i·lade (DEF-ĭ-layd) *v.*, to protect against enemy fire by using barricades

def·la·grate (DEF-lă-grayt) *v.*, to burn, especially suddenly and rapidly

de·glu·ti·tion (dee-gloo-TI-shŏn) *n.*, the act of swallowing

de·hisce (dĕ-HIS) or (dee-HIS) *v.*, to gape or burst open

de·hort (dee-HOHRT) *v.*, an archaic term meaning to discourage against

deic·tic (DĪK-tik) *adj.*, a term used in logic meaning offering direct proof

deil (DEEL) *n.*, a Scottish term for a devil

deip·nos·o·phist (dīp-NAHS-ŏ-fĭst) *n.*, a good dinner conversationalist

de·la·tor (dĕ-LAYD-ŏr) or (dĕ-LAY-tohr) *n.*, a professional informer

del·i·quesce (del-ĭ-KWES) *v.*, to melt away; to vanish

del·i·tes·cent (del-ĭ-TE-sĕnt) *adj.*, concealed; hidden

del·ti·ol·o·gy (del-tee-AHL-ŏ-jee) *n.*, the avocation of postcard collecting

de-mer-sal (dĕ-MĔR-săl) or (dee-MĔR-săl) *adj.*, living at the bottom, as a fish

de-mesne (dĕ-MAYN) or (dee-MAYN) *n.*, lawful ownership of land

de-mi-se-mi-qua-ver (de-mee-SE-mee-kway-vĕr) *n.*, a 1/32 note in music

de-mit (dĕ-MIT) *v.*, to resign or quit, as from a job or public office

de-mul-cent (dĕ-MŬL-sĕnt) or (dee-MŬL-sĕnt) *adj.*, soothing or softening, as a throat lozenge

de-my (dĕ-MĪ) *n.*, a gold coin of 15th-century Scotland

de-na-ry (DEE-nă-ree) or (DĔ-nă-ree) *adj.*, containing 10; tenfold

den-dri-form (DEN-drĭ-fohrm) *adj.*, resembling a tree

den-droph-i-lous (den-DRAHF-ĭ-lŭs) *adj.*, dwelling in or on a tree

den-gue (DENG-gee) or (DENG-gay) *n.*, an infectious fever transmitted by mosquitoes that causes severe pain in the joints and muscles; also called breakbone fever

de-on-tol-o-gy (dee-ahn-TAHL-ŏ-jee) *n.*, the study of duty and moral responsibility

de-perm (dee-PĔRM) *v.*, to demagnetize a ship's steel hull as a precaution against magnetic mines

de-phlo-gis-ti-cate (dee-flŏ-JIS-tĭ-kayt) *v.*, to remove from a substance the part of a combustible substance that causes burning

de-pone (dĕ-POHN) or (dee-POHN) *v.*, to testify under oath

de-raign (dĕ-RAYN) *v.*, an obsolete term meaning to prove a claim or settle an argument by personal combat

derf (DERF) *adj.*, a Scottish term meaning bold; fearless

de-sip-i-ence (dĕ-SIP-ee-ĕn(t)s) or (dee-SIP-ee-ĕn(t)s) *n.*, relaxed playfulness

de-spon-so-ries (dĕ-SPAHN-sŏ-reez) *n.*, an obsolete term for a written marriage announcement; betrothal

des-pu-mate (DES-pyoo-mayt) or (dĕ-SPYOO-mayt) *v.*, an archaic term meaning to clarify by removing scum, as with honey or wine

des-qua-mate (DES-kwă-mayt) *v.*, to pare off in scales, such as those present in certain skin diseases

des-ue-tude (DES-wee-tood) or (DES-wee-tyood) *n.*, the state of disuse and neglect; outmoded

de-tri-tion (dĕ-TRI-shŏn) *n.*, the act of wearing away by rubbing

deu-ter-og-a-my (d(y)ood-ĕ-RAHG-ă-mee) *n.*, a legal second marriage following the death or divorce of a first spouse

deu-ter-os-co-py (d(y)ood-ĕr-AHS-kŏ-pee) *n.*, an archaic term for clairvoyance

dex-tral (DEKS-trăl) *adj.*, of or relating to the right; right-handed

---

\a\ bat \ă\ about \e\ or \è\ check \ĕ\ letter
\é\ cafe \i\fish \ĭ\ tie \ī\ limit \o\ boat
\ō\ bacon \u\ sun \ŭ\ helpful \ü\ fool

dghai-sa (DĪ-să) *n.*, a small boat, common in Malta, that is similar to a gondola

dhar-na or **dhur-na** (DĂR-nă) *n.*, an Indian method of seeking justice by fasting on the doorstep of the offender

dhole (DOHL) *n.*, an Indian term for a fierce wild dog that hunts in packs

dho-ti (DOH-tee) *n.*, a loincloth worn by male Hindi

dhya-na (dee-AH-nă) or (DYAH-nă) *n.*, meditation upon a single object in the Hindu and Buddhist religions

di-ac-o-nate (dī-AK-ŏ-năt) or (dee-AK-ŏ-năt) *n.*, the office or term of office of a deacon

di-al-lel (DĪ-ă-lel) *adj.*, mating in accordance with a system that breeds each female to two or more males to determine how certain characteristics are transmitted

di-a-no-et-ic (dī-ă-noh-ED-ik) *adj.*, intellectual

di-a-pho-ret-ic (dī-ă-fŏ-RED-ik) *adj.*, able to induce sweating

di-aer-e-sis or **di-er-e-sis** (dī-ER-ĕ-sĭs) *n.*, a symbol represented by two dots placed over the second of two adjacent vowels to show separate pronunciation, such as in the word naïve

di-a-skeu-ast or **di-a-sceu-ast** (dī-ă-SKYOO-ast) or (dī-ă-SKYOO-ăst) *n.*, an editor; a person who revises

di-ath-e-sis (dī-ATH-ĕ-sĭs) *n.*, a tendency or predisposition toward a disease or abnormality

dib (DIB) *v.*, to fish by lightly bobbing and dipping the bait

dib-ble (DIB-ĕl) *n.*, a small gardening tool used to dig holes for planting

dick-cis-sel (dik-SIS-ĕl) *n.*, a common yellow-breasted finch found throughout the central U.S. that feeds on grasshoppers and weed seeds

dic-ty or **dick-ty** (DIK-tee) *adj.*, a U.S. slang term meaning snobbish

did-ger-i-doo or **did-jer-i-doo** (DI-jĕr-ee-doo) *n.*, a large, bamboo musical pipe used by Australian aborigines

did-y-mous (DID-ĭ-mŭs) *adj.*, in pairs; twin

dight (DĪT) *v.*, an archaic term meaning to decorate; beautify

dig-i-ti-grade (DIJ-ĭd-ĭ-grayd) *adj.*, walking on the toes with the heel raised

di-glot (DĪ-glaht) *adj.*, bilingual; expressed in two languages

di-go-neu-tic (dī-gŏ-N(Y)OOD-ik) *adj.*, having two broods within a single year

di-lamb-do-dont (dī-LAM-dŏ-dahnt) *adj.*, having two pointed and crossing ridges on the molar teeth

dim-ble (DIM-bĕl) *n.*, English dialect for a ravine with a waterway

di-mid-i-ate (dĭ-MID-ee-ayt) *adj.*, separated into two equal parts

di-nan-de-rie (dĭ-NAN-dĕ-ree) or (dee-nan-DREE) *n.*, decorative brass, copper, or bronze objects for church or home use, such as those made between the 13th and 15th centuries

din-dle (DIN-dĕl) *n.*, a Scottish term for a tremor or quake

din-gle (DING-gĕl) *n.*, a northern U.S. term for a storm door or protective covering at the entrance of a house

dink (DINGK) *n.*, a small boat, particularly one for duck hunting

din-key or **dink-y** (DING-kee) or (DING-ki) *n.*, a small locomotive, especially one for hauling freight and logs

din-mont (DIN-mahnt) *n.*, a Scottish term for a castrated male sheep between one and two years old or between the first and second shearing

di-oe-cious (dī-EE-shŭs) *adj.*, having separate sexes

di-oes-trum or **di-es-trum** (dī-ES-trŭm) or (dī-EE-strŭm) *n.*, the interval between the periods of sexual excitability, especially in female animals

di-or-tho-sis (dī-ohr-THOH-sĭs) *n.*, an archaic term for a rewriting, especially of text

di pet-to (dee-PED-oh) *adv.*, or *adj.*, from the chest, used in regard to singing

dip-lo-e (DIP-loh-ee) *n.*, the bony tissue between the tables of the skull

dip-sas (DIP-săs) *n.*, a serpent whose bite produced intense thirst, according to ancient beliefs

dir-dum (DIR-dŭm) *n.*, a Scottish term for blame; scolding

di-remp-tion (dī-REM(P)-shŏn) *n.*, separation into two

di-rhin-ous (dī-RĪ-nŭs) *adj.*, a zoological term for having paired nostrils

dis-bos-om (dis-BOOZ-ŏm) or (dis-BOO-zŏm) *v.*, to reveal or confess

dis-cal-ce-ate (di-SKAL-see-ăt) *adj.*, without shoes

dis-cerp-ti-ble (dĭ-SĔRP-tĭ-bĕl) *adj.*, able to be torn apart

dis-cinct (dĭ-SING(K)T) *adj.*, casually dressed; negligent

dis-cob-o-lus or **dis-cob-o-los** (dĭ-SKAHB-ŏ-lŭs) *n.*, a person who throws the discus

dis-em-bogue (dis-ĕm-BOHG) *v.*, to empty or discharge, as a river into a sea

di-seuse (dee-ZĔRZ) *n.*, a woman who recites verse or other text as an accompaniment to music

dis-limn (dĭs-LIM) *v.*, to dim; to fade

di-so-mus (dī-SOH-mŭs) *n.*, a monster with two bodies

dis-sil-i-ent (dĭ-SIL-yĕ-nt) or (dis-SIL-ee-ĕnt) *adj.*, exploding open

dis-tich (DI-stik) or (DI-steek) *n.*, two lines of verse that make complete sense; a couplet

dit-o-kous (DID-ŏ-kŭs) *adj.*, 1. producing two young or laying two eggs at each birth 2. producing two kinds of young, as is done by certain types of worms

dit-tol-o-gy (di-TAHL-ŏ-jee) *n.*, a double meaning

di-u-tur-nal (dī-yoo-TŬR-năl) *adj.*, long-lasting

di-va-gate (DĪ-vă-gayt) or (DIV-ă-gayt) *v.*, to wander or stray from one place or subject to another; to digress

di-vulse (dī-VŬLS) or (dĭ-VŬLS) *v.*, a surgical term meaning to pull or rip apart

dix-it (DIK-sit) *n.*, an utterance

di-zy-got-ic (dī-zī-GAHD-ik) *adj.*, developed from two fertilized eggs; fraternal, as applied to twins

diz-zard (DIZ-ărd) *n.*, U.S. dialect for a dimwit

do-bra (DOH-bră) *n.*, an 18th- and early 19th-century Portuguese coin, especially one made of gold

do-cent (DOHS-ěnt) *n.*, a college lecturer

doch-an-dor-rach or **doch-an-dor-ris** (D(Y)AHK-ăn-DOHR-ăs) or (D(Y)AHK-ăn-DAHR-ăs) *n.*, a Scottish and Irish term for a farewell drink

doc-i-ty (DAHS-ĭd-ee) *n.*, U.S. dialect for an apt willingness to learn

dod-dy or **dod-die** (DAH-dee) *n.*, a Scottish term for a cow or bull without horns

do-dec-a-gon (doh-DEK-ă-gahn) *n.*, a 12-sided polygon

dog-ber-ry (DAWG-be-ree) or (DAHG-be-ree) *n.*, a bungling official, after a character in Shakespeare's *Much Ado about Nothing*

dog-fall (DAWG-fahl) *n.*, 1. a fall in wrestling in which both competitors land together, so neither has the advantage 2. a draw or a tie

do-lab-ri-form (doh-LAB-ră-fohrm) *adj.*, in the shape of the head of an ax or hatchet

do-lent (DOH-lěnt) *adj.*, grieving

dol-i-chop-o-dous (dahl-ě-KAHP-ŏ-dŭs) *adj.*, having a long foot in proportion to the body

do-li-o-form (DOH-lee-ŏ-fohrm) *adj.*, barrel-shaped

do-lus (DOH-lŭs) *n.*, a Roman and civil law term for a deceitful act, especially one with evil intentions

dom-dan-iel (dahm-DAN-yěl) *n.*, an archaic term for a "den of iniquity" or an immoral place

don-nered (DAHN-ěrd) *adj.*, a Scottish term for stunned; dazed

don-sie or **don-sy** (DAHN(T)-see) *adj.*, U.S. dialect for slightly sick

doo-dle-bug (DOOD-ěl-bŭg) *n.*, a person who does not defend his beliefs

doo-dle-sack (DOOD-ěl-sak) *n.*, British dialect for a bagpipe

do-ra-do (dŏ-RAH-doh) *n.*, a dolphin found in tropical and temperate waters that is prized as food

do-ra-pho-bi-a (doh-ră-FOH-bee-ă) *n.*, an abnormal fear of coming into contact with the skin or fur of an animal

dor-ty (DOHR-ti) *adj.*, a Scottish term meaning sullen

doss (DAHS) *v.*, a British term meaning to sleep or lie down wherever convenient

dos-sal or **dos-sel** (DAHS-ăl) *n.*, a decorative cloth hung behind and above an altar

dos-ser (DAHS-ĕr) *n.*, a basket for carrying objects on the back

do-ta-tion (doh-TAY-shŏn) *n.*, an endowment

dot-tle or **dot-tel** (DAHD-ĕl) or (DAHT-ĕl) *n.*, tobacco residue caked in the bowl of a pipe

dou-blure (dŏ-BLUUR) or (doo-BLUUR) *n.*, a book cover lining, especially one of leather or brocade

dough-face (DOH-fays) *n.*, 1. a congressman from the North who did not oppose slavery during the Civil War 2. a mask

doup (DAUUP) or (DĂUUP) *n.*, a Scottish term for the end or bottom of something, especially the end of a burned candle; buttocks

dou-rine (DUU-reen) *n.*, a contagious disease of horses that affects the genitals and hind legs

draff-sack (DRAF-sak) *n.*, a Scottish term for a bag of the malt by-product of brewing

dra-gade (dră-GAYD) *v.*, to break up melted glass by pouring it into water

drag-o-man (DRAG-ŏ-măn) or (DRAIG-ŏ-măn) *n.*, an Arabic, Turkish, or Persian interpreter or tourist guide employed by an embassy

drail (DRAYL) *n.*, a hook used for fish trolling

dram-mock (DRAM-ŏk) *n.*, a Scottish term for a mixture of cold water and raw oatmeal

drave (DRAYV) *n.*, a Scottish term for a fishing expedition devoted to the catch of herring

drogue (DROHG) *n.*, an anchor that reduces a boat's speed

drom-o-ma-ni-a (drahm-ŏ-MAY-nee-ă) *n.*, an extreme desire to wander

drom-ond (DRAHM-ŏnd) or (DRŎM-ŏnd) *n.*, a large, fast-sailing ship of the Middle Ages

dron-go (DRAHNG-goh) *n.*, Australian slang for a novice

drosh-ky (DRAHSH-kee) or (DRAHSH-ki) *n.*, a light, low, four-wheeled open vehicle used mainly in Russia

drum-ble (DRUM-bĕl) or (DROOM-bĕl) *v.*, an archaic term meaning to move slowly and without energy

drupe (DROOP) *n.*, a one-seeded fruit, such as a peach, cherry, or plum, characterized by a thin outer skin and a seed encased in a hard shell

drux-y (DRŬK-see) *adj.*, knot-holed

dry-as-dust (DRĪ-az-dust) *n.*, a person who deals with boring subjects

dud-die or **dud-dy** (DŬ-dee) *adj.*, a Scottish term for shabby; tattered

\a\ bat \ā\ about \e\ or \è\ check \ĕ\ letter
\é\ cafe \i\ fish \ī\ tie \i\ limit \o\ boat
\ŏ\ bacon \u\ sun \ŭ\ helpful \ü\ fool

du-en-na (d(y)oo-EN-ă) *n.*, an elderly woman who works as chaperone or governess for a Spanish or Portuguese family

du-gong (DOO-gahng) *n.*, a plant-eating, fishlike water mammal found in the Red Sea and Indian Ocean; also called the sea cow

du-loc-ra-cy (doo-LAHK-ră-see) or (dyoo-LAHK-ră-see) *n.*, rule by slaves

du-lo-sis (dyoo-LOH-sĭs) *n.*, enslavement practiced by insects that seize and rear the young of another species

du-ma or **dou-ma** (DOO-mă) or (DOO-mah) *n.*, an elective committee in Russia

dum-ka (DUUM-kă) or (DOOM-ka) *n.*, a slow-tempoed, melancholy musical passage

dun-nage (DŬN-ij) *n.*, padding that protects fragile items from breakage while moving or shipping

dunn-ite (DUN-īt) *n.*, an explosive used in artillery shells

dunt (DŬNT) *v.*, to crack a ceramic object because of the quick temperature change during firing or cooling

duo-mo (DWAW-moh) *n.*, a cathedral

du-op-so-ny (dyoo-AHP-sŏ-nee) *n.*, a market situation in which only two buyers determine the demand for a product or service from many suppliers

dur-bar (DŬR-bahr) or (dŭr-BAHR) *n.*, 1. a court held by a East Indian prince 2. a gala for a maharajah's subjects at which they pledge loyalty to their host

du-roc (D(Y)UU-rahk) or (D(Y)OO-rahk) *n.*, a large, sturdy, red American hog

du-um-vir (dyoo-ŬM-vĭr) *n.*, one of two men jointly holding the same public office in ancient Rome

du-ve-tyn (DYOO-vĕ-tĭn) *n.*, a smooth, velvetlike fabric

dwai-ble (DWAY-bĕl) *adj.*, a Scottish term meaning weak and shaky

dys-cra-si-a (dĭ-SKRAY-zh(ee)-ă) or (dis-KRAY-zhee-ă) *n.*, an undefined disease or abnormal condition of the body, especially one of the blood

dys-gen-ics (dĭs-JEN-iks) *n.*, the study of racial deterioration

dys-lo-gis-tic or **dis-lo-gis-tic** (dis-lŏ-JIS-tik) *adj.*, uncomplimentary; belittling

dys-phe-mi-a (dĭs-FEEM-ee-ă) *n.*, stammering

dys-thy-mi-a (dĭ-STHĪ-mee-ă) *n.*, a mental state of anxiety, depression, and obsession

dys-to-ci-a (dĭ-STOH-sh(ee)-ă) *n.*, a slow or difficult labor or birth

dy-vour (DĪ-vŏr) *n.*, a Scottish term for a bankrupt man

dzeg-ge-tai (JEG-ĕ-tī) *n.*, a Mongolian wild ass

dzo or **zho** ((D)ZOH) or (ZHOH) *n.*, a cross between a yak and a domestic cow

E

ea-gre or **ea-ger** (EE-gĕ(r)) or (AY-gĕ(r)) *n.*, a tidal flood

ean-ling (EEN-ling) *n.*, an obsolete term for a young lamb

eb-e-ne-zer (eb-ĕ-NEE-zĕr) *n.*, U.S. dialect for anger

é-bou-le-ment (ay-BOOL-mahn) *n.*, a landslide

e-bur-ne-an (ĕ-BUR-nee-ăn) or (ee-BUR-nee-ăn) *adj.*, ivory-colored

e-cau-date (ee-KAW-dayt) *adj.*, tailless

ec-bol-ic (ek-BAHL-ik) *n.*, a drug that prompts labor by increasing uterine contractions

ec-chy-mo-sis (ek-ĕ-MOH-sĭs) *n.*, a bruise

ec-cle-si-ol-a-try (ĕ-klee-zee-AHL-ă-tree) *n.*, an abnormal devotion to the church

ec-dy-sis (EK-dĭ-sĭs) *n.*, the molting or shedding of the outer skin, as done by a reptile or insect

ec-dys-i-ast (ek-DIZ-ee-ast) *n.*, a stripper

e-ce-sis (ĕ-SEE-sis) *n.*, the acclimation of a plant to a new environment

ech-ard (E-kahrd) *n.*, the water in soil that is unavailable to plants

e-chi-nate (ĕ-KĪ-năt) or (ĕ-KĪ-nayt) *adj.*, prickly

e-chi-noid (ĕ-KĪ-noid) or (ee-KĪ-noid) *n.*, a sea urchin

ech-o-la-li-a (ek-oh-LAY-lee-ă) *n.*, the immediate, uncontrollable, and pathological repetition of words spoken by another person

ech-o-prax-i-a (ek-oh-PRAK-see-ă) *n.*, the uncontrollable repetition of the actions of another person

ec-logue (E-klawg) or (E-klahg) *n.*, an idyllic poem

e-clo-sion (ee-KLO-zhŏn) *n.*, 1. the hatching of an insect larva from its egg 2. the emergence of a full-grown insect from its pupa

é-cra-seur (ay-KRAH-zuur) *n.*, an instrument used in surgery when there is a risk of hemorrhage

ec-tad (EK-tad) *adv.*, outward

ec-ta-sis (EK-tă-sĭs) *n.*, the lengthening of an ordinarily short syllable

ec-type (EK-tīp) *n.*, a reproduction or copy

e-da-cious (ĕ-DAY-shŭs) or (ee-DAY-shŭs) *adj.*, with regard to eating; devouring

e-dac-i-ty (ĕ-DAS-ĭ-dee) *n.*, an appetite

ed-do (E-doh) *n.*, an African term for the edible root of the taro plant

e-den-tate (ee-DEN-tayt) *adj.*, toothless

e-dul-co-rate (ĕ-DUL-kŏ-rayt) *v.*, to purify by washing away acids or salts

ef-fa-ble (EF-ă-bĕl) *adj.*, able to be uttered or expressed

\a\ bat \ā\ about \e\ or \è\ check \ĕ\ letter
\é\ cafe \i\fish \ī\ tie \ĭ\ limit \o\ boat
\ŏ\ bacon \u\ sun \ŭ\ helpful \ü\ fool

eft (EFT) *n.*, a lizard or newt

eg-ger or **eg-gar** (EG-ĕr) *n.*, a tent caterpillar

ei-det-ic (ī-DED-ik) *adj.*, pertaining to photographic memory

ei-do-lon (ī-DOH-lŏn) *n.*, a phantom or image

eigne (AYN) *n.*, the oldest or first born

e-joo (EE-joo) *n.*, a Malaysian palm with large leaves that yields a sweet sap from which wine is made

el-a-pid (EL-ă-pĭd) *n.*, a snake characterized by permanently erect fangs in the front of the upper jaw, as the cobra, mamba, and coral snake

el-dritch or **el-drich** (EL-(d)rich) *adj.*, strange; spooky

el-ee-mos-y-nar-y (el-ĕ-MAHS-ĕn-er-ee) *adj.*, charitable; generous

el-e-mi (EL-ĕ-mee) *n.*, a fragrant resin used in making lacquers, varnishes, or perfumes

elf-lock (ELF-lahk) *n.*, matted hair

e-lo-de-a (ĕ-LOH-dee-ă) or (el-ŏ-DEE-ă) *n.*, a water herb native to North and South America; also called waterweed

e-loign (i-LOIN) *v.*, an archaic term meaning to distance one's self

e-lu-cu-brate (ee-LOO-k(y)ŭ-brayt) *v.*, to solve; to clarify

e-lute (ee-LOOT) *v.*, to extract or wash out

em-bon-point (ahn-bohn-PWAN) *n.*, excessive plumpness; stoutness

em-bosk (ĕm-BOSK) *v.*, to conceal, especially in regard to plants or greenery

em-bow (ĕm-BOW) *v.*, an archaic term meaning to make into a vault or arch

em-brac-er-y (ĕm-BRAY-sĕr-ee) *n.*, an attempt to influence a court, jury, or official corruptly by bribery, threats, or promises

em-bro-cate (EM-brŏ-kayt) *v.*, to apply liniment or lotion on the body

eme (EEM) *n.*, a Scottish term for uncle or friend

em-gal-la (em-GAL-lă) *n.*, the South African wart hog

em-mer (EM-ĕr) *n.*, a hard, red wheat grown chiefly in Russia and Germany

em-met (EM-ĕt) *n.*, U.S. dialect for an ant

em-ple-o-ma-ni-a (em-plee-oh-MAY-nee-ă) *n.*, a violent desire to hold public office

em-presse-ment (ahn-pres-MAHN) *n.*, emotional zeal or involvement

emp-tion (EM(P)-shŏn) *n.*, the act of purchasing

e-munc-to-ry (ĕ-MŬNG(K)-tŏ-ree) *n.*, an archaic term for an organ or a part of the body such as the skin or kidneys that purifies the body from wastes

e-nate (EE-nayt) *adj.*, 1. related on the mother's side 2. growing outward

en-chi-rid-i-on or **en-chei-rid-i-on** (en-kī-RID-ee-ŏn) *n.*, a handbook

en-cho-ri-al (en-KOH-ree-ăl) or (eng-KOH-ree-ăl) *adj.*, belonging to or used in a particular country, especially the popular, simplified writing of ancient Egypt

en-dog-a-my (en-DAHG-ă-mee) *n.*, marriage within a specific tribe or group as required by tradition or law

en-gas-tri-myth (ĕn-GAS-trĭ-mith) *n.*, an obsolete term for a ventriloquist

en-ne-ad (EN-ee-ad) or (EN-ee-ăd) *n.*, 1. a group of nine 2. in Egyptian religion, a group of nine gods

en-ne-a-style (EN-ee-ă-stīl) *adj.*, an architectural term for having nine columns

en-op-tro-man-cy (e-NAHP-trŏ-man(t)-see) *n.*, predicting the future by using mirrors

e-no-sis (ĕ-NOH-sĭs) or (ee-NOH-sĭs) *n.*, a union; specifically, a movement designed to bring about the political union of Greece and Cyprus

ens (ENZ) or (EN(T)S) *n.*, an abstract being or entity

en-si-form (EN(T)-sĭ-fohrm) *adj.*, shaped like a sword

en-sor-cell (ĕn-SOHR-sĕl) *v.*, to bewitch or fascinate

en-tad (EN-tad) *adj.*, inward

en-top-ic (en-TAHP-ik) *adj.*, an anatomical term meaning occurring in the usual place

en-tre-sol (EN-tĕ(r)-sahl) or (EN-trĕ-sahl) *n.*, the mezzanine of a building

ent-wick-lungs-ro-man (ent-vik-luung(k)s-roh-MAHN) *n.*, an autobiographical novel about a character's development from childhood to maturity

e-o-an (ee-OH-ăn) *adj.*, associated with the dawn or the east

e-o-li-an or **ae-o-li-an** (ee-OH-lee-ăn) *adj.*, moved, deposited, created, or eroded by the wind

e-on-ism (EE-ŏn-izĕm) *n.*, the wearing of women's clothes by a man

e-pact (EE-pakt) *n.*, the difference between the number of days in a solar year and a lunar year

e-pac-tal (ee-PAK-tăl) *adj.*, of or relating to a bone that occurs irregularly in the seams of the skull

e-pei-ric (ĕ-PĪ-rik) *adj.*, with regards to a shallow sea that covers a large part of a continent, yet remains connected with the ocean

e-pergne (ĕ-PĔRN) or (ee-PĔRN) *n.*, an elaborate table centerpiece of glass or silver that is used for serving or decoration

ep-ex-e-ge-sis (ep-eks-ĭ-JEE-sĭs) *n.*, an explanation following a word or passage that clarifies or limits its meaning

eph-od (EF-ahd) or (EE-fahd) *n.*, an apron worn by Hebrews in ancient religious ceremonies

\a\ bat \ā\ about \e\ or \ĕ\ check \ē\ letter \ê\ cafe \i\fish \ī\ tie \i\ limit \o\ boat \ō\ bacon \u\ sun \ŭ\ helpful \ü\ fool

eph-or (EF-ŏr) or (EF-ohr) *n.*, one of a magisterial body chosen by the Spartans to exercise control over their king

ep-i-cede (EP-ĭ-seed) *n.*, a dirge

ep-i-cene (EP-ĭ-seen) *adj.*, 1. having characteristics of the opposite sex 2. effeminate

e-pic-ri-sis (ĕ-PIK-rĭ-sĭs) *n.*, an analysis, especially of a medical case history

ep-i-deic-tic (ep-ĭ-DĪK-tik) *adj.*, rhetorically demonstrative

ep-i-der-moph-y-to-sis (ep-ĭ-dĕr-mahf-ĭ-TOH-sĭs) *n.*, a skin or nail disease caused by a parasitic fungus

ep-i-gam-ic (ep-ĭ-GAM-ik) *adj.*, attracting the opposite sex during mating season by colors, odors, behaviors, etc.

ep-i-ge-an (ep-ĭ-JEE-ăn) or **ep-i-ge-al** (ep-i-JEE-ăl) *adj.*, 1. growing above the ground 2. living near or on the ground, especially in regard to insects

ep-i-nas-ty (EP-ĭ-nas-tee) *n.*, a movement by which a plant part bends outward or downward, as a flower unfolding

ep-i-ni-ci-an (ep-ĭ-NI-shĭn) *adj.*, celebrating victory

e-piph-o-ra (ĕ-PIF-ŏ-ră) *n.*, an excessive tearing of the eyes

ep-i-stax-is (ep-ĭ-STAKS-ĭs) *n.*, a nosebleed

e-pis-te-mo-phil-i-a (ĕ-pis-tĕ-moh-FIL-ee-ă) *n.*, a preoccupation with knowledge

ep-i-tha-la-mi-um or **ep-i-tha-la-mi-on** (ep-ĭ-thă-LAY-mee-ŭm) or (ep-ĭ-thă-LAY-mee-ŏn) *n.*, a song or poem in honor of a bride and groom

ep-i-thu-met-ic (ep-ĭ-th(y)oo-MED-ik) *adj.*, associated with appetite or desire

ep-i-zo-ot-ic (ep-ĭ-zŏ-WAHD-ik) or (ep-ĭ-zoh-AHD-ik) *adj.*, relating to a disease that affects many animals of one kind at the same time

ep-on-y-mous (ĕ-PAHN-ĭ-mŭs) *adj.*, giving one's name to a tribe, place, etc.

ep-o-pee (EP-ŏ-pee) *n.*, an epic poem

ep-u-lo (EP-yŭ-loh) or (AYP-ŭ-loh) *n.*, a member of a group of ancient Roman priests in charge of sacrificial banquets

e-pure (AY-pyuur) *n.*, a complete, preparatory architectural drawing traced on a wall or floor as a pattern for work to be done

eq-ui-tant (EK-wĭd-ănt) *adj.*, of or relating to leaves that overlap at the base

eq-ui-voque or **eq-ui-voke** (EK-wĭ-vohk) *n.*, a pun or play on words

e-re-mic (ĕ-REE-mik) or (ĕ-RE-mik) *adj.*, associated with deserts or sandy areas

er-e-mite (ER-ĕ-mīt) *n.*, a hermit or recluse, especially one motivated by a religious vow

er-e-mo-phyte (ER-ĕ-moh-fīt) or (ĕ-REE-mŏ-fīt) *n.*, a plant that grows in the desert

e·rep·sin (ĕ-REP-sĭn) *n.*, an enzyme produced in the intestines

er·e·thism (ER-ĕ-thizĕm) *n.*, an abnormal sensitivity to stimulation, either generalized or restricted to a body part

er·gate (ĔR-gayt) *n.*, a worker ant

er·go·phobe (ĔR-gŏ-fohb) *n.*, a person who fears work

er·ic (ER-ik) or (AYR-ik) *n.*, a medieval Irish law term for a blood fine imposed on a murderer and his family

e·rig·er·on (ĕ-RIJ-ĕ-rŏn) *n.*, a plant resembling an aster whose leaves are used as a diuretic

er·i·na·ceous (er-ĭ-NAY-shŭs) *adj.*, like a hedgehog

er·is·tic (ĕ-RIS-tik) *adj.*, controversial

erl·king (ERL-king) *n.*, in German and Scandinavian mythology, a mischievous spirit that afflicts children

erne or **ern** (ĔRN) *n.*, a sea eagle

e·rose (ĕ-ROHS) or (ee-ROHS) *adj.*, a botanical term meaning uneven or irregular

er·rhine (ER-rīn) *adj.*, designed to increase nasal discharge or induce sneezing

e·ru·ci·form (ĕ-ROO-sĭ-fohrm) *adj.*, like a caterpillar

e·ruc·ta·tion (ĕ-rŭk-TAY-shŏn) *n.*, a belch

e·rum·pent (i-RŬM-pĕnt) *adj.*, bursting forth

e·ryn·go (ĕ-RING-goh) *n.*, the candied root of the seaholly

e·ryth·ro·pho·bi·a (ĕ-rith-rŏ-FOH-bee-ă) *n.*, 1. an abnormal fear of the color red 2. an abnormal fear of blushing

es·clan·dre (es-KLAHN-dră) *n.*, an unpleasant public scene

es·cu·lent (ES-kyŭ-lĕnt) *adj.*, able to be eaten

es·ker (ES-kĕr) *n.*, a narrow ridge of sand, gravel, or boulders thought to have been formed by a stream flowing under or in glacial ice

es·pal·ier (ĕ-SPAL-yĕr) *n.*, a railing or trellis on which fruit trees or shrubs are trained to grow flat

es·par·to (e-SPAHRD-oh) *n.*, Spanish or Algerian grass used to make shoes, baskets, paper, or cordage

es·piè·gle (e-SPYE-gĕl) *adj.*, playful

es·pring·al (ĕ-SPRING-ăl) *n.*, a young man

e·squa·mate (ee-SKWAY-mayt) *adj.*, having no scales

es·quisse (e-SKEES) *n.*, a rough sketch, usually for a painting or statue

es·ta·fette (es-tă-FET) *n.*, a messenger on horseback

es·ta·mi·net (e-sta-MEE-nay) *n.*, a small cafe or bistro

es·ti·vate or **aes·ti·vate** (ES-tĭ-vayt) *v.*, to spend the summer, usually at one place and in a state of inactivity

\a\ bat \ă\ about \e\ or \ĕ\ check \ĕ\ letter
\ē\ cafe \i\fish \ī\ tie \ĭ\ limit \o\ boat
\ŏ\ bacon \u\ sun \ū\ helpful \ü\ fool

es-trade (e-STRAHD) *n.*, a raised platform or dias

e-su-ri-ent (ĕ-SUU-ree-ĕnt) *adj.*, hungry; greedy

e-ta (AY-dă) or (EE-tă) *n.*, the seventh letter of the Greek alphabet

e-te-sian (ĕ-TEE-zhăn) *adj.*, occurring annually, in describing certain Mediterranean winds

eth-moid (ETH-moid) *adj.*, pertaining to one or more bones forming part of the walls of the nasal cavity

eth-narch (ETH-nahrk) *n.*, the ruler of a people, tribe, or nation

e-ti-o-late (EED-ee-ŏ-layt) *v.*, to bleach or whiten a plant by depriving it of light

et-na (ET-nă) *n.*, a device, originally used for heating liquids, that is a cup attached to a saucer in which alcohol is burned

et-tle (ED-ĕl) *v.*, a Scottish term meaning to plan or devise

e-tui or **et-wee** (ay-TWEE) or (et-WEE) *n.*, a small, often-decorated case for small necessities such as toiletries, glasses, scissors, etc.

et-y-mon (ED-ĭ-mahn) *n.*, the original form of a word

eu-cra-si-a (yoo-KRAY-zh(ee)-ă) *n.*, a normal state of physical health

eu-dae-mo-ni-a or **eu-dai-mo-ni-a** (yoo-dee-MOH-nee-ă) or (yoo-day-MOH-nee-ă) *n.*, well-being; happiness

eu-mor-phic (yoo-MOHR-fik) *adj.*, having a powerful, athletic body type

eu-o-nym (YOO-ŏ-nim) *n.*, an appropriate name for a person, place, or thing

eu-phu-ism (YOO-fyŭ-wizĕm) *n.*, an affected, artificially elegant style of speaking popular at the end of the 16th century

eup-ne-a or **eup-noe-a** (yoop-NEE-ă) *n.*, easy or normal breathing

eu-po-tam-ic (yoo-pŏ-TAM-ik) *adj.*, capable of living and growing in both still and flowing water

eu-ri-pus (yŭ-RĪ-pŭs) *n.*, a channel or strait

eu-sta-cy (YOO-stă-cee) *n.*, a worldwide fluctuation in sea level

eu-tex-i-a (yoo-TEKS-ee-ă) *n.*, the capability of being melted at a low temperature

eu-ther-mic (yoo-THĔR-mik) *adj.*, producing heat or warmth

eux-ine (YOOK-sĭn) *adj.*, relating to the Black Sea

e-va-ga-tion (ee-vă-GAY-shŏn) *n.*, an obsolete term for a straying of the mind

e-vag-i-nate (ĕ-VAJ-ĭ-nayt) *v.*, to turn inside out; to cause a protrusion

é-va-sé (ay-vah-ZAY) *adj.*, widening gradually, as a chimney

e-vec-tion (ĕ-VEK-shŏn) *n.*, an astronomical term for a periodic irregularity in the moon's motion caused by the attraction of the sun

ev-i-rate (EV-ĭ-rayt) or (ee-VĪ-rayt) *v.*, an archaic term meaning to castrate

ev-zone (EV-zohn) *n.*, a member of an elite corps of footsoldiers in the Greek army

ew-er-y (YOO-ĕ-ree) *n.*, a room for storing napkins and pitchers, especially in a royal palace

ex-an-them (ig-ZAN-thĕm) or (ek-SAN-them) *n.*, an eruptive disease such as measles or chicken pox, often associated with a fever

ex-arch (EK-sahrk) *n.*, the title or means of addressing a provincial ruler in the Byzantine empire

ex-clave (EK-sklayv) *n.*, a section of a country that is split off from its main part and is surrounded by an alien country, as West Berlin

ex-e-at (EK-see-at) *n.*, 1. permission allowing a priest to change his diocese 2. a British term for official permission for a person to be temporarily absent

ex-e-dra (EK-sĕ-dră) or (ek-SEED-ră) *n.*, an open room with seats for meetings and conversation in ancient Greece and Rome

ex-en-ter-ate (ek-SEN-tĕ-rayt) *v.*, to disembowel

ex-e-quy (EK-sĕ-kwee) *n.*, a funeral ceremony or procession

ex-her-i-date or **ex-her-e-date** (eks-HER-ĭ-dayt) *v.*, to cut off someone's inheritance

ex-ig-u-ous (eg-ZIG-yĕw-ŭs) *adj.*, meager; sparse

ex-im-i-ous (eg-ZIM-ee-ŏs) *adj.*, an archaic term meaning excellent or distinguished

ex-in-a-ni-tion (eg-zin-ă-NI-shŏn) *n.*, an obsolete term for extreme fatigue

ex-o-cu-late (eks-AH-kyoo-layt) *v.*, an obsolete term meaning to put out someone's eyes, especially as punishment

ex-o-pha-si-a (ek-soh-FAY-zh(ee)-ă) *n.*, speech uttered from the speech organs

ex-or-di-um (eg-ZOHR-dee-ŭm) *n.*, the beginning or introduction to something

ex-or-na-tion (ek-sohr-NAY-shŏn) *n.*, an embellishment or adornment

ex-per-ge-fac-tion (ek-spĕr-jĕ-FAK-shŏn) *n.*, an archaic term for an awakening

ex-pis-cate (EK-spĭ-skayt) or (ek-SPI-skayt) *v.*, a Scottish term meaning to find out by careful investigation

ex-po-ni-ble (ik-SPOH-nĭ-bĕl) *adj.*, able to be explained

ex-pro-mis-sion (eks-proh-MI-shŏn) *n.*, the act of assuming another's debt

ex-sic-cate (EK-sĭ-kayt) or (ek-SI-kayt) *v.*, to drain water from or dry up

ex-suc-cous (ek(s)-SŬK-ŭs) *adj.*, dried up; having no moisture

ex-suf-fli-cate (ik-SUF-li-kit) or (ik-SUF-li-kayt) *n.*, an obsolete term for forcible breathing or blowing out

ex-tra-for-an-e-ous (ek-stră-fohr-AYN-ee-ŭs) *adj.*, outside

\a\ bat \ă\ about \e\ or \ĕ\ check \ē\ letter
\é\ cafe \i\ fish \ī\ tie \ĭ\ limit \o\ boat
\ŏ\ bacon \u\ sun \ŭ\ helpful \ü\ fool

ex-un-da-tion (ek-sŭn-DAY-shŏn) *n.*, an archaic term for flooding

ex-u-vi-ate (ig-ZOO-vee-ayt) or (ig-SOO-vee-ayt) *v.*, to shed, as a snake's skin

eye-ser-vice (Ī-SĔR-vĭs) *n.*, an archaic term for work done only when the employer is watching

ey-ot (Ī-ŏt) *n.*, British dialect for a small island

ey-ra (AY-rǎ) *n.*, a reddish-colored wildcat

ey-rir (AY-rir) *n.*, a unit of money in Iceland

fab-li-au (FAB-lee-oh) *n.*, a short, comic, often coarse tale by a medieval minstrel

fa-cient (FAY-shĭnt) *n.*, a doer

fa-cin-o-rous (fǎ-SIN-ŏ-rŭs) *adj.*, an archaic term for very wicked

fac-u-la (FAK-yŭ-lǎ) *n.*, any of the unusually bright areas on the sun's surface

fac-und (FAK-ŭnd) or (fǎ-KŬND) *adj.*, eloquent

fadge (FAJ) *n.*, 1. a Scottish term for a rounded, thick bread loaf 2. an Irish term for a potato cake or bread

fa-got-to (fǎ-GAHD-oh) *n.*, a bassoon

faille (FĪL) *n.*, a soft, ribbed fabric of silk, rayon, or lightweight taffeta

fai-ne-ant (FAY-nee-ănt) *adj.*, doing nothing; idle

fai-tour (FAYD-ŏr) *n.*, an archaic term for a cheat or fraud

fal-ba-la (FAL-bǎ-lǎ) *n.*, a trimming for a woman's garment

fal-cate (FAL-kayt) *adj.*, curved as a sickle

fam-i-list (FAM-ĭ-lĭst) *n.*, a member of a mystical group in 16th- and 17th-century Europe

fam-u-lus (FAM-yŭ-lŭs) *n.*, an assistant or attendant, especially to a magician or scholar

fane (FAYN) *n.*, 1. an archaic term for a temple or church 2. an archaic term for a flag or banner

fan-far-o-nade (fan-FAR-ŏ-nayd) or (fan-FAR-ŏ-nahd) *n.*, bragging or boasting

fan-ion (FAN-yŏn) *n.*, a flag marker originally used by horse platoons and now by soldiers and surveyors

fan-toc-ci-ni (fahn-tŏ-CHEE-nee) or (fan-tŏ-CHEE-nee) *n.*, a string-operated puppet

fan-tod or **fan-tad** (FAN-tahd) or (FAN-tad) *n.*, a state of fretfulness or tension; sometimes, a state of worry

far-an-dole (FAR-ăn-dohl) or (far-ăn-DOHL) *n.*, a lively dance of southeastern France in which the dancers form a chain

far-ci or **far-cie** (fahr-SEE) *n.*, a cooking term meaning a stuffed dish such as poultry

fard (FAHRD) *n.*, 1. an archaic term for face paint 2. a brown date grown in California and eastern Arabia

far-fel (FAHR-fĕl) *n.*, in Yiddish cookery, a noodle dough formed like small pellets or crumbs

far-rag-i-nous (fă-RAJ-ĭ-nŭs) *adj.*, disordered

far-ra-go (fă-RAH-goh) or (fă-RAY-goh) *n.*, 1. a mixture or hodgepodge 2. a deceptive grouping

fas-ci-ate (FASH-ee-ayt) *adj.*, 1. having broad stripes of color 2. a botanical term meaning compressed into a bundle, as stems that have grown together

fas-ci-cle (FAS-ĭ-kĕl) *n.*, 1. a small collection or bundle 2. a section of a book published in installments and usually bound together later

fas-tig-i-um (fa-STI-jee-ŭm) *n.*, a summit or peak such as the ridge of a house or end of a gable

fas-tu-ous (FAS-chŭ-wŭs) *adj.*, haughty and insolent; pretentious

fa-tid-ic (fay-TID-ik) or (fă-TID-ik) *adj.*, prophetic

fau-tress (FAW-tres) *n.*, an obsolete term for a female patron or protector

fa-vil-la (fă-VIL-ă) *n.*, a small, glowing piece of volcanic lava

fa-vo-ni-an (fă-VOH-nee-ăn) *adj.*, 1. pertaining to the west wind 2. mild

fa-vus (FAY-vŭs) *n.*, a tile or marble piece cut into a hexagonal shape 2. a skin disease caused by fungus and usually found on the scalp

fa-zen-da (fă-ZEN-dă) *n.*, 1. a Brazilian coffee plantation 2. the house on such a plantation

feak (FEEK) *n.*, an obsolete term for a lock of hair

feaze (FAYZ) or (FEEZ) *v.*, British dialect meaning to become unraveled

feaz-ings (FEE-zingz) *n.*, an unraveled portion at the end of a rope

feb-ri-fuge (FEB-rĭ-fyooj) *n.*, something that reduces or cures a fever

feb-ru-a-tion (feb-rŭ-WAY-shŏn) *n.*, an archaic term for a purification by a religious rite

feck (FEK) *n.*, 1. a Scottish term for the majority 2. a Scottish term for value

fei-rie (FEE-ree) *adj.*, a Scottish term for being capable of walking

feist (FĪST) *n.*, U.S. dialect for a mongrel dog; a mutt

fe-li-form (FEE-lĭ-fohrm) *adj.*, catlike

fell-mon-ger (FELL-mŏn-gĕr) or (FELL-mahn-gĕr) *n.*, a person who, before tanning, removes hair or wool from skins or hides, especially those of sheep

fel-ly or **fel-loe** (FEL-(l)ee) or (FEL-oh) *n.*, the outside rim of a wheel reinforced by spokes

---

\a\ bat \ă\ about \e\ or \è\ check \ĕ\ letter \é\ cafe \i\fish \ī\ tie \ĭ\ limit \o\ boat \ŏ\ bacon \u\ sun \ŭ\ helpful \ü\ fool

fen·er·a·tion (fen-ĕr-AY-shŏn) *n.*, the practice of lending of money and charging interest

fen·land (FEN-land) or (FEN-lănd) *n.*, low, marshy ground

fe·ra·cious (fĕ-RAY-shŭs) *adj.*, fruitful; productive

fer·bam (FĔR-bam) *n.*, a black, powdered chemical compound used to kill crop fungus

fer·e·to·ry (FER-ĕ-toh-ree) *n.*, an ornate, portable case for storing the relics of saints

fe·ri·a·tion (fi-ree-AY-shŏn) *n.*, an archaic term for observing a holiday, especially when celebrated by not working

fer·i·ty (FER-i-tee) *n.*, the state of being wild or untamed

ferk or **firk** (FĔRK) *v.*, British dialect meaning to move fast

fern·tick·le (FERN-tik-ĕl) *n.*, a Scottish term for a freckle

fer·ri·tin (FER-ĭ-tĭn) *n.*, an amber-colored protein found in the liver, spleen, and bone marrow that helps the body store iron

fer·ru·mi·nate (fĕ-ROOM-ĭ-nayt) *v.*, to solder; to join metal together

fer·u·la (FER-(y)ŭ-lă) or **fer·ule** (FE-rŭl) *n.*, an object used to punish young students; specifically, a flat piece of wood like a rulei that is used on the hands

fes·cen·nine (FES-ĕn-īn) or (FES-ĕn-een) *adj.*, 1. obscene 2. sung or read at a rural festival or wedding in ancient Italy and often marked with obscenities

fes·ti·nate (FES-tĭ-nayt) *v.*, to hurry; to involuntarily speed one's gait, as a result of illness

fe·ta·tion or **foe·ta·tion** (fee-TAY-shŏn) *n.*, pregnancy

fet·er·i·ta or **fed·er·i·ta** (fed-ĕ-REED-ă) *n.*, a grain sorghum used for animal food

fe·tial or **fe·cial** (FEE-shăl) *adj.*, dealing with international relationships; diplomatic

fe·ti·cide or **foe·ti·cide** (FEED-ĭ-sīd) *n.*, an abortion

fe·tor or **foe·tor** (FEED-ŏr) *n.*, a stench; a strong, unpleasant smell

feuil·le·ton (FĔR-ee-tohn) *n.*, the feature section of a newspaper or magazine that is aimed at entertaining the average reader

fe·ver·few (FEE-vĕr-fyoo) *n.*, a perennial European herb with small, white flowers

few·ter·er (FYOO-tĕr-ĕr) *n.*, an obsolete term for a person who tends dogs, especially greyhounds

few·trils (FYOO-trĭlz) *n.*, British dialect meaning odds and ends

fi·a·cre (fee-AH-krĕ) or (fee-AHK-rĕ) *n.*, a small horse-drawn coach available for hire

fi·chu (FI-shoo) or (FE-shoo) *n.*, a woman's triangular scarf of muslin or lace worn over the shoulders as a shawl

fi·co (FEE-koh) *n.*, the least bit

fic·tile (FIK-tĕl) *adj.*, 1. able to be molded into a utensil or piece of art 2. made of or relating to pottery or earthenware

fid (FID) *n.*, a nautical term for a wooden or metal bar or pin used to support the topmast

fidg-in fain (FIJ-ĭn-fayn) *adj.*, a Scottish term meaning restless with excitement

fike (FĪK) *v.*, a British term meaning to fidget

fil (FIL) *n.*, a coin of Iraq

fi-la-ceous (fi-LAY-shŭs) *adj.*, made of threads or filaments

fi-lar (FĪ-lăr) *adj.*, having threads or lines across the field of vision, as a gunsight

fil-a-ree (FIL-ă-ree) or (fil-ă-REE) *n.*, a grass used as cattle forage in areas of southwestern United States; also called pin grass

fi-lar-i-a (fĭ-LAA-ree-ă) *n.*, a slender worm transmitted by a biting insect in its larval stage that becomes parasitic on the blood or tissues of mammals as an adult

fil-i-ate (FIL-ee-ayt) *v.*, to declare the paternity of an illegitimate child

fil-i-beg or **fil-le-beg** or **fil-a-beg** (FIL-ĭ-beg) or (FEEL-ĭ-beg) *n.*, a kilt worn by Scottish Highlanders

fil-i-col-o-gy (fil-ĭ-KAHL-ŏ-jee) *n.*, the study of ferns

fil-i-form (FIL-ĭ-fohrm) or (FĪL-ĭ-fohrm) *adj.*, threadlike

fil-i-pen-du-lous (fil-ĭ-PEN-dyoo-lŭs) *adj.*, strung on or hanging by a thread

fim-ble (FIM-bĕl) *n.*, a male hemp plant or its fiber

fim-bri-ate (FIM-bree-ăt) or (FIM-bree-at) *adj.*, fringed

fip-ple (FIP-ĕl) *n.*, a slitted plug in the end of a whistle, flute, or recorder through which the player blows

fire-fang (FĪ(E)R-fang) *v.*, to become dry or damaged because of the heat produced by decomposing organic matter such as manure or grain

firn-i-fi-ca-tion (fir-nĭ-fĭ-KAY-shŏn) *n.*, the process by which snow changes into the granular, partially compacted snow on a glacial surface

fis-si-lin-gual (fis-ĭ-LING-wăl) *adj.*, of or relating to a type of fork-tongued lizard

fis-si-ped (FIS-ĭ-ped) *adj.*, cloven-hoofed

fitch (FICH) *n.*, a European meat-eating mammal about two feet long and dark brown and black with white markings on its head

fiz-gig (FIZ-gig) *n.*, 1. an archaic term for a flirting girl or woman 2. a type of firework made of damp powder that fizzes or hisses when set off

fjeld (FYEL) or (FEE-el) *n.*, a rocky, stark plateau in Scandinavia

fla-bel-late (flă-BEL-ăt) or (FLA-bĕ-layt) *adj.*, fan-shaped

fla-bel-lum (flă-BEL-ŭm) *n.*, 1. a fan used in state or religious ceremonies 2. a body part that looks like a fan

\a\ bat \ă\ about \e\ or \è\ check \ĕ\ letter \é\ cafe \i\fish \ī\ tie \ĭ\ limit \o\ boat \ŏ\ bacon \u\ sun \ŭ\ helpful \ü\ fool

fla·gi·tious (flă-JI-shŭs) *adj.*, criminal; corrupt

fla·neur (flah-NĔR) *n.*, a self-centered and phony person

flap·drag·on (FLAP-drag-ŏn) *n.*, 1. an old game in which the players snatch and eat raisins, plums, etc., out of burning brandy 2. an obsolete, usually derogatory term for a German or Dutchman

fla·ves·cent (flă-VES-ĕnt) *adj.*, turning yellow; yellowish

fla·vin (FLAY-vĭn) or (FLA-vĭn) or **fla·vine** (FLAY-veen) *n.*, a yellow dye extracted from a certain type of bark

fleam (FLEEM) *n.*, 1. a sharp surgical instrument formerly used in bloodletting 2. the angle of bevel on a sawtooth edge

flech (FLEK) *n.*, a Scottish term for a flea

fleer (FLI(Ĕ)R) *v.*, to grin or laugh in a coarse or mocking manner; to sneer

flense (FLEN(T)S) *v.*, to strip the blubber or skin from an animal such as a whale or seal

fletch·er (FLECH-ĕr) *n.*, an arrow maker

flews (FLOOZ) *n.*, the large, hanging parts of the upper lip of some dogs such as bloodhounds

fley (FLĔI) or (FLAY) *v.*, a Scottish term meaning to frighten, especially by startling

flif·fis or **flif·fus** (FLIF-ĭs) *n.*, a twisting, double somersault on a trampoline

flink·ite (FLING-kīt) *n.*, a mineral of greenish brown manganese arsenate

flitch (FLICH) *n.*, 1. a salted and cured side of a hog 2. a strip of smoked fish

floc·cil·la·tion (flahks-sĭ-LAY-shŏn) *n.*, a delirious picking at bedclothes by people who are exhausted or feverish

floc·cule (FLAH-kyool) *n.*, a small clump of matter hanging in or concentrated from a liquid

floc·cu·lent (FLAHK-yoo-lĕnt) *adj.*, 1. looking like wool 2. covered with a soft, wooly substance

flodge (FLAHJ) *n.*, English dialect for a pool or puddle

flo·ta (FLOHD-ă) or (FLOH-tah) *n.*, a fleet of Spanish ships that formerly sailed annually from Spain to Mexico to pick up products from Spanish colonies

flump (FLŬMP) *v.*, to plop down suddenly or heavily

flysch (FLISH) *n.*, a deposit of sandstone found adjacent to a rising mountain belt that is common in the European Alpines

fodg·el (FAHJ-ĕl) *adj.*, a Scottish term meaning plump and solidly built; buxom

fo·di·ent (FOH-dee-ĕnt) *adj.*, capable of digging or burrowing

fo·gram or **fo·grum** (FOH-grăm) *n.*, an old-fashioned or conservative person

foin (FOIN) *v.*, a fencing term meaning to lunge

folk-moot (FOHK-moot) or **folk-mote** (FOHK-moht) *n.*, in early England, an assembly of the people

fon-ti-na (fahn-TEE-nă) or (fohn-TEE-nă) *n.*, a creamy-textured, mild-flavored soft cheese

foo-tle (FOO-dĕl) *v.*, 1. to wile away time 2. to speak or act foolishly

foo-ty (FOOD-ee) or (FUU-tee) *adj.*, U.S. dialect meaning worthless or unimportant

foo-zle (FOO-zĕl) *v.*, to handle or play clumsily; to bungle

fo-ram-i-nous (fŏ-RAM-ĭ-nŭs) *adj.*, having pores

forb (FOHRB) *n.*, any herb that is not a grass; a weed

for-by or **for-bye** (fohr-BĪ) *adv.*, a Scottish term meaning over and above; besides

force-meat (FOHRS-meet) *n.*, a mixture of chopped and seasoned meat or fish and eggs, grains, and vegetables used as a stuffing or served alone

for-do or **fore-do** (fohr-DOO) *v.*, an archaic term meaning to kill or terminate

for-el or **for-rel** (FAH-rĕl) *n.*, 1. a slipcover for a book 2. a poor-quality parchment used to make bookcovers

for-fend or **fore-fend** (fohr-FEND) *v.*, 1. to avert or turn aside 2. to guard or preserve

for-fic-i-form (fohr-FIS-ĭ-fohrm) *adj.*, shaped like a pair of scissors

for-fough-en or **for-fouch-en** (fŏr-FOHK-ĕn) or (fŏr-FAHK-ĕn) *adj.*, a Scottish term meaning tired out; exhausted

fo-rint (FOHR-int) *n.*, the basic monetary unit of Hungary

for-jes-ket or **for-jes-kit** (fŏr-JES-kĕt) *adj.*, a Scottish term meaning worn down; extremely tired

for-la-na (fohr-LAH-nah) *n.*, an old Italian dance

for-mic (FOHR-mik) *adj.*, pertaining to ants

for-mi-ca-ry (FOHR-mĭ-ke-ree) *n.*, an ant hill or ant colony

for-mi-ca-tion (fohr-mĭ-KAY-shŏn) *n.*, an abnormal feeling like the sensation of insects crawling on the skin

for-rit (FOHR-it) *adv.*, a Scottish term meaning forward

fosse or **foss** (FAHS) or (FAWS) *n.*, 1. a canal; ditch; trench 2. a castle moat

fou (FOO) *adj.*, a Scottish term meaning drunk

four-ra-gère (FOOR-ă-zhe(ĕ)r) *n.*, a braided cord, usually worn over the left shoulder, awarded to members of a military unit for distinguished service

fo-ve-a (FOH-vee-ă) *n.*, a small pit or depression

fo-ve-ate (FOH-vee-ayt) or (FOH-vee-ăt) *adj.*, pitted

\a\ bat \ă\ about \e\ or \è\ check \ĕ\ letter
\ē\ cafe \i\fish \ī\ tie \ĭ\ limit \o\ boat
\ŏ\ bacon \u\ sun \ū\ helpful \ü\ fool

fraise (FRAYZ) *v.*, a Scottish term meaning to flatter

fram·be·si·a or **fram·boe·si·a** (fram-BEE-zh(ee)ă) or (fram-BEE-zee-ă) *n.*, a tropical disease with lesions that look like raspberries; also called yaws

fram·pold (FRAM-pold) *adj.*, an obsolete term meaning irritable; quarrelsome

fran·gi·ble (FRAN-jĭ-bĕl) *adj.*, breakable; fragile

fran·ion (FRAN-yŏn) *n.*, an archaic term for a person who seeks pleasure; a merrymaker

frank·lin (FRANK-lĭn) *n.*, in 14th-and 15th-century England, a wealthy landowner not of noble birth

free·mar·tin (FREE-mahr-tĭn) *n.*, a usually sterile female calf born as a twin to a male

fremd (FREMD) *adj.*, a Scottish term meaning foreign; strange

fres·cade (fres-KAYD) or (fres-KAHD) *n.*, a shaded place

fre·tum (FREED-ŭm) or (FREE-tŭm) *n.*, a passageway connecting two large bodies of water

fri·a·ble (FRĪ-ă-bĕl) *adj.*, easily crushed or made into powder

frib·ble (FRI-bĕl) *adj.*, frivolous

fric·a·trice (FRIK-ă-trĭs) *n.*, 1. an archaic term for a slut or whore 2. an archaic term for a lesbian

frig·o·ri·fic (frig-ŏ-RIF-ik) *adj.*, causing coolness or cold

fri·jol (FREE-hohl) or (FREE-hawl) *n.*, a southwestern U.S. term for a bean such as a kidney bean or cowpea

frip·per·er (FRIP-ĕr-ĕr) *n.*, an archaic term for an old-clothes dealer

fri·sure (FRI-zhŭr) *n.*, a style of curling the hair; hairdo

frit·il·la·ry (FRID-ĭl-e-ree) *n.*, an orange-brown butterfly marked with black lines and dots and silver spots on the undersides of its wings

froe or **frow** (FROH) *n.*, 1. a tool for splitting shingles from a block 2. a steel log-splitting wedge

froise (FROIZ) *n.*, British dialect for a thick pancake, often eaten with bacon

fron·des·cence (frahn-DES-ĕn(t)s) *n.*, 1. the period when leaves unfold 2. foliage

fron·deur (FROHN-duur) *n.*, a rebel

frore (FROH(Ĕ)R) *adj.*, frozen

frot·tage (fraw-TAHZH) or (frŏ-TAHZH) *n.*, 1. masturbation by rubbing against something or someone 2. an artistic process done by rubbing lead, chalk, etc., over paper positioned on a textured surface

fro·ward (FROH-(w)ărd) *adj.*, disobedient

fru·giv·o·rous (froo-JIV-ŏ-rŭs) *adj.*, fruiteating, such as certain bats

fru·men·ta·ceous (froo-mĕn-TAY-shŭs) *adj.*, composed of or resembling wheat or other grain

fru-men-ty (FROO-měn-tee) *n.*, a British cereal of wheat cooked in milk and flavored with sugar, cinnamon, and raisins

frush (FRUSH) *n.*, 1. the triangular, elastic mass in the middle of the sole of a horse's foot 2. a discharge from it

fub-sy (FUB-zee) *adj.*, British dialect meaning short and chunky

fu-coid (FYOO-koid) *adj.*, resembling seaweed

fud (FŬD) *n.*, a Scottish term for the buttocks or an animal tail

fug (FUG) *n.*, warm, smelly air, especially that found in a crowded room, kitchen, etc.

fu-ga-cious (fyoo-GAY-shŭs) *adj.*, 1. a botanical term meaning falling or fading early 2. fleeting; transitory

fu-gle (FYOO-gĕl) *v.*, an archaic term meaning to act as a guide or leader

fu-gle-man (FYOO-gĕl-măn) *n.*, a soldier placed in front of a military company at drill as a model for others

fu-ji or **fu-gi** (F(Y)OO-jee) *n.*, 1. a spun-silk, plain-weave fabric made in Japan 2. a type of vine also called wisteria

ful-ci-ment (FUUL-sĭ-mĕnt) *n.*, an archaic term for a prop or a brace

ful-gent (FUUL-jĕnt) or (FŬL-jĕnt) *adj.*, glowing; dazzling

ful-gu-rous (FUUL-g(y)ŭ-rŭs) *adj.*, resembling flashes of lightning

ful-ham (FUUL-ăm) *n.*, an archaic term for a weighted die loaded at one corner

fu-lig-i-nous (fyoo-LIJ-ĭ-nŭs) *adj.*, sooty

ful-vous (FUUL-vŭs) *adj.*, yellowish brown or gray; tawny

ful-yie or **ful-zie** (FUUL-(y)ee) *n.*, a Scottish term for filth or street dirt

fu-ma-role or **fumerole** (FYOO-mă-rohl) *n.*, a hole in or near a volcano from which vapor and gas rise

fu-met or **fu-mette** (FYOO-mĕt) *n.*, a concentrated stock used as a flavoring and made by simmering fish, chicken, or game in wine or water

fu-mi-to-ry (FYUU-mĭ-toh-ree) *n.*, a European herb with purple flowers

fu-mu-lus (FYOO-myŭ-lŭs) *n.*, a thin cloud like a veil that can form at any altitude

fu-nam-bu-list (fyuu-NAM-byŭ-lĭst) *n.*, a tightrope walker or dancer

fu-nest (fyoo-NEST) *adj.*, causing evil or death; fatal

fun-gi-ble (FŬN-jĭ-bĕl) *adj.*, interchangeable

fu-nic (FYOO-nik) *adj.*, pertaining to the umbilical cord

fu-ni-cle (FYOO-nĭ-kĕl) *adj.*, 1. any body structure that resembles a cord 2. the stalk of a seed

\a\ bat \ă\ about \e\ or \è\ check \ĕ\ letter \é\ cafe \i\fish \ī\ tie \ĭ\ limit \o\ boat \ŏ\ bacon \u\ sun \ŭ\ helpful \ü\ fool

fu-ra-cious (fyŭ-RAY-shŭs) *adj.*, an archaic term meaning thieving

fu-ran (FYUU-ran) or (fyŭ-RAN) *n.*, a clear liquid compound used in making nylon-manufacturing chemicals

fur-cif-er-ous (fŭr-SIF-ĕ-rŭs) *adj.*, having a forked appendage

fur-fu-ra-ceous (fur-f(y)ŭ-RAY-shŭs) *adj.*, covered with scales

fur-fu-ra-tion (fur-f(y)ŭ-RAY-shŏn) *n.*, a flaking off, such as dandruff

furr-a-hin (FŬ-ră-HIN) *n.*, a Scottish term for a horse that walks on the right side of the furrow in plowing

furze (FŬRZ) *n.*, a spiny evergreen shrub with yellow flowers, common in Europe, that is often used for fuel and animal feed

fu-sain (FYOO-zayn) or (fyoo-ZAYN) *n.*, a component of coal similar to charcoal that causes dust in bituminous coal mines

fus-cous (FUS-kŭs) *adj.*, brownish gray; dusky-colored

fu-see or **fu-zee** (fyoo-ZEE) *n.*, 1. a wooden or paper match 2. a flare used to signal stalled trains and trucks

fu-si-form (FYOO-zĭ-fohrm) *adj.*, spindle-shaped; tapering at both ends

fu-sil (FYOO-zĭl) *n.*, a flintlock musket

fus-sock (FUS-ŏk) or (FŬS-ŏk) *n.*, 1. British dialect for a donkey 2. British dialect for a dumb person

fus-tic (FŬS-tik) *n.*, the yellow wood of a large tropical American tree that yields a yellow dye

fus-ti-gate (FŬS-tĭ-gayt) *v.*, 1. to bludgeon with a stick 2. to criticize

fus-ti-lugs (FŬS-tee-lŭgz) *n.*, an archaic term for a fat, unkempt woman

fu-thark or **fu-thorc** or **fu-thork** (FOO-thahrk) or (FOO-thohrk) *n.*, an alphabet used by the Germanic peoples from the 3rd to the 13th century

fyke or **fike** (FĪK) *n.*, a bag-shaped fish trap

fyl-fot (FIL-faht) *n.*, a swastika

fyrd (FĬRD) or (FURD) *n.*, England's militia before the Norman Conquest or the obligation to serve in it

gab-bard (GAB-ărd) or **gab-bart** (GAB-ărt) *n.*, a small ship or barge, formerly used in Scotland

ga-belle (gă-BEL) *n.*, a tax; specifically, one on salt

gab-er-lun-zie (GAB-ĕr-lun-zi) *n.*, a Scottish term for a a licensed, professional beggar

ga-bi-on (GAY-bee-ŏn) *n.*, a cylinder made of wicker and filled with dirt that is used as a military defense

gab-lock (GAB-lŏk) *n.*, 1. an archaic term for a spear or javelin 2 British dialect for a crowbar

ga-boon or **ga-bun** (gă-BOON) or (gah-BOON) *n.*, a soft, reddish brown African wood used in furniture making

ga-by (GAY-bi) or (GAW-bi) *n.*, British dialect for a fool

gad-di or **ga-di** (gă-DEE) or (GĂ-dee) *n.*, 1. an Indian term for a cushion, especially one for a throne 2. an Indian term for a high ruling status

ga-droon (gă-DROON) *n.*, an architectural ornament made by notching or carving a rounded molding

gad-wall (GA-dwawl) *n.*, a duck about the size of a mallard that is found in parts of North America

gair (GAYR) *adj.*, a Scottish term for greedy; stingy

ga-lac-to-phore (gă-LAK-tŏ-fohr) *n.*, a milk-carrying duct

ga-la-go (gă-LAY-goh) or (gă-LAH-goh) *n.*, a type of small, nocturnal African primate with long hind legs for leaping great distances

ga-lah (gă-LAH) *n.*, a gray and pink Australian cockatoo often kept as a pet

gal-an-tine or **gal-a-tine** (GAL-ăn-teen) *n.*, a dish made of boned meat or fish that is stuffed, cooked, pressed, jellied, and served cold

gal-ba-num (GAL-bă-nŭm) or (GAWL-bă-nŭm) *n.*, a gum resin with a strong odor derived from various Asian plants and used in medicine and incense

ga-le-ate (GAY-lee-ayt) *adj.*, helmet-shaped or hooded

ga-le-i-form (gă-LEE-ĭ-fohrm) or (GAY-lee-ĭ-fohrm) *adj.*, 1. helmet-shaped 2. resembling a typical shark

ga-lère (gă-LE(Ĕ)R) *n.*, a group of people who have a common quality or relationship

gal-i-ma-ti-as (gal-ĭ-MAY-shee-ăs) or (gal-ĭ-MAD-ee-ăs) *n.*, gibberish

gal-le-ass or **gal-li-ass** (GAL-ee-ăs) *n.*, a three-masted fighting ship used in the Mediterranean Sea from the 15th to the 18th centuries

gal-liard (GAL-yĭrd) *n.*, a spirited dance for two popular in the 16th and 17th centuries

gal-liar-dise (GAL-yĭ(r)-dīz) or (GAL-yĭ(r)-deez) *n.*, an archaic term for gaiety

gal-li-gas-kins (gal-ĭ-GAS-kĭnz) or (ga-lee-GAS-kĭnz) *n.*, loose trousers worn in the 16th and 17th centuries

gal-li-mau-fry (ga-lĭ-MAW-free) *n.*, a mixture; a hodgepodge

gal-li-na-ceous (gal-ĭ-NAY-shŭs) *adj.*, resembling a large, ground-based bird such as a pheasant or turkey

gal-li-nip-per or **gal-ly-nip-per** (GAL-ĭ-nip-ĕr) or (GAL-ee-nip-ĕr) *n.*, an insect that stings or bites such as a mosquito or bedbug

gal-li-on-ic or **gal-le-on-ic** (gal-ee-AHN-ik) *adj.*, careless; indifferent

---

\a\ b**a**t \ā\ **a**bout \e\ or \è\ ch**e**ck \ē\ l**e**tter \é\ caf**e** \i\f**i**sh \ī\ t**ie** \ĭ\ l**i**mit \o\ b**oa**t \ŏ\ bac**o**n \u\ s**u**n \ū\ helpf**u**l \ü\ f**oo**l

gal-li-pot (GAL-ĭ-paht) *n.*, a small-mouthed container used to hold medicines

gal-lo-glass or **gal-low-glas** (GAL-oh-glas) *n.*, a heavily armed Irish ground soldier

gal-loon (gă-LOON) *n.*, a gold or silver braid or a strip of lace or embroidery used to trim clothing

gal-lus (GAL-ŭs) *n.*, U.S. dialect for a pair of suspenders

gal-ways (GAWL-wayz) *n.*, whiskers along the chin from ear to ear

gal-yak (GAL-yak) *n.*, a sleek, flat fur made from the hide of a stillborn goat or lamb

ga-mash-es (gă-MASH-ĕz) *n.*, an archaic Scottish term for horseback riders' leggings

gamb or **gambe** (GAM(B)) or (GAAM(B)) *n.*, a leg or shank symbolized on a coat of arms

gam-ba-do (gam-BAY-doh) *n.*, 1. a pair of long boots strapped to a saddle to keep the rider's legs dry 2. the leap of a horse

gam-boge (gam-BOHJ) or (gam-BOOZH) *n.*, a gum resin from various southeast Asian trees that is used in medicine and yellow dyes

gam-brel (GAM-brĕl) or (GAWM-brĕl) *n.*, an animal's hock, such as a horse

gam-ic (GAM-ik) *adj.*, a biological term meaning needing fertilization

gam-ine (ga-MEEN) or (GAM-ĭn) *n.*, 1. a tomboy 2. a slightly built, likable girl, especially one who is pert or mischievous

gam-ma-cism (GAM-ă-sizĕm) *n.*, a difficulty pronouncing consonants such as G and K

gam-mer (GAM-ĕr) *n.*, an old woman

gam-mon (GAM-ŏn) *n.*, deceptive talk

gamp (GAMP) *n.*, a British term for a large umbrella

ganch or **gansh** (GANCH) *v.*, to kill by impalement

gang days (GANG-dayz) *n.*, the three days before Ascension Day, observed by some Christians with special prayer

gang-er (GANG-ĕ(r)) *n.*, a Scottish term for a person who travels by foot

gang-rel (GANG-(ĕ)rel) *n.*, a Scottish term for a vagabond or bum

gangue (GANG) *n.*, the worthless rock in which valuable metals or minerals are found

gan-is-ter (GAN-ĭs-tĕ(r)) *n.*, a fine-grained quartz used in making silica brick

gan-ja (GAHN-jă) *n.*, a term for marijuana

gan-net (GAN-ĕt) *n.*, a large, web-footed, fish-eating seabird that flies great distances and breeds in colonies on offshore islands

gan-oid (GA-noid) *adj.*, having scales with a bony core covered with a shiny material that resembles enamel

gan-y-mede (GAN-ĭ-meed) *n.*, a young man employed to pour and serve liquors

gape-seed (GAYP-seed) *n.*, a British term for something that causes observers to stare; a public spectacle

gap-o-sis (gap-OH-sis) *n.*, a gap or series of gaps between buttoned buttons or closed snaps on a garment

gar-boil (GAHR-boil) *n.*, an archaic term for a state of turmoil; confusion

gar-dant (GAHR-dănt) *adj.*, an animal positioned so that the observer is given a full-faced and side view

gar-dy-loo (gahr-di-LOO) *imper. v.*, a Scottish shout used to warn pedestrians that household slop was about to be thrown from an upstairs window

gar-lion (GAHR-lyen) *n.*, a vegetable hybrid derived from garlic and onion

garth (GAHRTH) *n.*, an archaic term for a small yard or garden

gar-vey (GAHR-vee) *n.*, a small boat used along the New Jersey coast

gas-con-ade (GAS-skŏ-nayd) *n.*, bragging

gas-o-gene (GAS-ŏ-jeen) *n.*, a device that attaches to a vehicle and produces combustible gas by partially burning charcoal or wood

gas-tril-o-quist (ga-STRIL-ŏ-kwĭst) *n.*, a ventriloquist

gaud (GAWD) or (GAHD) *n.*, 1. an archaic term for a trick 2. a flashy decoration or piece of jewelry

gaum (GAWM) or (GAHM) *v.*, U.S. dialect meaning to smear, especially with something tacky or oily

gaum-less (GOM-lĕs) *adj.*, U.S. dialect meaning unaware; stupid

gaur (GOWR) *n.*, a large East Indian wild ox with short, thick horns

gav-e-lock (GAV-lŏk) *n.*, British dialect for a crowbar

ga-vi-al (GAY-vee-ăl) *n.*, a large crocodile that inhabits the rivers of India

gaw-sie (GOW-see) *adj.*, a Scottish term for looking well-fed and healthy

ga-yal (gă-YAHL) *n.*, a domestic ox of India that has longer, more slender horns than its probable ancestor the gaur

geck (GEK) *v.*, a Scottish term meaning to be scornful or derisive

ged (GED) *n.*, a Scottish term for northern pike

ge-gen-schein (GAY-gĕn-shīn) *n.*, a faint, cloudy light best seen opposite the sun in the September or October sky

ge-la-da (JE-lă-dă) *n.*, an Ethopian ape characterized by the long mane of hair on the neck and shoulder of the adult male

ge-las-tic (jĕ-LAS-tik) *adj.*, 1. referring to the ability or inclination to laugh 2. funny

gem-eled (JEM-ĕld) *adj.*, paired

\a\ bat \ă\ about \e\ or \è\ check \ĕ\ letter
\é\ cafe \i\fish \ī\ tie \ĭ\ limit \o\ boat
\ŏ\ bacon \u\ sun \ŭ\ helpful \ü\ fool

gems-bok (GEMZ-bahk) *n.*, a large south African antelope similar to a gazelle or oryx

gen-et (JEN-ĕt) *n.*, a type of Old World, meat-eating mammal with retractable claws

ge-neth-li-ac (jĕ-NETH-lee-ak) *n.*, an archaic term for a calculator of birth statistics such as time, day, and astrological conditions

ge-nic-u-late (jĕ-NIK-yŭ-layt) *adj.*, bent at an angle, as a bent knee

gen-i-pap (JEN-ĭ-pap) *n.*, a tree of the West Indies and northern South America

gen-ro (gen-ROH) *n.*, the elder diplomat of Japan

gen-ti-li-tial (jen-tĭ-LI-shăl) *adj.*, characteristic of a people or family

gen-too (JEN-too) *n.*, a penguin native to the Falkland Islands

ge-nu (JEE-n(y)oo) *n.*, a kneelike part or bend

ge-o-duck (GOO-ee-dŭk) *n.*, a large, edible clam that weighs over five pounds and burrows deeply in the sandy mud along the Pacific coast of North America

ge-og-e-nous (jee-AHJ-ĕ-nŭs) *adj.*, growing in or on the ground

ge-o-phyte (JEE-ŏ-fīt) *n.*, a plant that bears fruit below the ground during winter

geor-gic (JAUR-jik) *adj.*, agricultural and rural; rustic

ge-rah or **ge-ra** (GI-ră) *n.*, an ancient Hebrew unit of weight

ge-rent (JI-rĕnt) *n.*, a person who governs or manages

ges-so (JE-soh) *n.*, a plaster-of-paris compound used in painting and other art forms

ges-tic (JES-tik) *adj.*, associated with body movements or gestures

gey (GĔI) *adv.*, an emphatic Scottish word that means very; quite

ghar-ry (GAR-ee) *n.*, a horse-driven cab in India

ghat (GAWT) or (GAHT) *n.*, an Indian term for a mountain range or pass

gha-wa-zee (gă-WAH-zee) *n.*, female Egyptian dancers who perform in the streets

gha-zi (GAH-zee) *n.*, a Muslim warrior, especially one victorious in battle defending Islam

ghee (GEE) *n.*, clarified cooking butter in India and surrounding countries, usually made from buffalo milk

ghil-lie (GIL-i) *n.*, 1. a male servant to a Scottish Highland chief 2. a type of shoe that laces up the front

ghur-ry (GĔR-ee) *n.*, a water clock in India

giaour (JAU(Ŏ)R) *n.*, one who does not believe in the Muslim faith

gib-bed (GIB-d) *adj.*, referring to a castrated cat

gi-bus (JĪ-bŭs) *n.*, an opera hat named after its 19th-century French designer

giff-gaff (GIF-gaf) *n.*, British dialect for banter

gigue (ZHEEG) *n.*, a lively dance movement in a musical work

gil-li-ver (JIL-lĭ-vĕ(r)) *n.*, British dialect for the sweet-smelling gillyflower

gil-py or **gil-pey** (GIL-pi) *n.*, a Scottish term for a lively young boy or girl

gil-rav-age (gĭl-RAV-ij) *v.*, to live immoderately with regard to food and drink

gim-bal (GIM-băl) or (JIM-băl) *n.*, an apparatus that allows an object to pivot freely yet maintain a balance, as a ship compass

gin-gel-ly (JIN-je-lee) *n.*, a sesame seed

gin-gly-form (JING-glĕ-fohrm) *adj.*, like or relating to an anatomical hinge joint

gir-an-dole (JIR-ăn-dohl) *n.*, 1. a radiating, showy composition like a cluster of sky rockets 2. a brass candleholder with figures and crystal

gir-a-sol or **gir-a-sole** (JIR-ă-sawl) *n.*, 1. a Jerusalem artichoke 2. a fire opal

girn (GIRN) *v.*, a Scottish term meaning to bare the teeth

gi-rou-ette (zhee-roo-ET) *n.*, a French term for a rooster-shaped weather vane

gi-ta-no (hee-TAH-noh) *n.*, a male gypsy in Spain

git-tern (GID-ĕrn) *n.*, a medieval stringed instrument like a guitar that was played with a thin piece of bone or metal

giv-y or **giv-ey** (GIV-ee) *adj.*, inclined to give; yielding

gizz (JIZ) *n.*, a Scottish term for a wig

giz-zen (GIZ-ĕn) *adj.*, a Scottish term meaning dried or shriveled

gjet-ost (JAYD-awst) *n.*, a dark brown cheese made from goat's milk

gla-bel-la (glă-BEL-ă) *n.*, the smooth area of the forehead between the eyebrows

gla-brous (GLAY-brŭs) *adj.*, having a smooth, hairless surface

gla-cis (GLA-see) *n.*, a gentle incline

glack (GLAK) *n.*, a Scottish term for a narrow ravine

glai-kit (GLAY-kĭt) *adj.*, a Scottish term meaning showing poor judgement; silly

glau-cous (GLAW-kŭs) *adj.*, having a powdery or waxen surface that appears white, but can be removed

gle-ba (GLEE-bă) *n.*, spore-making tissue in the reproductive structures of some fungi

glebe (GLEEB) *n.*, an archaic term for an area of cultivated land

gled (GLED) *adj.*, a Scottish term meaning glad

gleed (GLEED) *n.*, British dialect for a burning, glowing coal or an ember

gleek (GLEEK) *n.*, a card game for three players popular in England from the 16th to the 18th century

\a\ bat \ă\ about \e\ or \ĕ\ check \ē\ letter
\é\ cafe \i\fish \ĭ\ tie \ĭ\ limit \o\ boat
\ŏ\ bacon \u\ sun \ŭ\ helpful \ü\ fool

gleet (GLEET) *n.*, an inflammation of a body opening that is usually accompanied by an abnormal discharge

gleg (GLEG) *adj.*, a Scottish term meaning quick to perceive or act

gle-noid (GLE-noid) *adj.*, possessing the form of a smooth depression

gley (GLAY) *n.*, a bluish gray, sticky layer of clay formed beneath waterlogged soil

gli-a-din (GLĪ-ă-dĭn) *n.*, a protein in wheat and rye that is obtained by removing the gluten with weak alcohol

gliff (GLIF) *v.*, British dialect meaning to frighten

glime (GLĪM) *v.*, British dialect meaning to steal a glance

glop-pen (GLAH-pĕn) *v.*, English dialect meaning to surprise; to shock

glos-sa (GLAHS-ă) *n.*, the tongue of an insect

glos-so-la-li-a (GLAH-soh-lay-lee-ă) *n.*, the act of speaking in tongues

glos-sol-o-gy (GLAH-sŏl-ŏ-jee) *n.*, an archaic term for the study of language

glost (GLOST) *n.*, unfired glazed clayware

glot-to-gon-ic (GLAHD-oh-gahn-ik) *adj.*, relating to the origin of language

glout (GLOOT) *v.*, an archaic term meaning to frown

gloze (GLOHZ) *n.*, an archaic term for flattery

glump (GLŬMP) *v.*, U.S. dialect meaning to look glum; depressed

glu-ti-tion (gloo-TI-shŏn) *n.*, the act, power, or process of swallowing

gly-cin (GLĪ-sĭn) *n.*, a poisonous compound used as a fine-grain developer in photography

glyph (GLIF) *n.*, 1. an decorative vertical groove 2. a carved or incised symbol or character

glyph-ic (GLIF-ik) *adj.*, resembling an ornamental vertical groove

gnar (NAHR) *v.*, to snarl or growl, as a dog

gnath-ic (NATH-ik) *adj.*, associated with the jaw

gna-thi-on (NAY-thee-ahn) *n.*, the middle of the lower border of a human jaw

gna-thon-ic (NAY-thahn-ik) *adj.*, of or relating to a person who seeks favors by flattering wealthy or influential people

gneiss (NĪS) *n.*, a rock made up of many thin layers, similar to granite, and often named for its most abundant mineral component

gno-mist (NOH-mist) *n.*, a person who writes things that have no definite pattern or form

gno-mon-ic (noh-MAHN-ik) *adj.*, of or relating to the pointer shaft of a sundial or its use in telling time

goad-man (GOHD-man) or **goads-men** (GOHDZ-mĕn) *n.*, a person who herds animals by prodding them with a pointed stick

go-bang (GOH-bahng) *n.*, a Japanese board game

gob-bet (GAH-bĕt) *n.*, a piece of food or uncooked meat

gobe-mouche (gohb-MOOSH) *n.*, a person who believes anything he or she hears

go-by (GOH-bee) *n.*, a spiny-finned fish with a large mouth and a sucking disk that lives in shallow coastal waters

god-ling (GAHD-ling) *n.*, an inferior deity

god-wit (GAHD-wit) *n.*, a wading bird with a long, slightly curved bill

gof-fer (GAHF-ĕ(r)) *v.*, to crimp or flute with a hot iron

gog-let (GAHG-lĕt) *n.*, a long-necked, earthenware water vessel used in India

gom-er-al or **gom-er-el** (GAHM-(ĕ)r-ăl) *n.*, British dialect for a dunce; a fool

gom-phi-a-sis (gom-FĪ-ă-sis) *n.*, loose teeth

gon-fa-lon-i-er (GAHN-fă-lah-ni-(ĕ)r) *n.*, a person who carries a flag of state, especially the standard bearer for the Vatican

go-ni-on (GOH-nee-ahn) *n.*, the point of the angle on both sides of the human jaw

go-ni-um (GOH-nee-ŭm) *n.*, a primitive, undifferentiated germ cell

gon-o-cyte (GAHN-ŏ-sīt) *n.*, a cell that produces mature sex cells

gon-o-pore (GAHN-ŏ-poh(ĕ)r) *n.*, a pore on the genitals

goonch (GUUNCH) *n.*, a large, freshwater catfish found in India that can weigh up to 250 pounds and grow to six feet long

goo-ney (GOO-nee) *n.*, a black-footed albatross

gor-get (GAUR-jet) *n.*, a piece of armor for protecting the throat

gor-gon-ize (GAUR-gŏn-īz) *v.*, to have a paralyzing effect upon

gos-port (GAHS-poh(ĕ)rt) *n.*, a one-way speaking tube for use between separated cockpits of an airplane

gos-soon (gah-SOON) *n.*, an Irish term for a boy servant

gos-sy-pol (GAH-sў-paul) *n.*, a red or green pigment from cottonseed that is somewhat toxic to some animals before processing

gouache (GWAHSH) or (goo-AHSH) *n.*, a painting with colors that have been ground with water and mixed with gum

gowk (GŎUUK) or (GAHK) or (GOHK) *n.*, British dialect for a a fool or a cuckoo

grac-ile (GRAS-ĕl) *adj.*, graceful; slender; trim

gra-ci-o-so (grah-see-OH-soh) *n.*, a comic character in a Spanish comedy

gra-dine (GRAY-deen) *n.*, one of a row of steps or seats placed one above another

gra-dus (GRAY-dŭs) *n.*, a dictionary of Greek and Latin poetic phrases, used as an aid when writing Greek or Latin poetry

graip (GRAYP) *n.*, British dialect for a three-tined garden or manure fork

graith (GRAYTH) *n.*, a Scottish term for equipment; gear

gral-la-to-ri-al (gral-ă-TOH-ree-ăl) *adj.*, of or relating to the wading birds, such as cranes or storks

gral-loch (GRAL-lŏk) *n.*, a British term for animal entrails

gram-i-niv-o-rous (gram-ĭ-NIV-(ŏ)-rŭs) *adj.*, grass-eating

gram-ma-log or **gram-ma-logue** (GRAM-ă-lawg) *n.*, a word written with a single stroke in shorthand

gram-pus (GRAM-pŭs) *n.*, a marine mammal related to the blackfish and the killer whale

grau-pel (GROW-pĕl) *n.*, granulated snow pellets or soft hail

gray-lag or **grey-lag** (GRAY-lag) *n.*, a common gray goose of Europe thought to be a wild ancestor of the common domestic goose

gre-gal (GREE-găl) *adj.*, an archaic term meaning belonging to or typical of a company or crowd of people

gre-ga-le (gray-GAH-lay) *n.*, a cold, northeast wind of the central Mediterranean

gre-go (GREE-goh) *n.*, a warm, hooded seamen's jacket

greige (GRAY(ZH)) *n.*, an unbleached, undyed textile in the early stage of preparation

gre-mi-al (GREE-mee-ăl) *adj.*, of or relating to the lap or bosom

gres-so-ri-al (gre-SOH-ree-ăl) *adj.*, adapted for walking

grice (GRĪS) *n.*, a Scottish term for a young pig

gride (GRĪD) *v.*, to scrape or rub against something and so produce a harsh, grating sound

grif-fo-nage (grif-ŏ-NAHZH) *n.*, poor handwriting; an illegible scrawl

grig (GRIG) *n.*, a small person or creature; a dwarf

grilse (GRILS) *n.*, a young male salmon returning to spawn for the first time

gri-mal-kin (grĭ-MAL-kĭn) *n.*, 1. an elderly cat 2. a frumpy old woman

gri-saille (grĭ-ZĪ) *n.*, the act of painting in varying shades of one color, usually gray, sometimes as an underpainting for a glaze finish

gri-sette (grĕ-ZET) *n.*, 1. a French working-class girl 2. a young girl who supplements her income by prostitution

gris-kin (GRIS-kĭn) *n.*, a British term for the lean part of a pork loin

grith (GRITH) *n.*, 1. an obscure term meaning assured protection 2. an archaic term for sanctuary

griv-et (GRIV-ĕt) *n.*, a monkey of the upper Nile with an olive green back and white lower parts

gri-voi-se-rie (GREEV-wah-z-ree) *n.*, bold, improper behavior

gro-bi-an (GROH-bee-ăn) *n.*, a crude, slovenly person; a lout

gro-bi-an-ism (GROH-bee-ăn-izĕm) *n.*, the boorish behavior of a crude person

gro-schen (GROH-shĕn) *n.*, a German coin issued from the 13th to the 19th century

grosz (GRAUSH) *n.*, a unit of Polish currency

groyne (GROIN) *n.*, a small jetty extending from a shore to prevent erosion

gru-gru (GROO-groo) *n.*, a kind of spiny, tropical palm

grum (GRŬM) *adj.*, morose; sour

grume (GROOM) *n.*, a thick, sticky fluid, especially a blood clot

gru-mous (GROO-mŭs) *adj.*, resembling a thick, sticky fluid; clotted

grumph-ie (GRŬM(P)F-i) *n.*, a Scottish term for a sow

grunt-ling (GRŬNT-ling) *n.*, a young pig

grush-ie (GRŬSH-i) *adj.*, a Scottish term meaning flourishing

guai-a-cum (G(W)Ī-ă-kŭm) *n.*, a tropical tree with feathery leaves and blue flowers

gua-ni-dine (GWAH-nĭ-deen) *n.*, a colorless, crystalline, water-soluble chemical used in the manufacture of plastic and explosives

gua-no (GWAH-noh) *n.*, a substance made of partially decomposed bird droppings, found in areas frequented by sea birds, and often used as a fertilizer

guar (GWAHR) *n.*, a drought-resistant legume grown for forage and seed

gua-ra-ni (GWAH-ră-nee) *n.*, the basic monetary unit of Paraguay

gub-ber-tushed (GUUB-ĕr-tuusht) or (GŬB-ĕr-tĕsht) *adj.*, English dialect meaning buck-toothed

gud-dle (GŬD-ĕl) *v.*, to fish by groping in underwater hiding places

gud-geon (GŬ-jĕn) *n.*, a metal pivot at the end of a wooden shaft

gue-non (ge-NOH) or (ge-NAHN) *n.*, a long-tailed, tree-dwelling African monkey

guer-don (GŬR-dŏn) *n.*, something that one has received as a reward

gu-fa (GOO-fä) *n.*, a round, wicker boat used in ancient Mesopotamia

guimpe (GAMP) or (GIMP) *n.*, 1. a blouse worn beneath a jumper or pinafore 2. a wide, usually starched cloth used to cover the neck and shoulders in some religious orders

gui-pure (gee-P(Y)UU(Ĕ)R) *n.*, any hand- or machine-made lace with large sections joined by cutouts and used for trimming on women's clothes

gui-ro ((G)WEE-roh) *n.*, a Latin American percussion instrument made from a notched gourd and played by scraping a stick over its surface

guit-guit (GWIT-gwit) *n.*, a small, brightly colored tropical bird

---

\a\ bat \ă\ about \e\ or \è\ check \ĕ\ letter
\é\ cafe \i\fish \ī\ tie \ĭ\ limit \o\ boat
\ŏ\ bacon \u\ sun \ŭ\ helpful \ü\ fool

gul (GOOL) or (GUUL) *n.*, a rose

gules (GYOOLZ) *n.*, the color red

gu-los-i-ty (gyoo-LAHS-ĭd-ee) *n.*, a huge appetite; greediness

gum-ma (GŬ-mă) *n.*, a rubbery tumor characteristic of the third stage of syphilis

gun-nel (GŬN-ĕl) *n.*, a small, slimy fish found in the north Atlantic

gur-ry (GŬ-ree) *n.*, the parts leftover after cleaning fish

gut-ta-per-cha (GED-ă-PER-chă) *n.*, a gray to brown plastic substance made from latex that is used for electric insulation and in dentistry

gut-ta-tim (gŭ-TAYD-ĭm) *adv.*, a pharmaceutical term meaning drop by drop

gut-ti-form (GŬT-ĭ-fohrm) *adj.*, in the shape of a drop

gut-tle (GŬD-ĕl) *v.*, to eat or drink greedily

guy-ot (gee-OH) *n.*, a flat-topped, underwater mountain in the Pacific ocean

gy-as-cu-tus (gi-ă-SK(Y)OOD-ŭs) *n.*, a large, imaginary four-legged beast with legs that are longer on one side for walking on mountains

gyle (GĪ(Ĕ)L) *n.*, the fermenting malt solution added to stout or ale

gym-nos-o-phist (jim-NAHS-ŏ-fĕst) *n.*, a member of a sect of Hindu philosophers who went naked and practiced meditation

gy-nar-chy (JE-nahr-kee) *n.*, government by women

gyre (JI(Ĕ)R) *v.*, to cause to spin around; to whirl

gy-rene (JĪ-reen) *n.*, a slang expression for a Marine Corps member

gy-ro-man-cy (JĪ-rŏ-man(t)-see) *n.*, a method of predicting the future in which a person walks in circles until dizzy, then falls and reads the future from where he or she fell

gy-ro-vague (JĪ-roh-vayg) *n.*, a wandering, wanton monk of the early church

gy-rus (JĪ-rŭs) *n.*, a twisted ridge between grooves, especially a ridge of the brain

gyve (JĪV) *v.*, to bind and hold with fetters; to chain

haaf (HAHF) *n.*, a deep-sea fishing area off the coast of the Shetland Islands

hab-nab ((H)AB-nab) *adv.*, British dialect meaning by one means or another; by hook or crook

ha-boob (hă-BOOB) *n.*, a severe dust storm occurring in northern Africa or India

ha-bu (HAH-boo) *n.*, a dangerous, poisonous snake common to the Ryukyu Islands

ha-chure (ha-SHUU(Ĕ)R) *n.*, a short line used in mapmaking to show the direction and grade of a slope

hack-ee (HAK-ee) *n.*, a chipmunk

hade ((H)AYD) *n.*, an English term for a strip of land left unplowed in an otherwise plowed field

hadj (HAJ) *n.*, the Muslim pilgrimage to Mecca

haft (HAFT) *n.*, the handle of a weapon or tool

hag-born (HAG-bohrn) *adj.*, conceived by a witch

hag-don (HAG-dŏn) *n.*, a type of seabird found in the north Atlantic

ha-ha (HAH-hah) *n.*, a reinforced trench used to divide land without marring the landscape

haik (HĪK) *n.*, a large piece of usually white cloth worn as an outer garment by people in northern Africa

hake (HAYK) *n.*, a fish related to the cod

ha-ken-kreuz (HAH-kĕn-kroits) *n.*, the Nazi swastika

ha-kim (hă-KEEM) *n.*, a Muslim doctor

hal-berd (HAL-bĕrd) *n.*, a 15th- and 16th-century weapon made of a battle-ax and pike mounted on a six-foot handle

half-pace (HAF-pays) *n.*, 1. a raised floor at the top of steps 2. a staircase landing

hal-i-dom (HAL-ĭ-dŏm) *n.*, an archaic term for a holy place or relic

hal-i-eu-tic (hal-ee-(Y)OOD-ik) *adj.*, associated with fishing

hal-i-tus (HAL-i-tŭs) *n.*, an archaic term for breath

hal-lux (HAL-ŭks) *n.*, the big toe

hal-oid (HAL-oid) *adj.*, resembling or derived from fluorine, chlorine, bromine, iodine, or astatine

hal-sen (AHL-zĕn) *v.*, English dialect meaning to divine or predict

hal-tere (HAL-ti(ĕ)r) *n.*, a modified second set of wings that an insect uses for flight

ha-mar-ti-ol-o-gy (hă-MAHRD-ee-ahl-ŏ-jee) *n.*, a branch of theology dealing with sin

ham-ble (AM-(b)ĕl) *v.*, English dialect meaning to stumble or limp

hame-suck-en (HAYM-sŭk-ĕn) *n.*, a Scottish legal term for the act of assaulting a person in his own home

ha-mi-form (HAY-mĭ-fohrm) *adj.*, hook-shaped

ham-u-lus (HAM-yŭ-lŭs) *n.*, a hook or hooklike growth

han-a-per (HAN-ă-pĕ(r)) *n.*, a British term for a small wicker case used to store legal documents

hand-hab-end (HAND-hab-ĕnd) *adj.*, an old English law term meaning possessing stolen goods

hand-sel (HAN(T)-sĕl) *n.*, an obsolete term for a lucky token

ha-nu-man (HĂ-NUU-mahn) *n.*, a common Indian monkey protected as a protégé of a monkey deity

hap-har-lot (HAP-hahr-lŏt) *n.*, English dialect for a coarse bed covering

---

\a\ bat \ă\ about \e\ or \ĕ\ check \ĕ\ letter
\ĕ\ cafe \i\ fish \ĭ\ tie \ĭ\ limit \o\ boat
\ŏ\ bacon \u\ sun \ŭ\ helpful \ü\ fool

hap-log-ra-phy (ha-PLAHG-ră-fee) *n.*, the omission of one or more similar words, letters, or lines in writing

hap-lol-o-gy (ha-PLAHL-ŏ-jee) *n.*, a contraction of a word made by omitting one or more similar sounds in pronunciation

hare-bell (HA(Ĕ)R-bĕl) *n.*, a slim herb with blue flowers; also called a bluebell

ha-ren-gi-form (hă-REN-jĭ-fohrm) *adj.*, in the shape of a herring

har-i-jan (HAR-ĭ-jan) *n.*, a member of the outcasts of India; an untouchable

har-pac-toph-a-gous (HAHR-pak-tahf-ă-gŭs) *adj.*, predatory, especially when applied to insects

har-tal (hahr-TAHL) *n.*, a work stoppage used as a protest against a political situation

ha-rus-pex ((h)ă-RŬ-speks) *n.*, a person who predicts the future by interpreting natural events such as lightning

hat-te-ri-a (hă-TI-ree-ă) *n.*, a primitive, lizardlike reptile from islands near New Zealand

hau-berk (HAW-bĕrk) *n.*, a long tunic of ring or chain mail that served as defensive armor in the 12th to 14th centuries

haugh (HAW(K)) *n.*, a Scottish term for a low-lying meadow by a river side

haulm (HAWM) *n.*, the tips or stems of cultivated plants, especially those leftover after harvest

hau-sen (HAUU-zĕn) *n.*, a sturgeon from the Black or Caspian Sea that produces the roe for caviar

have-lock (HAV-lahk) *n.*, a cap or hat with long sides and back for protection from the elements

hav-ior (HAYV-yŏr) *n.*, U.S. dialect for the manner in which a person acts; behavior

hay-bote (HAY-boht) *n.*, the wood that English law allowed a tenant for the repair of his fences

heaume (HOHM) *n.*, a 13th-century helmet worn over a close-fitting steel cap and supported by the shoulders

heb-do-mad (HEB-dŏ-mad) *n.*, 1. a group of seven 2. a week

heb-dom-a-dal (heb-DAHM-ĕ-dăl) *adj.*, an obsolete term for something that lasts seven days

he-be-phre-ni-a (hee-bĕ-FREE-nee-a) *n.*, a schizophrenic state characterized by silliness, delusions, and hallucinations

heb-e-tate (HEB-ĕ-tayt) *v.*, to make dull

he-bet-ic (hi-BET-ik) *adj.*, relating to or occurring in puberty

heb-e-tude (HEB-ĕ-tood) *n.*, a state of lethargy

hec-a-tomb (HEK-ă-tohm) *n.*, an ancient Greek and Roman sacrifice, usually of 100 oxen or cattle

heel-ball (HEEL-bawl) *n.*, the underside of a foot's heel

he-gu-men (hĕ-GYOO-mĕn) *n.*, the leader of a religious group in the Eastern Church

hel·i·coid (HEL-ĭ-koid) *adj.*, spiral-shaped

hell·kite (HEL-kīt) *n.*, a person who acts with extreme cruelty

hel·minth (HEL-minth) *n.*, a parasitic worm, especially one in the intestine

he·lo·bi·ous (he-LOH-bee-ŭs) *adj.*, dwelling in marshy places

hel·ot·ry (HEL-ŏt-ree) *n.*, slavery

helve (HELV) *n.*, a tool or weapon handle

he·ma·gogue (HEE-mă-gawg) *adj.*, promoting the blood's flow

hem·a·to·poi·e·sis (hem-ăd-oh-poi-EE-sĭs) *n.*, the production of blood within the body

hem·er·a·lo·pi·a (HEM-ĕr-ă-loh-pee-a) *n.*, an eye defect indicated by reduced vision in bright lights or the sun

hemp·en (HEMP-ĕn) *adj.*, an archaic term meaning pertaining to a hangman's noose

hen·bane (HEN-bayn) *n.*, a foul-smelling Old World herb that is toxic to fowl

hen·bit (HEN-bit) *n.*, a weed with bean-shaped leaves and small purple flowers

hen·de·ca·syl·la·ble (hen-DE-kă-sil-ă-bel) *n.*, a poetic line with eleven syllables

hen·e·quen (HEN-ĕ-kĕn) *n.*, a strong, hard fiber made from the leaves of a tropical plant of Yucatan and used to make twine

hen·o·the·ism (HEN-oh-thee-izĕm) *n.*, the worship of more than one god

hent (HENT) *v.*, U.S. dialect meaning to catch or to seize

he·re·si·arch (hĕ-REE-zee-ahrk) *n.*, the head of a group who believes an idea that contradicts or opposes established religious beliefs

he·re·si·og·ra·phy (hĕ-REE-zee-ahg-ră-fee) *n.*, a paper written about an opinion contrary to orthodox beliefs

her·i·ot (HER-ee-ŏt) *n.*, a tribute owed a feudal lord upon the death of a tenant

her·me·neu·tics (hĕr-mĕ-N(Y)OOD-iks) *n.*, the study of the principles of interpretation and explanation

hes·y·chas·tic (HES-ĕ-kas-tik) *adj.*, referring to something soothing or calming

he·tae·rism (hĕ-TI-rizĕm) *n.*, sexual relations outside of marriage

het·er·och·tho·nous (hed-ĕ-RAHK-thŏ-nŭs) *adj.*, not formed in the place it currently resides; transported

het·er·o·clite (HED-ĕr-ŏ-klīt) *adj.*, deviating from the ordinary; irregular

het·er·o·nym (HET-ĕr-ŏ-nim) *n.*, a word spelled the same as another, but having a different sound and meaning

het·er·o·phe·my (HED-ĕr-ŏ-fee-mee) *n.*, the unconscious usage of words other than those originally intended

het·ero·telic (HED-ĕroh-telik) *adj.*, existing because of something else

het·man (HET-măn) *n.*, a leader of the cossacks

heugh (KYOOK) *n.*, a Scottish term for a steep ravine or cliff

hi·ber·nac·u·lum (hi-bĕ(r)-NAK-yŭ-lŭm) *n.*, the part of a plant that rests in the ground during the winter

hi·ber·ni·cism (hi-BĔR-nĭ-sizĕm) *n.*, something Irish in appearance or character

hi·drot·ic (hi-DRAHD-ik) *adj.*, causing sweat

hi·e·mal (HĪ-ĕ-măl) *adj.*, pertaining to winter

hi·er·o·dule (HĪ-(ĕ)r-ŏ-d(y)ool) *n.*, a slave in the service of a temple, especially an ancient Greek sacred prostitute

hil·ding (HIL-ding) *adj.*, an archaic term meaning lacking moral principles

hink (HINK) *n.*, an obsolete term for a wavering or a hesitation

hin·ny (HIN-ee) *n.*, the offspring of a stallion and an ass

hip·parch (HI-pahrk) *n.*, an ancient Greek calvary commander

hip·po·cam·pine (HIP-ŏ-kam-pīn) *adj.*, associated with sea horses

hip·po·crep·i·form (hip-ŏ-KREP-ĭ-fohrm) *adj.*, horseshoe-shaped

hir·ple (HIR-pĕl) *v.*, a Scottish term meaning to limp

his·pid (HIS-pĭd) *adj.*, rough; having bristles, spines, or stiff hair

hoa·tzin (wah(t)-SEEN) *n.*, a crested bird of South America that has a strong odor; also called the stinkbird

hob·ble·de·hoy (HAH-bĕl-dee-hoi) *n.*, an awkward, unsophisticated adolescent boy

ho·di·er·nal (HOH-dee-ĕr-năl) *adj.*, of this day

hog·gas·ter (HAWG-ăs-tĕ(r)) *n.*, an archaic term for a three-year-old boar

hog·ger·el (HAHG-(ĕ)r-ĕl) *n.*, a British term for a young sheep

hog·get (HAHG-ĕt) *n.*, a British term for an unshorn sheep that is younger than one year old

hog·ma·nay (HAHG-mă-nay) *n.*, a Scottish term for New Year's Eve

ho·go (HOH-goh) *n.*, British dialect for a distinctively strong smell

hoick (HOIK) *v.*, U.S. dialect meaning to jerk

hol·lus·chick (HAHL-ŭs-chik) *n.*, a young, male fur seal

holm (HOHM) or (HOHLM) *n.*, a British term for a small island in a river or lake

holm·gang (HOH(L)M-gang) *n.*, an archaic Scottish term for a duel, especially on an island

hol·o·graph (HAHL-ŏ-graf) *n.*, a document in the handwriting of the person in whose name it appears

ho·loph·ra·sis (hŏ-LAHF-ră-sĭs) *n.*, the expression of a complex idea with a single word

hom·i·nid (HAWM-ĭ-nĭd) *n.*, a man

hom-mock (HAHM-ŏk) *n.*, a ridge or heap of ice

ho-mo-erot-i-cism (HOH-moh-erahd-ĭ-sizĕm) *n.*, the obtaining of sexual gratification from a member of the same sex

ho-mun-cu-lus (hoh-MŬNG-kyŭ-lŭs) *n.*, a tiny man

hon-do (HAHN-doh) *n.*, a wide, low-lying brook or stream in the southwestern United States

hoo-poe (HOO-poo) or (HOO-poh) *n.*, an insect-eating bird in Europe, Asia, and northern Africa that has cinnamon and black feathers

hor-ni-to ((h)aw(r)-NEED-oh) *n.*, an oven-shaped mound that spews smoke and vapors in volcanic regions

hor-rent (HAW(R)-ĕnt) *adj.*, erect as bristles

hor-rip-i-la-tion (haw-rip-ĭ-LAY-shŏn) *n.*, the standing on end of the hair on the head or body when frightened or cold; goose bumps

hor-tu-lan (HAW(R)-chŭ-lăn) *adj.*, associated with a garden

hou-ri (HOO-ree) *n.*, according to Muslim belief, a beautiful, dark-eyed virgin that lives with the blessed in paradise

hou-sel (HAUU-zĕl) *n.*, an archaic term for Holy Communion and its rite

hui (HOOEE) *n.*, a Hawaiian term for a partnership

hum-dud-geon (hŭm-DŬJ-ĕn) *n.*, a Scottish term for a noisy complaint

hum-hum (HŬM-hŭm) *n.*, a rough, cotton fabric, formerly imported from India

hum-mum (HŬ-mŭm) *n.*, a Turkish bath

hum-strum (HŬM-strŭm) *n.*, any musical instrument that is untuned

hu-mu-hu-mu-nu-ku-nu-ku-a-pu-a-a (hoo-mŭ-HOO-mŭ-noo-kŭ-NOO-kŭ-ah-pŭ-wah-ah) *n.*, a small Hawaiian fish

hur-kle (HŬR-kĕl) *v.*, British dialect meaning to stoop or squat

hurst (HŬRST) *n.*, a grove or knoll with trees

hush-ion (HUSH-ŏn) *n.*, an archaic Scottish term for a footless stocking

hus-tle-ment (HŬS-ĕl-mĕnt) *n.*, U.S. dialect for household furnishings or goods; knickknacks

hwan ((H)WAHN) *n.*, a monetary unit of South Korea replaced by the won

hy-a-line (HĪ-ă-lĭn) or (HĪ-ă-līn) *adj.*, of or like glass

hy-e-tal (HĪ-ĕd-ĕl) *adj.*, associated with rain, rainfall, or rainy regions

hy-la (HĪ-lă) *n.*, a toad with enlarged toes that resemble claws, but are sticky pads for tree climbing

hy-lic (HĪ-lik) *adj.*, pertaining to matter

hy-pae-thral (hī-PEE-thrăl) *adj.*, open to the sky; roofless

\a\ bat \ă\ about \e\ or \ĕ\ check \ĕ\ letter
\é\ cafe \i\fish \ĭ\ tie \ī\ limit \o\ boat
\ŏ\ bacon \u\ sun \ŭ\ helpful \ü\ fool

hy·per·bo·re·an (HĪ-pĕ(r)-boh-ree-ăn) *adj.*, associated with an extreme northern region; frozen

hy·per·du·li·a (HĪ-pĕ(r)-d(y)oo-lee-ä) *n.*, the worship of the Virgin Mary as the holiest of beings

hy·per·gol (HĪ-pĕ(r)-gawl) *n.*, a self-igniting fluid for rocket propulsion

hy·perm·ne·si·a (hi-pĕrm-NEE-zh(ee)ä) *n.*, a vivid memory of impressions that seemed long forgotten

hy·per·on (HĪ-pĕr-ahn) *n.*, a term in physics for an elementary particle between a neutron and a deutron

hyp·no·pom·pic (hip-nŏ-PAHM-pik) *adj.*, of or relating to the semiconsciousness experienced before waking

hy·po·bu·li·a (hī-poh-BYOO-lee-ä) *n.*, the condition of being unable to act or make decisions

hy·po·ge·al (hī-poh-JEE-ăl) *adj.*, living under the surface of the ground

hyp·or·che·ma (hīp-ĕ(r)-KEE-mä) *n.*, an ancient Greek song and dance, usually in honor of Apollo

hy·pos·ta·sis (hī-PAHS-tă-sĭs) *n.*, something that settles at the bottom of a liquid

hyp·si·loid (HIP-sĭ-loid) *adj.*, resembling the Greek capital letter upsilon

hyte (HĪIT) *adj.*, a Scottish term meaning insane

I

iat·ro·gen·ic (Ī-A-troh-jen-ik) *adj.*, suffering from physician-induced ailments suggested to a patient during a physical examination

icar·i·an (i-KAR-ee-an) *adj.*, 1. flying beyond a safe height 2. unable to execute an ambitious project

ice-blink (ĪS-blink) *n.*, 1. a yellow or white glare in the sky above an ice field 2. a cliff of ice on a coastline

ich (IK) *n.*, a skin disease affecting freshwater fish that is especially damaging in aquariums and hatcheries

ich·neu·mon (IK-nyoo-mŏn) *n.*, a North African mongoose highly regarded in ancient times for its ability to eat crocodile eggs

i·chor (Ī-kawr) *n.*, 1. the fluid that flows through the veins of the gods of Greek mythology 2. a thin, blood-tinged discharge

ick·er (IK-er) *n.*, the fruit-bearing spike of cereal plants, especially an ear of corn

i·cosa·he·dron (Ī-KOSÄ-hee-drŏn) *n.*, a geometric figure with 20 faces

ic·tic (IK-tik) *adj.*, relating to the recurring stress or beat in rhythmic sounds

ic·tus (IK-tŭs) *n.*, a heartbeat or pulsation

id·e·o·plas·tic (id-ee-ŏ-PLAS-tik) *adj.*, 1. changed by mental activity 2. made symbolic in an art form through mental reconstruction of a natural subject

id·i·o·graph (ID-ee-ŏ-graf) *n.*, a mark or signature characteristic of a person

id·i·o·trop·ic (id-ee-ŏ-TROP-ik) *adj.*, turning inward

i·do·ne·ous (ī-DOH-nee-ŭs) *adj.*, an archaic term meaning appropriate

i·er·oe (EE-ĕ-roi) *n.*, a Scottish term for a great-grandchild

ig·nes·cent (ig-NES-ĕnt) *adj.*, 1. able to emit sparks 2. volatile

ih·ram (ee-RAHM) *n.*, 1. the devotion to religious duty assumed by Muslims on pilgrimage to Mecca 2. the clothing worn on a Meccan pilgrimage

ii·wi (ee-EE-wee) *n.*, a small Hawaiian bird with bright plumage formerly used to make feather cloaks

i·ke·ba·na (EE-ke-BAH-nah) *n.*, the Japanese art of flower arrangement

il·laq·ue·ate (ĭ-LAK-wee-ayt) *v.*, an archaic term meaning to snare or trap

il·la·tion (ĭ-LAY-shŏn) *n.*, an inference

illth (ILTH) *n.*, poverty or something that produces it

il·lu·mi·na·ti (ĭ-LOO-mĭ-nah-dee) *n.*, 1. members of an 18th-century secret German society who believed in republican principles 2. persons who claim to be extremely enlightened

il·men·ite (IL-mĕ-nīt) *n.*, an iron-black mineral compound

i·ma·go (ĭ-MAY-goh) *n.*, 1. an adult insect in its final, sexually mature stage 2. an idealized perception of anyone or of one's self

i·ma·ret (ĭ-MAH-ret) *n.*, a Turkish inn or hospice

im·bi·bi·tion (im-bĭ-BI-shŏn) *n.*, 1. a saturation or solution in liquid 2. the act of drinking

im·bri·ca·tion (im-brĭ-KAY-shŏn) *n.*, 1. an overlapping, especially of tiles, shingles, or layers of tissue 2. a decoration or pattern with such overlapping

im·brue (ĭm-BROO) *v.*, to drench

im·mar·ces·ci·ble (i(m)-mahr-SE-sĭ-bĕl) *adj.*, incapable of being destroyed

im·merd (i-MĔRD) *v.*, an archaic term meaning to cover with manure

im·mis·ci·ble (i-MIS-ĭ-bĕl) *adj.*, not capable of being mixed

im·mund (ĭ-mŭnd) *adj.*, dirty; filthy

im·pa·na·tion (im-pă-NAY-shŏn) *n.*, 1. the inclusion of Christ's body in the communion bread 2. the doctrine affirming Christ's presence in the Eucharist

im·par (IM-pahr) *adj.*, relating to or of an unpaired anatomical structure

im·pav·id (im-PAV-id) *adj.*, an archaic term meaning fearless

\a\ bat \ă\ about \e\ or \ĕ\ check \ē\ letter
\é\ cafe \i\fish \ī\ tie \ĭ\ limit \o\ boat
\ŏ\ bacon \u\ sun \ŭ\ helpful \ü\ fool

im-pec-cant (im-PEK-ănt) *adj.*, sinless; without error

im-pe-trate (IM-pĕ-trayt) *v.*, to obtain by asking or to request

im-pig-no-rate (ĭm-PIG-nŏ-rayt) *v.*, to promise; to mortgage

im-prest (ĭm-PREST) *v.*, an archaic term meaning to give an advance or a loan of money

im-prov-i-sa-to-re (im-prahv-ĭ-ză-TOH-ree) *n.*, a person who prepares and performs material spontaneously

in-bye (IN-bī) *adv.*, a Scottish term meaning in an inward direction

in-ca-les-cence (in-kă-LES-ĕn(t)s) *n.*, a becoming warm or fervent

in-ca-nous (ĭn-KAY-nŭs) *adj.*, gray or white from the growth of down

in-carn (ĭn-KAHRN) *v.*, an archaic term meaning to heal

in-car-na-dine (ĭn-KAHR-nă-dīn) *adj.*, 1. flesh-colored 2. red

inch-ling (INCH-ling) *n.*, a small being that is likely to grow bigger

in-con-cin-ni-ty (in-kŏn-SIN-ĕd-ee) *n.*, unsuitability; an awkward form or character

in-con-dite (ĭn-KAHN-dĭt) or (ĭn-KAHN-dīt) *adj.*, 1. badly organized or assembled 2. without manners

in-cras-sate (ĭn-KRA-sayt) *adj.*, 1. thickened 2. swollen or inflated in structure

in-cre-pa-tion (ĭn-krĕ-PAY-shŏn) *n.*, an archaic term for a chiding or a reproach

in-cus (ING-kŭs) *n.*, 1. the middle of three small bones in the ear of mammals 2. the top of a thundercloud that is shaped like an anvil

in-cuse (in-KOOZ) *v.*, to make an impression by striking, punching, or stamping

in-da-ba (in-DAH-bă) *n.*, a conference among representatives of native African tribes

in-de-his-cent (in-DĔ-his-sĕnt) *adj.*, staying closed; not bursting open

in-dign (ĭn-DĪN) *adj.*, 1. an archaic term for lacking worth; undeserving 2. an obsolete term for unbecoming; disgraceful

in-dite (ĭn-DĪT) *v.*, 1. to create or compose 2. an obsolete term meaning to dictate

in-doc-i-ble (ĭn-DAHS-ĭ-bĕl) *adj.*, unable to be taught

in-dri (IN-dree) *n.*, a large lemur on the island of Madagascar

in-duc-tile (ĭn-DŬK-tĕl) *adj.*, rigid; unbending

in-du-rate (ĬN-d(y)ŭ-răt) *adj.*, physically or morally calloused

in-e-nar-ra-ble (in-ee-NAR-ră-bĕl) *adj.*, not capable of being narrated or described

in-ex-pugn-a-ble (in-ek-SPYOON-ă-bĕl) *adj.*, not capable of being taken by assault or forcibly subdued

in-fare (IN-faĕr) *n.*, U.S. dialect for a reception for newlyweds given by the groom's family, usually a few days after the wedding

in-faust (ĭn-FAUUST) *adj.*, unfavorable; not lucky

in-fib-u-late (ĭn-FIB-yŭ-layt) *v.*, to fasten, as with a clasp or buckle

in-fib-u-la-tion (in-fib-yŭ-LAY-shŏn) *n.*, the act of sealing male or female genitals to prevent sexual intercourse

in-fi-cete (in-fĭ-SEET) *adj.*, without wit

in-fra-lap-sar-i-an (in-fră-lap-SER-ee-ăn) *n.*, a person who believes that God permitted the fall of man and predestined some souls to be saved

in-fra-pose (in-fră-POHZ) *v.*, to put under or beneath

in-fun-dib-u-lar (IN-fŭn-dib-yŭ-lăr) *adj.*, funnellike

ing (ING) *n.*, English dialect for a low pasture or meadow

in-ger-ence (IN-jĕr-ĕn(t)s) *n.*, an intrusion or interference

in-gle (IN-gĕl) *n.*, 1. a fire 2. a hearth or fireplace 3. an edge, angle, or corner

in-grav-i-date (ĭn-GRAV-ĭ-dayt) *v.*, an archaic term meaning to make pregnant

in-i-on (IN-ee-ahn) *n.*, the outer bump at the back of the skull

in-qui-nate (IN-kwĭ-nayt) *v.*, to corrupt

in-san-a-ble (in-SAN-ă-bĕl) *adj.*, unable to be cured

in-sci-ent (IN-sh(ee)-ĕnt) *adj.*, showing or based on a lack of knowledge

in-so-late (IN-soh-layt) *v.*, to put in the sunlight; to expose to the sun's rays for drying

in-spis-sate (inz-PIS-sayt) *adj.*, of a thick consistency

in-stau-ra-tion (inz-taw-RAY-shŏn) *n.*, the restoration after deterioration

in-sulse (ĭn-SŬL(T)S) *adj.*, an archaic term meaning lacking taste

in-tar-si-a (ĭn-TAHR-see-a) *n.*, a mosaic, usually of inlaid wood, popular as a decoration in 15th-century Italy

in-teg-u-ment (ĭn-TEG-yŭ-mĕnt) *n.*, 1. something that acts as a cover or enclosure 2. an outer coating

in-tem-er-ate (ĭn-TEM-ĕ-rayt) *adj.*, pure; unspoiled

in-tem-pes-tive (in-tem-PES-tiv) *adj.*, untimely; inopportune

in-ten-er-ate (ĭn-TEN-ĕ-rayt) *v.*, to soften

in-ter-am-ni-an (in-tĕ-(R)AM-nee-ăn) *adj.*, between or enclosed by rivers

in-ter-co-lum-ni-a-tion (in-te(r)-kŏ-lŭm-nee-AY-shŏn) *n.*, the space between the columns in a series

in-ter-fen-es-tra-tion (in-tĕ(r)-fen-ĕ-STRAY-shŏn) *n.*, windows arranged with relation to the distance between them

in-ter-la-cus-trine (in-tĕ(r)-lă-KŬS-trĭn) *adj.*, located between lakes

---

\a\ **bat** \ă\ **about** \e\ **or** \ĕ\ **check** \ē\ **letter**
\ē\ **cafe** \i\ **fish** \ī\ **tie** \ĭ\ **limit** \o\ **boat**
\ŏ\ **bacon** \u\ **sun** \ŭ\ **helpful** \ü\ **fool**

in·ter·lu·ca·tion (in-tĕ(r)-loo-KAY-shŏn) *n.*, the process of thinning trees to increase the growth of those remaining

in·tus·sus·cep·tion (in-tŭs-ŭ-SEP-shŏn) *n.*, the passing of one part into another

in·ter·mun·dane (in-tĕ(r)-MŬN-dayn) *adj.*, existing between worlds, as space

in·ter·nun·cio (in-tĕ(r)-NŬN-(t)see-oh) *n.*, a messenger

in·ter·si·de·re·al (in-tĕ(r)-sī-DEE-ree-ăl) *adj.*, interstellar

in·ter·tes·sel·late (in-tĕ(r)-TES-ĕ-layt) *n.*, an intricate interrelation like a mosaic design

in·ti·ma (IN-tĭ-mă) *n.*, the innermost layer of an organ that consists of blood vessels and tissue

in·tus·sus·cep·tion (in-tŭs-ŭ-SEP-shŏn) *n.*, the passing of one part another

in·us·tion (ĭ-NŬS-chŏn) *n.*, an archaic term for cauterization

in·var (IN-vahr) *n.*, an iron-nickel alloy

ip·se·dix·it·ism (ip-see-DIK-sĭd-izĕm) *n.*, the authoritative assertion of something as if it were fact

ip·se·i·ty (ip-SEE-ĭd-ee) *n.*, individual identity

i·ra·cund (Ī-ră-kŭnd) *adj.*, easily angered

i·ra·de (ee-RAH-dee) *n.*, a Muslim ruler's decree

ir·rep·ti·tious (i-rep-TI-shŭs) *adj.*, marked by or resulting from entering secretly or inadvertently

ir·ro·rate (IR-ŏ-rayt) *adj.*, speckled

ir·ru·ma·tion (i-roo-MAY-shŏn) *n.*, the act of fellatio

is·ba (ĭz-BAH) *n.*, a Russian hut made of logs

i·soch·ro·nous (ī-SAHK-rŏ-nŭs) *adj.*, referring to things equal in duration, interval, or length

i·soch·ro·ous (ī-SOK-roh-ŭs) *adj.*, possessing the same color throughout

i·so·gloss (Ī-soh-glahs) *n.*, a boundary between places or regions that have linguistic differences

i·son·o·my (ī-SAHN-ŏ-mee) *n.*, legal equality

i·so·pod (Ī-soh-pahd) *n.*, a small crustacean with a flat, oval body and seven pairs of legs

is·tle (IS-(t)lee) *n.*, a fiber used in basket-making and obtained from a Mexican plant

i·ter (I-ter) *n.*, an anatomical passage

i·thy·phal·lic (i-thĭ-FAL-ik) *adj.*, 1. having an erect penis, especially in artwork 2. obscene

ix·i·a (IKS-ee-a) *n.*, a South African iris with swordlike leaves and pink or purple flowers; also called the corn lily

i·zar (ĭ-ZAHR) *n.*, a billowing outer garment worn by Muslim women to cover the entire body

iz·zard (IZ-ă(r)d) *n.*, U.S. dialect for the letter Z

iz·zat (IZ-ăt) *n.*, 1. personal dignity or honor 2. the power of commanding admiration

J

jab-i-ru (jab-ĭ-ROO) *n.*, a large tropical American stork

ja-cal (hă-KAHL) *n.*, a crude house or hut with thatched roof and mud walls in Mexico and the southwestern U.S.

jac-a-mar (JAK-ă-mahr) *n.*, a brilliantly colored tropical bird found in Mexican and South American forests that feeds on insects it catches while flying

jac-a-na (JAK-ă-nă) *n.*, a wading bird whose long, slender legs and toes allow it to run on floating vegetation

ja-cinthe (JAY-sĭnth) *n.*, a moderate orange color

jack-e-roo (jak-ĕ-ROO) *n.*, an Australian term for a sheep rancher's new apprentice

ja-co-bus (jă-KOH-bŭs) *n.*, an old British commemorative coin celebrating the union of the English and Scottish thrones

jac-tance (JAK-tăn(t)s) *n.*, prideful bragging

jac-ta-tion (jak-TAY-shŏn) *n.*, 1. boasting 2. a throwing or tossing of the body

jac-ti-ta-tion (jak-tĭ-TAY-shŏn) *n.*, 1. an archaic term meaning a boastful public claim 2. jerking or twitching of body parts

jac-u-la-tion (JAK-yŭ-LAY-shŏn) *n.*, the act of pitching, tossing, or hurling

jakes (JAYKS) *n.*, 1. U.S. dialect for an outhouse 2. British dialect for a dirty mess

jal-ap (JAL-ăp) *n.*, a powerful drug made from the dried roots of a Mexican plant

ja-ma or **ja-mah** (JAH-mă) *n.*, a long-sleeved cotton coat worn by males of northern India and Pakistan

jam-beau (JAM-boh) *n.*, a plate of medieval armor for the shin and calf

jam-bee (JAM-bee) *n.*, an archaic term for a rattan walking stick popular during the late 17th century

jam-bone (JAM-bohn) *n.*, in the card game euchre, a lone hand played with the bidder's hand exposed on the table

jam-pan (JAM-pan) *n.*, an Indian term for a sedan with two poles

jan-i-ceps (JAN-ĕ-seps) *n.*, a double-headed monster with faces looking in opposite directions

jan-i-form (JAN-ĕ-fohrm) *adj.*, having two faces back to back

jan-nock (JAN-ŏk) *adj.*, British dialect meaning fair and decent

ja-ra-ra-cus-su (zha-ră-rah-kŭ-SOO) *n.*, a poisonous Brazilian snake

jar-bird (JAHR-bĭrd) *n.*, a nuthatch

jar-goon (jahr-GOON) *n.*, a clear, pale yellow or smoky zircon

---

\a\ bat \ă\ about \e\ or \ĕ\ check \ĕ\ letter \é\ cafe \i\fish \ī\ tie \ĭ\ limit \o\ boat \ŏ\ bacon \u\ sun \ŭ\ helpful \ū\ fool

ja-ri-na (zhă-REE-nă) *n.*, a South American ivory nut

jark-man (JAHRK-măn) *n.*, an archaic term for a wandering document counterfeiter

jarl (YAHRL) *n.*, a Scandinavian noble next in rank to the king

ja-ro-vize (yah-rŏ-VĪZ) *v.*, to stimulate the flowering of a plant by artificially shortening its dormant period

ja-sey (JAY-zee) *n.*, a British term for a wig made of hard, twisted yarn

ja-ta-ka (JAHD-ă-kă) *n.*, the birth stories recounting the incarnations of Guatama Buddha in Buddhist religious writings

jauk (JAWK) or (JAHK) *v.*, a Scottish term meaning to loaf or dawdle

jav-el (JAV-ĕl) *n.*, an archaic term for a vagrant

ja-wab (jă-WAHB) *n.*, a building built to balance another, such as the false mosque of the Taj Mahal

jawp (JAHP) or (JAWP) *n.*, a Scottish and northern English term for a splash of water or a stain

jaz-er-ant (JAZ-ĕr-ănt) *n.*, a coat of armor with small, overlapping metal plates on a cloth lining

je-hu (JEE-h(y)oo) *n.*, a driver of a cab or coach who speeds or drives recklessly

je-june (jĕ-JOON) *adj.*, 1. an obsolete term for hungry 2. inadequate as nourishment 3. lacking interest; dull

je-ju-nos-to-my (ji-joo-NAHS-tŏ-mee) *n.*, a surgery that creates a permanent hole through the abdominal wall into the small intestine

je-la-ba (jĕ-LAH-bă) *n.*, a full, loose, hooded garment worn chiefly in Morocco

jel-u-tong (JEL-ŭ-tawng) *n.*, a gluey, milky substance made from trees and used in rubber products, waterproofing, and chewing gum

jem-a-dar (JEM-ă-dahr) *n.*, an officer of the Indian army equivalent in rank to an English army lieutenant

jen-net (JEN-ĕt) *n.*, 1. a little Spanish horse 2. a female donkey or ass

jeo-fail (JE-fay(e)l) *n.*, an archaic term for a mistake or oversight in legal pleas

jer-bo-a (jer-BOH-ă) *n.*, a jumping rodent with long hind legs, a long tail, and large ears found in the dry regions of Asia and northern Africa

je-reed (jĕ-REED) *n.*, a wooden javelin used in some Muslim countries

jer-ri-can (JER-ee-kan) *n.*, a five-gallon container for fluids

jheel (JEE(Ĕ)L) *n.*, a pool, marsh, or lake, especially one left after a flooding

ji-ca-ra (HEE-kă-ră) *n.*, a cup or bowl made from the fruit of the tropical American calabash tree

jim-ber-jawed (JIM-bĕ(r)-jawd) *adj.*, having a lower jaw that projects

jimp (JIMP) *adj.*, 1. British dialect meaning slim 2. British dialect for meager

jing-bang (JING-bang) *n.*, a U.S. slang expression for the whole company or crowd

ji-pa-ja-pa (hee-pee-HAH-pă) *n.*, 1. a Central and South American plant that looks like a palm 2. a hat made from the fiber of the leaves of the plant

ji-va (JEE-vă) *n.*, a Hindu term for the essential energy of life; the soul

jna-na (jĕ-NAH-nă) *n.*, a Hindu term for knowledge acquired by meditation

jo-ba-tion (joh-BAY-shŏn) *n.*, a British term for a long, tedious scolding or a lecture

job-ber-nowl (JAH-bĕ(r)-nohl) *n.*, a British term for a numbskull or bonehead

jobe (JOHB) *v.*, an archaic term meaning to scold or lecture

jock-er (JAHK-ĕ(r)) *n.*, a U.S. slang term for a homosexual man

jo-kul (YOH-kuul) *n.*, a mountain covered with ice and snow in Iceland

jol-loped (JAHL-ŏpt) *adj.*, a term in heraldry meaning depicted with a wattle, a fleshy outgrowth like a rooster's comb

jo-se-phin-ite (JOH-zĕ-fee-nīt) *n.*, a natural iron-nickel alloy found in the gravel of streams

jos-kin (JAHS-kĕn) *n.*, an unsophisticated person or a bumpkin

joss (JAHS) *n.*, a Chinese god or cult image

jos-ser (JAHS-sĕ(r)) *n.*, a British term for a fellow; a chap

jouk (JOOK) *v.*, 1. U.S. dialect meaning to dodge 2. U.S. dialect meaning to avoid work

joule (JOOL) *n.*, a unit measure of energy

ju-ba (JOO-bă) *n.*, a Haitian dance for work or for the dead

ju-bate (JOO-bayt) *adj.*, fringed with long hair like a mane

ju-dex (JOO-deks) *n.*, a Roman law term for a private individual appointed to hear and determine a case 2. a judge

ju-gate (JOO-gayt) *adj.*, in pairs

ju-glan-da-ceous (joo-glan-DAY-shŭs) *adj.*, of or pertaining to walnuts and hickories

jug-u-late (JŬG-yŭ-layt) *v.*, to murder by slitting the throat

ju-jube (JOO-joob) *n.*, 1. the edible fruit from the Chinese date tree 2. a fruit-flavored candy drop

ju-mart (JOO-mahrt) *n.*, the mythical offspring of a bovine and an equine animal

jum-buck (JŬM-bŭk) *n.*, an Australian term for sheep

ju-ris-con-sult (juu-rĭ-SKAHN-sŭlt) *n.*, a man educated in law, especially international and public law

jus-sive (JŬ-siv) *adj.*, having the effect of an order

\a\ bat \ă\ about \e\ or \ĕ\ check \ĕ\ letter
\é\ cafe \i\fish \ī\ tie \ĭ\ limit \o\ boat
\ō\ bacon \u\ sun \ŭ\ helpful \ü\ fool

ju-ve-nes-cence (joo-vĕ-NES-ĕn(t)s) *n.*, the state of being young or youthful

kaa-ba (KAH-bă) *adj.*, pertaining to the Islamic shrine in Mecca that is the goal of all Islamic pilgrimage and the direction in which all Muslims pray

kaa-ma (KAH-mă) *n.*, an endangered African antelope; also called a hartebeest

ka-ba-ka (kă-BAH-kă) *n.*, the king of Buganda, a tribe in Uganda

ka-bel-jou (KAH-bĕl-yow) *n.*, a large South African fish whose liver is rich in vitamin A

kaf-fi-yeh (kă-FEE-(y)ĕ) *n.*, an Arab headdress folded to form a triangle and bound on the head with a cord of goat's hair

ka-gu (KAH-goo) *n.*, a New Caledonian flightless bird that is gray with an orange bill and feet

ka-ha (KAH-hah) *n.*, a large Bornean monkey with a long tail and a long nose; also called a proboscis monkey

ka-hu-na (kă-HOO-nă) *n.*, a Hawaiian term for a native master craftsman or medicine man

kai (KĪ) *n.*, an ethnic group of New Guinea

kail-yard (KAY(Ĕ)L-yahrd) *n.*, a Scottish term for a home garden

ka-ka-po (KAH-kă-poh) *n.*, a flightless New Zealand parrot that lives in burrows and ground holes; also called the owl parrot

ka-ki (KAH-kee) *n.*, a blackish, long-legged bird of New Zealand

kak-i-dro-sis (kak-ĭ-DROH-sĭs) *n.*, foul perspiration odor

kak-is-toc-ra-cy (kak-ĭ-STAHK-ră-see) *n.*, rule by the worst men in the state

kak-kak (KA-kak) *n.*, a small heron of Guam

ka-lam (kă-LAHM) *n.*, Muslim theology of a scholarly nature

ka-li-an (kah-lee-AHN) *n.*, a Persian pipe that draws smoke through water; a hookah

ka-lon (kă-LAHN) *n.*, the classical Greek ideal of physical and moral beauty

ka-long (KA-lawng) *n.*, a fruit-eating bat found in the Malay archipelago

kal-pa (KĂL-pă) *n.*, a Hindu term for the time span from the beginning to the destruction of the universe

ka-ma-ai-na (kah-mă-Ī-nă) *n.*, a person who has lived in Hawaii many years

ka-me-rad (kah-mĕ-RAHAHT) *interj.*, a cry of surrender used by German soldiers in World War 1

ka-mik (KAH-mik) *n.*, an Eskimo boat made of sealskin

ka-na (KAH-nă) *n.*, a Japanese system of writing from the 8th or 9th century that was used almost exclusively for foreign words

ka-na-ka (kă-NAH-KĂ) *n.*, a person from a South Sea island

ka-na-ra (kă-NAHR-ă) *n.*, a region in southwestern India

keit-lo-a (KĪT-lŏ-wă) *n.*, a black rhinoceros with horns of approximately the same length

kel-li-on (ke-LEE-ahn) *n.*, a small house of the Eastern Church lived in by no more than three monks and three lay brothers

kemp (KEMP) *n.*, British dialect for a strong warrior or athlete; a champion

ken-sing-ton (KEN-zing-tŏn) *n.*, U.S. dialect for a potluck dinner

ken-speck-le (KENZ-pek-ĕl) *adj.*, a Scottish term meaning noticeable; conspicuous

ke-pi (KAY-pee) *n.*, a type of French military cap

ke-ra-na or **ker-ra-na** (ke-RAH-nă) *n.*, a Persian trumpet

kerf (KERF) *n.*, a slit or cut made by a saw or cutting torch

ker-mis (KER-mĭs) *n.*, 1. a local outdoor festival of the Netherlands or Belgium 2. a fund-raising show and fair

kern (KĔRN) *v.*, to position typeset characters according to the space surrounding each letter's projections

ker-ri-a (KER-ee-a) *n.*, a Chinese shrub with a solitary yellow flower

ke-rug-ma or **ke-ryg-ma** (kĕ-RIG-mă) *n.*, the preaching of the gospel of the early Christian church

ke-tene (KEE-teen) *n.*, a colorless, poisonous gas with a sharp odor that is used to make acetic compounds

ke-tu-bah (ke-t(h)oo-VAH) *n.*, a formal Jewish marriage contract that grants the wife a money settlement in the case of marital dissolution through death or divorce

kev-el (KEV-ĕl) *n.*, a hammer for shaping or breaking stone

kex (KEKS) *n.*, a Mayan rite in which a sick person offers food to the force responsible for his illness in return for his health

khad-dar (KAHD-ĕ(r)) *n.*, a homespun cloth worn by proponents of autonomy for India

kham-sin (kam-SEEN) *n.*, a hot, southerly Egyptian wind that carries fine particles of sand from the Sahara

khan-da (KAHN-dă) *n.*, an Indian sword with a broad, single-edged blade

khed-a (KED-ă) *n.*, an enclosure used to capture wild elephants

khe-dive (kĕ-DEEV) *n.*, the ruler of Egypt from 1867 to 1914 under the sultan of Turkey

khid-mat-gar (KID-măt-gahr) *n.*, an Indian term for a male waiter

---

\a\ bat \ă\ about \e\ or \è\ check \ĕ\ letter \é\ cafe \i\fish \ī\ tie \ĭ\ limit \o\ boat \ŏ\ bacon \u\ sun \ŭ\ helpful \ü\ fool

ki-ang (kee-(Y)AHNG) *n.*, a wild ass from Asia with reddish sides, white belly, and a dusty stripe along the spine

kia ora (kee-a-OHR-ă) *interj.*, an Australian and New Zealand toast or salutation

kiaugh (KYAHK) *n.*, a Scottish term for trouble; anxiety

kibe (KĪB) *n.*, a crack in the skin caused by cold

kick-shaw (KIK-shaw) *n.*, a fancy culinary dish; a delicacy

kil-der-kin (KIL-dĕ(r)-kĭn) *n.*, an English unit of volume equal to 1/2 barrel

kil-erg (KIL-urg) *n.*, an obsolete term for a unit of energy

kang or **k'ang** (KAHNG) *n.*, a northern Chinese term for a brick platform for sleeping that is built across one side or end of a room and warmed by a fire underneath

kan-ga-ny (kăng-GAH-nee) *n.*, a labor overseer in India, Ceylon, and Malaya

kan-ji (KAHN-jee) *n.*, a Japanese system of writing that is based upon the Chinese system and incorporates most of its characters

kan-tar (kan-TAHR) *n.*, a unit of weight used in some Mediterranean countries

kan-te-le (KAHN-tĕ-lĕ) *n.*, a Finnish harp that originally had five strings but now has as many as 30

kao-liang (KOW-lee-ahng) *n.*, 1. a variety of sorghum grown chiefly in China and Manchuria for grain and fodder 2. a liquor distilled in China from the juice of the kaoliang stalks

kaph or **caph** (KAHF) *n.*, the 11th letter in the Hebrew alphabet

kar-mouth (kahr-MOOT) *n.*, an African fish that can survive out of water for a time

kar-ree (kă-REE) or (kă-RAY) *n.*, a plant of South Africa

karst (KAHRST) *n.*, a limestone region marked by sinks, ridges, caverns, and underground streams

kash-ruth (kah-SHROOT(H)) *n.*, the state of being observant of the Jewish dietary laws

kath-en-o-the-ist (kat-HEN-oh-thee-ĭst) *n.*, one who worships one superior god while not denying the existence of other gods

ka-tu-ka (kăd-ŭ-kă) *n.*, an extremely poisonous snake from southeast Asia with a pale brown body and black spots

ka-tun (KAH-toon) *n.*, a time period of the Mayan calendar equivalent to 20 tuns or 7,200 days

ka-va (KAH-vă) *n.*, a shrub pepper from Australia whose roots make an intoxicating drink

ka-vass (kă-VAHS) *n.*, an armed courier or policeman in Turkey

ke-a (KE-ă) or (KEE-ă) *n.*, the large, green, insect-eating parrot of New Zealand that sometimes preys on sheep for their kidney fat

keck (KEK) *v.*, to make a retching sound

keck-le (KEK-ĕl) *v.*, to wind with rope to prevent abrasion

kedge (KEJ) *n.*, a small anchor used in navigation

keech (KEECH) *n.*, English dialect for a lump of fat

keek (KEEK) *n.*, a Scottish term meaning to look; to peep

kee-li-vine (KEE-li-vīn) *n.*, a Scottish term for a pencil, especially a black-leaded one

kees-hond (KAYS-hahnd) *n.*, a small, heavy-coated dog similar to a Pomeranian, but larger

keest (KEEST) *n.*, a Scottish term for marrow

kef (KEF) or (KAYF) *n.*, a smokable substance that produces a state of sleepy contentment

kef-fel (KEF-ĕl) *n.*, British dialect for an old nag or worthless horse

kil-hig (KIL-hig) *n.*, a pole used in logging to control the fall of a tree

ki-lim (kee-LEEM) *n.*, a pileless, tapestry-woven rug, mat, or spread made in the Middle East

kin-cob (KIN-kahb) *n.*, an Indian brocade fashioned of gold, silver, or both

kine (KĪN) *n.*, an archaic term for cows or cattle

king-ling (KING-ling) *n.*, a small or petty king

kin-ka-jou (KING-kă-joo) *n.*, a nocturnal, carnivorous mammal from Mexico and Central and South America that has a long prehensile tail, large eyes, and soft, wooly, yellow-brown fur

kin-ni-kin-nick (KIN-ĕ-kĭ-nik) *n.*, a mixture of dried bark and leaves smoked by the Indians and pioneers of the Great Lakes region

kis-sar (KIS-ă(r)) *n.*, a five-stringed instrument from northern Africa and Ethiopia

kiss-me-quick (KISS-mee-kwik) *n.*, a small bonnet popular in the latter half of the 19th century and worn off the face

kit-tly-benders (KIT-lee-bend-ĕ(r)z) *n.*, thin, bending ice

ki-va (KEE-vă) *n.*, a round, partly subterranean structure used by the Pueblo Indians for ceremonial purposes or as a lounging room for men

kla-vier-stück (klah-VEER-shtoo(e)k) *n.*, a piano piece

klepht (KLEFT) *n.*, a Greek who belonged to one of several independent, armed communities formed after the Turkish conquest

klip-spring-er (KLIP-spring-ĕ(r)) *n.*, a small antelope of southern Africa

knack-er (NAK-ĕ(r)) *n.*, a British term for a dealer who buys and sells worn-out domestic animals and carcasses for nonfood products

knaw-el (NAW(E)L) *n.*, a low-spreading, Old World annual weed found in North America

kneipp-ism (NĪ-pizĕm) *n.*, the treatment of disease through various forms of water therapy such as baths

---

\a\ bat \ă\ about \e\ or \ĕ\ check \ē\ letter
\ē\ cafe \i\fish \ī\ tie \ĭ\ limit \o\ boat
\ŏ\ bacon \u\ sun \ŭ\ helpful \ü\ fool

knick-knack-a-to-ry (NIK-nak-ă-toh-ree) *n.*, an archaic term for small, trivial articles and ornaments

knout (NOWT) or (NOOT) *n.*, a flogging whip used for punishing criminals that has a lash of leather thongs twisted with wire

koa (KOHĂ) *n.*, a Hawaiian timber tree with grayish bark, crescent-shaped leaves, and small white flowers

ko-an (KOH-ahn) *n.*, a paradoxical statement used as a meditative technique to train Zen Buddhist monks to rely on intuitive enlightenment

ko-bold (KOH-bawld) *n.*, a gnome that inhabits underground places, according to German folklore

ko-el (KOH-ĕl) *n.*, a type of cuckoo that is found in India, Australia, and the East Indies; also called the long-tailed cuckoo

koft-ga-ri (KAWFT-gă-ree) *n.*, metalwork from India that features steel inlaid with gold

kohl (KOHL) *n.*, a substance used to darken the rims of the eyelids, especially in Egypt and Arabia

koi-me-sis (KEE-mee-sĭs) *n.*, a feast day in the Eastern Orthodox Church celebrating the death and assumption of the Virgin Mary

ko-kam (koh-KAHM) *n.*, a slow-moving, nocturnal lemur found in India and the East Indies; also called the slow loris

kok-sa-ghyz (KOHK-să-geez) *n.*, a perennial dandelion native to parts of Russia with more flower heads than the common dandelion of North America

ko-kum (KOH-kŭm) *n.*, an oil derived from the seed of a small East Indian tree and used in India as food; also called Goa butter

ko-lin-sky (kŏ-LIN-zkee) *n.*, the fur or pelt of any of several Asiatic minks; also called red sable

ko-lo (KOH-loh) *n.*, a folk dance from Central Europe in which a ring of dancers move slowly left or right around a solo dancer who performs complex steps in the center

ko-na (KOH-nă) *n.*, a Hawaiian storm of southerly or southwesterly winds and heavy rains

ko-nim-e-ter (koh-NIM-ĕd-ĕr) *n.*, a device used to measure the amount of dust in the air, as in a mine

koom-kie (KOOM-kee) *n.*, a trained, usually female elephant used in India as a decoy and to train wild male elephants

kor-dax (KAWR-daks) *n.*, a phallic dance of ancient Greece performed by nude, horned figures in orgies honoring the Greek god Dionysus

kra-sis (KRAH-sĭs) *n.*, the act of mixing water with wine in the Eastern Orthodox Eucharist

krat-o-gen (KRAD-ŏ-jen) *n.*, a region that remains undisturbed while an adjoining area has been affected by mountain-making movements

kreng (KRENG) or **krang** or **crang** (KRANG) *n.*, a whale carcass after the blubber and whalebone have been removed

kreut-zer (KROIT-sĕr) *n.*, a small silver or copper coin used in Austria, Germany, and Hungary from the 13th to the mid-19th century

kur-gan (kuu(ŭ)r-GAHN) *n.*, a burial mound in eastern Europe or Siberia

ku-rus (kŭ-ROOSH) *n.*, a Turkish monetary unit

kur-vey-or (kŭr-VAY-ŏ(r)) *n.*, an itinerant trader of southern Africa who carries his wares in a large ox wagon

k-vass (kĕ-VAHS) or (KFAHS) *n.*, a weak, homemade beer made in Eastern European countries

ky-ack (KĪ-ak) *n.*, a sack hung on either side of a pack saddle

ky-at (kee-(Y)AHT) *n.*, the basic monetary unit of Burma since 1952

ky-lie (KĪ-lee) *n.*, an Australian boomerang with one flat side and one convex side

kyte (KĪT) *n.*, a Scottish term for the stomach

L

laa-ger (LAH-gĕ(r)) *n.*, an African camp, especially one protected by a circle of wagons

lab-da-num (LAB-dă-nŭm) *n.*, an oil resin obtained from rockroses and used in making perfume

lab-e-fac-tion (lab-ĕ-FAK-shŏn) *n.*, a weakening, especially of the civil or moral order; a downfall

la-bret (LAY-bret) *n.*, an ornament worn by some primitive people in a hole in the lip

la-bur-num (lă-BŬR-nŭm) *n.*, a poisonous Eurasian tree shrub with three leaves and yellow flowers

la-cer-tid (lă-SĔRD-ĕd) *n.*, a land-dwelling, carnivorous Old World lizard

la-cin-i-ate (lă-SIN-ee-ayt) *adj.*, having a fringed border

la-con-i-cum (lă-KAH-nŏ-kŭm) *n.*, the sweating room an ancient Roman bath

la-cu-na (lă-K(Y)OO-nă) *n.*, a blank space

la-cu-nu-lose (LĂK-yoo-nyŭ-lohs) *adj.*, having tiny holes or gaps

la-cus-trine (lă-KŬS-trĭn) *adj.*, associated with lakes

la-di-no (lă-DEE-noh) *n.*, a westernized, Spanish-speaking Latin American not of pure Spanish lineage

la-drone (LAY-drŏn) or (LA-drŏn) *n.*, a Scottish term for a scoundrel

lag-an (LAG-ăn) *n.*, goods cast into the sea while attached to floats that mark the location

\a\ bat \ă\ about \e\ or \è\ check \ĕ\ letter \é\ cafe \i\ fish \ĭ\ tie \ī\ limit \o\ boat \ŏ\ bacon \u\ sun \ŭ\ helpful \ü\ fool

la-gniappe (LAN-yap) *n.*, a Louisiana term for a merchant's small gift to a customer making a purchase

la-i-cize (LAY-ĭ-sīz) *v.*, to put under the control of laymen

lakh (LAHK) *n.*, an East Indian term meaning one hundred thousand

lall (LAL) *v.*, to mispronounce the L or R sounds

lal-lan (LAL-ăn) *adj.*, a Scottish variation of lowland

lal-la-tion (la-LAY-shŏn) *n.*, 1. an infantile utterance in infants or adult speakers 2. an impaired articulation of the letter L

lam-bre-quin (LAM-bĕ(r)-kĭn) *n.*, a scarf with slashed edges used to protect a knight's helmet from the rain or sun

la-mel-la (lă-ME-lă) *n.*, 1. an organ, process, or part that looks like a plate 2. a small, medicated disk for the eye

la-mel-li-form (lă-MEL-ĭ-fohrm) *adj.*, having a form like a thin plate

la-mi-a (LAY-mee-ă) *n.*, a witch or a vampire

lam-pad (LAM-pad) *n.*, a candlestick or lamp

lam-pas (LAM-păs) *n.*, a brocade fabric of two or more colors used for upholstery

lam-pro-pho-ny (lam-PROF-ŏ-nee) *n.*, loudness and clarity of voice

la-nate (LAY-nayt) *adj.*, woolly

lan-ce-o-late (LAN(t)-sĭ-layt) *adj.*, shaped like a lance head

land-grave (LAN(D)-grayv) *n.*, 1. a German count with territorial authority 2. a country aristocrat in colonial Carolina

land-lop-er or **land-loup-er** (LAN(D)-lŏuu-pĕr) or (LAN(D)-loh-pĕr) *n.*, a wanderer or vagrant

lang-lauf (LAHNG-lowf) *n.*, cross-country running or skiing

lang-lau-fer (LAHNG-loi-fĕ(r)) *n.*, a cross-country skier

lan-gues-cent (LANG-gwe-sĕnt) *adj.*, becoming faint or tired

lan-gur (lăng-guu(ĕ)r) *n.*, a long-tailed Asiatic monkey with bushy eyebrows and a tuft of chin hair

la-ni-ate (LAY-nee-ayt) *v.*, to rip into pieces

la-ni-fer-ous (lă-NIF-ĕr-ŭs) *adj.*, wool-bearing

lan-ner (LAN-e(r)) *n.*, a southern European falcon similar to the American prairie falcon; specifically, the female of the species

lan-ta-na (lan-TAH-nă) *n.*, a tropical shrub with bright flowers and juicy fruit that is often grown as a potted plant

la-nu-gi-nous (lă-N(Y)OO-jĭ-nŭs) *adj.*, having a covering of soft down or fine, soft hair

lanx (LANG(K)S) *n.*, an ancient Roman term for a platter usually made of metal

la-od-i-ce-an (lay-AH-dĭ-see-an) *adj.*, 1. referring to an ancient city of Asia Minor that is the site of an early Christian church 2. indifferent in religious or political matters

lap-i-date (LAP-ĭ-dayt) *v.*, an archaic term meaning to stone someone

la-pid-i-fy (lă-PID-ĕ-fĩ) *v.*, an archaic term meaning to petrify or change into stone

lap-page (LAP-ij) *n.*, the amount by which one surface overlaps another, especially with regard to land

lar-es and **pe-na-tes** (LA-reez and pĕ-NAYD-eez) *n.*, a person's most precious personal and domestic articles

la-rith-mics (lă-RITH-miks) *n.*, the study of the quantitive features of populations

lar-moy-ant (lahr-MOI-ănt) *adj.*, 1. tearful 2. melancholy

lar-ri-gan (LAR-ĭ-găn) *n.*, an oil-tanned moccasin with leg coverings used by trappers and lumbermen

lar-ri-kin (LAR-ĭ-kĭn) *n.*, an Australian term for a noisy, rowdy fellow

lar-vate (LAHR-vayt) *adj.*, covered or hidden by a mask

las-car (LAS-kă(r)) *n.*, 1. an East Indian seaman 2. an East Indian native serving as a low-grade artilleryman in the British Army

lat-i-fun-di-um (lad-ĭ-FŬN-dee-ŭm) *n.*, a great landed estate held by an absentee landlord who farms with slave labor and primitive technology

lat-i-tu-di-nar-i-an-ism (lad-ĭ-too-dĭn-ER-ee-ă-nizĕm) *n.*, a broad and liberal belief system or condition

la-trant (LAY-trănt) *adj.*, an archaic term meaning barking or complaining

la-uan (lă-WAHN) *n.*, a Philippine timber with close-grained, brown wood of moderate strength and durability

lau-da-num (LAW-dă-nŭm) *n.*, a solution of opium in alcohol formerly used as a medicine

lau-wine (LO-win) *n.*, an avalanche

la-va-tion (lay-VAY-shŏn) *n.*, the act of washing or cleaning

lav-er-ock (LAV-(ĕ)-rŏk) *n.*, a Scottish word for lark

lay-boy (LAY-boi) *n.*, a machine that stacks sheets of pulp or paper into even piles

laz-a-ret-to (laz-ă-RED-oh) *n.*, 1. a hospital for people with contagious diseases 2. a building or ship for quarantines

leal (LEE(Ă)L) *adj.*, 1. a Scottish term meaning loyal; faithful 2. a Scottish term meaning accurate; true

leb-en or **leb-an** (LE-bĕn) *n.*, a North African food made from curdled milk

lec-a-no-man-cy (LEK-ă-noh-man(t)-see) *n.*, predicting the future by using water in a basin

le-chwe (LEE-chwee) *n.*, a tawny African antelope with a white belly and blackish legs

---

\a\ bat \ă\ about \e\ or \ĕ\ check \ĕ\ letter \ĕ\ cafe \i\fish \ĩ\ tie \ĩ\ limit \o\ boat \ŏ\ bacon \u\ sun \ŭ\ helpful \ü\ fool

lec-tion (LEK-shŏn) *n.*, a lesson or a selection from sacred writings read

lec-ti-ster-ni-um (lek-tĭ-STĔR-nee-ŭm) *n.*, an ancient Greek and Roman religious rite in which the images of gods are placed on couches and food is spread before them

lec-y-thus (LES-ĭ-thŭs) *n.*, a round, squat vase used to hold oils and ointments in ancient Greece

le-gist (LEE-jĭst) *n.*, a law specialist, especially in Roman or civil law

leg-u-le-ian (leg-yŭ-LEE-ăn) *n.*, an attorney whose methods are underhanded, petty, and disreputable

le-man (LE-măn) *n.*, 1. an obsolete term for a lover 2. an archaic term for a mistress

le-ni-fy (LE-nĭ-fĭ) *v.*, an archaic term meaning to soften; to alleviate

le-nit-ic (lĕ-NID-ik) *adj.*, relating to or living in still waters

len-tic-u-lar (len-TIK-yŭ-lă(r)) *adj.*, lentil-shaped or shaped like a double-convex lens

len-tig-i-nous (LEN-tij-ĭ-nŭs) *adj.*, relating to a small, dark spot on the skin unrelated to exposure to the sun and potentially malignant; freckled

lep-id (LEP-ĭd) *adj.*, an archaic term meaning witty

lep-i-dote (LEP-ĭ-doht) *adj.*, covered with flaky scales

lep-o-rine (LEP-ŏ-rīn) *adj.*, pertaining to or resembling a hare

lep-tor-rhine (LEP-tŏ-rīn) *adj.*, having a long, narrow nose

lep-to-some (LEP-tŏ-sohm) *adj.*, having a slender body

lev-i-gate (LEV-ĭ-gayt) *v.*, 1. an archaic term meaning to buff or smooth 2. to grind into a powder

lex-i-phan-ic (lek-sĭ-FAN-ik) *adj.*, using showy, hard-to-understand words

li (LEE) *n.*, 1. a Chinese unit of distance 2. a cardinal virtue in Confucianism that consists of correct behavior that expresses inner harmony 3. an ethnic group of southern China

li-a-na (lee-AH-nă) *n.*, a climbing plant found in tropical rain forests

li-ang (lee-AHNG) *n.*, an old Chinese unit of weight; also called a tael

li-ard (lee-AHR) *n.*, a 15th-century French coin

li-ber-ti-cide (lĭ-BĔRD-ĭ-sīd) *n.*, the annihilation of liberty

li-bra-to-ry (LĪ-bră-toh-ree) *adj.*, moving like a balance as it tends to evenly distribute weight

lic-i-ta-tion (lis-ĭ-TAY-shŏn) *n.*, the act of selling or bidding at an auction

lick-pen-ny (LIK-pe-nee) *n.*, an archaic term for something that costs money

lic-tor (LIK-tŏr) *n.*, a Roman officer who attended to magistrates, protected their safe passage, and caught and punished criminals

li-e-nal (li-EE-năl) *adj.*, associated with the spleen

li-erne (lee-ŬRN) *n.*, an architectural term for a short rib used in Gothic vaulting

lig-ro-in (LIG-rŏ-wĭn) *n.*, a petroleum product used chiefly as a solvent

lil-ly-low (LI-li-loh) *n.*, English dialect for a bright flame

lim-bate (LIM-bayt) *adj.*, having a part of one color that is edged with another color

lim-ber-ham (LIM-bĕ(r)-hahm) *n.*, an archaic term for a loose-jointed, servile person

li-men (LĪ-mĕn) *n.*, the threshold point at which a physical or psychological effect is produced

li-mic-o-lous (LI-mik-ŏ-lŭs) *adj.*, dwelling in mud

lim-i-trophe (LIM-ĭ-trohf) *adj.*, located on a border or frontier; adjacent

lim-mer (LI-mĕr) *n.*, a Scottish term for a worthless scoundrel or whore

limn (LIM) *v.*, to represent in drawing or painting; to delineate

limp-kin (LIMP-kĭn) *n.*, a large, brown wading bird with a curved bill, long neck and legs, and white stripes on the head and neck

lin-gam (LING-găm) *n.*, the stylized phallic symbol that serves as the emblem of the Indian god Siva and suggests virility and creative power

ling-tow (LING-toh) *n.*, a Scottish term for a rope that smugglers used to pack goods

lin-sey-wool-sey (LIN-zee-WUUL-zee) *n.*, 1. a wool and linen fabric 2. something disordered or nonsensical in speech or action

lip-o-gram (LIP-ŏ-gram) *n.*, a piece of writing that uses only words lacking a certain letter

lip-pen (LIP-ĕn) *v.*, a Scottish term meaning to believe in

lip-per (LIP-pĕ(r)) *n.*, 1. a slight choppiness of the sea 2. the light spray from small waves

lip-pi-tude (LIP-ĭ-tood) *n.*, an archaic term for tenderness or bleariness of the eye

lir-i-pipe (LIR-ĕ-pīp) *n.*, a long, trailing cloth attached to a sleeve, hood, or hat that became part of clerical and academic dress

lish (LISH) *adj.*, British dialect meaning nimble; quick

lisk (LISK) *n.*, British dialect for the groin

lis-sot-ri-chous (li-SAH-trĭ-kŭs) *adj.*, having straight, smooth hair

lit-e-ra-tim (lid-ĕ-RAYD-ĭm) *adv.*, letter for letter

li-thod-o-mous (lĭ-THAHD-ŏ-mŭs) *adj.*, refers to burrowing in rock

lith-o-glyph (LITH-ŏ-glif) *n.*, a stone engraving

\a\ bat \ă\ about \e\ or \è\ check \ĕ\ letter
\é\ cafe \i\fish \ī\ tie \ĭ\ limit \o\ boat
\ŏ\ bacon \u\ sun \ŭ\ helpful \ü\ fool

lith-o-man-cy (LITH-ŏ-man(t)-see) *n.*, predicting the future by using stones or charms or talismans of stones

li-thoph-a-gous (lĭ-THAHF-ĕ-gŭs) *adj.*, eating stones

li-to-tes (LĪD-ŏ-teez) *n.*, a statement that expresses an idea by negating its opposite

lit-u-rate (LICH-ŭ-rayt) *adj.*, a biological term meaning having spots

liv-yer (LIV-yĕr) *n.*, a northeastern Canadian term for a settler who lives by trapping, trading, or fishing

lob-cock (LAHB-kahk) *n.*, English dialect for an oaf

lo-be-li-a (loh-BEEL-yă) *n.*, a plant with long and clustered blue, red, yellow, or white flowers

lo-be-line (LOH-bĕ-leen) *n.*, a poisonous substance made from lobelia and used as a respiratory stimulant

lob-lol-ly (LAHB-lah-lee) *n.*, U.S. dialect for a thick gruel or muddy mess

lo-bo-la or **lo-bo-lo** (LOH-bŏ-lă) *n.*, the money or goods paid to the bride's family, especially by the prospective groom, among the Bantu people of southern Africa

lob-scouse (LAHB-skows) *n.*, a sailor's dish made of stewed meats with vegetables and biscuits

lo-chi-a (LOH-kee-ă) or (LAH-kee-a) *n.*, a uterine and vaginal discharge that occurs after childbirth

lo-co-fo-co (loh-koh-FOH-koh) *n.*, 1. a match or cigar invented during the 19th century that ignited by friction on any rough surface 2. a member of a radical New York Democratic organization of 1835

log-gia (LAHJ-(ee)ă) *n.*, a roofed, open gallery in the side of a building, especially one that faces an open court

lo-gi (LO-gee) *n.*, a Scandinavian mythological term for a personification of fire who defeated Loki in an eating contest

lo-gi-an (LOH-jee-ahn) *n.*, a short saying or perception, especially one made by a religious teacher

log-o-dae-da-ly (lahg-ŏ-DEED-ă-lee) *n.*, the random coinage of words

log-o-griph (LAWG-ŏ-grif) *n.*, a word puzzle

lol-lard (LAHL-ă(r)d) *n.*, a Protestant layman of the 14th and 15th centuries who traveled throughout Scotland and England preaching a biblically based religion

lo-ment (LOH-ment) *n.*, a dry, single-celled fruit that breaks into many segments when it matures

lon-ga-nim-i-ty (lahng-ă-NIM-ĭ-dee) *n.*, the patient endurance of injuries

long-ear (LOWNG-i(ă)r) *n.*, a western U.S. term for a calf with no brand

lon-gi-caud-al (lon-ji-KOD-ăl) *adj.*, having a long tail

lon-gil-o-quence (lahn-JIL-ŏ-kwĕn(t)s) *n.*, long-windedness

lon·gin·qui·ty (lahn-JING-kwĭd-ee) *n.*, an archaic term for distance in time or space

long-spur (LAWNG-spŭr) *n.*, a bird with long claws that migrates from the arctic regions and the plains of North America in huge flocks

loo·by (LOO-bee) *n.*, an awkward, bungling fellow, often one who is also lazy and stupid

loof (LOOF) *n.*, a Scottish term for the palm of the hand

lop·per (LAHP-ĕ(r)) *v.*, a northern U.S. term meaning to clot or curdle, especially milk

lo·quat (LOH-kwaht) *n.*, an Asian evergreen tree grown for its fruit that is used in jams and jellies

lo·ran (LOHR-an) *n.*, a navigational system that uses radio signals from two known positions to determine the geographical location of a ship or a plane

lor·do·sis (law(ĕ)r-DOH-sĭs) *n.*, an abnormal forward curvature of the spine

lo·ri·ca (lŏ-RĪ-kă) *n.*, 1. a Roman breastplate of leather or metal 2. a hard, protective case or shell

lor·i·cate (LAWR-ĭ-kayt) *v.*, to enclose or cover with a protective substance

lor·i·mer (LAWR-ĭ-mĕ(r)) *n.*, a person who makes bits, spurs, and the metal parts of bridles and saddles

lo·sel (LOH-zĕl) *n.*, a useless person

lo·toph·a·gous (lŏ-TAHF-ă-gŭs) *adj.*, lotus-eating

louch (LOWCH) *v.*, British dialect meaning to slouch

lou·troph·o·ros (loo-TRAHF-ŏ-rahs) *n.*, a tall, two-handled, long-necked water vase used in prenuptial ceremonies in ancient Athens

low-men (LOH-mĕn) *n.*, an obsolete term for dice loaded to show only low numbers

lub·ber fiend (LUB-ĕr-feend) *n.*, a helpful goblin that does housework after dark

luce (LOOS) *n.*, a full-grown pike

lu·cif·er·ous (LOO-sif-(ĕ)-rŭs) *adj.*, 1. an archaic term meaning shedding or bringing light 2. an archaic term meaning giving insight

lu·ci·vee (LOO-sĭ-vee) *n.*, a New England term for a Canadian lynx

lu·cu·brate (LOO-k(y)ŭ-brayt) *v.*, to write long, detailed works

lu·cu·lent (LOO-kyŭ-lănt) *adj.*, 1. an archaic term meaning giving off light; brilliant 2. very clear in expression; evident

lu·es (LOO-eez) *n.*, syphilis

lu·et·ic (loo-ED-ik) *adj.*, having syphilis

lull·i·loo (LŬL-ĭ-loo) *v.*, to shout joyously, as is the custom of African people

lu·mi·nif·er·ous (LOO-mĭ-nif-(ĕ)r-ŭs) *adj.*, transmitting or producing light

lu·nette (loo-NET) *n.*, a semicircular or crescent-shaped opening in a vaulted roof

\a\ bat \ă\ about \e\ or \ĕ\ check \ĕ\ letter \é\ cafe \i\fish \ī\ tie \ĭ\ limit \o\ boat \ŏ\ bacon \u\ sun \ŭ\ helpful \ü\ fool

lunt (LŬNT) *n.*, 1. a Scottish term for a slow game 2. a Scottish term for smoke

lu-nule (LOON-yool) *n.*, a body part that is crescent-shaped, as the whitish crescent at the base of the fingernail

lu-pa-nar (loo-PAY-nă(r)) *n.*, a whorehouse

lur-dane (LŬR-dăn) *n.*, an archaic term for an idle fellow

lu-so-ry (LOOS-(ŏ)-ree) *adj.*, 1. an archaic term meaning used in play 2. an archaic term meaning composed in a playful way

lus-tra-tion (lŭ-STRAY-shŏn) *n.*, a purification ceremony to cleanse an individual or society of the guilt of bloodshed

lu-te-ous (LOOD-ee-ŭs) *n.*, any of several colors from light to greenish yellow

lu-thern (LOO-thĕ(r)n) *n.*, a dormer window

lux (LŬKS) *n.*, a unit of illumination

lux-ate (LŬK-sayt) *v.*, to dislocate or throw out of joint

ly-art (LĪ-ărt) *adj.*, a Scottish term meaning streaked with gray

ly-can-thro-py (LĪ-kăn-thrŏ-pee) *n.*, the delusion that one has taken on the characteristics of or become a wolf or other predator

lydd-ite (LĪD-it) *n.*, an explosive made of picric

lyn-ce-an (lin-SEE-ăn) *adj.*, 1. associated with a lynx 2. having keen vision

ly-sin (LĪ-sĭn) *n.*, an antibody that can disintegrate certain blood cells and microorganisms

ly-sis (LĪ-sĭs) *n.*, the gradual lowering in fever

lys-sa (LI-să) *n.*, rabies or hydrophobia

lyss-o-pho-bi-a (lis-ŏ-FOH-bee-ă) *n.*, an abnormal fear of going insane

lyt-ta (LID-ă) *n.*, a band of cartilage that is part of the tongue of many carnivorous mammals

ma-ca-co (mă-KAH-koh) *n.*, a lemur or monkey

ma-caque (mă-KAK) or (mă-KAHK) *n.*, a short-tailed monkey found throughout Asia, Africa, and the East Indies

mac-a-ron-ic (mak-ă-RAHN-ik) *adj.*, distinguished by a blend of languages, usually Latin and non-Latin

mac-ca-boy (MAK-ă-boi) *n.*, a rose-scented snuff from Martinique

mac-é-doine (mas-ĕ-DWAHN) or (ma-SAY-dwahn) *n.*, a mixture of fruits or vegetables often served in a jelly and as a salad

mac·er·ate (MAS-ĕ-rayt) *v.*, to soften or separate into parts by steeping in liquid

mac·i·lent (MAS-ă-lănt) *adj.*, thin; emaciated

mack·le (MAK-ĕl) *n.*, a blur in printed material, as from a double impression

mac·ro·bi·an (ma-KROH-bee-ăn) *adj.*, long-lived

mac·rog·ra·phy (ma-KRAHG-ră-fee) *n.*, 1. a tendency to write in an unusually large hand 2. an examination by means of the naked eye

mac·rol·o·gy (ma-KRAHL-ŏ-jee) *n.*, the use of excessive, repetitious words in speaking or writing

ma·cron (MAY-krahn) or (MAY-krŏn) *n.*, a horizontal line placed over a vowel to indicate a long sound in pronunciation

mac·ros·mat·ic (MA-krahz-mad-ik) *adj.*, having a highly developed sense or organ of smell

mac·ro·so·ma·tous (mak-rŏ-SOH-măd-ŭs) *adj.*, having an unusually large body

mac·ro·tous (MA-krohd-ŭs) *adj.*, having big ears

ma·cru·ran (ma-KRUU-răn) *adj.*, pertaining to a type of crustacean such as a lobster, crayfish, shrimp, and prawn that has a well-developed abdomen

mac·ta·tion (mak-TAY-shŏn) *n.*, an act of slaughter, especially of a sacrificial victim

mac·u·late (MAK-yŭ-lăt) *adj.*, 1. spotted 2. impure

mad ap·ple (MAD-ap-ĕl) *n.*, the eggplant

mad·brained (MAD-braynd) *adj.*, hotheaded; reckless

ma·du·ro (ma-DUU-ro) *n.*, a strong, dark cigar

mae·nad (MEE-nad) *n.*, any frenzied or frantic, raging woman

maf·fick (MAF-ik) *v.*, to celebrate with joyfully extravagant and uproarious demonstration

maf·fle (MAF-ăl) *v.*, English dialect meaning to speak unclearly

magged (MAGD) *adj.*, used up; frayed

ma·hoe (ma-HOH) *n.*, a tropical tree with strong fibers used in making rope or mats

ma·ho·ni·a (ma-HOH-nee-ă) *n.*, a shrub with unarmed branches and featherlike leaves

ma·hout (mă-HOWT) *n.*, an elephant keeper or driver

ma·huang (MAH-hwahng) *n.*, a Chinese plant that yields the decongestant drug ephedrine

ma·ieu·tic (may-YOOD-ik) *adj.*, pertaining to the question-and-answer technique of logical inquiry used by Socrates

mai·gre (MAY-gră) *adj.*, containing neither meat nor blood, as those foods permitted on religious days of abstinence

\a\ bat \ä\ about \e\ or \ĕ\ check \ē\ letter \é\ cafe \i\fish \ī\ tie \ĭ\ limit \o\ boat \ŏ\ bacon \u\ sun \ŭ\ helpful \ü\ fool

ma·i·le (MAH-ee-lay) *n.*, a South Pacific vine whose fragrant leaves and bark are used to make Hawaiian leis

main·our (MAYN-ŏ(r)) *n.*, an Old English law term for a stolen article found on or near the thief

ma·jo (MAH-hoh) *n.*, a Spanish lower-class dandy

ma·jol·i·ca (mă-JAHL-ĭ-kă) *n.*, an early Italian earthenware that was covered and decorated with glaze before firing

make·bate (MAYK-bayt) *n.*, an archaic term for a person who starts quarrels

ma·ki·mo·no (mah-kĭ-MOH-noh) *n.*, a picture or story mounted on paper and rolled into a scroll

ma·lar (MAY-lăr) *adj.*, pertaining to the cheek or the side of the head

ma·lif·er·ous (mă-LIF-(ĕ)-rŭs) *adj.*, having an unhealthy effect

ma·line (mă-LEEN) *n.*, a delicate, stiff net with hexagonal mesh that is used in millinery

ma·lism (MAY-lizĕm) *n.*, the belief that the world is evil

mal·kin (MAW(L)-kĭn) *n.*, 1. English dialect for a slovenly woman 2. English dialect for a cat

mal·lee (MAL-ee) *n.*, an Australian dwarf eucalyptus

mal·le·muck (MAL-ĕ-mŭk) *n.*, a large seabird such as the petrel

mal·low (MAL-oh) *n.*, a hollyhock or okra with large, showy flowers and sticky juice in its stem, leaves, and roots

malm (MAHM) *n.*, a blend of clay and chalk that is used to make brick

malm·sey (MAHM-zee) *n.*, a fragrant, sweet Mediterranean wine

mal·ver·sa·tion (MAL-vĕ(r)-say-shŏn) *n.*, a civil law term for improper behavior in public office; corrupt rule

mam·e·lon (MAM-ĕ-lŏn) *n.*, a dome-shaped protrusion or elevation on the ground

mam·e·luke (MAM-ĕ-look) *n.*, an Egyptian military class of slaves

mam·mil·late (MA-mĭ-layt) *adj.*, having a nipple or a nipple-shaped protrusion

mam·mock (MA-mŏk) *n.*, U.S. dialect for a fragment; a scrap

mam·mose (MA-mohs) *n.*, a young sturgeon in Delaware and New Jersey

ma·na (MAH-na) *n.*, a supernatural force or power

ma·nav·el·ins (mă-NAV-ĕl-ĭnz) *n.*, U.S. slang for a meal's leftover food

man·bote (MAN-boht) *n.*, an Old English law term for the monetary compensation awarded to a lord whose servant was murdered

manche (MAHNCH) *n.*, a heraldic representation of a sleeve with a flaring end

man·ci·ple (MAN(T)-sĭ-pĕl) *n.*, a person authorized to buy provisions for a college or monastery

man-da-la (MĂN-dă-lă) *n.*, a circular, mystical representation of the cosmos used for meditation among Buddhists and Hindus

man-do-la (man-DOH-lă) *n.*, a three-stringed lute with a pear-shaped body

man-du-cate (MAN-jŭ-kayt) *v.*, an archaic term meaning to chew

man-go-nel (MANG-gă-nel) *n.*, a military engine that originally threw large stones or darts

ma-nille (mă-NIL) *n.*, the second highest trump in certain card games

man-i-ple (MAN-ĭ-pĕl) *n.*, the church vestment that hangs from the left arm to symbolize the napkin used by early deacons in their table services

man-quel-ler (MAN-kwel-ĕr) *n.*, an archaic term for a murderer

man-sue-tude (MAN(T)-swŭ-tood) *n.*, mildness; gentleness

ma-quis (ma-KEE) *n.*, the thick, stunted underbrush found along Mediterranean shores, especially on the island of Corsica

mar-a-bou (mar-ă-BOO) *n.*, a large African stork whose feathers trim hats and clothing

ma-ran-ta (mă-RAN-tă) *n.*, a starch derived from the American arrowroot

ma-ras-ca (mă-RAS-kă) *n.*, the bitter wild cherry whose juice produces the strong, sweet maraschino liqueur

mar-a-ve-di (mar-ă-VAY-dee) *n.*, a gold coin of Spain and Morocco

marc (MAHRK) *n.*, the residue left after juice has been extracted from fruit

mar-ces-cent (marh-SES-ĕnt) *adj.*, withering without dropping off, as a leaf

ma-rem-ma (mă-REM-ă) *n.*, a marshy region along a seashore

mar-ga-rite (MAHR-gă-rīt) *n.*, a mineral resembling mother-of-pearl

mar-gay (MAHR-gay) *n.*, a small, spotted cat like the ocelot that ranges from Texas to South America

mar-grave (MAHR-grayv) *n.*, a German nobleman equivalent in rank to a British marquess

ma-ric-o-lous (mă-RIK-ŏ-lŭs) *adj.*, living in the sea

mar-i-ol-a-try (ma(a)r-ee-AHL-ă-tree) *n.*, an excessive devotion to the Virgin Mary

mar-i-po-sa (mar-ĭ-POH-să) *n.*, a large, brilliantly colored fish found throughout warm and temperate seas

mar-khor (MAHR-kaw(ŏ)r) *n.*, a wild goat found in mountainous regions of Afghanistan and India

marl (MAHRL) *n.*, an earthy deposit containing dolomite that serves as a natural fertilizer for soils deficient in lime

mar-lock (MAH-lŏk) *n.*, English dialect for a prank

mar-ma-rize (MAHR-mă-rīz) *v.*, to change into marble

\a\ bat \ă\ about \e\ or \è\ check \ĕ\ letter \é\ cafe \i\fish \ī\ tie \ĭ\ limit \o\ boat \ŏ\ bacon \u\ sun \ŭ\ helpful \ü\ fool

mar-mo-re-al (MAHR-mohr-ee-al) *adj.*, of or like marble or a marble statue

ma-rou-flage (MAH-rŏ-flahzh) *n.*, a method of attaching canvas to a wall by using an adhesive substance

mar-plot (MAHR-plaht) *n.*, a person whose interference ruins a plan or process

mar-que-try (MAHR-kĕ-tree) *n.*, the elaborate inlaid patterns of various wood pieces that are used to decorate furniture

mar-ram (MAR-ăm) *n.*, a grass grown on beaches

mar-tin-gale (MAHR-tĭn-gayl) *n.*, a part of a horse's harness that restricts the movement of the animal's head

mas-con (MAHS-kahn) *n.*, a concentration of heavy material beneath the surface of the moon

mas-se-ter (mă-SEED-ĕ(r)) *n.*, the large muscle that helps close the jaw and aids chewing

mas-si-cot (MAS-i-kaht) *n.*, a lead compound that yields a yellow powder at certain temperatures

mas-ta-ba (MAS-tă-bă) *n.*, an ancient Egyptian tomb that connects with a mummy chamber

mas-ti-go-phor-ic (MAS-tĭ-goh-fawr-ik) *adj.*, having a long, whiplike tail

ma-ta-chin (mahd-ă-CHEEN) *n.*, a fantastically costumed sword dancer

ma-te-las-sé (MAHD-ĕl-ah-say) *n.*, a double-cloth fabric woven on a loom and distinguished by its raised designs and quilted appearance

mat-e-lote (MAD-ĕl-oht) *n.*, a highly seasoned sauce made from fish stock, wine, and onions

mathe-sis (mă-THEE-sĭs) *n.*, an archaic term for a mental discipline such as mathematics

ma-tri-lin-e-al (ma-trĭ-LIN-ee-ăl) *adj.*, associated with maternal lineage

mat-ri-po-tes-tal (MA-tree-poh-tes-tăl) *adj.*, pertaining to the authority of a mother

matro-cli-nous (MA-troh-klī-nŭs) *adj.*, inherited from the mother's side of the family

mat-ro-nym-ic (ma-trŏ-NIM-ik) *n.*, a family name taken from the name of the mother or other female ancestor

mat-ta-more (MAD-ă-moh(ĕ)r) *n.*, an underground storehouse

mat-tock (MAD-ŏk) *n.*, a tool that combines the characteristics of an ax and an adz with the point of a pick and is used for digging and chopping

mat-toid (MAD-oid) *n.*, a person on the edge of insanity

mat-u-res-cent (MACH-ŭ-res-ĕnt) *adj.*, becoming ripe

mat-zoon (maht-SOON) *n.*, a cultured milk food like yogurt

mau-met (MAW-mĕt) *n.*, British dialect for a figure built to resemble a human

mau-me-try (MAW-mĕ-tree) *n.*, an obsolete term for idolatry

maund (MAWND) *n.*, British dialect for a hand basket

maun-der (MAWN-dĕ(r)) *v.*, to talk or move in an aimless, disconnected way

maun-dy (MAWN-dee) *n.*, a rite that involves washing the feet of the poor on Holy Thursday

max-im-ite (MAKS-ĭ-mīt) *n.*, a powerful explosive used to penetrate tanks

ma-xixe (MĂ-sheesh) *n.*, a Brazilian ballroom dance

may-pop (MAY-pahp) *n.*, the bland fruit of a passionflower

maz-a-rine (MAZ-ă-reen) *n.*, a deep, metal dish, especially one used to line a serving plate

ma-zer (MAY-zĕ(r)) *n.*, a large drinking bowl or cup once fashioned from hardwood and later metal

maz-zard (MAZ-ă(r)d) *n.*, a wild sweet cherry

mea-cock (MEE-kahk) *n.*, an archaic term for a timid or effeminate man

mech-a-no-mor-phic (mekă-ă-noh-MAWR-fik) *adj.*, having the characteristics of a machine; described in terms of a machine

me-da-ka (mĕ-DAH-kă) *n.*, a small Japanese fish

me-di-e-ty (mĕ-DĪ-ĕd-ee) *n.*, a mathematical average

me-di-us (MEE-dee-ŭs) *n.*, the middle finger

med-lar (MED-lăr) *n.*, a meadowlark

meg-a-ce-phal-ic (meg-ă-sĕ-FAL-ik) *adj.*, having a skull with an abnormally large capacity

me-grim (MEE-grĭm) *n.*, a spontaneous or secret idea or emotion

me-ha-ri (mĕ-HAH-ree) *n.*, a camel of a breed noted for speed and used for riding

mein-y (MAY-nee) *n.*, an archaic term for a band of servants or disciples

mei-o-sis (MI-oh-sis) *n.*, an understated representation of a thing

mel (MEL) *n.*, a pharmaceutical term for honey

me-lan-geur (may-lahn-ZHŬR) *n.*, a machine that mixes the paste from coca beans with sugar to make chocolate

me-lan-ic (mĕ-LAN-ik) *adj.*, having a high amount of black pigment

mel-a-noc-o-mous (mel-ă-NAHK-ŏ-mŭs) *adj.*, having dark-colored or black hair

mel-ic (MEL-ik) *adj.*, pertaining to a melodic form of Greek poetry

mel-i-lot (MEL-ĭ-laht) *n.*, an aromatic clover that is grown for fertilizer throughout the world

me-line (MEE-līn) *adj.*, resembling a badger or comprised of badgers

me-lis-ma (mĕ-LIZ-mă) *n.*, a musical phrase or song

\a\ bat \ă\ about \e\ or \ĕ\ check \ĕ\ letter
\é\ cafe \i\fish \ī\ tie \ĭ\ limit \o\ boat
\ŏ\ bacon \u\ sun \ŭ\ helpful \ü\ fool

mel·liv·o·rous (me-LIV-ŏ-rŭs) *adj.,* depending on honey for food

mel·o·ma·ni·ac (mel-ŏ-MAY-nee-ak) *n.,* an abnormally dedicated musical fan

mel·o·poe·ia (mel-ŏ-PEE-(y)ă) *n.,* a tune

men·ac·me (měn-AK-mee) *n.,* the age period of a female's life characterized by the occurrence of menstruation

menald (MENĂLD) *adj.,* spotted; streaked

men·ha·den (men-HAYD-ĕn) *n.,* a fish similar to a shad that is found in abundance off the Atlantic coast and used for making oil and fertilizer

men·hir (MEN-hi(ĕ)r) *n.,* a lone, erect, rough stone, especially a prehistoric one

me·nis·cus (mě-NIS-kŭs) *n.,* a crescent or crescent-shaped object

me·nol·ogy (mě-NAHL-ŏ-jee) *n.,* a calendar of the feastdays of the saints and martyrs

men·o·pha·ni·a (men-oh-FAY-nee-a) *n.,* the first menstruation of puberty

mense (MEN(T)S) *n.,* British dialect for courteous behavior

mense·ful (MEN(T)S-fŭl) *adj.,* British dialect meaning orderly

men·ti·cide (MEN-tĭ-sīd) *n.,* an effort to replace an individual's belief structure with thoughts and emotions foreign to him or her

men·tum (MEN-tŭm) *n.,* a chin or chinlike projection

me·phit·ic (mě-FID-ik) *adj.,* having a smell that is offensive

mer·div·o·rous (měr-DIV-ŏ-rŭs) *adj.,* referring to something or someone who eats dung

mer·e·tri·cious (mer-ĕ-TRI-shŭs) *adj.,* pertaining to a prostitute

me·ris·tic (mě-RIS-tik) *adj.,* pertaining to or divided into parts

merk (MERK) *n.,* a Scottish term for an old English coin called a mark

mer·kin (MĔR-kĭn) *n.,* a hairpiece for the female pubic area

me·ro·pi·a (mě-ROH-pee-ă) *n.,* a state of partial blindness

merse (MĔRS) *n.,* a Scottish term for a marsh

me·si·al (ME-zee-ăl) *adj.,* in or directed toward the middle

mesne (MEEN) *adj.,* a legal term meaning intermediate: intervening

mes·o·gle·a (me-zoh-GLEE-ă) *n.,* a jellylike substance between the inner and outer walls of an animal like a sponge

me·son (ME-zahn) *n.,* a particle in the nucleus whose size is between that of an electron and a proton

me·soth·e·sis (mě-ZAHTH-ĕ-sĭs) *n.,* an agency or principle that mediates

me·so·thet·ic (me-zŏ-THED-ik) *adj.,* in the middle

mes·suage (MES-wij) *n.,* a house, its buildings, and its adjacent lands

met·age (MEED-ij) *n.,* the official measurement of an object's contents or weight

me-ta-grob-o-lize (med-ă-GRAHB-ŏ-līz) *v.*, to bewilder or mystify

me-ta-te (mĕ-TAHD-ee) *n.*, a stone used for grinding grain

me-tem-psy-cho-sis (mĕ-tem(p)-sĭ-KOH-sĭs) *n.*, the passage of the soul into another being upon death

mé-tis (may-TEE(S)) *n.*, a person of mixed ancestry

met-o-pos-co-py (med-ŏ-PAHS-kŏ-pee) *n.*, predicting the future by using the markings of the forehead

me-tri-cian (me-TRISH-ăn) *n.*, a composer or student of measured rhyme

met-ri-fi-ca-tion (me-trĭ-fĭ-KAY-shŏn) *n.*, a composition in measured rhythmical form such as verse

met-ro-ma-ni-a (me-troh-MAY-nee-ă) *n.*, an excessive enthusiasm for writing verse

mi-as-mic (mi-AZ-mĭk) *adj.*, having a noxious smell

mib (MIB) *n.*, U.S. dialect for a playing marble used as a target

mich (MICH) *v.*, U.S. dialect meaning to move secretly; to sneak

micher (MICH-ĕ(r)) *n.*, U.S. dialect for a truant

mi-cra-ner (MĪ-kră-ner) *n.*, an unusually small male ant

mi-cro-ceph-a-ly (mĪ-kroh-SEF-ă-lee) *n.*, a condition in which the skull capacity is abnormally small

mic-tu-ri-tion (MIK-chŭ-ri-shŏn) *n.*, the act of passing urine

mid-den (MID-ĕn) *n.*, 1. a dung hill 2. a refuse heap

mid-rib (MID-rib) *n.*, the vein at the center of a leaf

milch (MILK) *adj.*, of a domestic animal bred specifically for milk production

mil-les-i-mal (mĭ-LES-ĭ-măl) *adj.*, 1/1000

mil-lieme (mee(l)-YEM) *n.*, a Middle Eastern copper coin

mil-lime (mĭ-LEEM) *n.*, an aluminum coin of Tunisia

mil-line (MIL-līn) *n.*, a measurement of advertising space equivalent to a one-column line appearing in a million copies of a publication

mi-lo (MĪ-loh) *n.*, a small grain sorghum with yellow or pink seeds

mil-pa (MIL-pă) *n.*, a Central American, Mexican, or Asian tract of land cleared from the jungle, farmed, then abandoned

mim (MIM) *adj.*, U.S. dialect for timid or modest

mi-na-cious (mĭ-NAY-shŭs) *adj.* having a menacing or threatening effect

mi-nau-de-rie (mee-NOH-dree) *n.*, a flirtatious manner

min-bar (MIN-bahr) *n.*, a pulpit in a mosque

min-gy (MIN-jee) *adj.*, mean and stingy

min-i-ate (MIN-ee-ayt) *v.*, to paint with a red color

\a\ bat \ă\ about \e\ or \è\ check \ē\ letter \é\ cafe \i\fish \ī\ tie \ĭ\ limit \o\ boat \ŏ\ bacon \u\ sun \ŭ\ helpful \ü\ fool

min-im (MIN-im) *n.*, the smallest unit of liquid measure

min-i-mus (MIN-ĭ-mŭs) *n.*, a very small creature

min-ion-ette (min-yŏ-NET) *n.*, an old size of printers' type equal to approximately 6-1/2 points

min-i-ver (MIN-ĭ-vĕr) *n.*, a white or whitish fur worn as clothing by medieval nobles and used for robes of state today

miq-ue-let (MIK-ŭ-let) *n.*, a Spanish guerrilla who fought Napoleon's armies in the Peninsular War

mir-a-dor (MIR-ă-dohr) *n.*, a Spanish architectural term for any architectural structure such as a balcony that allows a person a broad view of the landscape

mird (MIRD) *v.*, a Scottish term meaning to flirt

mir-li-goes (MĬR-li-gohz) *n.*, a Scottish term for dizziness

mir-za (MIR-ză) *n.*, a Persian title commonly bestowed to honor an individual of note

mis-an-dry (MI-san-dree) *n.*, a hatred of men

mis-ci-ble (MIS-ĭ-bĕl) *adj.*, able to be mixed

mis-kal (mi-SKAHL) *n.*, a measure of weight in Muslim countries

mis-o-cai-ne-a (mis-oh-KĪ-nee-ă) *n.*, an abnormal dislike of new ideas

mi-sol-o-gy (mĭ-SAHL-ŏ-jee) *n.*, distrust or hatred of reason or reasoning

mis-o-ne-ism (mis-ŏ-NEE-izĕm) *n.*, a hatred of something new or changed

mis-o-pe-di-a (mis-ŏ-PEE-dee-ă) *n.*, a severe dislike of children, especially one's own

mis-pri-sion (mĭ-SPRI-zhŏn) *n.*, 1. misconduct or neglect of duty by a public servant 2. a misunderstanding

mis-sion-ate (MI-shŏ-nayt) *v.*, to carry on missionary work

mis-ti-gris (MIS-tee-gris) *n.*, a joker or wild card that can be played anytime

mith-ri-da-tism (MITH-rĭ-dayd-izĕm) *n.*, a tolerance to a poison that results from the repeated intake of gradually increasing doses

mix-ty-max-ty (MIKS-tee-MAKS-tee) *adj.*, muddled together; confused

miz-maze (MIZ-mayz) *n.*, 1. a maze 2. English dialect meaning a condition of confusion

miz-zle (MIZ-ĕl) *v.*, U.S. dialect meaning to rain in a fine mist

mlech-chha (mĕ-LECHĂ) *n.*, an Indian term for a person who does not practice Hinduism; specifically, a foreigner

mo-a (MOH-ă) *n.*, an extinct, flightless bird of New Zealand

mo-de-na (MAW-dĕ-nă) *n.*, an Italian hen pigeon

mo-doc (MOH-dahk) *n.*, an Indian tribe of southwest Oregon and northwest California

mog·gan (MAH-găn) *n.*, a Scottish term for a stocking, especially a long, footless stocking

mog·i·la·li·a (moj-ĭ-lay-LEE-ă) *n.*, a speech defect such as stuttering

mo·hock (MOH-hawk) *n.*, a member of a gang of rowdy noblemen who assaulted and abused people on the streets of early 18th-century London

moil (MOIL) *n.*, 1. drudgery 2. confusion

mo·jar·ra (moh-HAH-ră) *n.*, a South American fish

mo·lim·i·nous (mă-LĪ-mĕ-nŭs) *adj.*, unwieldy

mo·loch (MAH-lŏk) or (MO-lahk) *n.*, a dictatorial power to be gratified by human sacrifice

mome (MOHM) *n.*, an archaic term for a dimwitted person

mo·nad (MOH-nad) *n.*, a simple, single-celled organism

mon·ep·ic (mah-NEP-ik) *adj.*, having only one word or sentences of only one word

mo·ni·al (MOH-nee-ăl) *n.*, a slender vertical bar used to divide rows of windows, lights, or doors

mo·nil·i·form (mŏ-NIL-ĭ-fohrm) *adj.*, being joined or separated at intervals to look like a string of beads

mo·ni·tion (mŏ-NI-shŏn) *n.*, an instruction or counsel given as a warning

monks·hood (MŎNGKS-huud) *n.*, a very poisonous Eurasian herb

mo·noe·cious (mŏ-NEE-shŭs) *adj.*, having both male and female sex organs; hermaphroditic

mo·nog·e·nism (mŏ-NAHJ-ĕ-nizĕm) *n.*, the belief that all races originated from a single pair or common ancestral type

mo·nog·o·ny (mŏ-NAHG-ŏ-nee) *n.*, reproduction without sex

mon·or·chid (mah-NAWR-kĭd) *adj.*, having one testis or only one descended in the scrotum

mon·tane (mahn-TAYN) *adj.*, relating to a moist, cool zone of uplands just below the timberline, where large evergreens predominate

mon·teith (mahn-TEETH) *adj.*, a scalloped silver punch bowl

mon·te·ro (mahn-TE-roh) *n.*, 1. a game hunter 2. a cap worn by huntsmen

mon·ti·cle (MAHN-tĭ-kĕl) *n.*, a small hill

mool (MOOL) *n.*, British dialect for a soft, fertile soil rich in humus

moon·eye (MOON-ī) *n.*, a horse's eye that is affected with the inflammation caused by moon blindness

moon·let (MOON-lĕt) *n.*, a small satellite of a celestial body

moon·wort (MOON-wŏrt) *n.*, a fern

\a\ bat \ă\ about \e\ or \è\ check \ē\ letter
\é\ cafe \i\fish \ī\ tie \ĭ\ limit \o\ boat
\ŏ\ bacon \u\ sun \ŭ\ helpful \ü\ fool

moor-pun-ky (maw(r)-PŬNG-kee)
n., a large, ornamental pleasure
boat formerly used as the state
barge of India

moo-rup (moo-RUUP) *n.*, a large,
flightless bird with small, stout legs
that is found on the isle of New
Britain

mo-pus (MOH-pŭs) *n.*, a U.S. slang
term for cash

mo-quette (moh-KET) *n.*, 1. an
inexpensive machine-made
carpeting 2. an upholstery fabric

mor (MAW(Ĕ)R) *n.*, the layer of
organic matter found in the forest
that can be distinguished from the
mineral soil beneath it

mo-ra (MOH-ră) *n.*, a Roman and
civil law term for a blameworthy
delay in the execution of an
obligation

mo-raine (mŏ-RAYN) *n.*, the
mixture of earth and stones moved
and deposited by a glacier

mor-bi-dez-za (maw(r)-bĭ-DET-să)
n., an extreme softness and
delicacy in artwork

mor-bif-ic (maw(r)-BIF-ik) *adj.*,
causing illness

mor-cel-la-tion (maw(r)-sĕ-LAY-
shŏn) *n.*, the process of dividing
into parts and removing in small
pieces, as in the excision of a tumor

mor-da-cious (maw(r)-DAY-shŭs)
adj., biting

mor-dant (MAW(R)-dănt) *adj.*,
biting and sarcastic in manner,
thought, or style

mo-reen (mŏ-REEN) *n.*, an
upholstery fabric made of wool or
wool-cotton blend

mo-relles (mŏ-RELZ) *n.*, an
ancient strategic board game for
two players

mor-ga-nat-ic (maw(r)-gă-NAD-ik)
adj., referring to a legal marriage
between European royalty and
persons of lower rank

mor-gan-ize (MAW(R)-gă-nīz) *v.*,
to assassinate to prevent the release
of information

mor-gen (MAWR-gĕn) *n.*, an old
Dutch unit of land still used in
South Africa

mo-rig-er-ous (mŏ-RIJ-ĕr-ŭs) *adj.*,
an archaic term for obedient

mor-ris or **mor-rice** (MOR-ĭs) *n.*,
an English dance by costumed men
carrying bells, sticks, and
handkerchiefs in a traditional
feature of pageants, processions,
and May Day

mor-ro (MOR-oh) *n.*, a rounded hill

mor-sure (MAWR-shuur) *n.*, an
archaic term for a bite

mort-ling (MAWRT-ling) *n.*, the
wool obtained from dead sheep

mort-main (MORT-mayn) *n.*, a
legal term for the perpetual holding
of lands, especially by a corporation
or charitable trust

mos-chate (MOS-kayt) *adj.*,
having a musky smell

mo-tile (MOHD-īl) *adj.*, capable of
spontaneous movement

mou-lage (MOO-lahzh) *n.*, the
making of a plastic impression such
as a toothmark for use as evidence
in a criminal investigation

mou-ton (MOO-tahn) *n.*, sheepskin
cut and treated to resemble the fur
of another animal

moz-zet-ta or **mo-zet-ta** (MOHT-sed-ă) or (MOHT-zed-ă) *n.*, a short cape with an ornamental hood worn by some churchmen

msa-sa (ĕm-SAH-sa) *n.*, an African tree

mu-ci-lag-i-nous (MYOO-sĭ-laj-ĭ-nŭs) *adj.*, slimy; sticky

muck-er (MŬK-ĕ(r)) *v.*, to wander; to dawdle

muck-le (MŬK-ĕl) *n.*, a Scottish term for a large amount or sum

muck-worm (MŬk-wŏrm) *n.*, 1. a miser 2. a nontechnical term for a worm found in humus or manure

mud-sill (MŬD-sil) *n.*, a person of the lowest social class

mu-ez-zin or **mu-az-zin** (m(y)oo-EZ-ĭn) *n.*, a crier who summons Muslims to prayer five times daily from a high position

mug-gins (MŬG-ĭnz) *n.*, a rule in many English card games that allows a player to claim a score that his opponent fails to record

mu-gi-ent (MYOO-jee-ĕnt) *adj.*, making a mooing sound, as a cow

muj-ta-hid (mooj-TAH-hid) *n.*, a religious teacher acknowledged as an authoritative interpreter of the laws of Islam

mu-la-da (MOO-lah-dă) *n.*, a southwestern U.S. term for a drove of mules

mulct (MŬLKT) *n.*, 1. a fine 2. an arbitrary and coercive demand for money

mu-li-eb-ri-ty (myoo-lee-EB-rĭd-ee) *n.*, a womanly nature or qualities; womanhood

mul-lein or **mul-len** (MŬL-ĕn) *n.*, a tall American herb with yellow or white flowers

mul-li-grubs (MŬ-lee-grŭbz) *n.*, 1. a depressed, sullen, or bad-tempered mood 2. a sudden attack of intestinal spasms; colitis

mul-lion (MŬL-yŏn) *n.*, 1. a vertical divider between windows 2. an upright part of a frame

mul-lock (MŬL-ŏk) *n.*, 1. British dialect for trash 2. U.S. dialect for confusion

mulm (MŬLM) *n.*, the organic sediment found in fish tanks

mulse (MŬLS) *n.*, an obsolete term for a drink made from honey and blended with wine or water

mul-ti-grav-i-da (mŭl-tĭ-GRAV-ĭ-dă) *n.*, a woman who has become pregnant more than one time

mump-ish (MŬMP-ish) *adj.*, morose

mump-si-mus (MŬMP-sĭ-mŭs) *n.*, a bigoted adherent to a recognized, but customary, error

mum-ruf-fin (MOOM-ruf-in) *n.*, British dialect for a long-tailed bird

mun-div-a-gant (mŭn-DIV-ă-gănt) *adj.*, an archaic term for wandering worldwide

mun-dun-gus (mŭn-DUN-gŭs) *n.*, tobacco that burns with a foul odor

mun-go (MŬN-goh) *n.*, a poor quality of wool obtained from recycling wool goods and wastes

---

\a\ bat \ā\ about \e\ or \ĕ\ check \ē\ letter
\é\ cafe \i\fish \ī\ tie \ĭ\ limit \o\ boat
\ŏ\ bacon \u\ sun \ŭ\ helpful \ü\ fool

mu-ni-ment (MYOO-nĭ-mĕnt) *n.*, an archaic term for a method or line of defense

mu-ra (MOO-rä) *n.*, a country village in Japan

mur-en-ger (MYOO-rĕn-jĕ(r)) *n.*, the person in charge of a wall of a town and its repairs

mu-ri-cate (MYOO-rĭ-kayt) *adj.*, covered with sharp, hard points

mu-ri-form (MYOO-rĭ-fohrm) *adj.*, resembling a mouse or rat

mur-ra or **mur-rha** (MŬ-rä) *n.*, a material, probably semiprecious stone or porcelain, used to make vessels in ancient Rome

mur-rain (MŬR-ăn) *n.*, a deadly epidemic among domesticated plants or livestock

murre (MŬR) *n.*, a short-necked diving bird of the northern seas

mur-rey (MŬ-ree) *n.*, a purplish black color like the color of the mulberry

mus-ca (MŬS-kă) *n.*, a common housefly

mus-co-va-do (mŭs-kŏ-VAY-doh) *n.*, unrefined or raw sugar derived from the evaporated juice of sugarcane after molasses has been removed

mus-nud (MŬ-snŭd) *n.*, a cushioned seat used as a throne by East Indian princes

mus-quash (MŬ-skwahsh) *n.*, a muskrat

mus-si-ta-tion (mŭ-sĭ-TAY-shŏn) *n.*, the act of moving the lips as if speaking, but without making a sound

mutch (MŬCH) *n.*, a Scottish term for a close-fitting cap worn by old women or babies

mutch-kin (MŬCH-kĭn) *n.*, a Scottish unit of liquid measure

mut-sud-dy (mut-SŬ-di) *n.*, a native clerk or accountant in British India

mu-zhik (moo-ZHIK) *n.*, a Russian peasant

my-coph-a-gy (mī-KAH-fă-jee) *n.*, the eating of fungus like mushrooms

my-ia-sis (MĪ-(y)ă-sĭs) *n.*, a disease caused by fly maggots

my-ox-ine (mī-AHK-sīn) *adj.*, relating to small, Old World rodents known as dormice

myr-me-coid (MĬR-mĕ-koid) *adj.*, antlike

myr-me-col-o-gy (mĭr-mĕ-KAHL-ŏ-jee) *n.*, the study of ants

myr-mi-don (MĬR-mĭ-dahn) *n.*, an unquestioningly loyal follower who displays blind obedience to orders

my-so-pho-bi-a or **mi-so-pho-bi-a** (mī-sŏ-FOH-bee-ă) *n.*, an abnormal fear of contamination or uncleanliness

my-sost (MĪ-sahst) *n.*, a hard, mild cheese made from the whey of goat's milk

mys-ta-ci-al (mĭ-STAY-sh(ee)-ăl) *n.*, having a fringe of hair resembling a mustache

mys-ta-gogue (MIS-tă-gahg) *n.*, one who teaches mysticism

my-ta-cism (MĪD-ă-sizĕm) *n.*, the incorrect use of the letter M or the sound it represents

myth-o-ma-ni-a (mith-ŏ-MAY-nee-ă) *n.*, an abnormal tendency to lie and exaggerate

myx-o-ma (mik-SOH-mă) *n.*, a soft tumor of jellylike connective tissue

N

nab-cheat (NAB-cheet) *n.*, an obsolete slang term for a hat or cap

nack-et (NAK-ĕt) *n.*, a Scottish term for a mischievous boy

na-cre-ous (NAY-kree-ŭs) *adj.*, consisting of or resembling mother-of-pearl

nan-din (NAN-din) *n.*, an Oriental ornamental evergreen with red berries

nan-ism (NAY-nizĕm) *n.*, dwarfism

nan-keen (nan-KEEN) *n.*, a hand-woven cotton cloth from China with a natural yellow tinge

na-ol-o-gy (nay-AHL-ŏ-jee) *n.*, the study of sacred architectural structures

na-os (NAY-ahs) *n.*, an old shrine or temple

na-per-y (NAY-p(ĕ)-ree) *n.*, household table linen

na-pi-form (NAY-pĭ-fohrm) *adj.*, having the form, shape, or appearance of a turnip

na-poo (nă-POO) *v.*, British slang meaning to put an end to; to kill

nap-py (NA-pi) *n.*, a Scottish term for an ale or liquor

na-prap-a-thy (nă-PRAP-ă-thee) *n.*, a healing system based on massage

nar-co-syn-the-sis (nahr-ko-SIN(T)-thĕ-sĭs) *n.*, a psychiatric treatment using sedatives to enable the recovery of repressed memories

nar-ghi-le or **nar-gi-leh** (NAHR-gĭ-le) *n.*, an Oriental water pipe or hookah with long, flexible stems

narr (NAHR) *n.*, an archaic term for a statement in a legal case

nar-thex (NAHR-theks) *n.*, a porch or passageway set apart from the main body of a church, originally for those not entering the sanctuary such as women, the unbaptized, and penitents

nash-gab (NASH-gab) *n.*, an archaic Scottish term for a rude busybody

na-si-cor-nous (NAY-za-kawr-nŭs) *adj.*, having a horn on the nose, as a rhinoceros

na-sute (nay-SOOT) *adj.*, having a well-developed snout

natch-bone (NACH-bohn) *n.*, the hipbone on the rump of a cow

na-tes (NAY-teez) *n. pl.*, the buttocks or rump

na-ti-form (NAYD-ĭ-fohrm) *adj.*, resembling the buttocks

\a\ bat \ā\ about \e\ or \ĕ\ check \ē\ letter
\é\ cafe \i\fish \ī\ tie \ĭ\ limit \o\ boat
\ŏ\ bacon \u\ sun \ŭ\ helpful \ü\ fool

nat-ter-jack (NAD-ĕ(r)-jak) *n.*, a European toad with short hind legs that runs rather than hops

nau-ma-chi-a (naw-MAY-kee-ă) *n.*, a mock naval battle performed as a spectacle by ancient Romans

nau-pa-thi-a (naw-PA-thee-a) *n.*, seasickness

nau-sco-py (NAH-sko-pi) *n.*, the false art of discovering approaching ships or land at a considerable distance

nautch (NAWCH) *n.*, East Indian entertainment provided mainly by professional dancing girls

na-vette (na-VET) *n.*, a marquise-cut gemstone, gem cut, setting, or stone

na-vi-cert (NA-vĭ-sĕrt) *n.*, a British document certifying that a ship's cargo is free of contraband and may be shipped without search or seizure by blockade officers

na-vi-cu-lar (nă-VIK-yŭ-lă(r)) *adj.*, boat-shaped

ne-an-ic (NEE-an-ik) *adj.*, youthful; specifically, in relation to the pupal stage of insect development

ne-an-thro-pic (nee-an-THRAHP-ic) *adj.*, pertaining to the surviving species of mankind, as distinguished from earlier species known only through fossil remains

neat-herd (NEET-hĕrd) *n.*, an overseer, driver, or caretaker of livestock

neb (NEB) *n.*, the beak of a bird or tortoise; the bill

neb-neb (NEB-neb) *n.*, the pods of a native north African tree

ne-ces-si-tar-i-an-ism (nĕ-ses-ĭ-TER-ee-ă-nizĕm) *n.*, the doctrine that effects invariably follow from causes; determinism

ne-cro-mi-me-sis (nek-roh-mi-MEE-sis) *n.*, a mental disorder in which a person believes himself dead

ne-fan-dous (nĕ-FAN-dŭs) *adj.*, unmentionable

ne-fast (nĕ-FAST) *adj.*, evil

ne-gus (NEE-gŭs) *n.*, wine heated with hot water, sweetened, and often flavored with lemon juice and nutmeg

nek-ton or **nec-ton** (NEK-tŏn) *n.*, water animals that swim independent of waves or currents

ne-os-sol-o-gy (nee-ah-SAHL-ŏ-jee) *n.*, the study of young birds

ne-o-ten-ic (nee-ŏ-TEEN-ik) *adj.*, relating to the attainment of sexual maturity while in the larval stage

ne-o-ten-y (NEE-ŏ-tee-nee) *n.*, the retention of some larval or immature traits in adulthood

ne-pen-the (nĕ-PEN(T)-thee) *n.*, a drug or drink that induces forgetfulness of sorrow or trouble

neph-a-lism (NEF-ă-lizĕm) *n.*, total abstention from alcohol

neph-o-gram (NEF-ŏ-gram) *n.*, a photograph having a cloud or clouds as its subject

ne-phror-rha-phy (ne-FRAWR-ră-fee) *n.*, the suturing of a floating kidney to the posterior abdominal wall

ne-re-is (NI-ree-ĭs) *n.*, a large marine worm, usually green

ner-o-li (NER-ŏ-lee) *n.*, an oil derived from an orange tree and used in perfume

nes-ci-ence (NE-sh(ee)-ĕn(t)s) *n.*, ignorance

nes-ci-ent (NE-sh(ee)-ĕnt) *adj.*, believing that ultimate realities cannot be known through rationality

nes-khi or **nes-ki** (NES-kee) or **nas-khi** (NAS-kee) *n.*, Arabic script used in writing scientific or religious texts

ne-top (NEE-tahp) *n.*, a New England term for friend used as a greeting to an Indian by an American colonist

ne-tsu-ke (NET-skee) or (NET-sŭ-kay) *n.*, a small figurine made of ivory, wood, metal, or ceramic and used to attach personal objects to the sash of a Japanese kimono

neume (N(Y)OOM) *n.*, a symbol used in music notation during the Middle Ages

n-go-ko (ĕng-GOH-koh) *n.*, a dialect of Javanese used in addressing inferiors

nic-ta-tion (nik-TAY-shŏn) *n.*, the act of winking

nid-der-ing or **nid-er-ing** (NID-(ĕ)-ring) *n.*, an archaic term for a coward

nid-dick (NID-ik) *n.*, English dialect for the nape of the neck

nid-dle (NID-ĕl) *v.*, a Scottish term meaning to move swiftly

nid-get (NI-jĕt) *n.*, an archaic term for a fool

nid-i-fi-cate (NID-ĭ-fĭ-kayt) *v.*, to construct a nest

ni-dif-u-gous (nī-DIF-yŭ-gŭs) *adj.*, leaving the nest soon after birth

nid-nod (NID-nahd) *v.*, to allow the head to drop repeatedly from drowsiness

ni-dor-ous (NĪ-dŏr-ŭs) *adj.*, having the smell of rotting or burning flesh

nid-u-lant (NI-jŭ-lănt) *adj.*, lying free in a depression

ni-el-lo (nee-EL-loh) *n.*, a deep black alloy of sulfur with copper, lead, or silver

nieve (NEEV) *n.*, a woman born a serf

night-jar (NĪT-jahr) *n.*, a nocturnal European bird

ni-gres-cent (nī-GRES-ĕnt) *adj.*, tending toward black

nil-gai or **nil-ghai** (NIL-gī) *n.*, a large Indian antelope; also called a blue bull

ni-lom-e-ter (nī-LAHM-ĕd-ĕr) *n.*, a scale etched in rock or stone that measures the level of the Nile river, especially during floods

ni-mi-e-ty (ni-MĪ-ĕd-ee) *n.*, an excess; an overabundance

nim-i-ny-pim-i-ny (NIM-ĭ-nee-PIM-ĭ-nee) *adj.*, finicky

nim-mer (NIM-ĕr) *n.*, a petty thief in the northern U.S.

nim-shi (NIM(P)-shee) *n.*, a northern U.S. term for a foolish person

nip-cheese (NIP-cheez) *n.*, a slang term for a miser

\a\ bat \ä\ about \e\ or \è\ check \ĕ\ letter \é\ cafe \i\fish \ī\ tie \ĭ\ limit \o\ boat \ŏ\ bacon \u\ sun \ŭ\ helpful \ü\ fool

nip·per·kin (NIP-ĕ(r)-kĭn) *n.*, a liquor container that holds a half-pint or less

nip·ter (NIP-tĕr) *n.*, the Eastern Orthodox foot-washing ceremony performed on Holy Thursday

ni·si (NĪ-sī) or (NEE-see) *adj.*, pending

ni·sus (NĪ-sŭs) *n.*, a striving; an inclination

ni·val (NĪ-văl) *adj.*, associated with snow

nix·ie (NIK-see) *n.*, mail with an incorrect or illegible address

ni·zam (nĕ-ZAHM) or (nĭ-ZAM) *n.*, 1. an Indian ruler 2. a Turkish soldier

nob·ble (NAH-bĕl) *v.*, a British term meaning to disable race horses, especially through drugging

no·cake (NOH-cayk) *n.*, dried and powdered Indian corn

no·cent (NOH-sĕnt) *adj.*, harming or causing harm

noc·tiv·a·ga·tion (nahk-tiv-ă-GAY-shŏn) *n.*, roving after dark

noc·tu·ar·y (NAHK-chŭ-wer-ee) *n.*, a journal of incidents that occur at night

nod·dy (NAHD-dee) *n.*, a stupid person or fool

no·dose (noh-DOHS) or **no·dous** (NOH-dŭs) *adj.*, having many or noticeable bulges; knobbed

no·dus (NOH-dŭs) *n.*, 1. a complication 2. a central point

no·e·ma·tach·o·graph (noh-ee-mă-TAK-ŏ-graf) *n.*, a device used to measure reaction time

no·e·sis (noh-EE-sĭs) *n.*, a Greek philosophical term for reasoning

noi·some (NOI-sŏm) *adj.*, 1. unwholesome; destructive 2. offensive to the senses

no·li·tion (noh-LI-shŏn) *n.*, unwillingness

no·man·cy (NOH-măn(t)-see) *n.*, predicting the future by using letters

nom·arch (NAH-mahrk) *n.*, the chief administrator of a province in ancient Egypt or in modern Greece

nom·bril (NAHM-brĭl) *n.*, the center point or navel of the lower half of a shield bearing a coat of arms

nom·ic (NAHM-ik) or (NOHM-ik) *adj.*, valid or customary

no·mism (NOH-mizĕm) *n.*, the belief that moral law constitutes the basis of ethical or religious conduct

no·mog·ra·pher (noh-MAHG-ră-fĕr) *n.*, a person who writes or makes laws

no·na (NOH-nă) *n.*, sleeping sickness

non·age (NAHN-ij) or (NOHN-ij) *n.*, 1. the period of being a minor 2. any period of immaturity

no·ol·o·gy (noh-AHL-ŏ-jee) *n.*, 1. the study of the mind 2. the science of purely mental phenomena

no·o·scop·ic (noh-ŏ-SKAHP-ik) *adj.*, pertaining to the examination of the mind

no·ri·a (NOH-ree-ă) *n.*, a Persian device made of a wheel with a series of buckets that is used to raise water in Spain and the Orient

nos-ism (NOH-sizĕm) or (NAH-sizĕm) *n.*, an archaic term for the arrogance or pride of a group of individuals

no-sol-o-gy (noh-SAHL-ŏ-jee) *n.*, a branch of medical science concerned with the systematic classification of diseases

nos-o-pho-bi-a (nos-ĕ-FOH-bee-ă) *n.*, an abnormal fear of disease

nos-toc (NAH-stahk) *n.*, a type of blue-green algae that lives on damp ground or in the water

nos-tol-o-gy (no-STOL-ŏ-jee) *n.*, the science of caring for the elderly

nos-to-ma-ni-a (nos-tĕ-MAY-nee-ă) *n.*, intense homesickness

nou-me-non (NOO-mĕ-nahn) or (NOW-mĕ-non) *n.*, a philosophical term for an object inaccessible to direct experience, but understood through reason alone

no-vate (NOH-vayt) *v.*, to replace a previous duty or responsibility with a new one

no-ver-cal (nŏ-VĔR-kăl) *adj.*, pertaining to a stepmother

no-yade (nwah-YAHD) or (nwī-AHD) *n.*, a death penalty exacted by drowning or the simultaneous drowning of many people

n-rit-ya (en-RIT-yă) *n.*, a traditional dance of southern India that tells a story

nu-cha (N(Y)OO-kă) *n.*, 1. an obsolete term for the spinal cord 2. the rear part of an insect's middle section

nu-gac-i-ty (n(y)oo-GAS-ĭd-ee) *n.*, a triviality

nu-ga-to-ry (N(Y)OO-gă-toh-ree) or (N(Y)OO-gă-taw-ree) *adj.*, 1. worthless 2. invalid

nul-lah or **nul-la** (NŬ-lă) *n.*, an often-dry watercourse; a gully

nul-li-bic-i-ty (nŭ-lĭ-BIS-ĕd-ee) or **nul-li-bi-e-ty** (nŭ-lĭ-BĪ-ed-ee) *n.*, the condition or attribute of being nowhere

nul-li-fid-i-an (nŭ-lĭ-FID-ee-ăn) *n.*, a person who has neither faith nor religion; a skeptic

nul-lip-a-rous (nŭ-LIP-ă-rŭs) *adj.*, having never borne a child

num-bles or **nom-bles** (NŬM-bĕlz) *n.*, edible animal organs

nu-men (N(Y)OO-mĕn) *n.*, 1. a diety, especially one believed to inhabit a natural object or phenomenon 2. a genius

num-mu-lar (NŬM-yŭ-lăr) *adj.*, 1. circular- or oval-shaped 2. having circular or oval sores

nun-cheon (NUUN-shĕn) or **nunch** (NUUNSH) *n.*, English dialect for a light snack of bread, cheese, and beer

nun-cu-pate (NŬNG-kyŭ-payt) *v.*, to proclaim to the public

nun-di-nal (NŬN-dĭ-năl) *adj.*, of or relating to the market day held every ninth day according to ancient Roman custom

\a\ bat \ă\ about \e\ or \ĕ\ check \ĕ\ letter
\é\ cafe \i\fish \ī\ tie \ī\ limit \o\ boat
\ŏ\ bacon \u\ sun \ŭ\ helpful \ü\ fool

nu-ta-tion (n(y)oo-TAY-shŏn) *n.*, 1. the involuntary nodding of the head 2. a balancing motion of the earth's axis like the nodding of a top due to the combined gravitation of sun and moon

nu-tri-cism (N(Y)OO-trĭ-sizĕm) *n.*, a system of biological coexistence in which one organism is fed or protected without being of benefit to the other

nuz-zer (NŬZ-ĕr) *n.*, a ceremonial offering in India

nya-la (NYAH-lä) *n.*, a shaggy antelope of mountainous eastern central Africa

ny-an-za (nee-AN-ză) *n.*, a large body of water or lake in central and East Africa

nych-them-er-on or **nyc-them-er-on** (nik-THEM-ĕ-rahn) *n.*, the full day-and-night period

nyc-ta-lo-pi-a (NIK-tă-loh-pee-ă) *n.*, the inability to see in dim light or at night

nym-pho-lep-sy (NIM(P)-fŏ-lep-see) *n.*, 1. a type of devilish enthusiasm that the ancients believed resulted from possession or bewitchment by a beautiful female god 2. an emotional frenzy

oam (OHM) *n.*, a Scottish term for warm, misty air

oat-er (OHD-ĕr) *n.*, a Western movie or television or radio show; a "horse opera"

ob-duce (ahb-D(Y)OOS) *v.*, to enclose

o-be-ah (OH-bee-ă) or **o-bi** (OH-bee) *n.*, a charm used in the sorcery and magic rituals practiced by blacks of the West Indies, the Guianas, and southeastern United States

o-bex (OH-beks) *n.*, 1. an obstacle 2. a thin, triangular layer of gray matter in the roof of the fourth ventricle of the brain

ob-jur-gate (AHB-jŭ(r)-gayt) *v.*, to condemn officially or publicly

ob-last (ah-BLAST) *n.*, a subdivision of the U.S.S.R. that corresponds to an autonomous province or state and enables government

ob-la-tion (ŏ-BLAY-shŏn) *n.*, an inanimate religious or ritualistic offering that substitutes for a sacrifice of living things

ob-lec-ta-tion (ah-blek-TAY-shŏn) *n.*, a pleasure or a satisfaction

ob-mu-tes-cence (ahb-myŭ-TES-ĕn(ts)) *n.*, the act of becoming unable to speak or of keeping silent

ob-nu-bi-late (ahb-N(Y)OO-bĭ-layt) *v.*, 1. to obstruct vision as if by clouds 2. to befog or confuse

ob-ol (AHB-ŏl) or (OHB-ŏl) *n.*, 1. an ancient Greek unit of weight 2. an ancient Greek coin worth 1/5 of a drachma

o-bole (AH-bohl) *n.*, a small, medieval French coin

ob-rep-tion (ah-BREP-shŏn) *n.*, a term for fraudulently obtaining dispensation from church authority or a gift from a ruler

ob-ro-gate (AHB-rŏ-gayt) *v.*, to alter or nullify a law by enacting a new one

ob-ro-tund (AHB-rŏ-tŭnd) *adj.*, being nearly cylindrical, but having one diameter that exceeds the other

ob-se-crate (AHB-sĕ-krayt) *v.*, an archaic term meaning to beg

ob-sid-i-o-nal (ŏb-SĪD-ee-ŏ-năl) *adj.*, 1. pertaining to a siege 2. of a piece of money issued for a siege

ob-sig-na-tion (ahb-sig-NAY-shŏn) *n.*, an official ratification such as that conferred with an official seal

ob-ten-e-brate (ahb-TEN-ĕ-brayt) *v.*, to darken by shadowing

ob-test (ahb-TEST) *v.*, 1. to beg 2. to witness

ob-tund (ahb-TŬND) *v.*, to lessen the violence of; to dull

ob-tu-rate (AHB-t(y)ŭ-rayt) *v.*, to obstruct or shut

ob-ven-tion (ahb-VEN-chŏn) *n.*, something that occurs casually, as a passing advantage

ob-vo-lute (AHB-vŏ-loot) *adj.*, twisted together; coiled

ob-volve (ahb-VAHLV) *v.*, an archaic term meaning to wrap

o-ca or **o-ka** (OH-kă) *n.*, a South American wood sorrel cultivated for its edible, fleshy root

oc-ci-sion (ahk-SI-zhŏn) *n.*, a slaughter

o-cel-lat-ed (oh-SE-layd-ĕd) *adj.*, having or resembling simple eyes or eyelike spots

och-le-sis (ok-LEE-sis) *n.*, any disease caused by overpopulation

och-loc-ra-cy (ahk-LAHK-ră-see) *n.*, government by the mob

o-co-ti-llo (oh-kŏ-TEE-(y)oh) *n.*, 1. a shrub of southwestern United States and Mexico with thorny branches and clusters of scarlet flowers 2. a gray Mexican shrub used for making charcoal

oc-tan (OK-tăn) *adj.*, of a fever that occurs every eighth day

oc-to-na-ry (AHK-tŏ-ne-ree) *n.*, a stanza or group of eight verses

oc-troy (AHK-troi) *v.*, to authorize as a privilege

od (AHD) *n.*, a natural power once believed to reside in certain individuals or things and to underlie hypnotism, magnetism, and other phenomena

o-de-um (oh-DEE-ŭm) *n.*, 1. a small, ancient Greek or Roman theater in which music and poetry competitions were held for the public 2. a contemporary performing arts hall

o-do-nate (OH-dŏn-ayt) *n.*, a dragonfly

o-don-tal-gi-a (oh-dahn-TAL-j(ee)-ă) *n.*, a toothache

o-don-toid (oh-DAHN-toid) *adj.*, toothlike

\a\ bat \ă\ about \e\ or \è\ check \ĕ\ letter
\é\ cafe \i\fish \ī\ tie \ĭ\ limit \o\ boat
\ŏ\ bacon \u\ sun \ŭ\ helpful \ü\ fool

o-dor-i-vec-tor (OH-dahr-ĭ-vek-tŏr) *n.*, a substance that produces an odor

oe-cist (EE-sĭst) *n.*, one who colonizes

oeil-lade (ĕ(r)-YAHD) *n.*, a glance of the eye

oe-no-mel (EE-nŏ-mel) *n.*, an ancient Greek drink of wine and honey

oer-sted (ĔR-sted) *n.*, an electromagnetic unit of intensity

oes-trum (ES-trŭm) *n.*, a recurrent state of sexual excitability during which the female of most mammals will mate and conceive

og-do-ad (AHG-doh-ad) *n.*, 1. a Gnostic term for a group of eight eternal beings 2. a group of or the number eight

o-gee (oh-JEE) or (OH-jee) *n.*, a molding with an S-shaped profile

og-ham or **og-am** (AH-gŭm) *n.*, an old Irish alphabetic system that used lines and notches as symbols and appeared as inscriptions on memorial stones

o-gy-gi-an (oh-JI-jee-ŭn) *adj.*, ancient; primeval

oi-ti-ci-ca (oid-ĭ-SEE-kǎ) *n.*, a Brazilian tree whose pecanlike fruit yields an oil used in varnishes, paints, and printing inks

o-ka-pi (oh-KAH-pee) *n.*, an African mammal smaller than an ox that resembles a short-necked giraffe

old-wench (OHLD-wench) *n.*, a triggerfish found in tropical Atlantic and Indian Ocean waters

o-le-ate (OH-lee-ayt) *n.*, a salt used in making soaps and detergents

o-le-fin (OH-lĕ-fĕn) *n.*, a hydrocarbon with at least one double bond

o-lent (OH-lĕnt) *adj.*, an archaic term meaning having an odor

o-lib-a-num (oh-LIB-ă-nŭm) *n.*, frankincense

ol-id (AHL-ĭd) *adj.*, having a noxious smell

ol-i-goph-a-gous (ahl-ĭ-GAHF-ă-gŭs) *adj.*, eating only a few specific kinds of foods, especially in regard to an insect

ol-i-go-phre-ni-a (ahl-ĭ-goh-FREE-nee-ă) or (ŏ-lig-ŏ-FREE-nee-ă) *n.*, feeblemindedness

ol-i-gu-ri-a (ahl-ĭ-G(Y)UU-ree-a) *n.*, a condition marked by reduced excretion of urine

ol-i-to-ry (AHL-ĕ-toh-ree) *adj.*, associated with a home garden

ol-i-vet (AHL-ĭ-vet) *n.*, a fake pearl, especially one made for trading with primitive African peoples

ol-i-vine (AHL-ĭ-veen) *n.*, a mineral consisting of a silicate of magnesium and iron 2. a light greenish yellow

ol-la (AHL-ă) or (AW(L)-yă) *n.*, a large earthenware jar 2. a soup or stew

ol-la po-dri-da (ahl-ă-pŏ-DREE-dă) *n.*, 1. a soup or stew cooked in an olla 2. a hodgepodge

ol-pe (AHL-pee) *n.*, an ancient Greek leather flask for liquids; an ancient Greek wine pitcher

om-brol-o-gy (ahm-BRAHL-ŏ-jee) *n.*, a branch of meteorology concerned with rain

om-brom-e-ter (ahm-BRAHM-ĕd-ĕr) *n.*, a device that measures rainfall

om-broph-i-lous (ahm-BRAH-fĭ-lŭs) *adj.*, relating to a plant that can thrive in a lot of rain

om-broph-o-bous (ahm-BRAH-fŏ-bŭs) *adj.*, relating to a plant that cannot survive long-continued rain

o-mer (OH-mĕr) *n.*, an ancient Hebrew dry measurement unit

om-ne-i-ty (ahm-NEE-ĭd-ee) *n.*, the state of being complete

om-ni-far-i-ous (ahm-nĭ-FA(A)-ree-ŭs) *adj.*, of all kinds

om-nil-e-gent (AHM-nil-ĕ-jĕnt) *adj.*, being very well read

om-nist (AHM-nĭst) *n.*, one who believes in all faiths

o-mo-pha-gi-a (oh-mŏ-FAY-jee-ă) *n.*, the eating of raw flesh or raw food

o-moph-a-gist (oh-MOF-ă-jist) *n.*, a person who eats raw flesh or food

om-o-pla-tos-co-py (ohm-oh-plă-TAHS-kŏ-pee) *n.*, predicting the future by using a shoulder blade, usually one blotched or cracked from a fire

om-pha-cite (AHM(P)-fă-sīt) *n.*, a mineral

om-pha-lo-skep-sis (ahm(p)-fă-loh-SKEP-sĭs) *n.*, the contemplation of one's navel to induce a mental trance

on-a-ger (AHN-ă-jĕ(r)) *n.*, 1. a small, pale-colored Asiatic wild ass 2. a medieval war machine that threw stones

o-na-nism (OH-nă-nizem) *n.*, 1. the interruption of sexual intercourse 2. masturbation

on-cid-i-um (ahn-SID-ee-ŭm) *n.*, a showy tropical American orchid

o-nei-ric (oh-NĪ-rik) *adj.*, pertaining to dreams

o-nei-ro-crit-ic (oh-NĪ-roh-krid-ik) *n.*, a dream interpreter

o-ni-o-ma-ni-a (ohn-ee-oh-MAY-nee-ă) *n.*, an uncontrollable urge to buy things

on-o-mas-ti-con (ahn-ŏ-MAS-tĭ-kahn) *n.*, 1. a listing of words, especially those used in a specialized field 2. a collection of proper names or places

on-o-ma-to-ma-ni-a (ahn-ŏ-mad-ŏ-MAY-nee-ă) *n.*, an obsession with language, especially the repetition of certain words or sounds

on-tic (AHN-tik) or **on-tal** (AHN-tăl) *adj.*, pertaining to or having real being or existence

on-y-choph-a-gy (ahn-ĭ-KAHF-ă-jee) *n.*, the habit of nail biting

o-o (OH-oh) *n.*, a Hawaiian bird, especially one hunted to extinction for its feathers

o-o-a-a (OH-oh-AH-ah) *n.*, a Hawaiian honeyeater bird found only on the island of Kauai

---

\a\ **bat** \ă\ **about** \e\ **or** \ė\ **check** \ē\ **letter** \é\ **cafe** \i\ **fish** \ī\ **tie** \i\ **limit** \o\ **boat** \ŏ\ **bacon** \u\ **sun** \ŭ\ **helpful** \ü\ **fool**

o-o-cyte (OH-ŏ-sīt) *n.*, an egg before maturation

o-og-a-my (oh-AHG-ă-mee) *n.*, reproduction by the fusion of a small, active sperm with the larger, relatively immobile egg

o-oid (OH-oid) *adj.*, egg-shaped

o-ol-o-gy (oh-AHL-ŏ-jee) *n.*, a branch of zoology concerned with bird's eggs

oont (UUNT) *n.*, an Indian term for a camel

o-o-phyte (OH-ŏ-fīt) *n.*, the growth stage in which the sexual organs of a moss, fern, or liverwort develop

o-pa-cate (oh-PAY-kayt) or (OH-pă-kayt) *v.*, to make opaque; to darken or dim

o-per-cu-lum (oh-PĔR-kyŭ-lŭm) *n.*, a lid or flap

oph-e-lim-i-ty (ahf-ĕ-LIM-ĭd-ee) or (OHF-ĕ-lim-ĭd-ee) *n.*, economic gratification

o-phi-cleide (AH-fĭ-klīd) or (OH-fĭ-klīd) *n.*, 1. a deep-toned, brass wind instrument 2. an organ reed stop

oph-i-o-lo-gy (ah-fee-AH-lŏ-jee) or **oph-i-dol-o-gy** (ah-fĭ-DAH-lŏ-jee) *n.*, the study of snakes

o-phite (AH-fīt) *n.*, a type of green, blotched rock such as serpentine marble

o-pip-a-rous (oh-PIP-ă-rŭs) *adj.*, an archaic term meaning lavish

o-pis-the-nar (ŏ-PIS-thĕ-nahr) *n.*, the back part of the hand

o-pis-tho-graph (ŏ-PIS-thĕ-graf) *n.*, an ancient manuscript with writing or inscriptions on both sides

op-pi-dan (AH-pĭ-dăn) *n.*, 1. a person who lives in a town 2. an obsolete term for a nonstudent who lives in a university town

op-pig-no-rate or **op-pig-ne-rate** (ŏ-PIG-nŏ-rayt) *v.*, an archaic term meaning to pawn

op-pi-late (AH-pĭ-layt) *v.*, an archaic term meaning to block or obstruct

op-pug-nant (ŏ-PŬG-nănt) *adj.*, hostile; antagonistic

op-si-math-y (ahp-sĭ-MATH-ee) *n.*, the condition of beginning to learn late in life

o-pun-ti-a (oh-PŬN-ch(ee)-ă) *n.*, a prickly pear cactus found in America

o-pus-cule (oh-PŬ-skyool) or **o-pus-cle** (oh-PŬS-ĕl) *n.*, a minor work, as in literature

o-quas-sa (oh-KWAH-să) *n.*, a small, dark blue trout found in the Rangeley lakes in Maine

or-ache or **or-ach** (AWR-ăch) *n.*, an Asian herb like spinach that is used as greens or as a food seasoning

o-rad (OHR-ad) or (AW-rad) *adv.*, toward the mouth

o-rant (OHR-ant) or **o-ran-te** (oh-RAN-tee) *n.*, a female figure in ancient Greek art

o-ra-ri-on (aw-RAH-ree-ŏn) or **o-ra-ri-um** (oh-RA(A)-ree-ŭm) *n.*, a deacon's stole in the Eastern Orthodox Church

orc (AW(E)RK) or (AW(E)K) *n.*, 1. a member of the whale family 2. a mythical sea monster, giant, or ogre

or·chi·dec·to·my (aw(r)-kĭ-DEK-tŏ-mee) or **or·chi·ec·to·my** (aw(r)-kee-EK-tŏ-mee) *n.*, the surgical removal of a testicle

or·chi·tis (aw(r)-KĪD-ĭs) *n.*, an inflammation of the testicles

or·dure (AWR-jĕr) *n.*, 1. excrement 2. something that is morally degrading

o·re·ad (OH-ree-ad) *n.*, a mythological term for a mountain nymph

o·rec·tic (oh-REK-tik) *adj.*, pertaining to the desires

or·ga·non (AW(R)-gă-nahn) *n.*, a tool for acquiring or communicating knowledge

or·gu·lous (AW(R)-g(y)ŭ-lŭs) or **or·gil·lous** (AW(R)-gĭl-lŭs) *adj.*, 1. arrogant; haughty 2. ostentatious; splendid

or·i·bi (AWR-ĭ-bee) or **ou·re·bi** (UU-rĭ-bee) *n.*, a small, straight-horned antelope from southern and eastern Africa

o·ri·el (OH-ree-ĕl) or (AWR-ee-ĕl) *n.*, a large, semihexagonal or semisquare bay window that projects out from a wall

o·ri·en·cy (OH-ree-ĕn-see) *n.*, the state of being lustrous

or·i·flamme (AWR-ĭ-flam) or (AHR-ĭ-flam) *n.*, a banner or symbol that inspires loyalty or courage

o·ri·gan (AW-rĭ-găn) *n.*, the Old World wild marjoram

or·is·mol·o·gy (awr-ĭz-MAHL-ŏ-jee) or (ahr-ĭz-MAHL-ŏ-jee) *n.*, the science of providing definitions for technical terms

or·i·son (AWR-ĭ-sŏn) *n.*, a prayer or mystical contemplation

orle (awr(e)l) *n.*, 1. a term in heraldry for the small figures that form an inside border of a shield 2. the wreath on the knight's helmet that bears the crest

or·lop (AWR-lahp) *n.*, the lowest deck on a ship

or·mer (AWR-měr) *n.*, an abalone

or·mo·lu (AW(R)-mŏ-loo) *n.*, 1. an archaic term for gold used in gilding 2. brass made to imitate gold and used for decoration 3. something pretending to be more than its actual worth

or·ni·tho·cop·ros (aw(r)-nĭ-thoh-KAH-prŏs) *n.*, bird dung

or·ni·tho·rhyn·chus (aw(r)-ni-thŏ-RING-kŭs) *n.*, the egg-laying platypus

or·ni·troph·i·lous (aw(r)-nĭ-TRAH-fi-lŭs) *adj.*, liking birds

o·rol·o·gy (aw-RAHL-ŏ-jee) *n.*, the study of mountains

o·ro·tund (AW-rŏ-tŭnd) or (AH-ro-tŭnd) *adj.*, 1. characterized by fullness, strength, and clearness of voice or speech 2. unduly full and strong in delivery and style

orp (AWRP) *v.*, a Scottish term meaning to fret or sob morosely

or·phrey or **or·fray** or **or·frey** (AWR-free) *n.*, 1. embellished embroidery 2. an ornamental border on an ecclesiastical vestment

\a\ bat \ā\ about \e\ or \ě\ check \ē\ letter \é\ cafe \i\fish \ī\ tie \ĭ\ limit \o\ boat \ŏ\ bacon \u\ sun \ŭ\ helpful \ü\ fool

or-re-ry (AW-rĕ-ree) or (AH-rĕ-ree) *n.*, an apparatus of balls and wheels that represents the solar system

ort (AW(E)RT) *n.*, 1. a morsel remaining from a meal 2. a scrap

or-thi-con (AW(R)-thĭ-kahn) *n.*, a sensitive camera tube in videos

or-tho-dro-mics (aw(r)-thŏ-DRAH-miks) *n.*, the act or art of navigating a ship on a circular course

or-tho-e-py (AW(R)-thŏ-we-pee) or (aw(r)-THOH-ĕ-pee) *n.*, 1. the usual pronunciation of a language 2. the study of a language's pronunciation

or-thog-o-nal (aw(r)-THAHG-ŏ-näl) *n.*, an oceanographic term for an imaginary line at right angles to wave crests

or-thop-ter (aw(r)-THAHP-tĕr) *n.*, a mechanical bird

or-to-lan (AW(R)-dŏ-lăn) *n.*, a European bird related to the finch considered a table delicacy

o-ryc-tol-o-gy (ŏ-rik-TAHL-ŏ-jee) or (ohr-ik-TAHL-ŏ-jee) *n.*, the study of minerals

or-y-ziv-o-rous (awr-ĕ-ZIV-(ŏ)-rŭs) *adj.*, rice-feeding

os-cine (AHS-ĭn) or (AH-sĭn) *adj.*, relating to a family of perching birds with well-developed vocal organs

os-ci-tan-cy (AH-sĭd-ăn-see) *n.*, a drowsiness usually indicated by yawning

os-ci-ta-tion (ah-sĭ-TAY-shŏn) *n.*, 1. the act of not being attentive 2. the state of being drowsy

os-cu-late (AHS-kyŭ-layt) *v.*, 1. to kiss 2. a mathematical term meaning to have characters in common with two sets

os-cu-lum (AHS-kyŭ-lŭm) *n.*, a small, mouthlike opening like that of a sponge

ose (OHS) *n.*, a long, narrow ridge or mound of sand, gravel, and boulders deposited between ice walls

o-sier (OH-zhĕ(r)) *n.*, 1. a type of willow used to make wicker furniture or baskets 2. an American dogwood tree

os-ma-gogue (AHZ-mă-gahg) *adj.*, exciting to the sense of smell

os-mund also **os-mond** (AHZ-mŭnd) *n.*, a high-quality iron made in Sweden and used for making fishhooks and clockworks

os-phre-sis (ahs-FREE-sĭs) *n.*, the sense of smell

osse (AHS) *n.*, an obsolete term for a prophetic or forboding utterance

os-si-a (oh-SEE-ă) *conj.*, a term meaning or else used as a musical direction to indicate an alternative and usually simpler passage

os-su-ary (AH-shŭ-we-ree) *n.*, 1. a depository for bones 2. a communal burial spot

os-ti-a-ry (AHS-tee-ă-ree) *n.*, 1. a doorkeeper 2. an obsolete term for the mouth of a river

ost-mark (AWST-mahrk) *n.*, a monetary unit of East Germany

os-tre-oph-a-gous (ahs-tree-AHF-ă-gŭs) *adj.*, feeding on oysters

ot·a·cou·stic (ohd-ă-KOO-stik) *adj.*, aiding the sense of hearing

o·tal·gi·a (oh-TAL-j(ee)-ă) *n.*, an earache

o·ther·gates (Ŏ-thĕr-gayts) *adv.*, U.S. dialect meaning in a different manner

o·to·sis (oh-TOH-sĭs) *n.*, the misunderstanding of spoken sounds or an alteration of words because of such misunderstanding

ouch (OWCH) *n.*, 1. an obsolete term for a garment clasp or brooch 2. a setting for a precious stone 3. jewelry

oud (OOD) *n.*, an Arabian musical instrument that resembles a mandolin

ouph or **ouphe** (OWF) or (OOF) *n.*, an elf

ou·rie (OO-ri) *adj.*, 1. a Scottish term meaning depressing 2. a Scottish term meaning shivering

out·fang·thief (OWT-făng-theef) *n.*, a medieval English law term for the right of a lord to try a thief or felon who dwells in his manor but was caught outside it

out·li·er (OWT-lī-ĕr) *n.*, 1. one who sleeps outside or away from his business location 2. an animal not in its fold or enclosure

ou·tre·cuid·ance (ood-ĕ(r)-KWEED-ăn(t)s) *n.*, extreme vanity; presumption

ou·zel or **ou·sel** (OO-zĕl) *n.*, a European blackbird

o·vip·a·rous (oh-VIP-ă-rŭs) *adj.*, making eggs that develop and hatch outside the body

o·vo·vi·vip·a·rous (oh-voh-vĭ-VIP-(ă)-rŭs) *adj.*, producing eggs that develop inside the body and hatch within or immediately after expulsion from the parent

ow·el·ty (OH-ĕl-tee) *n.*, 1. equality 2. a payment made to achieve equality between two people who exchange property

ox·lip (AHK-slip) *n.*, a primrose

ox·peck·er (AHKS-pek-ĕr) *n.*, an African bird that feeds on ticks picked from the backs of animals

oy·er (OI-ĕr) *n.*, a criminal trial

o·zo·sto·mi·a (oh-zŏ-STOH-mee-ă) *n.*, foul breath

P

pa·ca (PAH-kă) or (PA-kă) *n.*, a large South and Central American rodent with white spots

pa·chin·ko (pă-CHING-koh) *n.*, a Japanese gambling machine similar to pinball

pach·ou·li or **patch·ou·li** or **patch·ou·ly** (PACH-ĕ-lee) or (pă-CHOO-lee) *n.*, an East Indian shrub mint that yields an aromatic oil

pach·y·ce·pha·li·a (pak-ă-se-FAY-lee-ă) or **pach·y·ceph·a·ly** (pak-ă-SEF-ă-lee) *n.*, head or skull thickness

pa-dauk or **pa-douk** (pă-DOWK) *n.*, an Asian tree with reddish wood that is similar to mahogany

pad-nag (PAD-nag) *n.*, a horse that moves at an easy pace

pad-u-a-soy (PAJ-ŭ-wă-soi) *n.*, a smooth, heavy silk fabric used for clothing and upholstery

pa-gle or **pai-gle** (PAY-gel) *n.*, English dialect for a cowslip or an oxslip plant

pa-gu-ri-an (pă-GYUU-ree-ăn) *n.*, a hermit crab

pa-ho-e-ho-e (pa-HOH-ee-hoh-ee) *n.*, cooled, hard lava that has a smooth, bright surface

pail-lette or **pai-lette** (pĭ-(Y)ET) or (pah-YET) *n.*, 1. small, shiny spangles, sequins, beads, or jewels applied in clusters as decorative trimming 2. a fabric woven or treated to give a spangled effect

pa-laes-tra or **pa-les-tra** (pă-LES-tra) *n.*, 1. in ancient Greece or Rome, a kind of gymnasium 2. athletic exercise, especially wrestling

pa-lae-ti-ol-o-gy (pă-LEED-ee-ahl-lă-jee) *n.*, the explanation of past events by causation

pal-a-fitte (PAL-ă-fit) or (PAL-ă-feet) *n.*, an ancient dwelling built on piles over a lake

pal-a-mate (PAL-ă-măt) or (PAL-ă-mayt) *adj.*, web-footed

pa-lan-quin (PA-len-keen) or **pal-an-keen** (PAL-ăn-keen) *n.*, an eastern Asian term for a transport vehicle carried on men's shoulders

pal-e-tot (PAL-ĕ-toh) or (PAL-toh) *n.*, a man's overcoat

pal-fre-nier (pawl-frĕ-NI(Ĕ)R) *n.*, an archaic term for a person who feeds, grooms, and stables horses

pal-frey (PAWL-free) *n.*, an archaic term for a saddle horse, especially one suitable for a lady

pal-i-kar or **pal-i-car** (PAL-ĭ-kahr) *n.*, 1. a mercenary of the sultan of Turkey 2. a Greek militiaman in the war of independence against Turkey

pal-i-la-li-a (pal-ĭ-LAY-lee-ă) or (pal-ĭ-LAY-lyă) *n.*, a speech defect in which the speaker repeats syllables, words, or sentences excessively

pal-imp-sest (PAL-ĭm(p)-sest) *n.*, a reusable piece of writing material such as a parchment or a tablet

pal-in-drome (PAL-ĭn-drohm) *n.*, a word, verse, sentence, or number that's the same backward or forward

pal-in-gen-e-sis (pal-ĭn-JEN-ĕ-sĭs) *n.*, 1. renewal or rebirth, such as by a Christian baptism 2. the creation of new rock by the refusion of old rocks deep within the earth

pal-in-ode (PAL-ĭ-nohd) *n.*, 1. a song that recants or retracts something in an earlier one 2. a retraction

pal-lette (PAL-ĕt) *n.*, the round plate at the armpit of a suit of armor

pal-liard (PAL-yĕ(r)d) *n.*, an archaic term for a rascal

pal-lion (PAL-yĕn) *n.*, a little piece or pellet

pal-ma-ry (PAL-mă-ree) or (PAHM-ă-ree) *adj.*, worthy of praise; outstanding

pal·mate (PAL-mayt) or (PAH-mayt) *adj.*, in the shape of a hand with the fingers spread

palm·er (PAH-měr) *n.*, a person who wears two crossed palm leaves to indicate completion of a pilgrimage to the Holy Land, especially during the Middle Ages

pal·mette (pal-MET) *n.*, an ornament of ancient origin that resembles an Egyptian lotus

pal·pe·bral (PAL-pě-brăl) *adj.*, pertaining to the eyelid

pal·ter (PAWL-te(r)) *v.*, 1. to act without sincerity 2. to bargain in order to create a delay or compromise

pa·lu·dal (pă-LOO-dăl) or (PAL-yŭd-ăl) *adj.*, marshy

pam (PAM) or (PA(Ě)M) *n.*, 1. the jack of clubs 2. a card game in which the jack of clubs is the highest trump card

pam·pe·ro (pam-PE-roh) *n.*, a strong, cold wind that sweeps over the prairies of South America

pam·poo·tie (pam-POOD-ee) *n.*, a shoe worn in the Aran islands of Ireland

pa·na·da (pă-NAH-dă) or (pă-NAY-dă) *n.*, a bread boiled in milk, broth, or water until pulpy 2. a paste used as a sauce base or as a thickener for a stuffing

pan·dect (PAN-dekt) *n.*, 1. a complete code of laws 2. a manuscript containing the entire Bible

pan·dic·u·la·tion (pan-dik-yŭ-LAY-shŏn) *n.*, a stretching and stiffening of the muscles, as when tired or sleepy

pan·dour (PAN-duu(ě)r) *n.*, a member of a Croatian regiment known for its cruelty in the 18th-century Austrian army

pan·du·rate (PAN-d(y)ŭ-răt) or (PAN-dŭ-rayt) *adj.*, fiddlelike; fiddle-shaped

pan·dy (PAN-di) *n.*, British dialect for a hit on the hand with a cane or stick

pan·ga (PAHNG-gă) *n.*, an African term for a machete

pa·niv·o·rous (pa-NIV-ěr-ŭs) *adj.*, living on bread

pan·nage or **pan·age** (PAN-ij) *n.*, 1. the act of pasturing hogs in a forest or woods, as in medieval England 2. the food available to swine in the forest

pa·no·cha (pă-NOH-chă) *n.*, a Mexican raw sugar

pan·op·tic (pan-AHP-tik) *adj.*, 1. all-inclusive 2. allowing everything to be seen

pan·sex·u·al·ism (PAN-sek-sh(ěw)-ă-lizěm) *n.*, the idea that all desire and interest arises from the sex drive

pan·tag·a·my (pan-TAG-ă-mee) *n.*, a type of marriage found in some communes in which every man is thought to be the husband of every woman and vice versa

pan·ta·gru·el·ism (pan-tă-GROO-ě-lizěm) *n.*, cynical humor

pan·tech·ni·con (pan-TEK-nĭ-kŏn) or (pan-TEK-nĭ-kahn) *n.*, a British term for a large warehouse

---

\a\ bat \ă\ about \e\ or \ě\ check \ě\ letter
\é\ cafe \i\fish \ī\ tie \i\ limit \o\ boat
\ŏ\ bacon \u\ sun \ŭ\ helpful \ü\ fool

pan-to-fle or **pan-tof-fle** (PAN-tŏ-fĕl) or (pan-TAHF-ĕl) *n.*, 1. a bedroom slipper 2. a woman's stiltlike shoe used as an overshoe in the 16th century

pan-toph-a-gous (pan-TAHF-ă-gŭs) *adj.*, eating or requiring a variety of foods

pan-urge (pan-URJ) *n.*, a rascal

pap-il-late (PAP-ĭ-layt) or (pă-PIL-ăt) *adj.*, covered with, having, or resembling nipples

pa-pi-o (PAH-pyoh) or **pa-pio-pio** (PAH-pyoh-pyoh) *n.*, a young Hawaiian fish highly prized for its food and sport value

pap-u-lif-er-ous (pap-yŭ-LIF-(ĕ)r-ŭs) *adj.*, pimply

par-a-bo-la-nus (par-ă-boh-LAH-nŭs) *n.*, a member of an early church brotherhood dedicated to the care of the sick, especially those with infectious diseases

par-a-clete (PAR-ă-kleet) *n.*, an advocate

par-a-go-ge (PAR-ă-goh-jee) *n.*, the addition of a sound or syllables to the end of a word to emphasize or change its meaning

par-a-gram (PAR-ă-gram) *n.*, a pun made by changing the letters of a word, especially its first letter

par-a-leip-sis (par-ă-LĪP-sĭs) or **par-a-lep-sis** (par-ă-LEP-sĭs) *n.*, a brief mentioning to emphasize what is not said

par-a-li-pom-en-a (par-ă-lĭ-PAHM-ĕn-ă) or (par-ă-lī-PAHM-ĕn-ă) *n.*, things left out, but added in a supplement

pa-ral-o-gism (pă-RAL-ŏ-jizĕm) *n.*, a reasoning contrary to logic

par-a-ment (PAR-ă-mĕnt) *n.*, a decorative religious tapestry or garment

pa-rang (pă-RAHNG) *n.*, a cutting blade such as a machete commonly used in Malaysia, British Borneo, and Indonesia

par-a-nymph (PAR-ă-nim(p)f) *n.*, 1. a friend who accompanied a bridegroom in ancient Greece when he brought home his bride 2. a best man or bridesmaid

par-aph (PAR-ăf) or (pă-RAF) *n.*, a flourish that ends a signature, sometimes used to prevent forgery

par-a-pher-na (par-ă-FĔR-nă) *n.*, a Roman and civil law term for a woman's property that remains hers alone after marriage

par-a-prax-i-a (par-ă-PRAK-see-ă) or **par-a-prax-is** (par-ă-PRAK-sĭs) *n.*, a blunder or mistake

par-a-sang (PAR-ă-săng) *n.*, a Persian unit of measurement, especially one approximately equal to four miles

pa-ra-shah (PAH-ră-shah) *n.*, one of the weekly lessons from the Torah read in the synagogue on the Jewish Sabbath

par-a-ton-ic (par-ă-TAHN-ik) *adj.*, resulting from outside stimuli

par-a-vane (PAR-ă-vayn) *n.*, a device towed from a ship to cut the moorings of mines

pa-rei-ra (pă-RE-ră) or (pă-RAY-ră) *n.*, a South American vine whose root is used as a diuretic, tonic, or laxative

par-en-ta-tion (pa(a)-rĕn-TAY-shŏn) *n.*, an archaic term for funeral rites for one's parents

par-get (PAHR-jĕt) *v.*, 1. to cover with plaster or ornamental plasterwork 2. to garnish with gilding or other surfacing 3. an archaic term meaning to whitewash

par-go (PAHR-goh) *n.*, a fish; also called the European porgy

par-i-sol-o-gy (par-ĭ-SAHL-ŏ-jee) *n.*, the use of ambiguous words

par-lan-do (pahr-LAHN-doh) or **par-lan-te** (pahr-LAHN-tay) *adj.*, delivered or performed in a manner suggesting speech

par-lous (PAHR-lŭs) *adj.*, 1. uncertain; dangerous 2. an obsolete term meaning dangerously shrewd or cunning

pa-rol (pa-ROHL) or (PA-rŏl) *n.*, 1. a verbal statement 2. an archaic term for the originally spoken pleadings in a law suit

par-o-no-ma-si-a (par-ŏ-noh-MAYZH-(ee)-ă) or (pă-rah-nŏ-MAYZH-(ee)-ă) *n.*, a pun

pa-ron-y-mous (pa-RAHN-ĭ-mŭs) *adj.*, 1. having the same derivation and some similarity of meaning 2. derived from a word in another language

par-o-rex-i-a (par-ă-REK-see-a) *n.*, a craving for unusual foods

pa-ro-toid (pă-ROH-toid) *adj.*, 1. looking like the salivary glands located near the ears 2. denoting certain glands that form warty masses near the ears of toads

par-rhe-si-a (pa-REE-zh(ee)-a) *n.*, boldness or freedom of speech

par-sec (PAHR-sek) *n.*, a unit of astronomical distance

par-terre (pahr-TE(Ĕ)R) *n.*, 1. a garden with beds or plots separated by paths 2. a level space with a site for a building 3. the part of the theater floor behind the orchestra

par-tu-ri-ent (pahr-TUU-ree-ĕnt) *adj.*, 1. about or in the process of giving birth 2. at the brink of producing or discovering something

par-tu-ri-fa-cient (pahr-tuu-rĭ-FAY-shĕnt) *adj.*, beginning or easing the process of birth

pa-rure (pă-RUU(E)R) *n.*, a set of matching jewelry or other ornaments worn together

pas-cu-al (PAS-kyoo-ăl) *adj.*, associated with pastures

pa-se (PAH-say) *n.*, the cape movement a matador makes to attract the bull

pash (PASH) *n.*, 1. English dialect for a heavy blow 2. a heavy rain or snow fall

pashm (PĂ-shĕm) or **pash-im** (PĂSH-eem) *n.*, the fleece from the underside of mountain goats in Kashmir and the Punjab

pa-sig-ra-phy (pă-SIG-ră-fee) *n.*, an international written language that uses signs or symbols rather than words

pas-quil (PAS-kwĕl) *n.*, 1. an unsigned lampoon posted in public 2. a political satire

---

\a\ bat \ă\ about \e\ or \è\ check \ĕ\ letter
\é\ cafe \i\fish \ī\ tie \ĭ\ limit \o\ boat
\ŏ\ bacon \u\ sun \ū\ helpful \ü\ fool

pas-quin-ade (pas-kwĕ-NAYD) *v.*, to criticize by means of satire

pas-sa-ca-gli-a (pah-să-KAHL-yă) *n.*, an instrumental composition in moderately slow triple time

pas-sant (PAS-ănt) *adj.*, 1. a term in heraldry meaning walking with the more distant forepaw raised 2. an archaic term meaning generally acceptable

pas-sim (PAS-ĭm) *adv.*, interspersed throughout

pa-ta-ca (pă-TAH-kă) *n.*, the basic monetary unit of Macao and Timor

pa-ta-gi-um (pă-TAY-jee-ŭm) *n.*, the wing membrane of tree-dwellling animals like the flying squirrel that supports them in long leaps

pat-a-mar or **pat-ta-mar** (PAD-ă-mahr) *n.*, 1. an obsolete term for a messenger 2. a sailing ship used in the trading business of Bombay and Ceylon

pat-en (PAT-ĕn) *n.*, 1. a precious metal plate used for the bread in the eucharistic service 2. a metal disk or something that looks like one

path-e-mat-ic (path-ĕ-MAD-ik) *adj.*, an archaic term meaning emotional

path-ic (PATH-ik) *n.*, 1. a boy kept for sexually deviant purposes 2. a passive person or a victim

path-og-no-my (pă-THAG-nŏ-mee) *n.*, the study of emotions or passions by their outward expressions

pa-tib-u-la-ry (pă-TIB-yŭ-le-ree) *adj.*, an archaic term meaning associated with the gallows or hanging

pat-ri-cen-tric (pa-trĭ-SEN-trik) *adj.*, gravitating toward or centered on the father

pat-ri-po-tes-tal (pa-trĭ-POH-tĕs-tăl) or (pay-trĭ-POH-tĕs-tal) *adj.*, deriving power from the father or a council of the father's relatives

pat-ro-cli-nous also **pat-ri-clin-ous** (pa-trŏ-KLĪ-nŭs) *adj.*, coming from the father or paternal line

pat-ten (PAT-ĕn) *n.*, 1. footwear used to increase the wearer's height or facilitate walking in mud 2. a British term for a wooden plate fastened to a horse's hooves to prevent them from sinking into soft ground 3. an early ice skate

pat-u-lous (PACH-ŭ-lŭs) *adj.*, widely spread apart

paughty (PAW-ti) or (PAHK-ti) *adj.*, a Scottish term for arrogant; pretentious

pa-vane (pă-VAHN) or **pav-an** (PAV-ĭn) *n.*, a ceremonial court dance for costumed couples in 16th-century Europe and England

pav-id (PAV-ĭd) *adj.*, afraid; timid

pav-is or **pav-ise** (PAV-ĕs) *n.*, a full-body shield used to protect crossbowmen and sometimes carried in front of a knight or archer

pav-o-nine (PAV-ŏ-nīn) or (PAV-ŏ-nĕn) *adj.*, pertaining to or resembling a peacock

paw-ky (PAW-ki) *adj.*, 1. a British term meaning shrewd 2. a Scottish term meaning without inhibitions 3. a Scottish term for unnecessarily fastidious

pay-nim (PAY-nĭm) *n.*, an archaic term for a pagan, especially a Muslim

peag or **peage** (PEEG) *n.*, a derivative of the Narraganset Indian term for wampum beads used by North American Indians as barter

pe-age (PAY-ij) *n.*, an archaic term for a toll paid to pass

pec-cant (PEK-ănt) *adj.*, 1. guilty of a moral wrong 2. transgressing a principle or rule 3. diseased

pec-ca-ry or **pec-a-ri** (PEK-ă-ree) *n.*, a nocturnal wild swine like a small pig found in herds ranging from Texas to Paraguay

pec-ca-to-pho-bi-a (pĕ-KAY-tŏ-FOH-bee-a) *n.*, an abnormal fear of sinning

pec-ky (PEK-ee) *adj.*, 1. marred by fungus or decay, especially lumber from trees with dry rot 2. having discolored and shriveled grains

pec-tate (PEK-tayt) *n.*, a salt of a pectic acid

pec-ti-nate (PEK-tĭ-nayt) *adj.*, comb-shaped; having projections or teeth like a comb

pec-u-late (PEK-yŭ-layt) *v.*, to embezzle

pec-u-la-tion (pek-yŭ-LAY-shŏn) *n.*, embezzlement

pe-dal-fer (pĕ-DAL-fĕ(r)) *n.*, a soil without a hardened layer of carbonates

pe-dim-a-nous (pĕ-DIM-ă-nŭs) *adj.*, 1. associated with the New World opossums 2. having the hand-shaped feet that characterizes some primates

ped-o-cal (PED-ŏ-kal) *n.*, a soil with a layer of accumulated carbonates

pe-do-don-ti-a (pee-doh-DAHN-ch(ee)-ă) *n.*, a branch of dentistry dealing with the care of children

pe-dun-cle (PEE-dŭng-kĕl) *n.*, 1. a flower 2. white matter joining parts of the brain 3. a narrow connecting stalk that attaches tumors or polyps to an organ

peery (PI-ree) or (PI-ri) *adj.*, curious; suspicious

pees-weep or **peese-weep** (PEEZ-weep) *n.*, British dialect for a crested bird with a wailing cry

peet-weet (PEE-tweet) *n.*, a spotted sandpiper

peev-er (PEE-vĕr) *n.*, a Scottish term for the stone used in playing hopscotch

pee-wit or **pe-wit** (PEE-wĭt) *n.*, 1. a crested bird, sometimes called a lapwing 2. a black-headed gull; also called a laughing gull

pei-ras-tic (pī-RAS-tik) or (pī-RAS-teek) *adj.*, experimental

pek-an (PEK-ăn) *n.*, a North American carnivorous mammal related to the marten and weasels; also called a fisher

\a\ bat \ă\ about \e\ or \ĕ\ check \ĕ\ letter \é\ cafe \i\fish \ĭ\ tie \ĭ\ limit \o\ boat \ŏ\ bacon \u\ sun \ŭ\ helpful \ü\ fool

pe-lag-ic (pĕ-LAJ-ik) or (pe-LAJ-eek) *adj.*, associated with the open sea; oceanic

pe-lar-gic (pĕ-LAHR-jik) *adj.*, pertaining to the stork

pelf (PELF) *n.*, 1. an archaic term for belongings, money, or wealth 2. a British term for trash 3. British dialect for compost 4. British dialect for a useless person

pel-lu-cid (pĕ-LOO-sĭd) or (pel-YOO-sĭd) *adj.*, 1. clear and translucent; without distortion 2. shining; iridescent 3. easy to understand; without ambiguity

pel-mat-o-gram (pel-MAD-ŏ-gram) *n.*, a footprint

pe-lo-ri-a (pĕ-LOH-ree-ă) *n.*, an unusual, hereditary regularity of structure that occurs in irregular flowers

pe-lo-rus (pĕ-LOH-rŭs) or (pĕ-LAW-rŭs) *n.*, a navigation instrument

pe-lo-ta (pĕLOHD-ă) *n.*, the Spanish court game jai-alai

pel-tast (PEL-tast) *n.*, an ancient Greek soldier who carried a small, light shield

pem-bi-na (pem-BEE-nă) or (PEM-bĭ-nă) *n.*, a cranberry tree

pe-nang or **pi-nang** (pĕ-NANG) *n.*, the betel palm

pen-di-cle (PEN-dĭ-kĕl) *n.*, 1. a hanging or suspended ornament 2. a Scottish term for property that is part of a large estate, especially if rented separately

pen-na (PEN-ă) *n.*, a feather that differs from down or plumes

pen-nate (PE-nayt) *adj.*, 1. winged or feathered 2. wing- or feather-shaped

pen-ni (PEN-ee) *n.*, a Finnish monetary unit

pen-sile (PEN(T)-sĭl) *adj.*, 1. hanging 2. having or making a hanging nest

pen-tad (PEN-tad) *n.*, 1. a group of five 2. a five-day period

pen-tarch-y (PEN-tahrk-ee) *n.*, government by five rulers or a union of five powers

pen-tom-ic (pen-TAHM-ik) *adj.*, 1. pertaining to an army division that comprises five battle groups 2. organized into five groups

pep-los or **pep-lus** (PEP-lŭs) *n.*, a women's garment in ancient Greece

per-coid (PĔR-koid) *adj.*, resembling a perch

per-cuss (pĕ(r)-KŬS) *v.*, to tap a body part or organ for medical diagnosis

per-du-el-lion (pĕr-d(y)oo-EL-yŏn) *n.*, a Roman law term for treason

per-dure (pĕr-D(Y)UU-(ĕ)r) *v.*, to continue; to survive

pe-ren-nate (PE-rĕ-nayt) *v.*, to persist from season to season

per-fla-tion (pĕ(r)-FLAY-shŏn) *n.*, ventilation

per-fri-ca-tion (pĕr-frĭ-KAY-shŏn) *n.*, an archaic term for a thorough rubbing

per-fuse (pĕr-FYOOZ) *v.*, to force liquid through a bodily part via the blood vessels

per-ga-me-ne-ous (pĕr-gă-MEE-nee-ŭs) *adj.*, resembling parchment

per-go-la (PĔR-gŏ-lă) or (pĕr-GOH-lă) *n.*, an arch covered by trailing vines

pe-ri (PI-ree) *n.*, 1. a supernatural being in Persian folklore that descended from the fallen angels and was excluded from paradise 2. a beautiful and graceful female

per-i-apt (PER-ee-apt) *n.*, a protective amulet

per-i-carp (PER-ĭ-kahrp) *n.*, the ripened walls of a plant ovary that have up to three distinct layers

pe-ric-li-tate (pĕ-RIK-lĭ-tayt) *v.*, to endanger

per-i-dot (PER-ĭ-doh) or (PER-ĭ-daht) *n.*, a variety of olivine used as a gemstone

per-i-e-ge-sis (per-ee-ĕ-JEE-sis) *n.*, a description of a region

pe-rip-e-ty (pĕ-RIP-ĕd-ee) or (PE-rĭp-ed-ee) *n.*, a reversal of a circumstance or situation in a literary work or in actual life

per-i-phras-tic (per-ĭ-FRAS-tik) *adj.*, associated with the use of longer phrasing in place of a shorter and more simple form of expression

pe-rip-ter-al (pĕ-RIP-t(ĕ)-răl) *adj.*, 1. with a row of columns on every side 2. associated with air motions around a moving body

pe-rique (pĕ-REEK) *n.*, a strong tobacco raised in St. James Parish, Louisiana

pe-ris-ci-i (pĕ-RIS-ee-ĭ) or (pĕ-RI-shee-ĭ) *n.*, persons who live within a polar circle

per-i-style (PER-ĭ-stīl) *n.*, 1. a colonnade around a building or court 2. the open space within a colonnade

per-jink (per-JINGK) *adj.*, a Scottish term meaning neat; exact

per-la-ceous (per-LAY-shŭs) *adj.*, pearly

per-lus-trate (pĕr-LŬ-strayt) *v.*, to examine carefully; to survey

per-nan-cy (PĔR-năn-see) *n.*, a collecting or accepting of something such as profits or rents

per-noc-ta-tion (pĕr-nahk-TAY-shŏn) *n.*, the act of staying up or out all night, especially to spend the night in vigil or prayer

per-o-ral (pĕr-OHR-ăl) *adj.*, through the mouth

per-pend (PĔR-pĕnd) *v.*, to consider carefully; to ponder

per-pent (PĔR-pĕnt) or **per-pend** (PĔR-pĕnd) or **par-pen** (PAHR-pĕn) *n.*, a brick or stone appearing on both sides of a wall

per-ron (PER-ŏn) or (pĕ-ROHN) *n.*, a stairway that leads to an entrance of a large building; a platform at the top of such a stairway

per-ru-quier or **pe-ru-ki-er** (pĕ-ROO-kee-e(r)) or (pe-rŭ-KI-(e)r) *n.*, a wigmaker

per-ry (PE-ree) *n.*, a British term for pear juice made into alcohol

---

\a\ bat \ă\ about \e\ or \ĕ\ check \ĕ\ letter
\ē\ cafe \i\ fish \ĭ\ tie \ī\ limit \o\ boat
\ō\ bacon \u\ sun \ŭ\ helpful \ü\ fool

perse (PĔRS) *adj.*, 1. an obsolete term for a light or pale blue and gray 2. dark grayish blue that looks like indigo

per-se-i-ty (pĕr-SAY-ĭd-ee) or (pĕr-SEE-ĭ-dee) *n.*, a self-sufficient being

pe-ruke or **pe-ruque** (pĕ-ROOK) *n.*, a wig, especially one popular from the 17th to 19th centuries

per-vi-ca-cious (pĕr-vĭ-KAY-shŭs) *adj.*, very stubborn

per-wits-ky (pĕ(r)-WITS-kee) *n.*, a tiger weasel of eastern Europe and northern Asia

pes (PEEZ) *n.*, 1. a segment of the hind leg of a vertebrate 2. a part resembling a foot

pe-sade (pĕ-SAYD) or (pĕ-ZAHD) *n.*, a maneuver in which a horse is trained to raise his forequarters without moving forward

pes-sa-ry (PES-ă-ree) *n.*, a vaginal suppository

pet-al-is-m (PED-ăl-izĕm) *n.*, an ancient Greek practice of banishing for five years citizens suspected of dangerous ambition or influence

pe-tard (pĕ-TAHRD) or (pĕ-TAHD) *n.*, 1. a case containing an explosive used for gaining entrance 2. a loud firework

pet-a-sus or **pet-a-sos** (PED-ă-sŭs) *n.*, a hat worn by ancient Greeks and Romans, especially the winged hat of Hermes or Mercury as represented in art

pe-te-chi-a (pĕ-TEE-kee-ă) or (pĕ-TEK-ee-ă) *n.*, a small hemorrhage caused by some infectious diseases

pe-tro-sal (pĕ-TROH-săl) *adj.*, 1. hard; stony 2. associated with the area of the hard, dense portion of the skull that houses the auditory organs

pet-ti-toes (PED-ee-tohz) *n.*, 1. pigs' feet when used as food 2. feet

pe-tun-tse or **pe-tun-se** (pĕ-TUUN-tsĕ) or (bĭ-DŬN-dzĕ) *n.*, a granite used in the manufacture of porcelain

pey-tral or **pey-trel** (PAY-trăl) *n.*, a piece of armor used to protect the breast of a horse

pfef-fer-ku-chen (FEF-ĕ(r)-koo-kĕn) *n.*, a German term for gingerbread

phae-och-rous (fee-AHK-rŭs) *adj.*, dusky

phal-a-cro-sis (fal-ă-KROH-sĭs) *n.*, baldness

phan-er-o-ma-ni-a (fan-ĕr-oh-MAY-nee-ă) *n.*, an obsessive picking, such as habitual nail biting

phat (FAT) *adj.*, capable of being quickly and easily typeset

phat-ic (FAD-ik) or (FAT-ik) *adj.*, speaking to socialize, rather than to communicate ideas

phen-a-kis-to-scope (fen-ă-KIS-tŏ-skohp) *n.*, an optical toy

phen-a-zine (FEN-ă-zeen) or (FEN-ă-zĭn) *n.*, a crystalline nitrogen base that is a parent compound for some dyes and antibiotics

phe-nol-o-gy (fĕ-NAHL-ŏ-jee) or (fĕ-NAHL-ŏ-ji) *n.*, the study of relations between climate and biological phenomena, such as the bird migrations and breedings or the flowering and fruiting of plants

phil·i·a·ter (FIL-ee-ayd-ĕ(r)) or (fil-ee-AYD-ĕ(r)) *n.*, a person interested in medicine

phil·o·pro·ge·ne·i·ty (fil-oh-proh-jĕ-NEE-ĕd-ee) *n.*, a love of offspring

phi·los·o·phas·ter (fĭ-LAH-sŏ-fas-tĕ(r)) *n.*, a person who dabbles in philosophy

phil·ter or **phil·tre** (FIL-tĕ(r)) *n.*, a magic or love potion

phil·trum (FIL-trŭm) *n.*, the vertical groove at the middle of the upper lip

phi·mo·sis (fĭ-MOH-sĭs) or (fĭ-MOH-sĭs) *n.*, a constriction of the foreskin of the penis that makes it impossible to bare the tip

phiz (FIZ) *n.*, a face

phon (FAHN) *n.*, a unit of loudness

phon·as·the·ni·a (fohn-ăs-THEE-nee-ă) *n.*, a feebleness or hoarseness of voice

phor·e·sy (FAWR-ĕ-see) *n.*, the association of one kind of animal with another for transportation

phos·gene (FAHZ-jeen) *n.*, a compound with an unpleasant odor that was used as poison gas in World War 1

phos·phene (FAH-sfeen) *n.*, a bright impression due to retinal excitation of the eye that is caused by something other than rays of light

phos·phine (FAH-sfeen) or (FAH-sfĕn) *n.*, 1. a colorless, poisonous gas mixture 2. an orange-yellow basic dye of a nitrate of chrysaniline

pho·toph·i·lous (foh-TAH-fĭ-lŭs) *adj.*, flourishing in bright light; requiring abundant light for complete growth

pho·to·phobe (FOHD-ŏ-fohb) *n.*, an organ or organism that thrives best in dark or that avoids the light

phre·at·ic (free-AD-ik) *adj.*, associated with a well

phron·tis·ter·y (FRAHN-tĭ-ste-ree) *n.*, a secluded location for thinking or study

phy·col·o·gy (fĭ-KAHL-ŏ-jee) or (fĭ-KAHL-ŏ-jĭ) *n.*, the study of algae

phyl·lite (FI-līt) *n.*, a thin-layered rock that is similar to slate

phyl·lode (FI-lohd) *n.*, a flat, expanded leafstalk that replaces the blade of a leaf and fulfills its functions

phyl·lo·man·cy (FI-lŏ-man(t)-see) *n.*, predicting the future by using leaves

phyl·lo·ge·net·ic (fil-ŏh-jĕ-NED-ik) *adj.*, associated with the growth of leaves

phys·i·an·thro·py (fiz-ee-AN(T)-thrŏ-pee) *n.*, the study of the make-up of man, his diseases, and their remedies

phy·tiv·o·rous (fĭ-TIV-(ĕ)-rŭs) *adj.*, feeding on plants, as insects

pi·a (PĪ-a) *n.*, the membrane of connective tissue of the nervous system

---

\a\ bat \ă\ about \e\ or \ĕ\ check \ĕ\ letter
\é\ cafe \i\fish \ĭ\ tie \ĭ\ limit \o\ boat
\ŏ\ bacon \u\ sun \ŭ\ helpful \ü\ fool

pi-a (PEE-a) *n.*, a perennial herb of India, Australia, and Polynesia cultivated for its starchy root

pi-ac-u-lar (pī-AK-yĕ-lĕ(r)) *adj.*, sacrificial; sinful

piaf-fer (PYAF-ĕr) *v.*, an obsolete term meaning to perform a trot in one place, as a show horse

pi-an (pee-AN) or (PYAHN) *n.*, a severe, contagious, nonvenereal tropical disease that is caused by a bacterium indistinguishable from the one that causes syphilis

pi-blok-to or **pi-block-to** (pĭ-BLAHK-toh) *n.*, a winter-related hysteria and depression among Eskimos, especially women

pi-broch or **piob-aireachd** (PEE-brahk) *n.*, complex variations on a traditional theme for a Scottish Highland bagpipe

pi-ca-cho (pĭ-KAH-choh) *n.*, a large, tapered, isolated hill

pic-a-ro (PIK-ă-roh) *n.*, a rogue; a wanderer

pic-a-roon or **pick-a-roon** (pik-ă-ROON) *v.*, to behave like a pirate searching for a prize or victim

pick-a-dil (PIK-ă-dil) or **pick-a-dil-ly** (pik-ă-DIL-lee) *n.*, 1. a decorative trim used as an edging for 16th- and 17th-century garments 2. a ruff or standing collar or a stiff support for it

pick-el-hau-be (PIK-ĕl-how-bĕ) *n.*, a helmet with spikes worn by German soldiers

pick-thank (PIK-thangk) *n.*, an archaic term for a person who tries to gain favor by flattery or gossiping

pi-cot (PEE-koh) *n.*, one of a series of small, ornamental loops that form the edge on lace or a ribbon

pic-o-tee (pik-ŏ-TEE) *n.*, a flower that has one basic color edged with another

pic-quet-er (PIK-ĕd-ĕ(r)) *n.*, a person who bundles artificial flowers

pic-ric (PIK-rik) or (PIK-reek) *n.*, a strong, toxic, yellow crystalline acid used in high explosives, as a dye, and as an antiseptic

pic-ul or **pic-ol** (PIK-ĕl) *n.*, a unit of weight in China and southeast Asia

pi-dan (pee-DAHN) *n.*, duck eggs that are preserved in brine with lime, ashes, and tea and aged for several months before eating

pif-fe-ro or **pif-e-ro** (PIF-ĕ-roh) *n.*, an old Italian wind instrument used by shepherds

pig-no-rate (PIG-nŏ-rĕt) *v.*, to give or deposit as a pledge for the payment of a loan or a debt or for the performance of an action

pig-nus (PIG-nŭs) *n.*, a Roman and civil law term for property held as security for a debt

pigs-ney (PIGZ-nee) *n.*, 1. a sweetheart 2. a small eye

pi-jaw (PĪ-jaw) *n.*, a British term for pious talk or moralizing

pi-ka (PĪ-kă) or (PEE-kă) *n.*, a small mammal found in the high, rocky areas of Asia and western North America that is closely related to rabbits

pi-ka-ke (PEE-kă-kay) *n.*, the Arabian jasmine

pi-lar (PĪ-lă(r)) *adj.*, hairy

pilch (PILCH) *n.*, 1. a wool or leather outer garment 2. an obsolete term for a saddle cover or a child's saddle 3. a covering over a baby's diaper

pil-crow (PIL-kroh) *n.*, a symbol indicating a paragraph break

pi-le-um (PĪ-lee-ŭm) *n.*, the top of a bird's head from the bill to the nape

pile-wort (PĪL-waw(ĕ)rt) *n.*, an herb once used for the treatment of piles

pil-gar-lic (pil-GAHR-lik) or **peel-gar-lic** (peel-GAHR-lik) *n.*, 1. a bald-headed man 2. a man looked upon with humorous disdain or false pity

pi-li (pee-LEE) *n.*, 1. an edible nut of a tree in the Philippines 2. the Java almond

pil-i-form (PIL-ĭ-fohrm) *adj.*, hairlike

pi-li-ki-a (pee-lee-KEE-ă) *n.*, a Hawaiian word for trouble

pil-lion (PIL-yŏn) *n.*, 1. a saddle for women 2. a pad behind a man's saddle for a woman to ride upon 3. a motorcycle or bicycle passenger saddle

pil-li-winks (PIL-ĭ-wingks) *n.*, a torture device used on the thumbs and fingers

pi-lo-e-rec-tion (pī-loh-ee-REK-shŏn) *n.*, the involuntary standing on end or bristling of hairs as a reflex to cold, shock, or fright

pi-lon (pee-LOHN) *n.*, a southwestern U.S. term for a bonus given with cash payment or a trade

pi-lose (PĪ-lohs) *adj.*, covered with hair, especially soft hair

pil-pul (PIL-pool) *n.*, critical analysis, especially the talmudic interpretations of Jewish scholars

pi-ly (PĪ-lee) *adj.*, having to do with a pile

pi-mo-la (pi-MOH-lă) *n.*, an olive stuffed with a sweet red pepper

pin-a-co-the-ca (pin-ă-KOH-thee-kă) *n.*, a picture gallery

pinch-beck (PINCH-bek) *n.*, 1. an alloy of copper and zinc that is used as imitation gold in cheap jewelry 2. anything fake or phony

pi-ne-tum (pī-NEED-ŭm) *n.*, 1. a plantation for pine trees 2. a scholarly written report on pines

pin-gle (PING-ĕl) *v.*, 1. a Scottish term meaning to strive or struggle 2. a Scottish term meaning to dawdle or play, especially with one's food

pin-go (PING-goh) *n.*, a small, low mound of earth or gravel, as in arctic regions, thought to be made by frost

pin-guid (PING-gwĭd) *adj.*, fat; fatty

pin-na (PIN-ă) *n.*, 1. the outer ear 2. a division of a featherlike leaf or frond 3. a feather, wing, or fin

pin-ni-ped (PIN-ĕ-ped) *adj.*, relating to a group of carnivores adapted to aquatic life, as seals and walruses

\a\ bat \ă\ about \e\ or \ĕ\ check \ĕ\ letter
\ĕ\ cafe \i\ fish \ī\ tie \ĭ\ limit \o\ boat
\ŏ\ bacon \u\ sun \ŭ\ helpful \ü\ fool

pin-nock (PIN-ŏk) *n.*, English dialect for a small bridge

pin-ta-no (pin-TAH-noh) *n.*, a small, bluish green to yellow fish with black, vertical stripes found in the warm, coastal seas of North and South America

pin-tle (PIN-tĕl) *n.*, an upright pivot pin

pinx-it (PINGK-sit) *v.*, a Latin word meaning "he or she painted it" that was formerly used as part of an artist's signature on paintings

pi-o-let (PEE-ŏ-lay) *n.*, a two-headed ax used in mountaineering

pi-on (PĪ-ahn) *n.*, a short-lived, unstable particle responsible for the nuclear force

pip-kin (PIP-kĭn) *n.*, a small metal or earthenware pot that usually has a horizontal handle

pip-sis-se-wa (pip-SIS-sĕ-wă) *n.*, an herb used by the Cree Indians as a tonic and diuretic

pi-quet or **pic-quet** (pee-KAY) or (pĭ-KAY) *n.*, a two-handed card game played with a deck of 32 cards

pi-ra-gua (pĭ-RAH-gwă) or (pĭ-RAG-gwă) *n.*, 1. a long canoe made out of a hollowed tree trunk 2. a dugout 3. a flat-bottomed sailing boat with two masts

pi-ra-ru-cu (pĭ-RAH-rŭ-koo) *n.*, a northern South American fish that is said to achieve a length of 15 feet and a weight of 500 pounds

pi-rogue (PEE-rohg) or **pi-roque** (PĪ-rohk) *n.*, a dugout canoe

pis-ca-ry (PIS-kă-ree) *n.*, 1. the legal right to fish, especially by net, at a certain place 2. a fishing place

pish-pash (PISH-pash) or (PISH-pahsh) *n.*, an East Indian term for a rice broth made with bits of meat

pi-si-form (PĪ-sĭ-fohrm) or (PĪ-zĭ-fohrm) *adj.*, similar to a pea in size or shape

pis-mire (PIS-mī(ĕ)r) or (PIZ-mī(ĕ)r) *n.*, 1. an ant 2. an insignificant or despicable person

pis-tic (PIS-tik) *adj.*, pertaining to or showing faith

pis-tol-o-gy (pĭ-STAHL-ŏ-jee) *n.*, a branch of theology concerned with faith

pith-e-col-o-gy (pith-ĕ-KAHL-ŏ-jee) *n.*, the study of apes

pi-ton (PEE-tahn) or (PEE-toh(n)) or (PĪ-toh(n)) *n.*, 1. a sharp mountain peak 2. an iron spike, wedge, or peg that is driven into the fissures or cracks of a mountain for support in climbing

piu (PYOO) or (pee-OO) *adv.*, a term for "more" that is used to qualify another adverb or adjective in musical direction

piz-zle (PIZ-ĕl) *n.*, the penis of an animal, especially a bull

pla-cet (PLAY-sĕt) *n.*, an approval; specifically, a ruler's permission for a bishop to function under the authority of the pope

plack (PLAK) *n.*, 1. a small, alloyed Scottish coin 2. an archaic term for a trifle

plac-oid (PLA-koid) *adj.*, a zoological term meaning having horny scales

pla-gal (PLAY-găl) *adj.*, in describing a religious melody, having a keynote on the fourth step of a scale

plaice or **plaise** (PLAYS) *n.*, 1. a European flounder 2. English dialect for a flattened, leaf-shaped worm

plan-gent (PLAN-jĕnt) *adj.*, 1. having a loud and vibrating sound, such as a bell 2. being expressive or plaintive

plan-gor-ous (PLANG-gŏr-ŭs) *adj.*, expressing sorrow loudly and vocally

plan-ti-grade (PLAN-tĭ-grayd) *adj.*, walking on the sole of the foot with the heel touching the ground

pla-num (PLA-nŭm) *n.*, a flat, bony surface, especially in the skull

plat-er-esque (plad-ĕ-RESK) or **plat-e-res-co** (plad-ĕ-RES-koh) *adj.*, relating to a 16th-century Spanish architectural style that used a lot of silver, platelike ornamentation

plec-tron (PLEK-trahn) *n.*, a musical instrument pick usually made of ivory, wood, metal, horn, quill, or plastic

pled-get (PLE-jĕt) *n.*, 1. a small, flat piece of gauze or cotton that is placed over a wound 2. a thread of tarred hemp used to caulk a boat

plei-on (PLĪ-ahn) *n.*, a region that shows a positive departure from the norm in meterological elements such as pressure, temperature, or rainfall

ple-o-nasm (PLEE-ŏ-nazem) *n.*, the use of more words than those necessary

ple-o-nex-i-a (plee-ŏ-NEK-see-ă) *n.*, greed

pleu-ra (PLUU-ră) *or* (PLOO-ră) *n.*, a thin membrane sac that lines one-half of the chest cavity and envelops the lung

pleu-ron (PLUU-rahn) *n.*, 1. a lateral part of a thorax of an insect 2. a lateral extension from a segment

pleus-ton (PLOOS-tŏn) *n.*, small, macroscopic floating organisms that form mats or layers on or near the surface of a body of water

plex-i-form (PLEK-sĭ-fohrm) *adj.*, 1. of, relating to, or having the form or characteristics of a plexus, a network of interlacing nerves or blood vessels 2. intricately interwoven

plex-or (PLEK-sŏ(r)) *n.*, a small, rubber-headed hammer that physicians use to test reflexes

pli-ca (PLĪ-kă) or **pli-ca po-lon-i-ca** (PLĪ-kă-pŏ-LAHN-ĭ-kă) *n.*, twisted, matted, and crusted hair, usually as a result of neglect, filth, or infestation

pli-cate (PLĪ-kayt) or (PLĪ-kăt) *v.*, 1. to fold or pleat 2. to perform the surgical procedure of tightening stretched or weakened body tissue by folding, tucking, and suturing

plook or **plouk** (PLOOK) *n.*, a Scottish term for a spot or blemish on the skin, especially one caused by infection

---

\a\ bat \ă\ about \e\ or \ĕ\ check \ē\ letter
\é\ cafe \i\fish \ī\ tie \ĭ\ limit \o\ boat
\ŏ\ bacon \u\ sun \ŭ\ helpful \ü\ fool

plu·mas·sier (PLOO-mă-si-(e)r) or (ploo-MA-see-ay) *n.*, a person who prepares or trades in ornamental plumes or feathers

plum·be·ous (PLŬM-bee-ŭs) *adj.*, 1. associated with lead 2. having a dull, lead-gray color

plum·bum (PLŬM-bŭm) *n.*, the element lead

plump·er (PLŬM-pe(r)) *n.*, 1. an act of falling suddenly or heavily, as from a horse 2. a British term for a vote given to one candidate only when the voter might select more than one nominee to the same office 3. U.S. dialect for a lie

plus·sage or **plus·age** (PLŬS-ij) *n.*, an amount in excess of another amount

plu·to·ma·ni·a (plood-ŏ-MAY-nee-ă) *n.*, an abnormal desire for wealth; a type of mental illness marked by delusions of wealth

plu·vi·ous (PLOO-vee-ŭs) *adj.*, rainy

pneu·ma (N(Y)OO-mă) *n.*, 1. the spirit of God 2. the life-giving principle in humans; the soul

po·chard or **poa·chard** (POH-chă(r)d) *n.*, a heavy-bodied diving duck with a large head; specifically, a common Old World duck similar to an American redhead

po·chette (poh-SHET) *n.*, 1. a small violin originally used by dancing masters 2. a handbag 3. a thin, transparent envelope that holds a postage stamp

po·co·cu·ran·te (poh-koh-kyŭ-RAN-tee) *adj.*, unconcerned; nonchalant

po·co·sin or **po·co·son** (pŏ-KOH-sĭn) or (POH-kŏ-sĭn) *n.*, a swamp or marsh, especially an elevated one in the area between streams of the coastal plain of southeastern United States

po·dag·ra (pŏ-DAG-ră) or (PAH-dăg-ra) *n.*, gout in the feet

pod·snap·pe·ry (pahd-SNAP-(ĕ)-ree) *n.*, an attitude of complacency toward life, characterized by a refusal to recognize unpleasant facts

pod·zol (PAHD-zahl) or (PAHD-sahl) *n.*, a type of infertile soil usually found in forests

poe·ci·log·o·ny (pee-sĭ-LAH-gŏ-nee) *n.*, a method of invertebrate-animal development in which the same species bears two kinds of young, although the adults are exactly alike

po·gey (POH-gee) *n.*, U.S. slang for a charitable institution for housing the aged, sick, and orphaned

pog·o·nip (PAH-gŏ-nip) *n.*, a dense winter fog with frozen particles that appears in the deep mountain valleys of the western United States

po·go·nol·o·gy (poh-gă-NAHL-ŏ-jee) *n.*, the study of beards

poh (POH) *interj.*, a term used to express contempt

poi·e·sis (poi-EE-sĭs) *n.*, the action or ability to produce or do something, especially creatively

poi·ki·lo·ther·mal (poi-ki-lŏ-THĔR-măl) *adj.*, pertaining to an animal whose body temperature approximates that of the environment, rather than being internally regulated

poi·lu (PWAH-loo) *n.*, a soldier in the French army, especially one at the front lines during World War 1

poind (POIND) or (PĪND) *v.*, a Scottish term meaning to take forcible legal possession of an object

poi·trel (POI-trĕl) *n.*, a decorated medieval piece of armor that protected the breast of a horse in battle

poke·lo·gan (POHK-loh-găn) or **poke·lo·ken** (POHK-loh-kĕn) *n.*, a New England term for a usually stagnant inlet or marshy place that branches off a stream or lake

pol·der (POHL-de(r)) *n.*, a tract of land recovered from the sea or another body of water through dikes or dams

po·leyn (POH-layn) *n.*, a piece of armor that covers the knee

po·li·o·sis (poh-lee-OH-sĭs) *n.*, the loss of hair color

pol·lard (PAHL-ă(r)d) *n.*, 1. a coin circulated in England in the 13th century and worth about a penny 2. an obsolete term for a hornless animal such as a cow, sheep, or a stag that has shed its antlers 3. wheat bran 4. a tree cut back to its trunk to produce a dense head of foliage

pol·lex (PAH-leks) *n.*, 1. the thumb 2. a unit measurement of length

pol·lic·i·ta·tion (pŏ-lis-ĭ-TAY-shŏn) *n.*, 1. an archaic term for the result or action of promising 2. a civil law term for an offer that is not accepted

pol·lin·i·um (pŏ-LIN-ee-ŭm) *n.*, a mass or body of pollen grains

po·ly·an·drous (pah-lee-AN-drŭs) *adj.*, 1. a botanical term meaning having many stamens 2. having multiple husbands

po·ly·chrest (PAH-lee-krest) *n.*, a drug or medicine that remedies more than one disease

po·ly·cot (PAH-lee-kaht) or **po·ly·cot·yl** (PAH-lee-kahd-ĕl) *n.*, a plant such as the pine and other conifers that has more than two primary leaf pairs

po·ly·his·tor (pah-lee-HIS-tŏ(r)) or **po·ly·his·to·ri·an** (pah-lee-hi-STOH-ree-ăn) *n.*, a person of encyclopedic knowledge

po·ly·lem·ma (pah-lee-LE-mă) *n.*, an argument similar to a dilemma in which more than three alternatives are presented in the major premise

po·lyn·ya or **po·lyn·ia** (PAH-lĭn-YAH) *n.*, a patch of open water in sea ice

pol·y·par·y (PAHL-ĭ-per-ee) *n.*, the common structure or tissue in which individual coral organisms are imbedded

pol·y·pha·gi·a (pah-lee-FAY-j(ee)-ă) *n.*, an excessive appetite; the act of eating voraciously

pol·y·phy·let·ic (pah-lee-fĭ-LED-ik) *adj.*, derived from more than one ancestral line, such as a group of animals

---

\a\ bat \ă\ about \e\ or \è\ check \ĕ\ letter \é\ cafe \i\ fish \ī\ tie \ĭ\ limit \o\ boat \ŏ\ bacon \u\ sun \ŭ\ helpful \ū\ fool

pome (POHM) *n.*, 1. a fruit such as an apple that consists of a central core of seeds enclosed within a bony or papery capsule and an outer, fleshy layer 2. a metal ball or globe

pom-mée (pah-MAY) *adj.*, having the end of each arm ending in a ball or disk, as certain types of crosses

po-mol-o-gy (poh-MAHL-ŏ-jee) or (poh-MAHL-ŏ-ji) *n.*, the science of fruit cultivation

ponce (PAHN(T)S) *n.*, British slang for a pimp

po-nent (POH-nĕnt) *adj.*, an obsolete term for western or occidental

pon-gid (PAHN-jĭd) *n.*, a primate of the family of apes that includes gorillas, chimpanzees, orangutans, and gibbons

pon-iard (PAHN-yă(r)d) *n.*, a dagger, usually with a slender square or triangular blade

pons (PAHNZ) *n.*, a band of nerve fibers in the brain

pon-tage (PAHN-tij) *n.*, 1. a duty or tax for building and reparing bridges 2. a toll users pay for bridge maintenance

pon-tif-i-cal-i-bus (pahn-tif-ĭ-KAL-ĭ-bŭs) *n.*, the uniform, costume, or vestments of one's office

pon-til (PAHN-tĭl) *n.*, a solid metal rod used for molding hot glass

poon (POON) *n.*, a hard, light wood from the East Indies and the Pacific islands that is used for ship masts

poor-tith (POHR-tith) *n.*, a Scottish term for poverty

pop-pet (PAH-pĕt) *n.*, 1. a British term of endearment for a girl 2. a midwestern U.S. term for a doll 3. a timber support at fore and aft ends of the ship that forms part of the launch cradle

por-noc-ra-cy (paw(r)-NAHK-ră-see) *n.*, government by prostitutes

por-ra-ceous (paw-RAY-shŭs) or (pŏ-RAY-shŭs) *adj.*, having the clear, light-green color of leek leaves

por-rect (pŏ-REKT) or (paw-REKT) *v.*, 1. an archaic term meaning to extend 2. to present; to tender

por-tance (POHR-tăn(t)s) *n.*, an archaic term for behavior or demeanor

po-sol-o-gy (pŏ-SAHL-ŏ-jee) *n.*, the study of drug dosage

pos-set (PAH-sĕt) *n.*, a hot drink made of sweetened, spiced milk with wine or ale and sometimes thickened with bread

post-ci-bal (pohs(t)-SĪ-băl) *adj.*, occurring after a meal

pos-til (PAHS-tĭl) *n.*, 1. a marginal note or comment; specifically, a marginal explanation of a biblical passage 2. an obsolete term for a short homily on scriptural passages

post-li-min-i-um (pohs(t)-lĭ-MIN-ee-ŭm) *n.*, a rule of international law under which things or persons seized by an enemy in wartime, as a general rule, regain their former rights when returned to the control of their own state

pos-tre-mo-gen-i-ture (pah-stree-moh-JEN-ĭ-chuu(e)r) *n.*, a system of inheritance by which the youngest son or daughter succeeds to the estate

po-ta-to-ry (POHD-ă-toh-ree) *adj.*, pertaining to drinking

po-teen (pah-TEEN) *n.*, a whiskey illegally distilled in Ireland from barley, potatoes, or sugar and molasses

po-to-ma-ni-a (pohd-ŏ-MAY-nee-a) *n.*, an uncontrollable, often periodic craving for alcoholic beverages

pot val-i-ant (POT-val-yănt) *adj.*, brave or courageous only as a result of being drunk

pot-wal-lop-er (PAH-twah-lŏ-pĕ(r)) *n.*, a voter in an English borough before the Reform Act of 1832 who qualified for suffrage as a householder by boiling his own pot at his own fireplace

poy-ou (POI-(y)oo) *n.*, an Argentinian armadillo

poz-zo-lan (PAHT-sŏ-lăn) *n.*, a material used by the ancient Romans to make mortar

prae-ci-pe or **pre-ci-pe** (PREE-sĭ-pee) or (PRES-sĭ-pee) *n.*, 1. a legal writ that commands a person to do something or to appear and show cause why he should not do what is ordered 2. a written order addressed to the court requesting issuance of a specified writ

prat (PRAT) *v.*, to push a person or thing with the buttocks

pra-tal (PRAYD-ăl) *adj.*, pertaining to the meadows

pra-tique (pra-TEEK) or (pră-TEEK) *n.*, the license or permission to use a port that is given to a ship after compliance with quarantine regulations or a presentation of a clean bill of health

prau (PROW) *n.*, an Indonesian boat propelled by sails, oars, or paddles

prax-e-ol-o-gy (prak-see-AHL-ŏ-jee) *n.*, the study of human conduct

pre-ag-o-nal (pree-AG-ŏ-năl) *adj.*, immediately preceding the agony of death

pre-ci-bal (pree-SĪ-băl) *adj.*, occurring before meals

pre-co-nize (PRE-kŏ-nīz) *v.*, 1. to announce; to commend publicly 2. a Roman Catholic term meaning to approve publicly by papal proclamation

pre-da-cious or **pre-da-ceous** (pree-DAY-shŭs) or (prĕ-DAY-shŭs) *adj.*, 1. preying on other animals 2. devouring

pree (PREE) *v.*, a Scottish term meaning to taste tentatively; to sample

pre-morse (pree-MAWRS) *adj.*, a biological term meaning having the end unnaturally terminated, as if bitten or broken off

pren-der or **pren-dre** (PREN-dĕ(r)) *n.*, the legal power or right to take a thing without its being offered

---

\a\ bat \ă\ about \e\ or \ĕ\ check \ĕ\ letter \é\ cafe \i\fish \ī\ tie \ĭ\ limit \o\ boat \ŏ\ bacon \u\ sun \ŭ\ helpful \ü\ fool

pre-pran-di-al (pree-PRAN-dee-ăl) *adj.*, relating to the time immediately before dinner

pre-puce (PREE-pyoos) *n.*, the foreskin of the penis; a similar fold enveloping the clitoris

pres-by-o-phre-ni-a (prez-bee-ŏ-FREE-nee-ă) *n.*, a form of senile dementia affecting women that is characterized by considerable mental alertness despite memory loss to the point of disorientation

pre-scind (pree-SIND) *v.*, an archaic term meaning to sever; to cut

prest (PREST) *n.*, 1. an obsolete term for a forced loan to the sovereign 2. an English legal term for a duty formerly paid by the sheriff on his account into the exchequer

pret-er-ist (PRED-ĕr-ĭst) *n.*, a person who believes that the prophecies of the Apocalypse have already been fulfilled

pre-ter-mit (preed-ĕ(r)-MIT) *v.*, 1. to let pass without mention, attention, or notice 2. to leave unsaid, undone, or unused 3. to interrupt or break off

pri-a-pism (PRĪ-ă-pizĕm) *n.*, 1. an abnormal, often painful erection of the penis 2. a phallic figure 3. a lewd act or exhibition

prick-mad-am (PRIK-mad-ăm) *n.*, English dialect for a stonecrop plant used in folk medicine to expel or destroy parasitic intestinal worms

prid-i-an (PRID-ee-ăn) *adj.*, pertaining to a previous day or yesterday

pri-me-ro (prĭ-ME-roh) or (prĭ-MI-roh) *n.*, an old card game popular in 16th- and 17th-century England

pri-mine (PRĪ-min) *n.*, a botanical term for the outer covering envelope of the ovary of seed plants

pri-mip-a-ra (prī-MIP-ă-ră) *n.*, 1. an individual that has only one offspring 2. one who bears a first offspring

prin-ceps (PRIN-seps) or (PRING-keps) *n.*, 1. the head of state during the Roman Empire 2. a chief official among ancient Teutons and Anglo-Saxons 3. a first edition of a work

prin-cock (PRIN-kahk) *n.*, an archaic term for a self-confident youth

prink (PRINGK) *v.*, English dialect meaning to walk or act in an affected or mincing manner

pris-iad-ka (pris-YAHD-kă) *n.*, a Slavic dance step for males executed by extending alternate legs from a squatting position

pris-tane (PRI-stayn) *n.*, a saturated, liquid hydrocarbon obtained from the liver oils of various sharks

proa (PROH-ă) *n.*, a sailing craft of Indonesia

pro-al (PROH-ăl) *adj.*, having a forward motion of the lower jaw in chewing

pro-bang (PROH-bang) *n.*, a thin, flexible rod with a small piece of sponge on one end that is used for applying medicine or removing obstructions

pro-bou-leu-tic (proh-boo-LOOD-ik) *adj.*, concerned with the preliminary deliberation on and discussion of something submitted later to another group of voters

pro-ca-cious (proh-KAY-shŭs) *adj.*, bold; impertinent

pro-cel-lous (proh-SEL-ŭs) *adj.*, stormy, as the sea

pro-cer-i-ty (proh-SER-ĕd-ee) *n.*, an archaic term for tallness or height

pro-cho-os (PROH-kŏ-wahs) *n.*, a tall, ancient Greek jug used to hold water for washing hands

pro-cryp-tic (proh-KRIP-tik) *adj.*, relating to or marked by protective coloration in insects

proc-tal-gi-a (prahk-TAL-j(ee)-a) *n.*, pain of the rectum

pro-cum-bent (proh-KŬM-bĕnt) *adj.*, 1. having ground-trailing stems without putting down roots 2. lying stretched out 3. slanting forward

prod-i-to-ri-ous (prahd-ĭ-TOH-ree-ŭs) *adj.*, an archaic term meaning likely to betray secret thoughts

prod-ro-mal (PRAHD-rŏ-măl) *adj.*, precursory, especially in relation to the premonitory symptoms of a disease

pro-fec-ti-tious (proh-fek-TISH-ŭs) *adj.*, a Roman law term meaning derived as property from an ancestor

pro-fic-u-ous (proh-FIK-yoo-ŭs) *adj.*, an obsolete term for profitable or useful

prog (PRAHG) *v.*, 1. U.S. dialect meaning to poke or search around, especially in order to steal or obtain something profitable 2. U.S. dialect meaning to prowl

prog-na-thous (PRAHG-nă-thŭs) *adj.*, 1. having jaws that protrude 2. relating to an insect that has its mouth parts in front of the cranium

pro-lapse (proh-LAPS) or (PROH-laps) *n.*, the falling down or slipping of a body part from its usual position

pro-le-gom-e-non (proh-lĕ-GAHM-ĕ-nahn) or (proh-lĕ-GAHM-ĕ-nŏn) *n.*, 1. introductory observations or remarks 2. a group of readings or intellectual exercises leading to further understanding in the knowledge of a subject matter

pro-li-cide (PROH-li-sīd) *n.*, the killing of one's child or children

pro-line (PROH-leen) or (PROH-lĕn) *n.*, an amino acid found in all proteins

pro-lu-sion (proh-LOO-zhŏn) or (prohl-YOO-zhŏn) *n.*, 1. an exercise before a contest or performance 2. a preface; a prologue

pro-no-tum (proh-NOH-tŭm) *n.*, the dorsal plate of an insect's thorax

pro-pae-deu-tic (proh-pee-D(Y)OOD-ik) or (proh-pee-D(Y)OOT-ik) *adj.*, needed as preparation for learning

\a\ bat \ă\ about \e\ or \ĕ\ check \ĕ\ letter
\ē\ cafe \i\ fish \ī\ tie \ĭ\ limit \o\ boat
\ŏ\ bacon \u\ sun \ŭ\ helpful \ü\ fool

pro-pale (proh-PAY(Ĕ)L) *v.*, an archaic term meaning to reveal or divulge

pro-pend (proh-PEND) *v.*, an obsolete term meaning to hang forward or downward

pro-phage (PROH-fayj) *n.*, a bacterial virus that is harmless to the host, but protects it from attack by active, harmful viruses

prop-o-lis (PRAHP-ŏ-lĭs) *n.*, a brownish material collected by bees from tree buds and used as a cement

pro-pug-na-tion (proh-pŭg-NAY-shŭn) *n.*, an obsolete term for a defense

pro-pyl (PROH-pĕl) or (PROH-pil) *n.*, a chemical component of propane and isopropane used as a solvent

pro-rogue (proh-ROHG) or (prŏ-ROHG) *v.*, 1. an archaic term meaning to extend the duration of or to postpone 2. to adjourn

pros-o-pog-ra-phy (prahs-ŏ-PAHG-ră-fee) *n.*, 1. a description of someone's appearance, character, and career 2. a collection of biographical sketches

pro-so-po-lep-sy (prŏ-SOH-pŏ-lep-see) *n.*, partiality

pro-so-po-poe-i-a (prŏ-soh-pŏ-PEE-ă) *n.*, 1. a representation of an imaginary, absent, or dead person as speaking or acting 2. a personification, as of inanimate things

prot-a-sis (PRAHD-ă-sĭs) *n.*, 1. the first part of an ancient drama in which the characters and their situations are introduced 2. a proposition that serves as a premise in reasoning

pro-ter-vi-ty (prŏ-TĔR-vĭd-ee) *n.*, peevishness

pro-tha-la-mi-on (proh-thă-LAY-mee-ăn) or (proh-thă-LAY-mee-ahn) *n.*, a song that celebrates a marriage

pro-thon-o-ta-ry (prŏ-THAN-ŏ-te-ree) or (proh-thŏ-NAHD-ăr-ee) *n.*, 1. a chief clerk in the English court in some countries of Europe 2. the principal court secretary

pro-tog-e-nal (proh-TAHJ-ĕ-năl) *adj.*, relating to a hypothetical unit believed to be the forerunner of living beings

pro-vine (proh-VĪN) *v.*, to layer, as in plant propagation

pru-ri-go (pruu-RĪ-goh) *n.*, a chronic, inflammatory skin disease marked by small, itching pimples

pru-rit-ic (pruu-RID-ik) *adj.*, pertaining to, marked by, or producing itching

psam-mite (SA-mīt) *n.*, a rock made of sandy particles or sandstone

pschent ((P)SKENT) *n.*, the headdress of the later Egyptian pharoahs that combined the crowns of pharoahs of Upper and Lower Egypt when the country became united under one rule

psel-lism (SEL-izĕm) *n.*, the condition or instance of stuttering; stammering

pse-phite (SEE-fīt) *n.*, a coarse rock composed of rounded pebbles

pse-phol-o-gy (see-FAHL-ŏ-jee) *n.*, the study of elections

pse-pho-man-cy (SEE-fŏ-man(t)-see) *n.*, predicting the future by using pebbles

pseud-an-dry (SOO-dan-dree) *n.*, the use of a masculine name as a pseudonym for a woman

pseud-e-pig-ra-phous (sood-ĕ-PIG-ră-fŭs) *adj.*, of or relating to writings falsely ascribed to biblical characters

pseu-do-cy-e-sis (soo-doh-SĪ-ee-sĭs) *n.*, a false pregnancy

pseu-dog-y-ny (soo-DAHJ-ĭ-nee) *n.*, the use of a feminine name as a pseudonym for a man

pseu-dol-o-gist (soo-DAHL-ŏ-jĭst) *n.*, a liar

pseu-do-man-cy (SOO-dŏ-man(t)-see) *n.*, false or counterfeit fortune telling

psi-lo-sis (sĭ-LOH-sĭs) *n.*, hair loss

psit-ta-cism (SID-ă-sizĕm) *n.*, repetitive, meaningless speech

pso-as (SOH-ăs) *n.*, either of two internal muscles of the loin that together form the tenderloin of animals and are used as food

psy-chal (SĪ-kăl) *adj.*, relating to the mind

psych-as-the-ni-a (SĪK-as-THEE-nee-ă) *n.*, a character weakness in which one feels unable to resolve doubts or uncertainties or to resist phobias, obsessions, or compulsions

psyl-la (SIL-ă) *n.*, a jumping plant louse

psy-war (SI-waw(e)r) *n.*, psychological warfare

ptar-mic (TAHR-mik) *n.*, something that causes sneezing

pter-ic (TER-ik) *adj.*, pertaining to or resembling a wing

pte-ro-pod (TE-rŏ-pahd) *n.*, a small mollusk that swims at or near the surface of the sea

pti-san (tĭ-ZAN) or (TIZ-ăn) *n.*, a liquid made by boiling barley with other ingredients in water; a tea

pto-sis (TO-sĭs) *n.*, a drooping of the upper eyelid

puc-coon (pŭ-KOON) *n.*, an American plant that yields a red or yellow pigment

puck-fist (PŬK-fīst) or (PŬK-fist) *n.*, 1. a puffball mushroom 2. a braggart

pu-den-cy (PYOO-dĕn-see) *n.*, modesty; prudishness

pu-er-i-cul-ture (PYUU-(ĕ)r-ĭ-kŭl-chŭ(r)) *n.*, the rearing or care of children; specifically, prenatal care of unborn children through attention to the health of the mother

pu-er-pe-ri-um (pyoo-ĕ(r)-PI-ree-ŭm) *n.*, 1. the state of a woman immediately following childbirth 2. the period between childbirth and the return of the uterus's normal size

\a\ bat \ă\ about \e\ or \ĕ\ check \ĕ\ letter
\ê\ cafe \i\fish \ī\ tie \ĭ\ limit \o\ boat
\ŏ\ bacon \u\ sun \ŭ\ helpful \ü\ fool

pug-mark (PŬG-mahrk) *n.*, a spoor or track of a wild animal

pug-ree (PŬG-ree) *n.*, 1. a turban worn in India 2. a light scarf wrapped around a sun helmet or used as a hatband on a straw hat

puis-ne (PYOO-nee) *adj.*, 1. an obsolete term meaning unimportant; petty 2. subordinate

puk-ka (PŬ-kă) *adj.*, genuine; authentic; complete

pul (POOL) *n.*, 1. a Russian copper coin issued from the 15th to 19th century 2. an Afghani coin

pule (PYOOL) *v.*, 1. to whine or whimper 2. an obsolete term meaning to chirp weakly

pul-er (PYOO-lĕr) *n.*, an archaic term for a person who whines or whimpers

pu-li (PUU-lee) or (PYOO-lee) *n.*, an intelligent, medium-sized, Hungarian farm dog with a long, corded coat

pu-li-cous (PYOO-lĭ-kŭs) *adj.*, an archaic term meaning infested with fleas

pul-lu-lant (PŬL-yĕ-lănt) *adj.*, budding; sprouting

pul-que (POOL-kay) or (POOL-kee) *n.*, a Mexican fermented drink that is made from the juice of various cactuses and is the source of mescal

pul-ta-ceous (pŭl-TAY-shŭs) *adj.*, having the consistency of porridge; pulpy

pul-vil (PŬL-vil) *n.*, an archaic term for perfumed or cosmetic powder

pul-vi-nar (pŭl-VĪ-nĕ(r)) *n.*, a cushion

pul-vi-nate (PŬL-vĭ-nayt) *adj.*, 1. curved; swelled 2. cushion-shaped

pum-e-lo (PŬM-ĕ-loh) *n.*, a grapefruit

pu-na-lu-a (poo-nă-LOO-ă) *n.*, 1. a group marriage, formerly practiced in Hawaii, in which a group of brothers marries a group of sisters

pun-cheon (PŬN-chĕn) *n.*, 1. a pointed tool for working with stone 2. a short, upright piece of timber 3. a figured stamp, die, or punch used especially by goldsmiths and engravers

punc-tate (PŬNG(K)-tayt) *adj.*, 1. pointed; resembling a point 2. applied to a point on an object 3. dotted with tiny spots or depressions

punc-ti-form (PŬNG(K)-tĭ-fohrm) *adj.*, 1. having the form of a point 2. pertaining to points or dots that represent words in reading material prepared for the blind

pun-do-nor (puun-dŏ-NAW(E)R) *n.*, a point of honor

pung (PŬNG) *n.*, a New England term for an oblong box on runners or a sleigh with a box-shaped body

pun-gled (PŬNG-gĕld) *adj.*, shrunken or shriveled, especially when referring to grain robbed of its juices by insects

pu-pil-lar-i-ty or **pu-pil-ar-i-ty** (pyoo-pĭ-LAR-ĕd-ee) *n.*, the period of growth prior to puberty

pur-blind (PŬR-blīnd) *adj.*, 1. dim- or short-sighted 2. lacking in vision, insight, or understanding

pur-dah or **par-dah** (PŬR-dă) *n.*, a Hindu and Muslim practice in which women are secluded from public view by means of concealing clothing, high-walled enclosures, and screens within the home

pur-fle (PŬR-fĕl) *v.*, 1. to ornament or trim the edges of 2. to ornament with fine embroidery threads, jewels, or fur

pur-li-cue (PŬR-lĭ-kyoo) *n.*, a Scottish term for a summary or recapitulation of a series of sermons or addresses given at its close

pur-lin or **pur-line** (PŬR-lĭn) *n.*, a horizontal piece of roof supported on the frame principals and supporting the common rafters

pur-pres-ture (pŭr-PRES(H)-chŭr) *n.*, a wrongful appropriation of land that is subject to the rights of others

pur-pu-rate (PŬR-pyŭ-rayt) *v.*, an archaic term meaning to robe in purple

purse-proud (PŬRS-prowd) *adj.*, proud or arrogant because of one's wealth, especially when there are no other distinctions

pur-sy (PŬ-see) or (PŬRS-see) or **pus-sy** (PŬ-si) *adj.*, 1. tending to be short-winded or asthmatic due to stoutness 2. fat; puffy

puss-ley or **pus-ley** (PŬS-lee) or (PŬS-li) *n.*, an herb of both hemispheres that is both troublesome as a weed and edible as a salad green or stew seasoning

pu-ta-men (pyoo-TAY-mĕn) *n.*, 1. an outer, reddish layer of the larger, external nucleus of the nerve tissue mass of the brain 2. the tough membrane that lines the shells of birds eggs

putch-er (PŬCH-ĕr) or (PUUCH-ĕr) *n.*, English dialect for a wicker trap used to catch salmon

pu-tri-lage (PYOO-trĭ-lij) *n.*, matter that is decomposing

put-tock (PŬD-ŏk) *n.*, a bird of prey such as a kite, a buzzard, or a marsh harrier

putz (PUUTS) *n.*, a Nativity scene under the Christmas tree in a Pennsylvania Dutch home

puz-zle-pat-ed (PŬZ-ĕl-payt-ĕd) *adj.*, having or based on confused attitudes or ideas

pya (pee-AH) or (PYAH) *n.*, a monetary unit of Burma

pye (PĪ) *n.*, 1. a table or collection of church rules used in England before the Reformation to determine the proper service or office for the day 2. an obsolete term for an alphabetical index or catalogue

py-e-li-tis (pī-ĕ-LĪD-ĭs) *n.*, inflammation of the funnel-shaped part of the kidney that leads into the ureter, or duct, to the bladder

py-e-mi-a or **py-ae-mi-a** (pĭ-EE-mee-ă) *n.*, a blood infection that is caused by pus-forming microorganisms and characterized by abscesses

\a\ bat \ä\ about \e\ or \è\ check \ĕ\ letter \é\ cafe \i\fish \ī\ tie \ĭ\ limit \o\ boat \ŏ\ bacon \u\ sun \ŭ\ helpful \ü\ fool

py·gal (PĬ-găl) *adj.*, pertaining to the region of the rump or posterior end of the back

py·gid·i·um (pĭ-JID-ee-ŭm) *n.*, the tail structure of various invertebrates

pyk·nic or **pyc·nic** (PIK-nik) *adj.*, characterized by short stature, broad girth, and powerful muscularity

py·lon (PĪ-lahn) or (PĪ-lĕn) *n.*, 1. a large gateway with flanking towers 2. a tower for supporting either end of a wire over a long span 3. a post or tower marking an airplane's prescribed flight path

py·lo·rus (pī-LOH-rŭs) or (pĕ-LOH-rŭs) *n.*, the opening from the stomach into the intestine in a vertebrate

py·o·sis (pī-OH-sis) *n.*, the formation of pus

py·ret·ic (pī-RED-ik) *adj.*, associated with a fever

pyr·i·form (PIR-ĭ-fohrm) *adj.*, pear-shaped

py·rog·ra·phy (pī-RAH-gră-fee) *n.*, 1. the process or art of producing designs or pictures by burning or scorching with hot instruments, as on wood or leather 2. an ornamentation produced by this burning technique

pyr·rho·tism (PIR-ŏ-tizĕm) *n.*, the condition or characteristic of being red-headed

py·tho·gen·ic (pĭ-thŏ-JEN-ik) *adj.*, produced by or originating from filth or decomposition

py·u·ri·a (pī-YUU-ree-ă) *n.*, the presence of pus in the urine

pyx (PIKS) *n.*, 1. the vessel, tabernacle, or container used to hold the Eucharist on the altar or to carry it to the sick 2. a box used in the U.S. and British mints as a repository for sample coins reserved for testing of weight and fineness 3. a small chest

qadi (KAH-dee) *n.*, a Muslim judge who interprets and administers Islamic religious law

qaid (kah-EETH) or (KĪTH) *n.*, an officer in charge of a castle or fortress

qa·si·da or **ka·si·da** (kă-SEE-dă) *n.*, a poem of praise, mourning, or satire in the literatures of Arabia and Persia

qin·tar (kin-TAHR) *n.*, a unit of Albanian currency

qoph or **koph** or **coph** (KOHF) *n.*, the 19th letter of the Hebrew alphabet

qua (KWAH) *n.*, a Scottish term for a quagmire

quack·le (KWAK-el) *v.*, a British term meaning to constrict the throat

quad·dle (KWAH-dĕl) or (KWAW-dĕl) *n.*, English dialect for a muttering complainer

quad·ra·ges·i·mal (kwahd-ră-JES-ĭ-măl) *adj.*, consisting of 40; specifically, in regard to a 40-day fast occurring during Lent

qua·dri·ga (kwah-DRĪ-gă) *n.*, an ancient Roman two-wheeled cart, drawn by four horses abreast

qua·drig·a·mist (kwah-DRIG-ă-mĭst) *n.*, a person married four times, especially one having four spouses at the same time

quae·re (KWI-ree) *n.*, an archaic term for an inquiry

quae·si·tum (kwee-SĪD-ŭm) *n.*, 1. an aim or goal that is sought for 2. the true or actual mathematical quantity

quaes·tor or **ques·tor** (KWES-tŏ(r)) or (KWEES-tŏ(r)) *n.*, 1. a Roman official responsible for managing public funds 2. an emissary of a pope or bishop with authority to collect alms and to grant indulgences

quaes·tu·ary (KWES(H)-chŭ-we-ree) or (KWEES(H)-chŭ-we-ree) *adj.*, an archaic term meaning concerned with or engaged in monetary gain or profit

quag·ga (KWA-gă) *n.*, a South African wild ass related to the zebra

qua·hog or **quo·hog** (KWAW-hawg) or (K(W)OH-hahg) *n.*, a thick-shelled clam found in America or the north Atlantic

quaich or **quaigh** (KWAYK) *n.*, a Scottish term for a small, shallow bowl or drinking cup with ears for handles

quam·ash (KWAHM-ish) *n.*, a lilylike plant found in the western United States that can poison grazing livestock; also called death camas

quan·dong or **quan·dang** or **quon·dong** (KWAHN-dahng) *n.*, a small, shrubby Australian tree with edible fruit

quant (KWANT) or (KWAHNT) *n.*, English dialect for a boat-propelling pole with a disk near the end that keeps the tool from sinking in the mud

quar·en·tene (KWAW-rĕn-teen) or (KWAHR-ĕn-teen) *n.*, an archaic term for a measure of land area equal to 40 square rods

quarl or **quarle** (KWAWRL) *n.*, a large brick or tile, especially a curved, fire-resistant piece used to support zinc-melting pots

quar·tan (KWAWR-tăn) or (KWAW(E)-tăn) *n.*, an intermittent malarial fever that recurs at 72-hour intervals

quarte (KAHRT) *n.*, 1. a term in fencing for the fourth of eight defensive positions 2. a sequence of four, same-suited playing cards

quar·ter·pace (KWAWR-dĕr-pays) *n.*, a staircase landing at which the stair flights form a right angle

quar·to·dec·i·man (kwawr-doh-DES-ĭ-măn) *n.*, an early British Christian who celebrated Easter on a day different from that observed in continental Europe

---

\a\ bat \ă\ about \e\ or \è\ check \ĕ\ letter \é\ cafe \i\fish \ī\ tie \ĭ\ limit \o\ boat \ŏ\ bacon \u\ sun \ŭ\ helpful \ü\ fool

quas·sia (KWAH-sh(ee)a) or (KWAH-see-a) *n.*, a drug extracted from the heartwood of various tropical trees and used as a roundworm treatment, as an insecticide, and as a substitute for hops in brewing

quas·sin (KWAH-šn) *n.*, the bitter, crystalline active element of quassia

quaw (KWAH) *n.*, a Scottish term for a soft, wet land that gives way when stepped on

quea·chy (KWEE-chee) or (KWEE-chǐ) *adj.*, English dialect meaning swampy; boggy

que·ma·de·ro (kay-mǎ-DE-roh) *n.*, a site for execution by burning

queme (KWEEM) *adj.*, English dialect for pleasant; comfortable

que·nelle (kě-NEL) *n.*, a drop of chopped meat and seasoning boiled in water or stock and served alone or as a garnish

quer·cine (KWĚR-sin) or (KWĚR-sīn) *adj.*, relating or pertaining to an oak tree

que·rent (KWI-rěnt) *n.*, a questioner; specifically, one who seeks the advice of an astrologer

quer·i·mo·ni·ous (kwer-ǐ-MOH-nee-ǔs) *adj.*, whining; peevish

querk·en (KWĚRK-ěn) *v.*, English dialect meaning to suffocate; to cause to gasp

quern (KWĚRN) or (KWĚN) *n.*, a primitive mill for grinding grain

quetch (KWECH) *v.*, 1. U.S. dialect meaning to twitch; to jerk 2. to break a silence; to make a sound

quet·zal (ket-SAHL) or (ket-SAL) *n.*, 1. a large, Central American bird of brilliant plumage and tail feathers that often exceed two feet in length

qui·a·qui·a (KEE-ǎ-kee-ǎ) *n.*, a small, narrow-bodied fish of the western Atlantic; also called the round scad or cigarfish

quid·di·ty (KWID-ěd-ee) or (KWID-ǐ-tee) or (KWID-ǐ-ti) *n.*, 1. an eccentricity 2. the essential nature or ultimate form of a thing; the distinguisher that makes a thing what it is

quid·dle (KWID-ěl) *n.*, U.S. dialect for a finicky or meticulous person

quid·nunc (KWID-nǔngk) *n.*, an unusually curious individual who is fond of petty speculations and gossip

quiff (KWIF) *n.*, U.S. slang for girl or female

qui·llai (kee-(Y)Ī) *n.*, a Chilean tree whose bark yields a soapy lather used in cleaning and emulsifying oils

quill·back (KWIL-bak) *n.*, a carpsucker fish with a long first ray on its dorsal fin

quill·er (KWIL-ěr) *n.*, a machine or its operator that transfers yarn from spools and cones to bobbins

quil·let (KWIL-ět) *n.*, U.S. dialect for a small expanse of land

quin·cunx (KWIN-kǔng(k)s) *n.*, an array of five objects, such as plants or trees, arranged with one item at each corner and one in the middle of a square or rectangle

quin-de-cen-ni-al (kwin-di-SEN-ee-ăl) *adj.*, of or pertaining to a 15-year period or the 15th occurrence in a series, such as an anniversary

quink (KWINGK) *n.*, a small, dark wild goose that breeds in the arctic regions and migrates southward along the coasts

quin-nat (KWIN-ĕt) *n.*, a large salmon of the northern Pacific whose red flesh has considerable commercial value; also called the king salmon

qui-noa (kee-NOH-ă) or **quin-na** (KEEN-wah) *n.*, a South American pigweed whose seeds are used as a cereal in the high Andes of Peru

quin-qua-ges-i-mal (kwin-kwă-JES-ĭ-măl) *adj.*, occurring in a 50-day season; consisting of 50 days

quin-sy (KWINZ-ee) or (KWINZ-ĭ) *n.*, an abscess in the region of the tonsils

quin-tain (KWIN-tĕn) *n.*, an object designed for tilting

quin-tal (kwin-tĕl) *n.*, a unit of weight used variously in Latin American and Mediterranean countries

quin-tic (KWIN-tik) *n.*, a polynomial equation of the fifth degree

quin-ton (ka-toh) *n.*, a violin whose five strings are tuned to g, d′, a′, d″, g″, respectively

qui-pu (KEE-poo) or **qui-po** (KEE-poh) *n.*, an ancient Peruvian calculating and record-keeping aid that consists of a main cord with smaller, varicolored strings attached and knotted together

quire (KWĪ(E)R) or (KWI-ĕ) *n.*, a set of 24 or 25 sheets of paper of the same dimensions and stock

quirl (KWER(Ĕ)L) *n.*, a midwestern U.S. variant term meaning a ringlet of hair

quitch (KWICH) *n.*, a creeping European grass that has spread throughout North America as a weed; also called quack grass, quick grass, or couch grass

quit-rent (KWIT-rent) *n.*, a small, fixed fee paid to a lord in lieu of feudal services

quit-tor (KWID-ĕ(r)) or (KWIT-ĕ(r)) *n.*, a pus-forming inflammation of horses' feet

quoc-ngu (kwahk-ĕng-GOO) or (KWAHK-noo) *n.*, a writing system that uses the Roman alphabet with additional letters and diacritics to express the Vietnamese language

quod (KWAHD) *v.*, British slang meaning to imprison

quod-li-bet (KWAHD-lĭ-bet) *n.*, 1. a subtle, moot point, especially a scholastic or theological issue proposed for argument 2. a whimsical, harmonious combination of melodies

quoin (K(W)OIN) or **coign** (KOIN) *n.*, 1. an angle; a corner 2. a wedge 3. a stone, brick, or wood piece that forms the exterior angle or corner at the juncture of two walls 4. a diamond-shaped facet on a cut gem

---

\a\ bat \ă\ about \e\ or \è\ check \ĕ\ letter \é\ cafe \i\ fish \ī\ tie \ĭ\ limit \o\ boat \ŏ\ bacon \u\ sun \ü\ helpful \ü\ fool

quo-mo-do (KWOH-mŏ-doh) *n.,* the method or way; the capacity

quon-dam (KWAHN-dăm) or (KWAHN-dam) *adj.,* having been earlier; sometime

quonk (KWAHNGK) or **quonk-ing** (KWAHNG-king) *n.,* a noise that disrupts a radio or television broadcast because of its closeness to the microphone or camera

quop (KWAHP) *v.,* U.S. dialect meaning to pulsate abnormally; to throb

quo-tha (KWOH-thă) *interj.,* an archaic term expressing surprise, contempt, or assertiveness

quoz (KWAHZ) *n.,* an archaic term for something peculiar or contrary to sense

qursh (KU(Ĕ)RSH) *n.,* a monetary unit of Saudi Arabia

qutb (KUD-ĕb) *n.,* an Islamic saint of utmost holiness who is regarded within some schools of Islamic mysticism as responsible for the invisible government of the world

R

rab (RAB) *n.,* a wooden beater that mixes hair with mortar

rab-at (RAB-ăt) *n.,* a polishing material made from unglazed, imperfectly fired potter's clay

ra-ceme (ray-SEEM) or (ră-SEEM) *n.,* a flower cluster of small, individually stemmed blossoms regularly spaced on a larger stalk

rack or **racke** (RACH) *n.,* British dialect meaning a dog or hound that tracks its prey by scent

ra-chis (RAY-kĕs) *n.,* the vertebral column; the backbone

ra-chi-tis or **rha-chi-tis** (ră-KĪD-ĭs) or (ră-KĪT-ĭs) *n.,* rickets, a nutritional deficiency caused by a lack of vitamin D or insufficient sunlight

rack rent (RAK-rent) *n.,* an annual tenant's fee equal or nearly equal to the full value of the property

ra-con (RAY-kahn) or (RAY-kĕn) *n.,* a radar beacon whose coded signal allows a navigator to identify the beacon and from it determine his craft's bearing and range from it

rad-i-cle (RAD-ĭ-kĕl) or (RAD-ee-kĕl) *n.,* the root portion of a plant embryo or seedling

ra-di-o-lu-cent (ray-dee-oh-LOO-sent) *adj.,* partly or wholly capable of being penetrated by X rays or other types of radiation

ra-dix (RAY-diks) *n.,* 1. a number that is raised to a power 2. the initial cause

ra-fale (ră-FAL) *n.,* a burst of artillery fire from a gun battery

raf-ty (RAF-ti) *adj.,* British dialect meaning rancid, especially when applied to bacon

rag-a-bash (RAG-ă-bash) or **rag-a-brash** (RAG-ă-brash) *n.*, British dialect for the rabble; the lowest, most disreputable class of society

rag-gee or **rag-gi** or **rag-gy** (RAG-ee) *n.*, an East Indian cereal grass whose seeds yield a bitter flour that is a staple in the Orient; also called finger millet

rah-dar (RAH-dahr) *n.*, an Indian term for a keeper of a toll road

ra-ia (RAY-(y)ă) *n.*, a synonym for raja, an Indian prince and ruler

raith (RAYTH) *n.*, a Scottish term for a quarter of a year

ra-ki (ră-KEE) or (RA-kee) or (RAH-kee) *n.*, a strong, sweet Turkish liquor, usually distilled from raisins and flavored with aniseed

rale (RAL) or (RAHL) *n.*, an abnormal respiratory sound heard during a physical examination of the chest

ra-mate (RAY-mayt) *adj.*, having branches

ram-bu-tan (ram-BOO-tăn) *n.*, a bright red, oval, Malayan fruit with a pleasant-tasting, acidic pulp

ra-men-tum (ră-MEN-tŭm) *n.*, a minute particle scraped off a surface; a piece or fragment produced by paring

ra-met (RAY-mĕt) *n.*, a plant that results from cloning

ram-fee-zled (ram-FEE-zĕld) *adj.*, a Scottish term meaning tired out; deprived of strength, patience, or endurance

ram-ie or **ram-ee** (RAM-ee) or (RAYM-ee) *n.*, a tall, perennial herb of eastern Asia, commercially cultivated for its strong, bast fibers that are spun and woven to make smooth, lustrous fabrics similar to linen or silk

ram-il-lie (RAM-ĭ-lee) *n.*, an 18th-century wig with a long back braid that is tied at top and bottom

ra-mo-neur (ra-mŏ-NĚR) *n.*, a British term for a person who cleans chimneys

ram-pal-lian or **ram-pal-lion** (ram-PAL-yŏn) *n.*, a worthless, reprehensible character

ram-pike (RAM-pīk) *n.*, a dead tree; a tree broken by the wind and left with a splintered trunk

rams-horn (RAMS-haw(ĕ)rn) *n.*, a snail often used as an aquarium scavenger

ram-til (RAM-til) *n.*, a tropical African herb cultivated in India for its niger seed that yields a commercially valuable oil

ran-dan (RAN-dan) or (ran-DAN) *n.*, a rowboat for three oarsmen pulling four oars

ra-ni or **ra-nee** (rah-NEE) *n.*, the wife of an Indian rajah

rant-i-pole (RANT-ee-pohl) or (RANT-ĭ-pohl) *v.*, to act in a wild and rakish fashion

ra-phe or **rha-phe** (RAY-fee) *n.*, the seam between the right and left halves of an organ or part

\a\ bat \ă\ about \e\ or \è\ check \ě\ letter \é\ cafe \i\fish \ī\ tie \i\ limit \o\ boat \ŏ\ bacon \u\ sun \ŭ\ helpful \ü\ fool

rap-pa-ree (ra-pă-REE) *n.*, a 17th-century Irish guerrilla

rap-pen (RAH-pĕn) *n.*, a Swiss coin of little value

rap-pi-ni (ra-PEE-nee) *n.*, baby turnips harvested early for their greens

rap-to-ri-al (rap-TOHR-ee-ăl) *adj.*, related to the seizure of prey

rar-ee-show (RAR-ee-shoh) or (RER-ee-shoh) *n.*, a small, portable exhibit viewed through a glass or opening

ras (RAHS) *n.*, 1. a tapering land mass that extends into an ocean, lake, or sea 2. an Italian Fascist official who exercised absolute authority in his locality

ras-bo-ra (raz-BOH-ră) or (RAZ-bŏ-ră) *n.*, a small, brightly colored, freshwater fish often included tropical aquariums

ra-so-ri-al (ră-SOH-ree-ăl) *adj.*, relating or referring to birds that habitually scrape at the earth for their food

ras-ter (RAS-tĕ(r)) *n.*, the pattern of parallel lines on the cathode-ray tube of a television that receives the incoming signals and produces the picture

rat-a-fia (rad-ă-FEE-ă) *n.*, a liqueur made by steeping plum, peach, and apricot kernels and bitter almonds with a base of brandy and fruit juices

rat-a-plan (rad-ă-PLAN) *n.*, the repetitive sound of beating, as from a drum or the hooves of a galloping horse

ra-tel (RAYD-ĕl) or (RAHD-ĕl) *n.*, a powerful, carnivorous mammal that resembles the badger

rath (RAHTH) or (RAH) *n.*, a circular, earthen structure that provided a stronghold and residence for an ancient Irish chief

rat-i-ha-bi-tion (rad-ee-hă-BISH-ŏn) *n.*, a validation

ra-toon (ra-TOON) *v.*, to grow or spring from the root

rat-teen (ra-TEEN) *n.*, an archaic term for a coarse, woolen fabric

rat-ten (RAT-ĕn) *v.*, a British term meaning to damage or harm a factory, its machinery, or its workers during a labor dispute

raun (RAWN) *n.*, the mass of eggs carried or deposited by a female fish

rau-wol-fi-a (row-WUUL-fee-a) or (raw-WUUL-fee-a) *n.*, a sedative extracted from the roots of an Indian tree and used to treat hypertension and some mental disorders

ra-ven-ing (RA-vĕn-ing) *n.*, an object nabbed or eaten as prey

rax (RAKS) *v.*, a Scottish term meaning to extend the limbs of one's body

ra-ya or **ra-yah** (RĪ-ă) *n.*, a Christian agricultural laborer under the rule of the Ottoman empire

raz-zi-a (RA-zee-ă) *n.*, a rapacious attack

re-a-ble (ree-AY-bĕl) *v.*, a British term meaning to restore to one's former condition or capacity

re-al-gar (ree-AL-gahr) or (ree-AL-gĕr) *n.*, an arsenic mineral compound that emits a sulfurous odor when burned

re-a-li-a (ree-AY-lee-ă) or (ray-AHL-ee-ă) *n.*, 1. a philosophical term for objects of experience 2. the materials or pursuits a teacher uses to relate classroom theories and fact to daily experience

re-bar-ba-tive (ree-BAHR-băd-iv) or (ree-BAH-băd-iv) *adj.*, repugnant; annoying

re-ba-to (rĕ-BAHD-oh) *n.*, a wide cloth collar of the 17th century that draped over the shoulders to lie open at the front

re-bec or **re-beck** (REE-bek) *n.*, a pear-shaped, slender-necked musical instrument whose three strings are played with a bow

reb-o-a-tion (reb-ŏ-WAY-shŏn) *n.*, a loud echo

re-cen-sion (rĕ-SEN-chŏn) *n.*, an explanatory or critical examination

re-cheat (rĕ-CHEET) or **re-chate** (rĕ-CHAYT) *n.*, a call sounded on the horn that summons the hounds for a hunt

reck-ling (REK-lĭng) or (REK-ling) *n.*, English dialect for the smallest or weakest of a litter, brood, or family

rec-li-vate (REK-lĭ-vayt) *adj.*, an entomological term meaning curved; having the shape of the letters C or S

re-coct (rĕ-KAHKT) or (ree-KAHKT) *v.*, an obsolete term meaning to prepare for eating or heat again

rec-re-ment (REK-rĕ-mĕnt) *n.*, extraneous material separated from what is more useful

re-cru-des-cent (ree-kroo-DES-ĕnt) *adj.*, appearing again; recurring with severity

rec-ti-grade (REK-tĕ-grayd) *adj.*, following a straightaway course

rec-trix (REK-triks) *n.*, a female leader

rec-um-ben-ti-bus (rek-ŭm-BEN-tĭ-bŭs) *n.*, an incapacitating punch

rec-u-sant (REK-yĕ-zĕnt) or (rĕ-KYOO-zĕnt) *adj.*, rejecting of or disagreeing with authority

re-dar-gue (rĕ-DAHR-gyoo) *v.*, to overcome through argument or evidence

red-ar-gu-tion (red-ahr-GYOO-shŏn) *n.*, an archaic term for disproof; confutation

red-di-tion (rĕ-DISH-ŏn) *n.*, 1. an archaic term for a restoration to a previous condition 2. an obsolete term for a comparative explanation

red-hi-bi-tion (red-(h)ĭ-BISH-ŏn) *n.*, in civil law, the voiding of a sale and return of an object to its seller because of material defect

red-in-gote (RED-ing-goht) *n.*, an outer coat or coatdress that is fitted to the figure

red-in-te-grate (rĕ-DIN-tĕ-grayt) or (ree-DIN-tĕ-grayt) *v.*, an archaic term meaning to fix or reassemble

red-i-vi-vus (red-ĭ-VĪ-vŭs) *adj.*, resuscitated; regenerated

---

\a\ bat \ā\ about \e\ or \ĕ\ check \ĕ\ letter
\é\ cafe \i\fish \ī\ tie \ĭ\ limit \o\ boat
\ŏ\ bacon \u\ sun \ŭ\ helpful \ü\ fool

re-fec-tion (rĕ-FEK-shŏn) or (ree-FEK-shŏn) *n.*, an animal's ingestion of its own feces

re-foc-il-late (ree-FAHS-ĭ-layt) or (ree-FOHS-ĭ-layt) *v.*, to invigorate; to renew

re-fran-gi-ble (rĕ-FRAN-jĭ-bĕl) *adj.*, capable of being deflected from a straight line

re-ful-gent (rĕ-FŬL-jĕnt) *adj.*, emitting a radiance; resplendent

reg-let or **rig-let** (REG-lĕt) *n.*, a flat, narrow architectural molding

reg-ma (REG-mă) *n.*, a dry fruit of three or more sections that breaks away from the flower's axis at maturity

reg-o-lith (REG-ŏ-lith) *n.*, the soft, unconsolidated surface that results from rock weathering and covers the solid bedrock; also called mantlerock

re-grate (rĕ-GRAYT) or (ree-GRAYT) *v.*, to purchase items at a market or fair in order to profit by reselling them in or near the same place

reg-u-lus (REG-yŭ-lŭs) *n.*, an impure metal by-product of ore smelting

re-i-fy (REE-ĭ-fī) *v.*, to treat an abstraction or intangible as a concrete, material object

re-lict (rĕ-LIKT) or (rĕ-LEEKT) *n.*, 1. a widow 2. a plant or animal that exists in a particular area as a survivor

rel-i-gate (REL-ĭ-gayt) *v.*, to tie together; to force

rem-a-net (REM-ă-net) *n.*, something left over; specifically, a case or proceeding postponed for hearing at a later date

rem-i-form (REM-ĕ-fohrm) *adj.*, oar-shaped

rem-i-ped (REM-ĕ-ped) *n.*, a crustacean or insect that uses its feet or legs as oars

re-mo-lade (ray-mŏ-LAHD) *n.*, a spicy sauce or dressing similar to mayonnaise, but made with hard-boiled egg yolks and seasoned with herbs

rem-o-ra (REM-ŏ-ră) *n.*, 1. a fish with a suction disk on the top of the head that allows it to adhere to sharks, other large fish, or ships 2. anything that deters or retards

ren-dzi-na (ren-JEE-nă) *n.*, an intrazonal group of dark, grayish brown soils coated with a fine deposit of calcium carbonate

re-ni-fleur (re-nĭ-FLĔR) *n.*, a person who satisfies his sexual desires through smells

ren-i-form (REN-ĭ-fohrm) or (REEN-ĭ-fohrm) *adj.*, like or resembling a mammalian kidney; having the outline of a bean

re-nin (REE-nĭn) *n.*, a kidney enzyme

ren-i-ten-cy (REN-ĭd-ĕn-see) or (rĕ-NĪ-tĕn-see) *n.*, the ability to withstand constraint or pressure

re-pand (rĕ-PAND) or (ree-PAND) *adj.*, of or referring to a leaf with scalloped edges

re-pine (rĕ-PĪN) or (ree-PĪN) *v.*, to feel or utter fretful and melancholy unhappiness

re-pris-ti-nate (ree-PRIS-tĭ-nayt) *v.*, to recover or return to an original state or condition

re-pul-lu-late (ree-PŬL-yŭ-layt) *v.*, an archaic term meaning to again send out shoots or show signs of growth

re-re-dos (RE-rĕ-dahs) or (RI-rĕ-dahs) *n.*, an ornamental screen or partition of wood or stone that forms the wall behind a church altar

re-seau (ray-ZOH) or (rĕ-ZOH) *n.*, an interconnected arrangement of elements in a controllable system

resh (RAYSH) *n.*, the 20th letter in the Hebrew alphabet that corresponds to the modern English R

re-sile (re-ZĪL) or (ree-ZĪL) *v.*, to return to an earlier shape or original position after being extended or compressed

res-i-pis-cence (res-ĭ-PIS-en(t)s) *n.*, a modification of belief or emotion that often results in readopting a previously abandoned correct view, position, or interpretation

res-or-cin (rĕz-AWR-sĭn) or (rez-AWR-sĭn) *n.*, resorcinol, a sweetish, crystalline phenol used to make dyes, pharmaceuticals, adhesives, and rubber products

re-staur or **re-stor** (rĕ-STAW(ĕ)r) *n.*, the legal options available to insurers against the shipmasters who incur loss through negligence

res-ur-rec-tion-ist (rez-ŭ-REK-shŏn-ĭst) *n.*, 1. a person who steals corpses 2. a person who revives a rejected or discarded idea or theory

ret (RET) *v.*, 1. to dampen or saturate woody tissue with water or chemicals to promote the loosening and softening of fiber 2. to damage or cause decomposition by exposing material to dampness

re-ta-blo (ray-TAH-bloh) *n.*, an offering of a painted panel depicting religious figures or saints that is hung in a Spanish or Mexican chapel because of a vow

re-ti-a-ry (REE-shee-e-ree) *adj.*, wielding a net or any entangling device

re-tic-u-lum (rĕ-TIK-yĕ-lŭm) *n.*, 1. the second stomach of a ruminant animal 2. a structure that resembles netting

ret-i-form (RED-ĭ-fohrm) *adj.*, composed of crosshatches and intervening spaces

re-trad (REE-trad) or (RE-trad) *adv.*, toward the rear or back

ret-ro-choir (RE-troh-kwī(e)r) *n.*, the area of a church behind the high altar

ret-ro-min-gent (re-trŏ-MIN-jĕnt) or (ree-trŏ-MIN-jĕnt) *adj.*, passing urine in a backward direction

re-trorse (rĕ-TRAW(Ĕ)RS) *adj.*, curved down or toward the back

ret-te-ry (RET-ĕ-ry) *n.*, the site or establishment for soaking fibers

re-tund (rĕ-TŬND) *v.*, an archaic term meaning to force off; to weaken the impact of

\a\ bat \ă\ about \e\ or \ĕ\ check \ĕ\ letter
\é\ cafe \i\fish \ĭ\ tie \ī\ limit \o\ boat
\ŏ\ bacon \u\ sun \ŭ\ helpful \ü\ fool

re-us (REE-ŭs) *n.*, a legal term for the person required to answer to a suit or criminal action

re-val-o-rize (ree-VAL-ŏ-rīz) *v.*, to assign a new and arbitrary market value to assets or currency after a period of inflated prices

rev-e-hent (REV-ĕ-hĕnt) or (rĕ-VEE-hĕnt) *adj.*, transporting back to the source

rev-e-nant (REV-ĕ-nĕnt) or (rev-ĕ-NAH) *n.*, a person whose character embodies qualities and traits appropriate to an earlier era

re-vers (rĕ-VI-(ĕ)r) or (ree-VI-(ĕ)r) *n.*, a hem, collar, edging, or other part of an article of clothing that is turned back and attached to show its underside

re-ver-so (rĕ-VĔR-soh) *n.*, the side to be read second when written material appears on both sides of a sheet

re-vet (ree-VET) *v.*, to reinforce a bank or obstruction with a layer of material such as stone, rock, or cement

rhab-dom (RAB-dahm) or (RAB-dŏm) *n.*, a tiny structure found in the neural receptors of an arthropodan compound eye

rhab-do-man-cy (RAB-dŏ-man(t)-see) *n.*, predicting the future by using wands

rhag-a-des (RAG-ă-deez) *n.*, the tiny, painful cracks in the skin that occur at the corners of the mouth

rhat-a-ny (RAT-ă-nee) *n.*, the dehydrated root of two South American shrubs that has medical uses as an astringent and tonic

rhe-a (REE-ă) *n.*, 1. a large, tall, flightless, South American bird that is smaller than, but similar to, the African ostrich

rhe-mat-ic (ri-MAT-ik) *adj.*, of or relating to the structure or arrangement of words

rhe-ni-um (REE-nee-ŭm) *n.*, a rare, heavy, polyvalent, metallic element usually used as a catalyst

rhe-o-base (REE-oh-bays) *n.*, the least amount of electrical current needed to stimulate bodily tissue

rhe-ol-o-gy (ree-AHL-ŏ-jee) *n.*, the study of changes in the shape and flow of matter

rhi-no-cer-i-cal (RĪ-nŏ-SER-ĭ-kăl) *adj.*, an archaic term meaning wealthy

rhip-i-date (RIP-ĭ-dayt) *adj.*, having the shape of a fan, often including the radiate parts similar to fan supports

rhi-pip-ter-ous (rĭ-PIP-tĕr-ŭs) *adj.*, of or relating to a type of minute insect that undergoes many different structural changes in the stages between molts

rhi-zo-pod (RĪ-zŏ-pahd) *n.*, a protozoan that uses temporarily extended protoplasm as its organs of locomotion

rhom-bo-he-dron (rahm-boh-HEE-drŏn) *n.*, a prism whose faces are equilateral parallelograms

rhon-chus (RAHNG-kŭs) *n.*, a rattling sound like snoring heard while listening to the chest when the air channels are partly obstructed

rho-pa-lism (ROH-pă-lizĕm) *n.*, a successive increase in the size or length of each unit in a work of prose

rho-ta-cism (ROHD-ă-sizĕm) *n.*, mispronunciation of the letter R, especially by replacing it with another sound

rhy-o-lite (RĪ-ŏ-līt) *n.*, an acid, volcanic rock that has the same composition as granite when in its lava form

rhy-pa-rog-ra-phy (rī-pă-RAHG-ră-fee) *n.*, 1. an artistic or literary work that portrays or characterizes vulgar, ignoble subjects 2. the painting of realistic, representational art depicting scenes and objects in daily life

rhy-ton (RĪ-tahn) *n.*, an ancient Greek drinking vessel of horn-shaped pottery

ri-at-a (ree-AD-ă) or (ree-AH-da) *n.*, a long, light, strong rope used with or without a running noose in driving or grazing livestock

ri-cer-car (ree-chĕr-KAHR) *n.*, a contrapuntal 16th- and 17th-century instrumental composition characterized by imitative treatment of themes

ric-in (RĪS-ĭn) or (RIS-ĭn) *n.*, a violently poisonous substance in the castor bean

ric-i-nus (RIS-ĭ-nŭs) *n.*, the castor-oil plant

ric-tus (RIK-tŭs) *n.*, 1. the wide-open gape of a bird's mouth 2. the aperture at the mouth; an open-mouthed, toothy facial expression of pleasure or pain

ri-deau (rĭ-DOH) *n.*, a small strip or patch of ground slightly higher than the surrounding area

ri-dent (RĪ-dĕnt) *adj.*, an archaic term meaning expressing mirth, glee, or good humor

ridge-ling or **ridg-ling** (RIDJ-ling) *n.*, a male animal whose testicles have not descended

ri-dot-to (rĭ-DAHD-oh) or (rĭ-DAWD-oh) *n.*, a public music-and-dance show, often performed in costume, that originated in Italy and became popular in 18th-century England

riel (REE(E)L) *n.*, a Kampuchean monetary unit

ri-fa-ci-men-to (ree-fah-chee-MEN-toh) *n.*, a remaking or refashioning of a literary work or musical composition

rigs-by (RIGZ-bi) *n.*, English dialect for a coarse or wanton female

rijks-daal-der (RĪKS-dahl-(d)ĕ(r)) *n.*, 1. an old Dutch unit of currency 2. the modern Dutch 2-1/2 guilder token

rin-con (ring-KOHN) *n.*, a southwest U.S. term for an isolated lowland tucked among hills or along a watercourse

rin-gent (RIN-jĕnt) *adj.*, with widely separated lips and a gaping mouth

---

\a\ bat \ă\ about \e\ or \ĕ\ check \ē\ letter
\ė\ cafe \i\fish \ī\ tie \ĭ\ limit \o\ boat
\ŏ\ bacon \u\ sun \ŭ\ helpful \ü\ fool

ring-straked (RING-straykt) *adj.*, an archaic term for having circular, striped markings

ri-par-i-an (ri-PER-ee-ăn) or (rī-PER-ee-an) *n.*, a person who resides or owns acreage on a riverbank

ri-pie-no (rĭ-PAY-noh) *n.*, a musical instrument, group, or performer added to an orchestra solely to increase the musical effect

rir-o-ri-ro (rir-ŏ-REE-roh) *n.*, a small, plain-colored songbird of New Zealand; also called the gray warbler

ri-sor-gi-men-to (ree-saw(r)-jĕ-MEN-toh) *n.*, a period of renewed interest and vigorous activity

ris-sole (rĭ-SOHL) or (RI-sohl) *n.*, finely diced meat or fish that is wrapped in pastry and deep fried

rive (RĪV) *v.*, 1. to tear into pieces 2. to arouse by strong emotion

riv-i-ère (RIV-ee-e(ĕ)r) or (rĭv-YE-(ĕ)r) or (reev-YE-(ĕ)r) *n.*, a string of diamonds or other precious stones that is worn around the neck

riz-zar (RIZ-ăr) *n.*, a Scottish term for a haddock cured by drying in the sun

ro-bomb (ROH-bahm) *n.*, a pilotless, explosive-laden jet plane that is electronically or mechanically directed to a target and drops as an aerial weapon

ro-bo-rant (RAH-bŏ-rănt) *n.*, a refreshing, stimulating medicine or physical agent

roc (RAHK) *n.*, a fabulous, huge bird of prey that inhabits the Indian Ocean area, according to Arabian legend

roc-am-bole or **roc-om-bole** (RAHK-ĕm-bohl) *n.*, a European plant related to the onion and used as a vegetable or seasoning

roch-et (RAHCH-ĕt) *n.*, a white linen ceremonial garment like a surplice that bishops and other ranking ecclesiastics wear during some rites

rod-o-mon-tade (RAHD-ŏ-mahn-TAYD) *n.*, 1. prideful, overstated talk 2. an arrogantly pretentious boaster

ro-ga-tion (roh-GAY-shŏn) *n.*, a proposal from an ancient Roman consul or tribune submitted to a popular vote

ro-ga-to-ry (RAH-gă-toh-ree) *adj.*, gathering knowledge about an incident or condition; specifically, having authorization to question witnesses or learn facts

rois-ter or **roys-ter** (ROIS-tĕ(r)) *v.*, to participate in uproarious, unrestrained activity, especially while drinking alcohol

roi-te-let (ROID-ĕl-et) or (RWAH-tlay) *n.*, an archaic term for an unimportant monarch

ron-dure (RAHN-jĕ(r)) *n.*, a spherical object or surface

ron-yon (RŎN-yŏn) *n.*, an obsolete term for an animal with bald, raw, and crusted patches on its skin

roor-back or **roor-bach** (RUUR-bak) or (RUU(E)-bak) *n.*, a damaging deceit issued near election time to sway the popular vote

roque (ROHK) *n.*, the game of croquet played on a paved or tamped field surrounded by an elevated rim for making bank shots

roq-ue-laure (RAHK-ĕ-loh(ĕ)r) or (ROHK-ĕ-loh(ĕ)r) *n.*, a loose, buttoned-in-front outer garment that fell to the knees and was especially popular in the 18th and early 19th centuries

ro-ral (ROH-răl) *adj.*, an archaic term for moist from morning condensation

ror-qual (RAWR-kwăl) *n.*, a large whale with baleen instead of teeth, such as the blue whale, finback, or sei, that lives in waters of the southern hemisphere

ro-sa-ce-a (roh-ZAY-shee-ă) *n.*, a chronic inflammation of the oily glands of the nose, forehead, and cheeks that is common in middle age; also called brandy nose

ros-i-nan-te (rahz-ĭn-AN-tee) or (rohz-ĭn-AN-tee) *n.*, an old or unhealthy horse

ros-iny (RAHZ-ĭn-ee) *adj.*, like or having the smell of a resin obtained from pine trees and used in varnishes and lacquers

ros-ma-rine (RAHS-mă-reen) *n.*, an obsolete term for an aromatic mint used in cooking and perfumes

ro-so-li-o or **ro-so-gli-o** (roh-ZOH-lee-oh) or (roh-ZOHL-yoh) *n.*, a liqueur made of alcohol, water, and sugar and flavored with rose petals, orange blossoms, cinnamon, or cloves

ro-so-ri-al (roh-ZOH-ree-ăl) or (roh-SOH-ree-ăl) *adj.*, persistent, repeated biting, chewing, or nibbling

ros-tel-lum (rah-STEL-ŭm) *n.*, a small, beaklike growth or projection

rotl (RAHD-ĕl) *n.*, a unit of weight in various Mediterranean and Near Eastern countries

ro-tu-ri-er (roh-TUU-ree-ay) or (roh-TYUU-ree-ay) *n.*, 1. a commoner who rents his land and is free of feudal duties 2. a wealthy individual with little education or refinement

roun-ce-val (ROWN(t)-sĕ-văl) *n.*, an overbearing, nagging woman

row-an (ROW-ăn) or (ROH-ăn) *n.*, the mountain ash tree of America and Europe

row-en (ROW-ĕn) *n.*, harvested cropland with vegetation left at the surface as grazing material for cattle

roz-zer (RAH-zĕ(r)) *n.*, British slang for an officer of the law

rsi or **ri-shi** (RI-shee) *n.*, a sacred and revered wise man, saint, or divinely influenced poet

rta or **ri-ta** (RID-ă) *n.*, the Vedic idea of order that serves as the basis for righteous conduct

ru-ba'i (roo-BAH-ee) *n.*, a verse unit of four lines

ru-basse (roo-BAS) *n.*, quartz given a ruby-red stain

ru-ba-to (roo-BAH-doh) or (roo-BAH-toh) *n.*, a changing musical tempo played against a steady rhythm

\a\ bat \ă\ about \e\ or \ĕ\ check \ĕ\ letter
\é\ cafe \i\fish \ĭ\ tie \ĭ\ limit \o\ boat
\ŏ\ bacon \u\ sun \ŭ\ helpful \ü\ fool

ru·big·i·nous (roo-BIJ-ĭ-nŭs) *adj.*, rusty or reddish-brown in color

ruche (roosh) *n.*, a folded, ridged, or gathered piece of fabric trimming women's garments

ruck (RŬK) *n.*, racehorses that fall behind those setting the pace

ruc·ta·tion (rŭk-TAY-shŏn) *n.*, an archaic term meaning the oral expulsion of stomach gas

ruc·tion (rŭk-shŏn) *n.*, a loud and intense argument within a group of people

ru·das (ROO-dăs) *n.*, a Scottish term for a hideous, vile, and loathsome old woman

rud·dle (RŬD-ĕl) *n.*, a red iron ore used to make pigment

rud·dock (RŬD-ŏk) *n.*, a European robin redbreast

ru·elle (roo-EL) *n.*, a morning function at which 17th- and 18th-century French women received visitors

rum·mer (RŬM-ĕ(r)) *n.*, a large, tall vessel for drinking wine

run·a·gate (RŬN-ă-gayt) *n.*, a person who abandons one cause or principle for another, often opposing one

run·ca·tion (rŭn-KAY-shŏn) *n.*, an obsolete term for the act of weeding

runch (RŬNCH) *n.*, a wild mustard plant

run·ci·ble (RŬN(T)-sĭ-bĕl) *n.*, a three-pronged utensil used for serving pickles or canapés

run·dle (RŬN-dĕl) *n.*, the winding part of a cable-driven machine for moving or hoisting

rund·let (RŬND-lĕt) *n.*, a small, barrel-shaped cask

run·nel (RŬN-ĕl) *n.*, a small channel or depression formed underwater in the ground near shore by current or wave movement

ru·pes·tri·an (roo-PES-tree-ăn) *adj.*, made of rock; engraved on rock

ru·pic·o·line (roo-PIK-ŏ-līn) or (roo-PIK-ŏ-līn) *adj.*, appearing on rocks

ru·rig·e·nous (ruu-RIJ-ĕ-nŭs) *adj.*, originating from or dwelling in the country

ru·then·ic (roo-THEN-ik) or (roo-THEEN-ik) *adj.*, of, relating to, or derived from a rare metallic element

ruth·ful (ROOTH-fŭl) *adj.*, 1. full of pity; compassionate 2. sorrowful

ru·ti·lant (ROOD-ĭ-lănt) *adj.*, having a bluish radiance

ru·tile (ROO-teel) or (ROO-tĕl) *n.*, a mineral of titanium dioxide that is used to coat welding irons

ry·ot or **rai·yat** (RĪ-ŏt) *n.*, a person bound to the soil in India through birth or occupation

ry·ot·war (RĪ-ŏ-twahr) *n.*, a revenue system in which the government collects land rent or taxes directly from the peasants

sab-a-ton or **sab-ba-ton** (SAB-ă-tahn) *n.*, a broad, blunt-toed steel shoe that accompanied a suit of armor

sa-bin (SAY-bǐn) or (SAB-ǐn) *n.*, a fixed measurement of sound absorption

sab-u-lous (SAB-yǔ-lǔs) *adj.*, having the feel or composition of sand or grit

sac-cad-ic (sa-KAHD-ik) *adj.*, twitchy

sa-chem (SAY-chĕm) *n.*, 1. a North American Indian chief who presided over the Algonquin tribes 2. a political party leader

sack-but (SAK-bǔt) *n.*, a medieval instrument like the trombone

sac-ra-men-tar-i-an-ism (sak-ră-men-TER-ee-ăn-izĕm) *n.*, the religious doctrine that sacraments are in themselves efficacious, necessary for salvation, and capable of granting grace to their recipient's soul

sa-crar-i-um (să-KRA(A)-ree-ŭm) *n.*, the most hallowed area of a church or temple

sade (SAYD) *v.*, English dialect meaning to tire

sad-i-ron (SA-dī-r(ĕ)n) *n.*, a flat, smooth-surfaced iron with points at both ends and a removable handle

saf-ra-nin (SA-fră-nǐn) *n.*, a type of red to blue azine dye

saf-role (SA-frohl) *n.*, a poisonous, oily ether found in sassafras oil and used for perfuming and flavoring

sa-ga-ci-ate (să-GA-shee-ayt) or (să-GAY-shee-ayt) *v.*, a southern U.S. term meaning to flourish

sag-a-more (SAG-ă-moh(ĕ)r) *n.*, an Algonquin Indian war chief

sa-gene (SAH-zhen) *n.*, a Russian unit of measurement equal to seven feet

sag-gar or **sag-ger** (SAG-e(r)) *n.*, a fire-clay box that protects fine or delicate ceramic pieces while they are fired

sag-i-nate (SAJ-ĭ-nayt) *v.*, an archaic term meaning to make plump

sag-it-tal (SAJ-ĭd-ăl) *adj.*, of or relating to the connecting seam between the two large membrane bones at the roof of the skull

sag-it-tate (SAJ-ĭ-tayt) *adj.*, having the shape of an arrowhead

sa-gum (SAY-gŭm) *n.*, a rectangular outer garment of coarse wool that Gauls, early Germans, and Roman soldiers wore fastened on the right shoulder

sain-foin (SAYN-foin) *n.*, an American plant with three-leafed foliage and rough, dry, and sticky fruit; also called tick trefoil

saithe (sayth) *n.*, an important and highly esteemed food fish of the north Atlantic that is related to and resembles the cod

\a\ bat \ă\ about \e\ or \è\ check \ĕ\ letter
\é\ cafe \i\fish \ī\ tie \ĭ\ limit \o\ boat
\ŏ\ bacon \u\ sun \ŭ\ helpful \ü\ fool

sa-lep (SA-lĕp) or (să-LEP) *n.*, a dried starchy tuber used for food, as tapioca, and to remedy inflamed and irritated mucous membranes

sal-let (SAL-ĕt) *n.*, a simple, light helmet of the 15th century that extended over the neck

sal-ma-gun-di (sal-mă-GŬN-dee) *n.*, a salad dish of meats, anchovies, hard-boiled eggs, pickled vegetables, olives, radishes, endive, and watercress dressing or vinaigrette sauce

sa-loop (să-LOOP) *n.*, a hot beverage of sassafras steeped in milk and sugar

sal-pinx (SAL-pingks) *n.*, the tube through which ova descend from the ovaries to the uterus; also called the fallopian tubes

salse (SAL(T)S) *n.*, an opening in the earth that allows the emission of vapor through a pool of mud or with the ejection of mud

sal-si-fy (SAL-sĭ-fee) or (SAL-sĭ-fī) *n.*, a European biennial herb with a long, edible root; also called the oyster plant

sal-sil-la (sal-SIL-lă) *n.*, a tropical American plant whose edible roots can be boiled as a substitute for potatoes

sal-ta-tion (sal-TAY-shŏn) *n.*, an obsolete term meaning an outpouring with intermittent surges

sal-tim-ban-co (sal-tĭm-BANG-koh) *n.*, a charlatan; a swindler

sal-tire (SAL-tĭ(ĕ)r) or (SAWL-tĭ(ĕ)r) *n.*, a cross in the shape of an X

sam-a-ri-form (SAM-ă-rĭ-fohrm) or (să-MA(A)R-ĭ-fohrm) *adj.*, having the form of a one-seeded, winged fruit like that of the elm tree

sam-bar (SAHM-bĕ(r)) *n.*, a large Asiatic deer that has long, coarse throat hair and strong, three-pointed antlers; also called the elk

sam-bu-ca (sam-B(Y)OO-kă) *n.*, an ancient, triangular harp with four strings and a shrill tone that is used for banquet music

sam-buk or **sam-bouk** or **sam-buq** (sahm-BOOK) *n.*, a small Arab boat of the Indian Ocean

sa-mekh or **sa-mech** or **sa-mek** (SAH-mek) *n.*, the 15th letter of the Hebrew alphabet that corresponds to an S

sam-i-sen (SAM-ĭ-sen) *n.*, a three-stringed musical instrument of Japan that resembles a banjo

sam-let (SAM-lĕt) *n.*, a young salmon

sam-my (SAM-mee) *adj.*, British dialect for water-logged

sam-sa-ra (săm-SAH-ră) *n.*, in Hinduism and Buddhism, the infinitely recurring cycles of birth, death, and rebirth that all beings undergo

san-a-ble (SAN-ă-bĕl) *adj.*, an obsolete term meaning able to be cured, healed, or remedied

san-be-ni-to (san-bĕ-NEED-oh) *n.*, a garment of goat or camel hair worn by penitents who become reconciled to the church

san-da-rac or **san-da-rach** (SAN-dă-rak) *n.*, the resin of a north African cypress pine that is used as incense

san-dek (SAHN-dek) or **san-dik** (SAHN-deek) *n.*, the man who holds the infant during the Jewish ceremony of circumcision

san-gar or **sun-gar** (SANG-gĕ(r)) or (SÄNG-gĕ(r)) *n.*, a small temporary fortification, often constructed of boulders around a natural hollow, that shelters a few men

san-ga-ree (sang-gă-REE) *n.*, a drink of sweetened, strong alcoholic liquor that is served in a tall tumbler of cracked ice and garnished with nutmeg

san-gui-niv-o-rous (sang-gwĭ-NIV-(ĕ)-rŭs) *adj.*, obtaining nourishment from blood, as some insects or vampire bats

san-jak (san-JAK) or (SAN-jak) *n.*, an administrative district or subdivision in Turkey

san-nup (SA-nup) *n.*, the mate of an American Indian squaw

sann-ya-si (săn-YAH-see) *n.*, a wandering, begging Hindu who devotes himself to self-denial and mortification

san-sei (sahn-SAY) *n.*, a second-generation Japanese-American who is born and educated in the U.S.

san-tims (SAHN-tĭmz) *n.*, a pre-World War 2 monetary unit of Latvia

san-tir (san-TI(Ĕ)R) or **san-tour** (san-TUU(Ĕ)R) *n.*, a Persian wire-stringed musical instrument played with two curved sticks

san-tol (sahn-TOHL) *n.*, an Indo-Malayan tree with reddish wood and red, acid fruits that are used in preserves and pickles

san-to-nin (SAN-tŏ-nĭn) *n.*, a poisonous, bitter, crystalline compound found naturally in European wormwood and formerly used for expelling intestinal parasites

sa-phe-na (să-FEE-nă) *n.*, either of two main, large veins of the leg

sa-pid-i-ty (să-PID-id-ee) or (să-PID-ĭ-tee) *n.*, a highly noticeable taste

sa-pi-ent (SAY-pee-ĕnt) or (SA-pee-ĕnt) *adj.*, possessing a learned wisdom

sap-o-na-ceous (sap-ŏ-NAY-shŭs) *adj.*, having the slippery, soft, and smooth qualities of soap

sa-pon-i-fy (să-PAHN-ĭ-fī) *v.*, to make into soap

sap-o-rous (SAP-ŏ-rŭs) *adj.*, having a marked and exhilarating taste or flavor

sa-po-ta (să-POHD-ă) *n.*, a large, tropical North American tree

sap-phism (SA-fizĕm) *n.*, female homosexuality

\a\ bat \ă\ about \e\ or \ĕ\ check \ē\ letter
\ē\ cafe \i\fish \ī\ tie \ī\ limit \o\ boat
\ŏ\ bacon \u\ sun \ŭ\ helpful \ü\ fool

sa-pre-mi-a (sa-PREE-mee-ă) *n.*, a toxic condition of the body caused by the blood absorption of poisons from the decomposing bacteria that accompany gangrene

sap-robe (SAP-rohb) *n.*, an organism that lives in a relatively oxygen-free environment rich in organic matter

sap-ro-gen-ic (sap-rŏ-JEN-ik) *adj.*, producing decay or decomposition

sa-proph-a-gous (să-PRAHF-ă-gŭs) *adj.*, gaining nourishment from decay or decomposition

sar-a-band or **sar-a-bande** (SAR-ă-band) or (SAR-a-baa(ĕ)nd) *n.*, a slow, stately court dance of the 17th and 18th centuries that evolved into a movement of the classical suite

sa-ran (să-RAN) or (să-RAA(Ĕ)N) *n.*, a sturdy, pliant thermoplastic that provides a waterproof protective coating

sar-coid (SAHR-koid) *adj.*, having the characteristics of flesh

sar-col-o-gy (sahr-KAHL-ŏ-jee) *n.*, a theory that animal body parts, when eaten by humans, strengthen or modify their corresponding human parts

sard (SAHRD) *n.*, a deep orange-red variety of quartz

sark (SAHRK) *n.*, British dialect for a unisex body garment

sa-rod or **sa-rode** (să-ROHD) *n.*, a bowed string instrument of northern India that resembles a lute

sar-wan (sah-WAHN) *n.*, a person who drives camels

sa-shoon (sa-SHOON) *n.*, a leg pad worn to ease pressure on a tender spot under a boot

sas-tru-ga or **zas-tru-ga** (SAS-trŭ-gă) or (ZAS-trŭ-gă) *n.*, a snaking ridge of hard, wind-formed snow

sat-is-pas-sion (sad-ĭ-SPASH-ŏn) *n.*, pain or distress suffered in repentance

sa-ty-ri-a-sis (sayd-ĕ-RĪ-ă-sĭs) or (sa-tĕ-RĪ-ă-sĭs) *n.*, uncontrollable male sexual desire

sau-ger (SAW-gĕ(r)) *n.*, 1. a small pike perch like the walleye 2. the freshwater walleye pike

saul-ie (SAWL-i) *n.*, a Scottish term for one paid to attend funerals as a mourner

sau-rel (SAW-rĕl) *n.*, a long, compressed fish with a series of bony plates along its lateral line, such as a horse or jack mackerel

sau-ri-an (SAW-ree-ăn) *adj.*, resembling a long-bodied, legged reptile with a tapering tail

sau-ro-pod (SAW-rŏ-pahd) *n.* a small-headed, herbivorous dinosaur with a long neck and tail that is included among the largest of land animals of any period

sa-vate (să-VAT) *n.*, a form of the sport of boxing in which combatants deliver blows with either their feet or hands

sax-a-tile (SAKS-ă-tīl) *adj.*, living or flourishing among rocks

sax-aul (SAK-sawl) *n.*, a small, leafless Asian shrub with green branches that is adapted for life in an arid climate and is used in the stabilization of desert soil

say-yid (SĪ-(y)ĕd) *n.*, a Muslim title of respect for one of outstanding achievement or noble birth

scac-chite (SKA-kīt) *n.*, a mineral of native manganese chloride occurring in volcanic regions

scagl-io-la (skal-YOH-lă) *n.*, an imitation ornamental marble made from finely ground gypsum and glue that is used for decorative interior work

sca-lar-i-form (skă-LA(A)R-ĭ-fohrm) *adj.*, having bars or stripes in a ladder-shaped pattern

scal-pri-form (SKAL-prĭ-fohrm) *adj.*, chisel-shaped

scam-mo-ny (SKA-mŏ-nee) *n.*, a twining, thick-rooted plant of Asia Minor

scan-da-roon (skan-dă-ROON) *n.*, a domestic carrier pigeon with a long body and legs and a curved beak

scan-so-ri-al (skan-SOH-ree-ăl) or (skan-SAW-ree-ăl) *adj.*, possessing the capacity for climbing

scant-ling (SKANT-ling) or (SKAANT-ling) *n.*, an archaic term for a part or section of an object that exemplifies the whole

scaph-oid (SKA-foid) *adj.*, concave

scap-u-li-man-cy or **scap-u-lo-man-cy** (SKAP-yŭ-lĭ-man(t)-see) *n.*, predicting the future by using a shoulder blade

scar-row (SKA-roh) *n.*, a Scottish term for a shaded or dim illumination

sca-toph-a-gy (skă-TAHF-ă-jee) *n.*, the eating of bodily wastes or other filth as a religious ceremonial practice or as a mentally ill act

sca-tu-ri-ent (skă-TUU-ree-ĕnt) *adj.*, copiously spouting forth

scaup (SKAHP) or (SKAWP) *n.*, U.S. dialect for the part of the human head that is covered with hair

scau-per (SKAW-pĕr) *n.*, an engraving tool with a U-shaped blade that is used as a gouge

scav-en-ger's daugh-ter (SKAV-ĕn-jĕrz-DAWD-ĕr) *n.*, an instrument of torture that squeezes the body so forcefully that blood flows from the nostrils, ears, hands, and feet

scel-er-at (SEL-ĕ-rat) *n.*, an archaic term for a felonious blackguard or criminal

scend (SEND) *v.*, to move or swell upward as a result of a naturally occurring force

scha-den-freu-de (SHAH-dĕn-froi-dĕ) *n.*, the pleasure derived from the misfortunes of others

schat-chen or **shad-chan** (SHAHT-kĕn) *n.*, a person who handles or arranges a marriage contract between a Jewish man and woman, in return for a fee or other consideration

scherm (SKE(Ĕ)RM) *n.*, an African term for a protective partition

---

\a\ bat \ă\ about \e\ or \ĕ\ check \ē\ letter \ê\ cafe \i\fish \ī\ tie \ĭ\ limit \o\ boat \ŏ\ bacon \u\ sun \ŭ\ helpful \ü\ fool

sche·sis (SKEE-sis) or (SKE-sĭs) *n.*, an obsolete term for the usual condition of the body or mind

schip·per·ke (SKIP-ĕ(r)-kee) *n.*, a small, stocky, black dog from a Belgian working breed developed originally as watchdogs on canal boats

schiz·o·thy·mi·a (skits-ŏ-THĪ-mee-a) *n.*, a withdrawn, self-reflective temperament that somewhat resembles schizophrenia

schlen·ter (S(H)LEN-tĕ(r)) *n.*, an African term for an artificial likeness or phony, especially in reference to a diamond

schnec·ke (SHNEK-ĕ) *n.*, a cinnamon roll

schnitz or **snits** or **snitz** (SHNITZ) *n.*, dehydrated sections of fruit, especially apple slices

scho·li·um (SKOH-lee-ŭm) *n.*, an explanation or commentary written in the margins of a book

schrik (SKRIK) *n.*, a south African term for a sudden, engulfing fear

schuyt (SKOIT) or (SKĪT) *n.*, a Dutch sailing boat with a broad, flat bow that is used on waterways

sci·ae·nid (sī-EE-nĭd) *adj.*, of or relating to the flesh-eating food and sport fish of the croaker family

sci·a·lyt·ic (sī-ă-LID-ik) *adj.*, causing shadows to disappear

sci·am·a·chy (sī-AM-ă-kee) *n.*, a struggle with a shadow; a pretend or pointless skirmish

sci·ap·o·dous (sī-AP-ŏ-dŭs) *adj.*, large-footed

sci·li·cet (SI-lĭ-set) or (SĪ-lĭ-set) or (SKEE-lĭ-ket) *adv.*, an expression meaning "namely" that precedes an explanation of a word or passage

sci·u·rine (SĪ-yoo-rīn) or (SĪ-yoo-rin) *adj.*, squirrel-like

sci·o·lism (SĪ-ŏ-lizĕm) *n.*, a shallow understanding

scis·sel (SIS-ĕl) or (SIZ-ĕl) *n.*, leftover metal pieces from various machine operations such as die punching

sci·u·roid (SĪ-(y)ŭ-roid) or (SĪ-(y)uu-roid) *adj.*, having the shape of a squirrel's tail, especially when referring to ears of grain

sclaff (SKLAF) *n.*, a golf shot in which the golf club head nicks the ground before the ball

scob·i·form (SKAHB-ĭ-fohrm) or (SKOHB-ĭ-fohrm) *adj.*, having the fine consistency of shavings or filings

scod·gy (SKAH-jee) *n.*, a Scottish term for one who works hard at a menial, unpleasant, or boring job

sco·li·on or **sko·li·on** (SKOH-lee-ahn) *n.*, an ancient Greek banquet song sung, and possibly improvised, by each participant in turn

scol·o·pen·dra (skahl-ŏ-PEN-dră) *n.*, a long, flat invertebrate with poisonous fangs and a pair of legs per body segment

sco·pa (SKOH-pă) *n.*, the brushlike hairs on the body of an insect that usually serve to gather something such as pollen

scop·u·la (SKAHP-yŭ-lă) *n.*, a thick cluster of hairs on the bodies of arthropods

scor-bu-tic (skaw(r)-BYOOD-ik) *adj.*, suffering from scurvy

scor-da-tu-ra (skaw(r)-dă-TUU-ră) *n.*, the nontraditional tuning of a stringed musical instrument to achieve some special effect

sco-ri-a (SKOH-ree-ă) or (SKAW-ree-ă) *n.*, a frothy, bubble-filled volcanic lava

scot-o-graph (SKAHD-ŏ-graf) or (SKOHD-o-graf) *n.*, a photograph produced by X rays or gamma rays

scram-a-sax (SKRAM-ă-saks) *n.*, a large hunting knife or weapon used by early Germanic peoples

scran-nel (SKRAN-ĕl) *adj.*, disagreeable to the ears

scraw (SKRAW) *n.*, a Scottish and Irish term for a piece of a surface layer of earth

screed (SKREED) *n.*, an informal prose piece of any form

screeve (SKREEV) *n.*, a British term for a letter that asks for money or general assistance

scrip-tur-i-ent (SKRIP-chŭr-ee-ĕnt) *adj.*, an obsolete term meaning having an overriding desire to write

scri-vel-lo (skrĭ-VE-loh) *n.*, a small elephant tooth commonly used to produce billiard balls

scro-bic-u-late (skroh-BIK-yŭ-layt) or (skroh-BIK-yŭ-lĕt) *adj.*, having a surface covered with many small, rounded indentations

scrog (SKRAWG) *n.*, British dialect for a dwarfed hedge

scroop (SKROOP) *n.*, the sound made by garments of silk and similar fabrics in motion

scro-ti-form (SKROHD-ĭ-fohrm) *adj.*, having the rounded shape of a pouch

scroyle (SKROI(E)L) *n.*, an archaic term for a worthless rascal

scrump (SKRŬMP) or (SKRUUMP) *n.*, English dialect for a wrinkled and dried or charred item

scry-ing (SKRĪ-ĭng) *n.*, predicting the future or gaining hidden knowledge through the interpretation of signs and omens

scud-dy (SKĔD-i) *adj.*, a Scottish term meaning nude

scul-pin (SKŬL-pĭn) *n.*, 1. a spiny, large-headed, scaleless fish with little edible flesh 2. a useless being

scum-ble (SKŬM-bĕl) *v.*, to mute the colors or soften the outlines of a drawing by lightly rubbing with a finger or a pointed roll of paper

scup-paug (skŭ-PAWG) *n.*, a small marine fish found along the Atlantic coast from South Carolina to Maine that is prized by anglers

scur-fy (SKŬR-fee) *adj.*, having, producing, or covered with thin, dry, flaky scales

scutch (SKŬCH) *v.*, U.S. dialect meaning to thrash

scute (SK(Y)OOT) *n.*, an archaic term for a metal token of currency that has little worth

scu-tif-er-ous (sk(y)oo-TIF-(e)r-ŭs) *adj.*, having large scales or horny plates

---

\a\ bat \ä\ about \e\ or \ĕ\ check \ē\ letter
\é\ cafe \i\fish \ī\ tie \i\ limit \o\ boat
\ŏ\ bacon \u\ sun \ŭ\ helpful \ü\ fool

scyb-a-lum (SIB-ă-lŭm) *n.*, a dried, solid piece of fecal excrement

sdruc-cio-la (ZDROO-chĕ-lah) *adj.*, having a triple rhyme that accents the third syllable from the end

sec-ta-ry (SEK-tă-ree) or (SEK-tă-ri) *n.*, a supporter or follower of a dissenting religious group

sec-tile (SEK-tĕl) or (SEK-tīl) or (SEK-til) *adj.*, capable of being separated into small divisions by a smooth-cutting knife

sec-un-dip-a-ra (sek-ŭn-DIP-ă-ră) *n.*, a woman whose two children were products of separate pregnancies

se-di-le (sĕ-DI-lee) *n.*, one of three seats near the altar of a church that is occupied by officiating clergy at intervals during the service

see-ly (SEE-lee) *adj.*, an archaic term meaning arousing contemptuous pity because of physical or mental weakness

see-see (SEE-see) *n.*, a small, Asiatic sand partridge with protective coloration adapted to sandy wasteland

seiche (SAYSH) *n.*, a back-and-forth movement of the waters in a lake or land-locked sea that varies in duration and may result from changes in atmospheric pressure

se-i-ty (SEE-ĭd-ee) *n.*, a personal, individual quality

se-jant (SEE-jănt) *adj.*, a term in heraldry meaning resting on the haunches; sitting

se-le-ni-an (sĕ-LEE-nee-ăn) *adj.*, referring to the moon

sel-e-nog-ra-phy (sel-ĕ-NAHG-ră-fee) *n.*, the recording, description, and study of the moon's landscape and physical features

self-heal (SELF-heel) *n.*, a plant believed to possess curative powers, especially an Asian mint with blue flowers now found throughout North America

sel-syn (SEL-sin) *n.*, a motor-generator system that transmits currents, rotates the motor to the same relative position as the generator, and remotely controls the instrument and valve settings

sel-vage (SEL-vij) or (SEL-veej) *n.*, the finished edge of a woven or flat-knitted fabric that prevents unraveling

se-mas-i-ol-o-gy (sĕ-may-see-AHL-ŏ-jee) *n.*, the study of the meanings of signs and symbols

se-mat-ic (sĕ-MAD-ik) *adj.*, providing a warning or signal of danger, especially when referring to the distinctive coloration of a poisonous or preying animal

se-mei-ol-o-gy (see-mī-AHL-ŏ-jee) *n.*, the study of indicators or symptoms of disease or physical disturbances

sem-eme (SE-meem) *n.*, the meaning of a linguistic unit constructed according to a system of signs

se-mi-qua-ver (se-mee-KWAY-vĕ(r)) *n.*, a musical note with one-sixteenth the value of a whole note

sem-per-vi-rent (sem-pĕ(r)-VĪ-rĕnt) *adj.*, remaining green with fresh vegetation

sem·pi·ter·nal (sem-pĭ-TĔR-năl) *adj.*, endless

sem·ple (SEM-pĕl) *adj.*, a Scottish term meaning born to a low social or political rank

sen·a·ry (SEEN-ă-ree) or (SEN-ă-ree) *adj.*, composed of or consisting of six elements or sections

se·nec·ti·tude (sĕ-NEK-tĭ-tood) *n.*, the final phase of the average life span

sen·e·schal (SEN-ĕ-shăl) *n.*, a representative of a medieval lord or king who manages and superintends a feudal estate and its populace

sen·net (SEN-ĕt) *n.*, a trumpet or cornet signal that indicates a stage entrance or exit

se·poy (SEE-poi) *n.*, an Asian Indian native in military service to a European power, especially a soldier in the British army

sep·pu·ku (se-POO-koo) *n.*, disembowelment as a means of suicide; also called hara-kiri

sep·ul·ture (SEP-ŭl-chŭr) *n.*, the act of interring a body

se·qua·cious (sĕ-KWAY-shŭs) or (see-KWAY-shŭs) *adj.*, an archaic term meaning abjectly compliant and obedient

se·rac (sĕ-RAK) or (say-RAK) *n.*, a pointed or sharp piece of ice appearing among the splits and rifts of a glacier

se·re·na (sĕ-RAY-nă) *n.*, a love song played in the evening

se·ri·ceous (sĕ-RI-shŭs) *adj.*, 1. silklike 2. having a short-haired, fuzzy surface

ser·mo·ci·na·tion (se(ĕ)r-moh-sĭ-NAY-shŏn) *n.*, an obsolete term for a method of speech-making in which a speaker poses a question, then immediately answers or comments on his remarks

ser·o·tine (SER-ŏ-tīn) *adj.*, late blooming

ses·qui·al·ter·al (ses-kwee-AWL-tĕ(r)-ăl) *adj.*, in the proportion of 1 to 1-1/2

se·ta·ceous (sĕ-TAY-shŭs) or (see-TAY-shŭs) *adj.*, 1. having bristles 2. bristlelike

sfer·ics or **spher·ics** (SFIR-iks) *n.*, 1. radio-receptor distortion produced by electrical activity in the atmosphere 2. an electronic storm detector that plots electrical discharges

sfu·ma·to (sfoo-MAH-toh) *n.*, the delineation of contour using delicate gradations in color and tone instead of sharp outlines

sga·bel·lo (zgah-BE-loh) or (skah-BE-loh) *n.*, an Italian Renaissance stool with a simple, upright back

sgraf·fi·to (zgrah-FEE-toh) or (skrah-FEE-toh) *n.*, an ornamental decoration achieved by scraping or cutting away areas of a surface layer to reveal the different colors and textures underneath

sha·doof or **sha·duf** (shă-DUUF) or (shah-DUUF) *n.*, a counterbalanced pole-and-post device used in Egypt to raise water for irrigation

---

\a\ bat \ä\ about \e\ or \ĕ\ check \ĕ\ letter \é\ cafe \i\ fish \ĭ\ tie \ĭ\ limit \o\ boat \ŏ\ bacon \u\ sun \ŭ\ helpful \ü\ fool

sha-drach (SHA-drak) *n.*, a mass of unblended materials remaining in a blast-furnace hearth; also called a salamander

shag-a-nap-pi (SHAG-ă-nap-ee) *n.*, a rawhide strand, strap, or rope

sha-green (sha-GREEN) *n.*, an untanned, brightly colored leather with a rough, granular surface

sha-ko (SHA-koh) or (SHAY-koh) *n.*, a high-crowned, stiff military dress hat with a front metal plate and a plume

shal-loon (shă-LOON) *n.*, a light, twilled fabric of wool used to line coats and uniforms

shal-lop (SHAL-ŏp) *n.*, a small, open boat equipped with oars, sails, or both for navigation in shallow waters

sha-mal (shă-MAHL) *n.*, a wind blowing northwest through Iraq and the Persian Gulf

shan-dy-gaff (SHAN-dee-gaf) *n.*, a beverage made from beer and ginger beer or ginger ale

sha-poo (SHAH-poo) or **sha-po** (SHAH-poh) *n.*, a wild sheep found in Kashmir and Tibet

shard-born (SHAHRD-baw(ĕ)rn) *adj.*, an archaic term referring to a beetle born in manure

shave-ling (SHAYV-ling) or (SHAVE-leeng) *n.*, 1. a belittling term applied to a man whose shaven head identifies him as a cleric 2. an immature lad

sha-wab-ti (shă-WAB-tee) *n.*, a small figure inscribed with religious passages and placed in an ancient Egyptian tomb to represent the servants of the deceased in the land of the dead

shawm or **shalm** (SHAWM) *n.*, an early double-reeded, straight-bodied woodwind that preceded the oboe

she-been (shĕ-BEEN) *n.*, an Irish term for an illegally run bar or tavern

shend (SHEND) *v.*, an archaic term meaning to abash

sher-ry-val-lies (SHER-ee-val-eez) *n.*, protective leg coverings of heavy cloth or leather, once used for horseback riding

sheugh (SHOOK) *n.*, a Scottish term for a small, steep-sided valley formed by water erosion

shi-kar (shĭ-KAHR) *n.*, an Indian term for the sport of game hunting

shi-ko (shi-KOH) or (SHI-koh) *n.*, a Burmese kneeling posture with clasped hands and bowed head that is assumed when in the presence of a superior

shil-la-ber (SHIL-ă-bĕ(r)) *n.*, a confederate who acts as a decoy and lures others into participation by his enthusiasm, good fortune, or example

shil-li-beer (SHIL-ĭ-bi(e)r) *n.*, a horse-drawn hearse equipped with seats for mourners

shil-pit (SHIL-pĭt) *adj.*, a Scottish term for having an emaciated appearance

shi-nar-ump (shĭ-NAR-ŭmp) *n.*, a southwestern U.S. term for wood that resembles agate in color, hardness, and pattern

shite-poke (SHĪT-pohk) or (SHĪD-pohk) *n.*, a type of heron that was traditionally believed to defecate when forced to take wing

shit-tim (SHID-ĭm) or (SHIT-ĭm) *n.*, an unspecified tree that is believed to have supplied the hard, fine-grained wood used in building the Ark and various pieces of the Hebrew tabernacle

shive (SHĪV) *n.*, a thin wood stopper for the fill-and-drain opening of a cask

shode (SHOHD) *n.*, English dialect for a piece of ore removed from bedrock by a natural agency and lying in the surface soil

shog (SHAHG) *v.*, U.S. dialect meaning to push and shove

sho-ji (SHOH-jee) *n.*, a temporary, paper folding-partition for a house or room

sho-neen (shoh-NEEN) or (SHOH-neen) *n.*, an Irish term for a man who pompously attempts to be a gentleman

shriev-al-ty (SHREEV-ăl-tee) *n.*, a British term for the office of a sheriff

shroff (SHRAHF) *v.*, to examine, evaluate, and cull coins

shruff (SHRŬF) *n.*, a metal impurity left after smelting

shu-ba (SHOO-bă) *n.*, a Russian outer garment made of or lined with fur

si-a-mang (SEE-ă-mang) or (SEE-ă-mawng) *n.*, a black tree-dwelling ape of Sumatra and the Malay Peninsula that has webbing between its second and third toes

sib-ship (SIB-ship) *n.*, a group of people descended from a single ancestor

sib-yl-line (SIB-ĕ-līn) or (SIB-ĕ-leen) *adj.*, enigmatic

sic-ca-tive (SIK-ăd-iv) or (SIK-ă-tiv) *adj.*, promoting water loss

sif-fi-late (SIF-ĭ-layt) *v.*, to speak in soft, sibilant tones

si-gan-id (sĭ-GAN-ĭd) or (sĭ-GAYN-ĭd) *adj.*, referring to a type of tropical Pacific fish with strong fin spines that can severely wound

sig-il (SIJ-yl) *n.*, an astrological or magical token possessing supposed supernatural power

sig-il-late (SIJ-i-layt) *adj.*, trimmed with imprinted designs or patterns

sig-los (SI-glahs) *n.*, an ancient Persian silver coin

sig-mate (SIG-mayt) *adj.*, S-shaped

sig-moi-dal (sig-MOI-dăl) *adj.*, 1. having a single curve like the letter C 2. having a double curve like the letter S

si-kin-nis (sĭ-KIN-ĭs) *n.*, a bizarre, wild dance performed in conjunction with the satyric drama of ancient Greece

---

\a\ bat \ă\ about \e\ or \ĕ\ check \ē\ letter
\é\ cafe \i\fish \ī\ tie \ĭ\ limit \o\ boat
\ō\ bacon \u\ sun \ŭ\ helpful \ū\ fool

sile (SĪ(E)L) *n.*, a Scottish term for a long, thick piece of building material

si·len·ti·ar·y (sī-LEN-chee-er-ee) *n.*, a person given the authority to maintain the quiet order necessary for a trial or other public assembly

sil·la·bub or **syl·la·bub** (SIL-ă-bŭb) *n.*, a beverage or dessert of sweetened milk or cream soured with wine, liquor, or other acidic potables

sil·log·ra·pher (sĭ-LAHG-ră-fĕ(r)) *n.*, a satirist

si·mar or **sy·mar** (sĭ-MAHR) *n.*, an archaic term for a woman's light, loosely hanging garment with a full skirt and train, popular during the Renaissance

si·mo·ny (SĪ-mŏ-nee) or (SIM-ŏ-nee) *n.*, the exchange of religious items, offices, or favors for money

si·moom (sĭ-MOOM) or (sī-MOOM) *n.*, a scorching, strong wind that bears sandy dust from the deserts of Asia and Africa

si·mous (SI-mŭs) *adj.*, an obsolete term meaning curved and hollow; blunt

sim·u·la·crum (sim-yŭ-LAY-krŭm) or (sim-yŭ-LA-krŭm) *n.*, a vague likeness

si·murgh or **si·murg** (see-MUU(E)RG) or (SEE-muu(ĕ)rg) *n.*, in Persian legend, a large, ancient bird thought to possess great wisdom

sin·ar·quism (SI-nahr-kizĕm) or (sĭ-NAHR-kizĕm) *n.*, a Mexican reactionary movement of peasants and workers opposed to U.S. influence in Latin America

sin·gul·tus (sing-GŬL-tŭs) *n.*, a sudden, uncontrollable diaphragm spasm; also called hiccup

sin·is·tral (SIN-ĭs-trăl) or (sĭ-NIS-trăl) *n.*, a person who prefers to use the left hand

sip·id (SIP-ĭd) *adj.*, flavorful; savory

si·roc·co (sĭ-RAH-koh) *n.*, a hot, humid wind from the Libyan desert that affects the northern Mediterranean coast

sir·rah or **sir·ra** (SI-ră) *n.*, an obsolete form of address that implies lower rank or standing

sis·co·wet (SIS-kŏ-wet) *n.*, a large lake trout found in the deeper waters of the Great Lakes

sis·e·ra·ra (sis-ĕ-RA(A)-ră) *n.*, U.S. dialect for an intense berating

si·tol·o·gy (sī-TAHL-ŏ-jee) or (sĭ-TAHL-ŏ-jee) *n.*, the study of foods and their nutritional values

si·to·pho·bi·a (sī-tŏ-FOH-bee-ă) *n.*, pathological avoidance and rejection of food

six·mo (SIK-smoh) *n.*, the dimensions of a piece of paper that is one-sixth of a sheet

siz·ar or **siz·er** (SĪZ-ĕr) *n.*, a college student given a reduction in his educational expenses, originally for performing servants' duties for other students

sjam·bok (sham-BAHK) or (sham-BŎK) *n.*, a South African term for a heavy whip of rhinoceros hide

skean or **skeen** or **skene** or **skhian** (S(H)KEE(A)N) *n.*, a bronze, double-bladed knife once used in Ireland

skeg-ger (SKEG-ĕr) *n.*, an immature salmon

skel-lum (SKEL-ŭm) *n.*, a Scottish term for a villain

skelp (SKELP) *n.*, British dialect for a quick, stinging stroke delivered by the flat of the hand

skep (SKEP) *n.*, a round wicker basket

sker-ry (SKER-ee) *n.*, an archaic term for a small, shallow two-seated boat

skew-bald (SKYOO-bawld) *adj.*, having spotty patches of white and some other color as markings

skey (SKAY) *n.*, a wedge-shaped bar of an ox yoke

ski-ag-ra-phy (skī-AG-ră-fee) *n.*, the technique of obtaining a photographic image, especially by means of X rays

ski-jor-ing (SKEE-johr-ing) or (skee-JOHR-ing) *n.*, a winter sport in which a skier towed by a horse or vehicle glides over snow or ice

skil-li-ga-lee (SKIL-ĭ-gă-lee) *n.*, a British term for a soupy, soft food of boiled oatmeal

skim-ming-ton (SKIM-ing-tŏn) *n.*, a person who publicly ridicules the husband of a nagging, unfaithful wife

skink (SKINGK) *n.*, a liquid food of simmered beef shinbones or hocks

skip-ken-nel (SKIP-ken-ĕl) *n.*, a young, low-ranking male servant

skip-pet (SKIP-ĕt) *n.*, a small, round case for protecting an official or personal seal

skirr (SKĬR) *v.*, to run away hurriedly

skive or **scive** (SKĪV) *v.*, to slice off in thin strips or pieces

sklent (SKLENT) *v.*, a Scottish term meaning to look at with distrust or suspicion

skoo-kum (SKOO-kŭm) *adj.*, strong or powerful

sku-a (SKYOO-ă) *n.*, a large, rapacious bird of the northern seas that robs food from weaker birds

sky-bald or **sky-bal** (SKĪ-băl) *n.*, British dialect for a lazy, worthless person

slade (SLAYD) *n.*, a shovel-like implement with an L-shaped blade for removing blocks of peat from turf

slais-ter (SLAYS-tĕr) *v.*, British dialect meaning to work with or handle messy, sloppy materials

slib-ber-sauce (SLIB-ĕr-saws) *n.*, an obsolete term for a disgusting blend of ingredients prepared as food, medicine, or as a cosmetic

slip-slop (SLIP-slahp) *n.*, an archaic term for a blundering, humorous misuse of a word

slock (SLAWK) *n.*, a Scottish term for an amount of drinkable liquid

slojd or **sloyd** (SLOID) *n.*, a Swedish program of manual training that emphasizes wood carving

sloom (SLOOM) *n.*, British dialect for a catnap

\a\ bat \ă\ about \e\ or \è\ check \ĕ\ letter
\é\ cafe \i\fish \ī\ tie \ĭ\ limit \o\ boat
\ŏ\ bacon \u\ sun \ŭ\ helpful \ü\ fool

slub-ber (SLŬB-ĕ(r)) v., to do carelessly and sloppily

slub-ber-de-gul-lion (SLŬB-ĕ(r)-dĕ-gŭl-yŏn) n., U.S. dialect for a knave

slum-gul-lion (slŭm-GŬL-yŏn) or (SLŬM-gŭl-yŏn) n., a mixture of blood, oil, and brine that collects on a whaler's deck during butchering

slum-mock (SLŬM-ŏk) n., a clumsy, crude, or messy person

slype (SLĪP) n., a narrow corridor

small-clothes (SMAWL-kloh(th)z) n., short, close-fitting trousers that end at the knee, especially those popular in the 18th and early 19th centuries

smal-to (SMAHL-toh) n., the colored glass or enamel used to make inlaid pictures or designs

sma-rag-dine (smă-RAG-dĭn) adj., having the yellowish green color of an emerald

smear-case or **smier-case** (SMIR-kays) n., a midwestern U.S. term for the soft cheese made from sour-milk curds; also called cottage cheese

smeech (SMEECH) n., British dialect for thick, heavy smoke

smeeth (SMEETH) v., British dialect meaning to remove lumps and unevennesses

smell-feast (SMEL-feest) n., a person who lives off the gratuitous support and sustenance of another

smell-fun-gus (SMEL-fŭng-gŭs) n., a person who criticizes petty flaws and inadequacies

smolt (SMOHLT) n., a silvery, two-year-old salmon or sea trout

snaf-fle (SNAF-ĕl) v., to limit or restrict in a gentle fashion

snash (SNASH) v., a Scottish term meaning to sass

snath (SNATH) or (SNETH) n., the long handle of a bladed tool used for mowing grass or grain

sneap (SNEEP) v., an archaic term meaning to injure or damage by exposure to cold

sneck (SNEK) n., British dialect for the device that fastens or holds a door shut

sneck-draw (SNEK-draw) n., a Scottish term for a sneaky person who insidiously tries to gain an advantage

sned (SNED) v., a Scottish term meaning to cut back excessive or superfluous vegetation

snib (SNIB) n., a Scottish term for a purposeful slight or injury

snick-er-snee (snik-ĕ(r)-SNEE) v., an archaic term meaning to take part in slash-and-jab combat with knives

snip-snap-sno-rum (snip-snap-SNOH-rŭm) n., a simple, rank-matching card game; also called Earl of Coventry

snod (SNAHD) adj., a Scottish term meaning tidy

snol-ly-gos-ter (SNAHL-ee-gahs-tĕ(r)) n., an unethical, canny person

snudge (SNŬJ) n., an archaic term for a stingy, grasping person

so-ja (SOI-(y)a) n., a legume cultivated worldwide for its nutritional value; also called the soybean

soke (SOHK) or (SAHK) *n.*, an Anglo-Saxon and early English legal term for the right to hear legal cases and administer justice

so-la-no (sŏ-LAH-noh) *n.*, a hot, humid, easterly wind of the Mediterranean region that originates in Spain

so-la-ti-um (soh-LAY-shee-ŭm) *n.*, something that eases or makes up for suffering or loss

sol-dan (SAHL-dăn) or (SOHL-dăn) or (SOH-děn) *n.*, a Muslim sovereign or prince

so-le-i-form (sŏ-LEE-ĭ-fohrm) or (SOH-lee-i-fohrm) *adj.*, slipper-shaped

sol-fa-ta-ra (sahl-fă-TAH-ră) or (sohl-fă-TAH-ră) *n.*, a volcanic area emitting only hot vapors and gases

sol-fège (sahl-FEZH) *n.*, the use of syllables like do-re-mi in singing musical exercises or melodies

sol-i-da-go (sahl-ĭ-DAY-goh) *n.*, a North American herb like goldenrod

so-li-fid-i-an (soh-lĭ-FID-ee-ăn) or (sahl-ĭ-FID-ee-ăn) *n.*, a person who holds that faith alone without good works guarantees salvation

sol-i-on (SAHL-ĭ-ŏn) or (SAHL-ī-ahn) *n.*, an electronic detect and amplify device that uses ions moving in a solution to operate

sol-mi-za-tion (sahl-mĭ-ZAY-shŏn) *n.*, a system of using syllables instead of letters to represent tones of a musical scale

som-nil-o-quist (sahm-NIL-ŏ-kwĭst) *n.*, a person who speaks aloud while sleeping

som-nip-a-thy (sahm-NIP-ă-thee) *n.*, irregular or dysfunctional sleep

soot-er-kin (SUUD-ĕ(r)-kĭn) or (SOOD-ĕ(r)-kĭn) *n.*, 1. the placental and fetal membranes once believed to be expelled by Dutch women after giving birth 2. something that is flawed or failed

so-phros-y-ne (sŏ-FRAHS-ĕn-ee) *n.*, 1. self-restraint 2. the exact combination of elements that results in a desired state

sor-dine (SAW(Ĕ)R-deen) or (saw(ĕ)r-DEEN) *n.*, a pipe placed into the mouth of a trumpet to dull its sound

sor-dor (SAWR-dŏr) or (SAWR-daw(ĕ)r) *n.*, useless, discardable material

sor-i-cine (SAWR-ĭ-sīn) *adj.*, shrewlike

so-ri-tes (sŏ-RĪD-eez) *n.*, a logical argument based on the linkage of its premises

sorn (SAW(E)RN) *v.*, a Scottish term meaning to exploit a relationship for the sake of personal gain

so-ro-che (sŏ-ROH-chee) *n.*, the illness that results from oxygen deficiency at high altitudes; also called mountain sickness

so-ror-i-cide (sŏ-RAWR-ĭ-sīd) *n.*, the act of putting one's sister to death

sor-ti-lege (SAW(R)D-ĭ-lij) or (SAW(R)-tĭ-lij) *n.*, fortune telling by lots

---

\a\ bat \ă\ about \e\ or \ĕ\ check \ē\ letter \é\ cafe \i\ fish \ĭ\ tie \ī\ limit \o\ boat \ŏ\ bacon \u\ sun \ŭ\ helpful \ü\ fool

soss (SAHS) *n.*, British dialect for a heavy blow

so-te-ri-ol-o-gy (soh-ti-ree-AHL-ŏ-jee) *n.*, the theological study of salvation as a result of divine intervention

so-tol (SOH-tohl) or (soh-TOHL) *n.*, a distilled northern Mexican liquor

sou-a-ri (soo-AH-ree) *n.*, a South American tree whose strong wood is used for furniture and shipbuilding

sou-brette (soo-BRET) *n.*, a young, flirtatious lady's maidservant

sough (SOW) or (SĔF) *v.*, to make a low, murmuring sound

soum (SUUM) *n.*, a Scottish term for the number of livestock that can be pastured on a given piece of land

sou-tache (soo-TASH) *n.*, a narrow, herringbone-patterned braid used as a decorative trim for clothing

sou-tane (soo-TAHN) *n.*, a long, close-fitting garment worn by lay deacons in the Roman Catholic Church

sov-khoz (sŏf-KAWZ) or (sawv-KAWZ) or (sahv-KAWZ) *n.*, a Russian state-owned farm that pays wages to its workers

so-war (soh-(W)AHR) *n.*, a cavalry soldier in the Indian military

spa-do (SPAY-doh) *n.*, a man or beast deprived of the ability to reproduce

spae (SPAY) *v.*, a Scottish term meaning to predict the future

spa-gyr-ic (spă-JIR-ik) *adj.*, of or relating to the health-promoting combination of chemistry and medicine

spa-hi or **spa-hee** (SPAH-hee) *n.*, a native Algerian cavalry soldier in the French army of Africa

spal-peen (spal-PEEN) *n.*, an Irish term for a scoundrel

spang-hew (SPANG-hyoo) *v.*, British dialect meaning to hurl something forcefully into the air

sparge (SPAHRJ) *v.*, to dampen by scattering drops of water upon

spar-id (SPAR-ĭd) *n.*, an abundant, widespread marine fish that has molars among its teeth

spar-ple (SPAHR-păl) *v.*, an archaic term meaning to strew

sparth (SPAHRTH) *n.*, a large, broad-bladed ax used by medieval Irish warriors

spar-tle (SPAHR-tĕl) *v.*, a Scottish term meaning to lie in an awkward, outstretched position

spatch-cock (SPACH-kahk) *n.*, a fowl that is cut and broiled immediately after being butchered

spa-ti-ate (SPAY-shee-ayt) *v.*, to take a leisurely or random walk

spat-u-la-man-cy (SPACH-ŭ-lă-man(t)-see) *n.*, predicting the future by using an animal's shoulder blade

spawl (SPAWL) *v.*, an archaic term meaning to expel saliva from the mouth

spay-ard (SPAY-ă(r)d) *n.*, a three-year-old male red deer

spec·u·lar (SPEK-yŭ-lă(r)) *adj.*, mirrorlike

speer (SPEER) *v.*, a Scottish term meaning to seek information about

spelt (SPELT) *n.*, a type of wheat grown primarily in Germany and Switzerland

spe·rate (SPI-rayt) *adj.*, an archaic term meaning confidently desired

sper·mo·phile (SPĔR-mŏ-fĭl) *n.*, a striped North American ground squirrel

sphac·e·late (SFAS-ĕ-layt) *v.*, to affect with tissue decay

sphe·nog·ra·phy (sfĕ-NAHG-ră-fee) *n.*, the technique or method of writing in or interpreting wedge-shaped symbols

sphra·gis·tics (sfră-JIS-tiks) *n.*, the study of the history and function of engraved identifying devices such as seals and signets

spic·ule (SPI-kyool) *n.*, a tiny, thin, needlelike body or projection

spin·or (SPIN-ŏr) or (SPI-naw(e)r) *n.*, a quantity resembling a vector that is used in the higher mathematics of the theory of relativity

spin·stry (SPIN-stree) *n.*, the activity or product of making fiber into yarn

spis·si·tude (SPIS-ĭ-tood) or (SPIS-ĭ-tyood) *n.*, an archaic term for the state of being closely packed together

spis·sa·tus (spi-SAY-tŭs) *adj.*, a meteorological term meaning having a density that blocks or dims the sun

spitch·cock (SPICH-kahk) *n.*, a cut and broiled eel

spiz·zer·inc·tum (spi-zĕ-RING(K)-tŭm) *n.*, personal drive or motivation

splack·nuck (SPLAK-nŭk) *n.*, an unusual or peculiar person or animal

splake (SPLAYK) *n.*, a hybrid trout produced in fish hatcheries

splanch·nol·o·gy (splangk-NAHL-o-jee) *n.*, the anatomical study of the internal organs of the body

splore (SPLOH(E)R) or (SPLAW(E)R) *n.*, a Scottish term for a drinking spree

spof·fish (SPAH-fish) *adj.*, upset at trifles

spon·sa·li·a (spahn-SAY-lee-a) *n.*, a formal contract to marry in the future

spon·toon (spahn-TOON) *n.*, a policeman's nightstick

sprach·ge·fühl (SHPRAK-gĕ-foo(ĕ)l) *n.*, an awareness of the grammar and idioms of a language

sprag (SPRAG) or (SPRAA(E)G) *n.*, a piece of wood or metal used as a support or stop

spraing (SPRAYNG) *n.*, a Scottish term for a bright strip of color or light

spraints (SPRAYNTS) *n.*, the excrement of an otter

spring·ald (SPRING-ăld) *n.*, a teen-aged boy

\a\ bat \ă\ about \e\ or \è\ check \ĕ\ letter \é\ cafe \i\ fish \ī\ tie \ĭ\ limit \o\ boat \ŏ\ bacon \u\ sun \ŭ\ helpful \ü\ fool

sproat (SPROHT) *n.*, a light, wide, and slightly flattened hook for catching fish

sprod (SPRAHD) *n.*, a sea trout in its second year

sprug (SPRŬG) *n.*, a Scottish term for an English sparrow

spud-der (SPŬD-ĕr) *n.*, the operator of a well-drilling machine

spuf-fle (SPŬF-ĕl) *v.*, English dialect meaning to make much ado

spu-mes-cent (spyoo-MES-ĕnt) *adj.*, having masses of tiny, white bubbles

spur-tle (SPŬRD-ĕl) *n.*, a Scottish term for a flat, dull-edged cooking utensil used to turn food

squa-bash (SKWAW-bash) or (SKWAH-bash) *v.*, to devastate with criticism

squa-li-form (SKWAY-lĭ-fohrm) *adj.*, sharklike in shape

squa-ma-ceous (skwă-MAY-shĕs) *adj.*, covered with thin, overlapping protective plates, as fish or reptiles

squar-son (SKWAHR-sŏn) *n.*, a landowner who is also an ecclesiastic of the Church of England

sque-teague or **squi-teague** (skwĕ-TEEG) *n.*, a sport and food fish common along the eastern coast of the U.S.; also called the gray trout

sra-va-ka (S(H)RAH-vă-kă) *n.*, a person who hears the teachings of the Buddha and becomes an immediate disciple

sri or **shri** (S(H)REE) *n.*, a title of respect in India

stad-dle (STAD-ĕl) *n.*, the frame or base that supports a stack

staf-fage (stă-FAHZH) *n.*, the minor figures and objects added to an artistic work, especially the subordinate human or animal figures painted in a landscape

sta-gi-ar-y (STAY-jee-er-ee) *n.*, a resident clergyman

stag-nic-o-lous (stag-NIK-ŏ-lŭs) *adj.*, living in motionless, stale water

stam-mel (STAM-ĕl) *n.*, an obsolete term for a coarse, red wool fabric used to make undershirts for penitents

stang (STANG) *n.*, British dialect for a long, slender rod

stan-na-ry (STAN-ă-ree) *n.*, a tin-processing area of England once under the jurisdiction of a special court

sta-pe-li-a (stă-PEE-lee-ă) *n.*, an evil-smelling African plant with large, oddly colored flowers; also called carrion flowers

stas-i-mon (STAS-y-mahn) *n.*, a choral ode in Greek tragedy

staum-rel (STAM-rĕl) *adj.*, a Scottish term meaning silly

stau-rol-a-try (staw-RAHL-ă-tree) *n.*, a devotion to and reverence for the cross or crucifix

ste-ap-sin (stee-AP-sĭn) *n.*, the pancreatic enzyme that accelerates the breakdown and synthesis of fats

ste-a-rin (STEE-ă-rĭn) or (STIR-ĭn) *n.*, a chemical compound of glycol and stearic acid

ste·a·to·py·gi·a (stee-ăd-ŏ-PI-jee-a) *n.*, an abnormal fatness of the buttocks

steg·o·don (STEG-ŏ-dahn) *n.*, a prehistoric mammal intermediate between elephants and mastodons

stele (STEEL) or (STEE-lee) *n.*, an inscribed memorial slab or pillar of stone

stel·late (STE-layt) *adj.*, starlike

stel·li·form (STEL-ĭ-fohrm) *adj.*, star-shaped

stel·li·fi·ca·tion (stel-y-fī-KAY-shŭn) *n.*, a lofty exaltation

stel·lion·ate (STEL-yĕ-nĕt) or (STEL-yĕ-nayt) *n.*, a Roman and Scottish legal term for a fraud involving the sale of one property to multiple buyers or the sale of property misrepresented as one's own

steph·a·ne (STEF-ă-nee) *n.*, a metal headband, wide at the middle and narrow toward the temples, that is often seen in ancient Greek statues of the gods

ster·co·ric·o·lous (stĕr-kŏ-RIK-ŏ-lŭs) *adj.*, living in excrement

ster·e·og·no·sis (ster-ee-ahg-NOH-sĭs) or (stir-ee-ahg-NOH-sĭs) *n.*, the ability to recognize an object by handling or lifting it

ster·e·og·ra·phy (ster-ee-AHG-ră-fee) *n.*, the art, process, or technique of delineating the forms of solid, three-dimensional bodies in two-dimensional space

ster·let (STĔR-lĕt) *n.*, a small sturgeon found in the Caspian Sea system and prized for its flavor and caviar

ster·nu·ta·tion (stĕr-nyŭ-TAY-shŭn) or (stĕr-nyoo-TAY-shŭn) *n.*, a sudden, involuntary exhalation of breath from the nose and mouth; a sneeze

ster·to·rous (STĔRD-ŏ-rŭs) *adj.*, characterized by a loud, laborious snoring

sthen·ic (STHEN-ik) or (STHEN-eek) *adj.*, having great strength and vitality

stil·la·ti·tious (stil-ă-TISH-ŭs) *adj.*, falling as droplets

stin·go (STING-goh) *n.*, a British term for a strong, fermented brew

stir·pi·cul·ture (STĔR-pĭ-kŭl-chŭr) *n.*, the selective breeding of special lines of descent or hereditary characteristics

sti·ver or **stui·ver** (STI-vĕ(r)) *n.*, a unit of monetary value in the Netherlands

sto·a (STOH-ă) *n.*, an ancient Greek roofed colonnade that provided a sheltered strolling area or a meeting place

sto·chas·tic (stŏ-KAS-tik) *adj.*, without a regular plan or purpose

stock·er (STAHK-ĕr) *n.*, a person who handles scrap and loads the open hearth in an iron or steel plant

sto·ke·si·a (stoh-KEE-zh(ee)ă) *n.*, a perennial herb with yellow or purple flower heads; also called a cornflower aster

---

\a\ bat \ă\ about \e\ or \ĕ\ check \ĕ\ letter \ĕ\ cafe \i\fish \ī\ tie \ĭ\ limit \o\ boat \ŏ\ bacon \u\ sun \ŭ\ helpful \ü\ fool

sto-la (STOH-lă) *n.*, a long, draped outer garment worn by women of ancient Rome

stol-len (S(H)TOHL-ĕn) *n.*, a sweet yeast bread with fruit and nuts

sto-ma (STOH-mă) *n.*, a surgically created permanent opening in the abdominal wall

stook (STUUK) or (STOOK) *n.*, a pillar of coal left unmined as a roof support

stoo-ter (STOHD-ĕr) *n.*, an old Dutch coin of low-grade silver

stoss (STAHS) *adj.*, facing in the direction of a glacial impact

stot (STAHT) *n.*, a Scottish term for a bounding step in dancing

sto-tin-ka (stŏ-TING-kă) *n.*, a monetary unit of Bulgaria

stound (STOWND) or (STOON(D)) *n.*, an archaic term for an indefinite period of time

stoup or **stoop** (STOOP) *n.*, a basin for holy water at the entrance of a Roman Catholic Church

stour-y or **stour-ie** (STUUR-i) *adj.*, a British term meaning like a forceful and violent snowstorm

strake (STRAYK) *n.*, an iron band that fastens together the outer segments of a wheel

stra-min-e-ous (stră-MIN-ee-ŭs) *adj.*, an archaic term meaning worthless

strid-u-lous (STRIJ-ŭ-lŭs) *adj.*, making a harsh, rasping sound

strig-il (STRIJ-ĭl) *n.*, a metal or ivory tool used by ancient Greeks and Romans to scrape the skin after athletic exercises and the bath

stri-gine (STRĪ-jīn) or (STRĪ-jĕn) *adj.*, resembling an owl

strob-ic (STRAHB-ik) *adj.*, spinning

stroud (STROWD) or **stroud-ing** (STROWD-ing) *n.*, the heavy, woolen blanketing material that Britain used in trade with North American Indians

stru-thi-an (STROO-thee-ăn) *adj.*, having a flat breastbone, as ostriches or emus

stull (STŬL) *n.*, a round piece of wood that supports the sides of a mine

stum (STŬM) *v.*, grape juice kept unfermented or partly fermented by artificial means

stum-mel (S(H)TUU-mĕl) *n.*, the stem and bowl of a smoking pipe

stump-age (STŬM-pij) or (STŬM-peej) *n.*, standing timber suitable for market

stu-pa (ST(Y)OO-pă) *n.*, a rounded, steepled tower or mound of earth, brick, or stone that serves as a Buddhist shrine

stu-pra-tion (st(y)oo-PRAY-shŏn) *n.*, a sexual assault made on a woman

sturt (STŬRT) *n.*, a Scottish term for an outbreak of disorder

sty-lite (STĪ-līt) *n.*, a medieval religious hermit who lived at the top of a pillar

sty-lo-graph (STĪ-lŏ-graf) *n.*, a fountain pen that allows the flow of ink to vary according to the pressure used in writing

su-ant (SOO-ănt) *adj.*, U.S. dialect meaning consistent

sub-au-di-tion (sŭ-baw-DI-shŏn) *n.*, the understanding of something implied, but not expressed

sub-bo-re-al (sŭ-BOH-ree-ăl) *adj.*, extremely cold

sub-do-lous (SŬB-dŏ-lŭs) *adj.*, wily

su-ber-in (SOO-bĕr-ĭn) *n.*, a complex, fatty substance in cork cell walls

sub-fusc (sŭb-FŬSK) *adj.*, dark and dim

sub-in-tel-lig-i-tur (sŭ-bin-tĕl-IJ-ĭd-ŭr) *n.*, an archaic term for an implied, but not expressed, understanding

sub-sul-tive (sŭb-SŬL-tiv) *adj.*, moving in an irregular way

sub-tra-hend (SŬB-tră-hend) *n.*, the quantity deducted in the mathematical operation of subtraction

sub-u-late (SŬB-yŭ-lăt) or (SOOB-yŭ-layt) *adj.*, long, narrow, and tapering to a point

sub-ur-bi-car-i-an (sŭb-ŭr-bĭ-KA(A)R-ee-ăn) *adj.*, suburban

sub-ven-tion (sŭb-VEN-chŏn) *n.*, the provision of support and monetary aid

suc-ce-da-ne-um (sŭk-sĕ-DAY-nee-ŭm) *n.*, a person who takes the place of another

suc-cor-ance (SŬK-ŏr-ăn(t)s) *n.*, the state of needing assistance from another

suc-cur-sal (sŭ-KŬR-săl) *adj.*, providing additional, limited support, as an offshoot or branch

su-dar-i-um (soo-DA(A)R-ee-ŭm) *n.*, a portrait of Christ done on a piece of cloth and used as an aid to worship

su-da-to-ri-um (soo-dă-TOH-ree-ŭm) *n.*, a room in a bath that is designed to promote perspiring

sudd (SŬD) *n.*, a floating mat of papyrus stems and aquatic grass that obstructs the upper White Nile River of Africa

su-do-rif-er-ous (soo-dŏ-RIF-ĕr-ŭs) *adj.*, sweat-producing

suf-fra-go (sŭ-FRAY-goh) *n.*, the horse's hock that corresponds to the ankle in man

sug-gil-la-tion (sŭ(g)-jĭ-LAY-shŏn) *n.*, a black-and-blue mark, especially one that develops after death

sul-lage (SŬL-ij) *n.*, liquid waste matter and refuse

sum-mist (SŬM-ĭst) *n.*, 1. a medieval philosopher who wrote comprehensive philosophical or theological treatises 2. an archaic term for a person who condenses a larger work

sumph (SŬMF) *n.*, a Scottish term for a slow or sluggish person

sum-pi-tan (SŬM-pĭ-tan) *n.*, a Malaysian weapon that ejects darts from a slender tube through the force of the breath

sump-si-mus (SŬMP-sĭ-mŭs) *n.*, a corrected expression or usage that replaces an old, common error

---

\a\ bat \ă\ about \e\ or \ĕ\ check \ĕ\ letter
\ĕ\ cafe \i\fish \ī\ tie \ĭ\ limit \o\ boat
\ŏ\ bacon \u\ sun \ŭ\ helpful \ü\ fool

sump-ter (SŬM(P)-tĕ(r)) *n.*, an animal used to carry heavy burdens or perform heavy work

sump-tu-a-ry (SŬM(P)-chĕ-wer-ee) *adj.*, monitoring expenses

su-per-e-rog-a-to-ry (SOO-pĕr-ĕ-RAHG-ă-toh-ree) *adj.*, over and above what is necessary

su-per-nac-u-lum (soo-pĕ(r)-NAK-yŭ-lŭm) *n.*, something of the highest quality; specifically, an alcoholic beverage

su-per-nal (soo-PĔR-năl) *adj.*, heavenly

su-pi-nate (SOO-pĭ-nayt) *v.*, to turn the hand and forearm so that the palm of the hand faces upward

sup-pe-da-ne-um (sŭp-ĕ-DAY-nee-ŭm) *n.*, a shelf attached to the upright of a cross as a support for the feet of those crucified

su-ra (SOO-ră) *n.*, a chapter or passage of the Muslim Koran

su-rah (SOO-ră) *n.*, a soft, lustrous, silk or rayon fabric in twill weave

su-ral (SUU-răl) *adj.*, relating to the calf area of the leg

sur-bate (SŬR-bayt) *v.*, an obsolete term meaning to make the feet tired and tender

sur-cin-gle or **cir-cin-gle** (SŬR-sing-gĕl) *n.*, a belt or band around the body of a horse used to attach something to the horse's back

surd (SŬRD) *adj.*, pronounced without a voiced sound

sur-re-but-ter (sŭr-ree-BŬD-ĕr) *n.*, a step in the process of common-law pleading in which a plaintiff addresses the defendant's previous statement

sus-lik (SŬS-lik) *n.*, a large, short-tailed eastern European ground squirrel with hairy feet and spotted grayish black fur

sus-pir-i-ous (sŭ-SPIR-ee-ŭs) *adj.*, producing a long, audible breath

su-sur-rus (sŭ-SŬR-ŭs) *n.*, a low, soft, continuous sound

su-tile (SOO-til) *adj.*, an archaic term meaning made by a continuous line of individual stitches

sut-ler (SŬT-lĕ(r)) *n.*, an army-post supplier, especially one who maintains a store on the post

sut-tee or **sa-ti** (sŭ-TEE) *n.*, a Hindu custom requiring a widow to be cremated on her husband's funeral pyre

swack (SWAK) *adj.*, a Scottish term meaning agile

swal-let (SWAH-lĕt) *n.*, English dialect for a brook that flows underground

swan-i-mote (SWAWN-ĭ-moht) or **swain-mote** (SWAYN-moht) *n.*, an assembly of forest officers held three times a year in medieval England to try offenses and hear grievances

swa-raj (swă-RAHJ) *n.*, national or local political autonomy

sward (SWAW(E)RD) or (SWAW(E)D) *n.*, the grassy surface layer of soil

swarf (SWAWRF) *n.*, a sudden, partial or total loss of consciousness; a faint

swee-ny or **swee-ney** (SWEE-nee) or (SWEE-ni) *n.*, a muscular wasting that occurs in a horse

sweet-sop (SWEET-sahp) *n.*, a sweet, pulpy tropical American fruit; also called the custard apple

sweet-wort (SWEET-wŏrt) or (SWEET-waw(e)rt) *n.*, unfermented malt steeped in liquid

swev-en (SWEV-ĕn) *n.*, an archaic term for something seen by means other than normal sight, as a dream

swive (SWĪV) *v.*, an archaic term meaning to indulge in sexual intercourse

sya-gush (SYAH-goosh) *n.*, an African and Asian wildcat with reddish brown fur and long, black tufted ears

syke (SĪK) *n.*, a term in heraldry for a circular emblem with six wavy lines in alternating silver and blue colors

sym-po-si-arch (sim-POH-zee-ahrk) *n.*, the moderator or chair of a symposium

syn-al-lag-mat-ic or **sin-a-lag-mat-ic** (sin-ă-lag-MAD-ik) *adj.*, affecting both sides equally with mutual and reciprocal rights or obligations

syn-co-pe (SING-kŏ-pee) *n.*, a temporary loss of consciousness due to inadequate blood flow to the brain

syn-cre-tize (SIN-krĕ-tīz) *v.*, to blend together or become one

syn-es-the-si-a or **syn-aes-the-si-a** (sin-ĕs-THEE-zh(ee)-ă) *n.*, a secondary, subjective experience of a sense different from the one being stimulated

syn-to-ny (SIN-tŏ-nee) *n.*, the normal emotional responsiveness to and harmony with the environment

syn-troph-ic (sin-TRAHF-ik) *adj.*, mutually dependent for the supply of nutritional needs

syr-tis (SĔRD-ĕs) *n.*, an archaic term for soft, wet, miry ground

syz-y-gy (SIZ-ĭ-jee) or (SIZ-ĭ-ji) *n.*, an astronomical phenomenon in which three celestial bodies fall into a straight-line configuration

szmik-ite (SMI-kīt) *n.*, a mineral consisting in part of manganese sulfate

T

tab-a-nid (TAB-ă-nĭd) *n.*, a horsefly

ta-bi (TAH-bee) *n.*, a Japanese foot covering like a sock

tab-la-ture (TAB-lă-chuu(ĕ)r) or (TAB-lă-chuuĕ) or (TAB-la-chĕ(r)) *n.*, a musical notation system that uses letters and other signs to indicate the string, fret, key, or finger to be played

ta-chyg-ra-phy (ta-KIG-ră-fee) or (tă-KIG-ră-fee) *n.*, the technique of writing rapidly

---

\a\ bat \ă\ about \e\ or \è\ check \ĕ\ letter
\é\ cafe \i\fish \ī\ tie \ĭ\ limit \o\ boat
\ŏ\ bacon \u\ sun \ŭ\ helpful \ü\ fool

tae-ni-a (TEE-nee-ă) or (TEE-nyă) *n.*, a flat strip of tissue

tae-ni-a-fuge (TEE-nee-ă-fyooj) or (TEE-nyă-fyooj) *n.*, a substance that causes the expulsion of tapeworms

tahr or **thar** (TAHR) *n.*, a beardless wild goat of the Himalayas with short, back-curving horns and a dark, reddish brown mane

tai-ga (tī-GAH) or (TĪ-gă) *n.*, the evergreen forest of Eurasia

taisch (TAYSH) or (TĪSH) *n.*, a Scottish term for a ghostly appearance of a person near death

taj (TAHZH) or (TAHJ) *n.*, a tall, cone-shaped hat worn by respected persons in Muslim countries

ta-ka-he (tă-KĪ) *n.*, a flightless bird of New Zealand

ta-kin (tă-KEEN) or (TAH-keen) *n.*, a heavily built Tibetan goat antelope related to the musk ox

ta-la (TAH-la) *n.*, the yellowish gray hardwood from an Argentinian timber tree

ta-la-ri-a (tă-LA(A)R-ee-a) *n.*, the winged sandals strapped to the ankles of the gods Hermes and Mercury

tal-i-grade (TAL-ĭ-grayd) *adj.*, walking with the body's weight borne on the foot's outer side

tal-i-on (TAL-ee-ŏn) *n.*, the principle of retaliation in kind, in accordance with the biblical "an eye for an eye, and a tooth for a tooth"

ta-luk (tah-LUUK) *n.*, an inherited estate in India

ta-man-du-a (tă-MAN-dŭ-wah) *n.*, a tree-dwelling anteater of Central and South America

tam-a-rau (TAM-ă-row) *n.*, a small, dark water buffalo found on the Philippine island of Mindora

tam-a-rin (TAM-ă-rĭn) or (TAM-ă-ran) *n.*, a small, squirrel-like South American monkey with a long, nonprehensile tail

tam-is (TAM-ee) or (TAM-ĭs) *n.*, a sieve made from open-weave worsted cloth

tam-pa-la (tam-PA-lă) *n.*, an Oriental herb cultivated for its spinachlike leaves

tam-pan (TAM-pan) *n.*, a disease-transmitting tick, especially the chicken tick

tang-an-tang-an (tang-ahn-TAHNG-ahn) *n.*, an herb whose poisonous seeds yield the cathartic castor oil; also called the castor-oil plant

tan-gram (TANG-grăm) or (TAN-grăm) *n.*, a Chinese puzzle of five triangles, a square, and a rhomboid cut from a square and reassembled into different geometric shapes and designs

tan-ist (TAN-ĭst) or (THAWN-ist) *n.*, an early Irish ruler chosen from his predecessor's relatives and elected by the people

tan-ka (TAHNG-kă) *n.*, a Tibetan religious painting done on cloth and mounted on a scroll-like brocade border for use as a processional banner

tan-ti-vy (tan-TI-vee) *n.*, the loud, harsh sound of a trumpet or similar horn

taph·e·pho·bi·a (taf-ee-FOH-bee-a) *n.*, an abnormal fear of being interred while still alive

tap·lash (TAP-lash) *n.*, U.S. dialect for stale or low-proof beer

tar·an·tism (TAR-ăn-tizĕm) *n.*, an uncontrollable passion for dancing among late-medieval Europeans that was believed the result of a tarantula bite

tar·boosh or **tar·bush** or **tar·boush** (tahr-BOOSH) or (tahr-BUUSH) *n.*, a close-fitting, brimless red hat similar to the fez worn by eastern-Mediterranean Muslim men, either alone or as part of a turban

tar·di·grade (TAHR-dĭ-grayd) *adj.*, moving at a slow rate of speed

tare (TA(A)(Ĕ)R) or (TE(Ĕ)R) *n.*, the weight of a container deducted from the total weight to determine the weight of the container's contents

tarn (TAHRN) *n.*, a small mountain lake or pool

ta·tha·ga·ta·gar·bha (tă-tah-gă-tă-GĂR-bă) *n.*, the essential, eternal Buddha-like nature inherent to all living beings

tau·ri·form (tawr-Ĭ-fohrm) *adj.*, shaped like the head or horns of a bull

tau·ro·mach·i·an (taw-rŏ-MAYK-ee-ăn) *adj.*, of or relating to bullfighting

taw (TAW) *n.*, 1. a partner in square dancing 2. a monetary investment made in hope of an increased return

taw·ny (TAW-nee) *n.*, an archaic term for a Western-hemisphere Indian native

taw·pie or **taw·py** (TAW-pee) or (TAW-pi) *n.*, a Scottish term for a silly or gawky adolescent

taz·za (TAHT-să) *n.*, a shallow, decorative bowl set on a pedestal or pillar

tea·sel or **tea·sle** (TEE-zĕl) *n.*, the dried flower head of a prickly, coarse plant whose barbed, leaflike structures are used to raise the nap of woolen fabrics

tec·ti·form (TEK-tĭ-fohrm) *n.*, a roof-shaped design found in paleolithic cave art and interpreted as a symbol of a dwelling

tec·trix (TEK-triks) *n.*, a small feather at the base of the wing and tail feathers of a bird

ted (TED) *v.*, to distribute over a surface as an aid to drying

tee·ter·tail (TEED-ĕ(r)-tayl) or (TEE-tĕ(r)-tayl) *n.*, a North American sandpiper with a continually bobbing head and tail

tee·to·tum (tee-TOHD-ŭm) or (tee-TOH-tŭm) *n.*, a small, conical, spinning children's toy

teff (TEF) *n.*, an African cereal grass that provides flour, hay, and forage

teg or **tegg** (TEG) *n.*, a two-year-old unshorn sheep

teg·men (TEG-mĕn) *n.*, something that covers or encloses

\a\ bat \ā\ about \e\ or \è\ check \ĕ\ letter
\é\ cafe \i\fish \ī\ tie \i\ limit \o\ boat
\ŏ\ bacon \u\ sun \ŭ\ helpful \ü\ fool

te-gua (TAY-gwă) *n.*, a rawhide moccasin popular in the southwest U.S. and Mexico

teig-lach or **taig-lach** (TAYG-lĕk) or (TĪG-lĕk) *n.*, small dough pieces cooked in honey

tei-id (TEE-(y)ĕd) *adj.*, of or relating to a family of tropical American lizards having a forked tongue

tek-non-y-my (tek-NAHN-ĕ-mee) *n.*, a custom in which a parent assumes the name of the child

tek-tite (TEK-tīt) *n.*, a rounded, indefinitely shaped, glassy body of meteoric origin

tel-a-mon (TEL-ă-mahn) or (TEL-ă-mŏn) *n.*, a male figure used as an architectural support or column

tel-e-du (TEL-ĕ-doo) *n.*, a small Javanese and Sumatran badger that secretes a foul-smelling substance; also called the Javanese skunk

tel-e-gno-sis (tel-ĕ-NOH-sĭs) or (te-leg-NOH-sĭs) *n.*, the knowledge of distant or future events obtained by supernatural means

te-leg-o-ny (tĕ-LEG-ŏ-nee) *n.*, the supposed transfer of one sire's genetic characteristics to the offspring of the dam and other males

tel-e-ost (TEL-ee-ahst) *n.*, a jawed, bony fish

te-les-tic (tĕ-LES-tik) or (TE-lĕ-stik) *adj.*, occult

tel-lu-ri-an (tĕ-LUU-ree-ăn) or (tĕl-YUU-ree-ăn) *n.*, an earthling

tel-ma-tol-o-gy (tel-mă-TAHL-ŏ-jee) *n.*, a specialized area of physical geography that studies wet lands such as marshes or bogs

tem-blor (TEM-blŏ(r)) or (TEM-blaw(ĕ)r) *n.*, a vibration or shaking of the earth

tem-er-ar-i-ous (tem-ĕ-RA(A)-ree-ŭs) *adj.*, impetuous

tem-pe-an (TEM-pee-ăn) *adj.*, picturesque and charming

tench (TENCH) *n.*, a European freshwater fish that can survive out of water for some time and is noted for its excellent flavor

ten-e-brif-ic (ten-ĕ-BRIF-ik) *adj.*, dark and shadowy

te-nes-mus (tĕ-NEZ-mŭs) *n.*, a painful inability to urinate or defecate

ten-on (TEN-ŏn) *n.*, a projecting piece of wood that fits into a mortise to form a joint

ten-rec (TEN-rek) *n.*, a small, spiny, tailless insect-eating mammal of Madagascar

ten-ty or **ten-tie** (TEN-ti) *adj.*, a Scottish term meaning mindful

ten-u-is (TEN-yĕ-wĭs) *n.*, a voiceless stop consonant

te-o-cal-li (tee-ŏ-KAL-ee) or (tay-ŏ-KAHL-ee) *n.*, an ancient Mexican or Central American temple, usually constructed atop a truncated pyramidal mound

te-o-sin-te (tay-ŏ-SIN-tee) *n.*, a tall grass of Mexico and Central America, believed to be related to maize and Indian corn

tep·i·dar·i·um (tep-ĭ-DA(A)-ree-ŭm) *n.*, a heated sitting room in the public baths of ancient Rome

ter·aph (TER-ăf) *n.*, an idol of one of the household gods worshiped by the ancient Jews and other Semites and later used in fortune telling

ter·a·to·sis (ter-ă-TOH-sĭs) *n.*, a fascination with wonders and the supernatural

ter·a·tol·o·gy (ter-ă-TAHL-ŏ-jee) *n.*, the biological study of abnormalities in bodily growth or structure

ter·e·bin·thine (ter-ĕ-BIN(T)-thĕn) *adj.*, turpentine-like

te·re·do (tĕ-REE-doh) *n.*, a long, wormlike marine clam that burrows in and damages piers and ships; also called a shipworm

ter·gi·ver·sa·tion (tĕr-jĭ-vĕr-SAY-shŏn) *n.*, double-talk

ter·ma·gant (TĔR-mă-gănt) *n.*, a domineering, nagging woman

ter·mi·tar·i·um (tĕr-mĭ-TER-ee-ŭm) *n.*, a nest of termites

ter·mor (TER-mŏr) *n.*, a person who owns an estate for a specific period of years or for life

ter·nate (TĔR-nayt) or (TĔR-năt) *adj.*, ordered in groups of threes

terp (TE(Ĕ)RP) *n.*, a large, man-made prehistoric mound on the flood plains of the Netherlands

terr·a·que·ous (ter-AYK-wee-ŭs) *adj.*, composed of both land and water

tes·sa·ra·glot (TES-ă-ră-glaht) *adj.*, written or spoken in four languages

tes·sel·lat·ed (TES-ĕ-layd-ĕd) *adj.*, mosaic-like

tes·ta (TES-tă) *n.*, the hard outer covering surrounding a seed

tes·ta·ceous (te-STAY-shŭs) *adj.*, 1. composed of a shell-like material 2. brick-colored

tes·ton (TES-tŏn) or (TE-stahn) *n.*, an old European coin

teth or **tet** (TAYT) or (TAYS) *n.*, the ninth letter of the Hebrew and other Semitic alphabets

tet·ra·gram (TE-tră-gram) *n.*, a four-letter word

te·tral·o·gy (te-TRAHL-ŏ-jee) or (te-TRAL-ŏ-jee) *n.*, a group of four related compositions

te·tra·skel·i·on (te-tră-SKEL-ee-ŏn) *n.*, a four-armed figure whose branches bend in the same direction

tha·li·an (thă-LĪ-ăn) *adj.*, wryly amusing

thal·pot·ic (thal-PAHD-ik) *adj.*, arousing the sensation or experience of warmth

thal·weg (TAAL-veg) or (TAAL-vayk) *n.*, the line along the deepest channel of a valley

than·a·to·ma·ni·a (than-ă-toh-MAY-nee-ă) *n.*, 1. an obsession with committing suicide 2. death caused by autosuggestion

tharm (THAHRM) *n.*, a Scottish term for the strong cord made from sheep intestine or catgut

---

\a\ bat \ă\ about \e\ or \ĕ\ check \ĕ\ letter
\ê\ cafe \i\ fish \ī\ tie \ī\ limit \o\ boat
\ŏ\ bacon \u\ sun \ŭ\ helpful \ü\ fool

thau·ma·turge (THAW-mă-tŭrj) *n.*, a person who performs wonders and miracles

the·an·thro·pism (thee-AN(T)-thrŏ-pizĕm) *n.*, the bestowal of human qualities and characteristics upon God or the gods

the·ca (THEE-kă) *n.*, a biological term for a pouchlike protective container

the·lyt·o·kous (thĕ-LID-ŏ-kŭs) *adj.*, bearing only female offspring

the·o·lo·gou·me·non (thee-ŏ-loh-GOO-mĕ-nahn) *n.*, a belief or idea about God and religion based on ecclesiastical teaching

the·om·ach·ist (thee-AHM-ă-kĭst) *n.*, a person resistant to God or divine will

the·oph·a·gy (thee-AHF-ă-jee) *n.*, the symbolic eating of a god, typically in the form of an animal or image, in a religious ritual that emphasizes communion with or empowerment by the god

the·or·bo (thee-AWR-boh) *n.*, an obsolete, 17th-century lute with two necks, two sets of strings, and two sets of pegs

the·ri·a·cal (thĕ-RĪ-ă-kăl) *adj.*, having a curative or remedial effect upon the body

the·ri·an·throp·ic (thi-ree-an-THRAHP-ik) *adj.*, having the physical characteristics of both man and beast

the·rol·o·gy (thi-RAHL-ŏ-jee) *n.*, the zoological study of mammals

thes·mo·thete (THEZ-mŏ-theet) *n.*, a legislative magistrate of ancient Athens

thet·i·cal (THED-ĭ-kăl) *adj.*, declared dogmatically

the·ur·gy (THE-ŭr-jee) *n.*, the technique of forcing or convincing a god or kindly spirit to do what one wants

thig (THIG) *v.*, a Scottish term meaning to plead for charitable assistance

thi·on·ic (thī-AHN-ik) *adj.*, sulfuric

thirl (THĔR(Ĕ)L) *v.*, a British term meaning to limit

thir·lage (THĔR-lij) *n.*, a feudal arrangement requiring tenants to grind their grain at a particular mill and pay its customary fees

thorp (THAWRP) *n.*, an archaic term for a very small community

thrall·dom (THRAWL-dŏm) *n.*, enslavement

thra·son·i·cal (thray-SAHN-ĭ-kăl) *adj.*, self-congratulatory; self-glorifying

thrave (THRAYV) *n.*, 1. a British unit of measurement of unthreshed grain 2. an ample amount

thraw (THRAW) *n.*, a Scottish term for wrath

threap (THREEP) *n.*, a Scottish term for an allegation of wrongdoing

threm·ma·tol·o·gy (threm-ă-TAHL-ŏ-jee) *n.*, the biological study of the breeding of domesticated animals and plants

thren·o·dy (THREN-ŏ-dee) or (THREN-ŏ-di) *n.*, a mourning song for the dead

thrim-ble (THRIM-běl) *v.*, a British term meaning to handle or toy with in a hesitating manner

throp-ple (THRAHP-ěl) *n.*, U.S. dialect for the neck area in front of the spine that holds the passages from the mouth and nose to the lungs

thu-ri-fi-ca-tion (th(y)uu-rĭ-fĭ-KAY-shŏn) or (thŭr-ĭ-fĭ-KAY-shŏn) *n.*, the act of adding a perfumed smell to an area by burning incense

thwaite (THWAYT) *n.*, U.S. dialect for a section of cleared forest land used for cultivation

tick-len-burg (TIK-lěn-bŭrg) *n.*, a coarse fabric made of linen

tic-po-lon-ga (tik-pŏ-LAWNG-gă) *n.*, a venomous snake found in Ceylon and India; also called Russell's viper

tid (TID) *n.*, a Scottish term for an appropriate time or season, especially in regard to an agricultural activity

tid-dle-dies (TID-ěl-deez) or (TID-ěl-diz) *n.*, pieces of ice floating on the surface of a body of water

tif-fin (TIF-ĭn) *n.*, a light noon meal or lunch

tik-o-loshe or **tik-o-losh** (TIK-ŏ-lahsh) or (TIK-ŏ-lawsh) *n.*, a playful spirit in south African folklore who takes the form of a water-dwelling little man who likes children

til-i-kum or **til-li-cum** (TIL-ĭ-kŭm) *n.*, a northwestern U.S. term for a nonhostile individual

tim-bal or **tym-bal** (TIM-băl) *n.*, an orchestral percussion instrument; also called the kettledrum

ti-mo-neer (TĪ-mŏ-ni(ě)r) or (TIM-ŏ-ni(ě)r) *n.*, a person who steers a ship

tin-a-mou (TIN-ă-moo) *n.*, a flightless, short-tailed bird of Central and South America

tin-chel (TING-kěl) *n.*, a Scottish term for a circular arrangement of hunters attempting to entrap deer

tinc-to-ri-al (tingk-TOH-ree-ăl) *adj.*, transmitting a color

tin-e-a (TIN-ee-ă) *n.*, a fungous skin disease, especially ringworm, affecting various parts of the body

tin-e-id (TIN-ee-ĭd) *n.*, a common clothes moth

tin-ta-marre or **tin-ta-mar** (TIN-tă-mahr) *n.*, a loud and distracting confusion of noises

tirl (TĬRL) *v.*, a Scottish term meaning to rattle at the door fastener

ti-tho-ni-a (tĭ-THOH-nee-ă) or (tĭ-THOH-nyă) *n.*, a tall, ornamental herb that resembles a sunflower; also called the Mexican sunflower

ti-ti (TĪ-tĭ) or (TĪD-ĭ) *n.*, a tree of the southern U.S. with glossy leaves and fragrant white flowers; also called buckwheat tree

\a\ bat \ä\ about \e\ or \ě\ check \ě\ letter \é\ cafe \i\ fish \ī\ tie \ĭ\ limit \o\ boat \ŏ\ bacon \u\ sun \ŭ\ helpful \ü\ fool

ti-ti (tĭ-TEE) or **tee-tee** (tee-TEE) *n.*, a small, tree-dwelling South American monkey that resembles a squirrel monkey

tit-i-va-tion (tid-ĭ-VAY-shŏn) *n.*, the act of adding minor touches to enhance one's clothes and appearance

tit-tup (TID-ŭp) *n.*, active, playful behavior

tit-tup-py (TID-ŭp-ee) *adj.*, unstable

tit-u-ba-tion (tich-ŭ-BAY-shŭn) *n.*, a reeling, stumbling walk present in some nervous-system diseases

tjae-le (CHAY-lee) or (CHAY-lĕ) *n.*, ground that is permanently frozen

tme-sis ((tĕ)-MEE-sĭs) *n.*, the separation of compound-word parts by placing one or more words between them

tnoy-im (tĕ-NOI-(y)ĭm) or (tĕ-NOI-eem) *n.*, a Jewish engagement party

toad-eat-er (TOHD-eed-ĕr) *n.*, an archaic term for a quack's assistant who supposedly eats poisonous toads so that his boss can demonstrate his healing skills

to-a-to-a (TOH-ă-toh-ă) *n.*, an ornamental New Zealand pine with celery-like leafage and striking whorled branches; also called the adventure bay pine

to-col-o-gy (toh-KAHL-ŏ-jee) *n.*, the medical study of the physical events and circumstances surrounding birth

tod-dick (TAH-dik) or (TAH-deek) *n.*, a southern U.S. term for or an amount of flour meal taken by the miller as a charge for services

toff (TAHF) or (TAWF) *n.*, a British term, often used as a slight, for a smartly dressed, fashionable member of the upper class

toft (TAHFT) or (TAWFT) *n.*, a British term for a small hill appropriate for a construction site

to-gate (TOH-gayt) *adj.*, 1. dressed in a toga 2. impressive in greatness or rank

togue (TOHG) *n.*, a large North American trout important as a commercial food resource in the northern lakes; also called the lake trout

to-hu-bo-hu (TOH-hoo-boh-hoo) *n.*, total disorder

to-hun-ga (TOH-huung-gă) *n.*, a New Zealand term for a tribal shaman

to-la (TOH-lă) *n.*, 1. an Indian weight 2. an Ecuadoran or Peruvian burial mound

to-lan (TOH-lan) *n.*, a crystalline hydrocarbon derived from stilbene hydrocarbon

tole (TOHL) *n.*, a decorative, lacquered metal used for trays, lamps, and boxes

tol-ly (TAH-lee) or (TAH-lĭ) *n.*, a wax or tallow candle

to-lu (tŏ-LOO) or (toh-LOO) *n.*, a yellowish brown aromatic resin obtained from a South American tree and used as a cough-medicine and perfume ingredient

to-mal-ley (tŏ-MAL-ee) or (TAHM-al-ee) *n.*, a lobster's liver

tom-bac or **tom-bak** (TAHM-bak) *n.*, a copper-zinc alloy used to make junk jewelry

tom-bo-lo (TAHM-bŏ-loh) *n.*, a sand or gravel strip joining an island to the mainland or another island

to-men-tose (tŏ-MEN-tohs) or (TOH-men-tohs) *adj.*, covered with thickly tangled hairs

tom-nod-dy (TAHM-nahd-ee) *n.*, a Scottish term for a North Atlantic puffin 2. an idiot

ton-do (TAHN-doh) *n.*, 1. a round painting 2. a hand-sculpted commemorative medal

to-nit-ru-ous (tŏ-NI-trŭ-wŭs) *adj.*, raging

ton-let (TŎN-lĕt) *n.*, a horizontal plate that overlapped others to form the skirt of a late medieval suit of armor

ton-nish (TAHN-ish) *adj.*, chic

ton-tine (TAHN-teen) or (tahn-TEEN) *n.*, a group-insurance arrangement in which participants share annuities and agree to distribute each member's death benefits among the survivors

toom (TOOM) *n.*, a Scottish term for a scrap heap; a garbage dump

toon (TOON) *n.*, an Asian tree that yields cedar for carpentry and construction

to-pha-ceous (tŏ-FAY-shŭs) *adj.*, having the characteristics of gritty deposits of uric acid salts found in cases of gout

to-pi (TOH-pee) *n.*, a light, curved-brim pith hat of India

top-i-nam-bou (tahp-ĭ-NAM-boo) *n.*, the root of an American sunflower plant; also called a Jerusalem artichoke

to-pon-y-my (tŏ-PAHN-ĕ-mee) or (toh-PAHN-ĕ-mee) *n.*, the etymological study of the names given to geographical locations within a region or language

torc (TAW(Ĕ)RK) or (TAW(Ĕ)K) *n.*, a chain-metal neckpiece worn by the ancient Gauls, Germans, and Britons

to-reu-tic (tŏ-ROOD-ik) *adj.*, of or relating to wrought metalwork, especially small and highly finished

tor-i-i (TOH-ree-ee) or (TAW-ree-ee) *n.*, a delicately curved Japanese gateway near a Shinto shrine

to-rose (TOHR-ohs) or (TAW-rohs) *adj.*, having a knobby surface

tor-re-fy or **tor-ri-fy** (TAW-rĕ-fī) *v.*, to remove moisture by exposure to dry heat

tor-sade (tawr-SAHD) or (tawr-SAYD) *n.*, an ornamental twist of cords or ribbons

tosh (TAHSH) *adj.*, a Scottish term for comfortably neat and orderly

to-ti-pal-mate (tohd-ĕ-PAL-mayt) or (tohd-ĕ-PAH-mayt) *adj.*, having webbing between all four toes

to-tip-o-tent (toh-TIP-ŏ-dĕnt) *adj.*, capable of developing any inherent possibilities of its kind

tour-bil-lion (tuur-BIL-yŏn) *n.*, 1. a whirling, spiraling object 2. the coil of hair at the highest point of the human head

---

\a\ bat \ā\ about \e\ or \ĕ\ check \ĕ\ letter \ē\ cafe \i\fish \ī\ tie \ĭ\ limit \o\ boat \ŏ\ bacon \u\ sun \ū\ helpful \ü\ fool

tour-nure (tuur-NYUU(Ĕ)R) *n.*, a pad or other device that adds fullness to the skirts of some women's fashions

tow-mond (TOW-mŏnd) *n.*, a Scottish term for a twelve-month period of time

tow-y (TOH-ee) *adj.*, having the short, broken fibers taken from flax before spinning

tox-oph-i-ly (tahk-SAHF-ĭ-lee) *n.*, the technique of shooting with a bow and arrow

to-yo (TOH-yoh) *n.*, the Japanese rice-paper straw used to make hats

toy-on or **to-llon** (TOI-ahn) or (TOH-yŏn) *n.*, an ornamental American Pacific evergreen with hardy, bright red berries; also called the Christmasberry

tra-be-ate (TRAY-bee-ayt) or (TRAY-bee-ăt) *adj.*, an architectural term meaning having a horizontal-beamed design or construction

trac-tate (TRAK-tayt) *n.*, a formal, detailed written explanation of controversial subject matter

trac-tile (TRAK-tĭl) or (TRAK-tīl) *adj.*, capable of being drawn or lengthened by stretching

trad-i-tor (TRAD-ĭd-ŏ(r)) *n.*, a Christian informant who provided names and religious objects to the Romans during the persecutions

trag-o-pan (TRAG-ŏ-pan) *n.*, a brightly colored Asian pheasant

tra-gus (TRAY-gŭs) *n.*, the small mass of cartilage in front of the external opening of the human ear

trai-teur (TRAY-tĕr) *n.*, the proprietor of a small French or Italian restaurant

tral-a-ti-tious (tral-ă-TI-shŭs) *adj.*, 1. having meaning or quality derived from something extraneous 2. passed on through time

tra-mon-tane (tră-MAHN-tayn) or (TRA-mŏn-tayn) *adj.*, notably different or unfamiliar

tran-sil-i-ent (tran-SIL-ee-ĕnt) *adj.*, having gaps or sudden changes in geological structure

trans-pa-dane (tranz-pă-DAYN) *adj.*, at a position north of the river Po

trans-pon-tine (tranz-PAHN-tīn) *adj.*, 1. at a position on the other side of a bridge 2. resembling a melodrama once popular in London theaters south of the Thames

tran-sump-tion (tran-SŬM(P)-shŏn) *n.*, duplication

trans-u-ran-ic (tran(t)s-yŭ-RAN-ik) *adj.*, relating to an element with an atomic number higher than uranium

trans-vase (tran(t)s-VAYS) *v.*, to transfer liquid from one vessel into another

tra-pe-zi-um (tra-PEE-zee-ŭm) *n.*, a four-sided figure with no parallel sides

trau-lism (TRAW-lizĕm) or (TROW-lizĕm) *n.*, the involuntary disruption of vocal communication by repetition and blocked speech

trau-ma-to-pho-bi-a (traw-măd-ŏ-FOH-bee-a) *n.*, an abnormal fear of war or physical injury that usually results from combat experience

trave (TRAYV) *n.*, a structure that restricts an animal's movement during shoeing

treb·u·chet (TREB-yŭ-shet) *n.*, 1. a medieval weapon designed to hurl stones mechanically and with great force 2. a small, accurate chemist's balance or scale

treg·et·our (TREJ-ĕd-ĕ(r)) *n.*, an archaic term for a person with great manual dexterity such as a juggler or magician

tre·ha·la (trĕ-HAH-lă) *n.*, the sweet, edible substance secreted by an Asiatic beetle as a pupal covering

treil·lage (TRAY-lij) *n.*, a latticed support for vines or other foliage

trem·el·lose (TREM-ĕ-lohs) *adj.*, jellylike in appearance or texture

tren·cher·man (TREN-chĕr-măn) *n.*, 1. a voracious eater 2. an archaic term for a parasite

tren·tal (TREN-tăl) *n.*, a series of 30 Roman Catholic masses offered for the dead, usually over a 30 consecutive-day period

tre·pan (trĕ-PAN) or (tree-PAN) *n.*, a heavy tool for boring into materials

tre·pang (trĕ-PANG) or (tree-PANG) *n.*, a large, wormlike aquatic animal used by the Chinese as a soup base

tre·phine (TREE-fīn) or (trĕ-FĪN) or (trĕ-FEEN) *n.*, a cylindrical surgical saw for cutting circular sections of bone from the skull

tret (TRET) *n.*, a four-pound weight allowance added to 104 pounds of net weight of various commodities to compensate for spoilage in transit

trews (TROOZ) *n.*, the close-fitting, tartan shorts sometimes worn under the Scottish kilt

trib·a·dism (TRIB-ă-dizĕm) *n.*, the mutual masturbation practiced among homosexual women in simulation of heterosexual intercourse

tri·ce·ri·on (trī-SI-ree-ahn) *n.*, a three-armed candelabrum used by bishops in the Eastern Orthodox Church

trich·ite (TRI-kīt) *n.*, a tiny, needlelike body

tri·chome (TRI-kohm) *n.*, a hair structure on the surface layer of plants

trich·o·til·lo·ma·ni·a (trik-ŏ-til-ŏ-MAY-nee-ă) *n.*, an uncontrollable urge to tear out one's hair

tri·clin·i·um (trī-KLIN-ee-ŭm) *n.*, a couch extending around three sides of a dining table that allowed ancient Romans to recline at meals

tri·ens (TRĪ-enz) or (TREE-ayn(t)s) *n.*, an ancient bronze coin

tri·ga (TREE-gă) or (TRĪ-gă) *n.*, an ancient Roman chariot drawn by three horses

tri·go (TREE-goh) *n.*, a wheat field

tri·gon (TRĪ-gahn) *n.*, an ancient, four-stringed harp used to provide banquet music

tri·met·ro·gon (trī-ME-trŏ-gahn) *n.*, an aerial mapping-system that uses three adjacent cameras filming in different directions simultaneously

---

\a\ bat \ă\ about \e\ or \è\ check \ĕ\ letter
\é\ cafe \i\fish \ī\ tie \ĭ\ limit \o\ boat
\ō\ bacon \u\ sun \ŭ\ helpful \ü\ fool

tri·o·let (tre-ŏ-LAY) *n.*, an eight-line poem or stanza that repeats the first line three times

tri·ose (TRI-ohs) or (TRI-ohz) *n.*, a simple sugar that has three carbon atoms

tri·phib·i·ous (trī-FIB-ee-ŭs) *adj.*, referring to the coordinated use of military land, naval, and air forces in attack

trip·tyque (trip-TEEK) *n.*, a customs pass allowing an automobile to be imported into a specified country

tri·tag·o·nist (trī-TAG-ŏ-nĭst) *n.*, the actor who performs the role third in importance to a play

troch·le·ar (TRAHK-lee-ă(r)) *adj.*, a botanical term for pulley-shaped

troke (TROHK) *v.*, a Scottish term meaning to trade by exchanging one type of goods for another

trone (TROHN) *n.*, a Scottish term for a machine that weighs heavy goods

troph·ic (TRAHF-ik) or (TRAHF-eek) *adj.*, concerned with nourishment

tro·pine (TROH-peen) or (TROH-pĕn) *n.*, a poisonous, crystalline amino alcohol

tro·poph·i·lous (troh-PAHF-ĭ-lŭs) *adj.*, adapted to life in an environment of marked periodic changes

trop·po (TRAH-poh) *n.*, U.S. slang for the mental confusion or stress afflicting troops serving in tropical climates

tro·tyl (TROH-dĭl) *n.*, explosive TNT

truck·le (TRŬK-ĕl) *n.*, a small wheel or roller used to move a heavy object

trut·ta·ceous (trŭ-TAY-shŭs) *adj.*, troutlike

tsan·tsa (TSAHN-tsă) *n.*, a human head shrunk by a Jivaro Indian of Peru or Ecudor

tsu·bo ((T)SOO-boh) *n.*, a Japanese measurement of area

tsu·na·mi ((t)soo-NAH-mee) or ((t)soo-NA-mee) *n.*, an unusually high ocean wave produced by volcanic eruption or seismic disturbance

tsu·tsu·ga·mu·shi ((t)soo-tsŭ-gă-MOO-shee) *n.*, a sudden, severe febrile form of typhus caused by rickettsia and transmitted by larval mites

tu·a·ta·ra (too-ă-TAH-ră) *n.*, a large, nearly extinct New Zealand reptile similar to an iguana

tu·chun (doo-JOON) *n.*, a warlord of an area in China

tuck·et (TŬK-ĕt) *n.*, an unripened ear of corn

tuck·y (TŬK-ee) *n.*, a common yellow water lily of eastern and central North America that thrives in sluggish water

tuff (TŬF) *n.*, a soft, porous rock formed by the consolidation of volcanic ash and dust

tuft·hun·ter (TŬFT-hŭn-tĕr) *n.*, a pretentious social climber

tu·i (TOO-ee) *n.*, a glossy black-with-white New Zealand honey eater often kept as a cage bird for its parroting ability

tu-la-si (TOO-lă-see) *n.*, an Indian term for the herb basil, believed sacred to the Indian deity Vishnu; also called holy basil

tulle (TOOL) or (TUUL) or (TŬL) *n.*, a sheer, machine-made net mesh of silk, rayon, or nylon used as veiling

tul-nic (TOOL-neek) *n.*, a long, wooden horn used to sound warning signals among Romanian villages

tum-brel or **tum-bril** (TŬM-brĕl) *n.*, a cart or wagon for transporting those sentenced to death to their execution site

tump-line (TĔM-plīn) *n.*, a sling for a backpack made by a strap around the chest or forehead

tum-tum (TŬM-tŭm) *n.*, the repeated plucking of a string

tun (TŬN) *v.*, an archaic term meaning to gulp down in huge swallows

tu-pik or **tu-pek** (TOO-pik) *n.*, an Eskimo summer residence; specifically, a tent made of sealskin

tuque (T(Y)OOK) *n.*, a warm, close-fitting cap made by folding a knitted stocking cap in on itself to double its thickness

tur-ba-ry (TŬR-bă-ree) *n.*, an area of peat accumulation

tur-bi-nate (TŬR-bĭ-năt) or (TŬR-bĭ-nayt) *adj.*, top-shaped

tur-di-form (TŬR-dĭ-fohrm) *adj.*, having the shape of a thrush

turn-ver-ein (TŬRN-vĕ-rīn) or (TŬRN-fĕ-rīn) *n.*, an association founded for the practice of gymnastics and physical exercise

tusche (TUUSH-ĕ) *n.*, a greasy liquid used to capture lithographic ink

tus-sah (TŬ-să) *n.*, an undomesticated Oriental silkworm that produces a coarse, durable brownish silk

tut-ty (TŬ-ti) *n.*, British dialect for a small bunch of flowers

tu-yere (too-YE(Ĕ)R) or (twee-YE(Ĕ)R) or (TWI(E)R) *n.*, a projecting vent that delivers a blast of air to a forge or blast furnace

tuz-zy-muz-zy (TŬ-zee-MŬ-zee) *n.*, an archaic term for a wreath or decorative chain of flowers

twi-bil (TWĪ-bil) or (TWĪ-bĭl) *n.*, English dialect for a hand tool with a hooked blade for harvesting beans

twitch-el (TWICH-ĕl) *n.*, English dialect for a clearing allowing passage between hedges

ty-chism (TĪ-kizĕm) *n.*, a theory that chance is a real factor in the universe

tzi-gane ((t)see-GAHN) *n.*, a member of the itinerant tribe of gypsies

---

\a\ bat \ă\ about \e\ or \è\ check \ĕ\ letter
\é\ cafe \i\fish \ī\ tie \ĭ\ limit \o\ boat
\ŏ\ bacon \u\ sun \ŭ\ helpful \ü\ fool

U

ua-ka-ri (wah-KAH-ree) *n.*, a short-tailed South American monkey with long, silky white or yellow hair

ua-yeb (WĪ-eb) *n.*, a five-day period in the 365-day year of the Mayan dating system

u-bi-e-ty (yoo-BĪ-ĕ-dee) *n.*, an archaic term for the state of being situated

u-dom-e-ter (yoo-DAHM-ĕd-ĕ(r)) *n.*, a device that measures rainfall

ug-gle-some (ŬG-ĕl-sŏm) *adj.*, an archaic term meaning ghastly

uh-lan (OO-lahn) or (YOO-lăn) *n.*, a Tatar lancer in the armies of Europe

uit-land-er (AYT-land-ĕ(r)) *n.*, a foreigner, especially a British settler in the Boer republics of Dutch South Africa

u-le-ma or **u-la-ma** (OO-lĕ-mah) *n.*, a group of Muslim theologians and scholars concerned with Muslim legal theory

u-le-tic (yoo-LED-ik) *adj.*, pertaining to the soft tissue surrounding the teeth

u-lig-i-nous (yoo-LIJ-ĭ-nŭs) *adj.*, growing in sodden or water-logged land

ul-lage (ŬL-ij) *n.*, the weight difference between a container's capacity and its contents

u-lot-ri-chous (yoo-LAHT-rĭ-kŭs) *adj.*, having curly, brittle hair

ul-ti-mo-gen-i-ture (ŭl-tĭ-moh-JEN-i-chŭr) *n.*, an inheritance system in which the youngest is heir

ul-tra-ism (ŬL-tră-izĕm) *n.*, extremism or an extremist act

ul-tra-mon-ta-nism (ŭl-tră-MAHN-tă-nizĕm) *n.*, a Roman Catholic term for the advocacy of an increase in the power of the pope

ul-tra-mun-dane (ŭl-tră-MŬN-dayn) or (ŭl-tră-mŭn-DAYN) *adj.*, positioned beyond the earth or beyond the boundaries of the solar system

ul-tro-ne-ous (ŭl-TROH-nee-ŭs) *adj.*, a Scottish legal term meaning voluntarily offered, as testimony

u-lu-a (oo-LOO-wă) *n.*, a Hawaiian food and sport fish

ul-u-late (ŬL-ŭ-layt) or (YOOL-yu-layt) *v.*, to make a prolonged, mournful sound

um-bles (ŬM-bĕlz) *n.*, the bowels or guts of an animal such as a sheep that are used as food

um-bra-geous (ŭm-BRAY-jŭs) *adj.*, 1. providing shade 2. easily offended

u-mi-ak or **oo-mi-ak** (OO-mee-ak) *n.*, a wooden-framed Eskimo boat covered with skins

u-nau (yoo-NAW) or (YOO-naw) *n.*, a two-toed sloth found in tropical America

un-cial (ŬN-chăl) *n.*, a style of handwriting used in early Greek and Latin manuscripts

un-ci-form (ŭn(t)-sĭ-fohrm) *adj.*, hook-shaped

un-ci-nate (ŬN(T)-sĭ-năt) or (UN(T)-sĭ-nayt) *adj.*, hallucinating flavors or aromas

un-co (ŬNG-koh) *adj.*, a Scottish term meaning incredible; bizarre

un-dec-a-gon (ŭn-DEK-ă-gahn) *n.*, an 11-sided geometric figure

un-der-croft (ŬN-dĕr-crawft) *n.*, an underground room or vault, especially one under a church

un-guic-u-late (ŬNG-gwik-yŭ-lit) or (ŬNG-gwik-yŭ-layt) *adj.*, possessing nails or claws

un-hou-seled (ŭn-HOW-zĕld) *adj.*, an archaic term for not having received the sacrament of Holy Communion

u-nic-i-ty (yoo-NIS-ĭd-ee) or (yoo-NIS-ĭ-tee) *n.*, the state of being one of its kind

u-ni-grav-i-da (yoo-nĭ-GRAV-ĭ-dă) *n.*, a woman pregnant for the first time

un-mew (ŭn-MYOO) *v.*, to liberate

un-par-a-goned (ŭn-PAR-ă-gawnd) *adj.*, unrivaled

un-son-sy (ŭn-SAHN(t)-see) *adj.*, British dialect meaning adverse

un-wemmed (ŭn-WEMD) *adj.*, an obsolete term meaning unstained

u-paith-ric (yoo-PĪTH-rik) *adj.*, roofless

u-pey-gan (oo-PAY-găn) *n.*, the common black rhinoceros

up-po-woc (ŭ-POH-wahk) *n.*, an archaic term for tobacco

u-ra-nism (YUU-ră-nizĕm) *n.*, male homosexuality

u-ra-nol-o-gy (yuu-ră-NAHL-ŏ-jee) *n.*, the study of celestial bodies

ur-ce-o-late (ŬR-see-ŏ-lit) or (ŬR-see-ŏ-layt) *adj.*, urn-shaped

u-ro-lag-ni-a (yuu-roh-LAG-nee-ah) *n.*, sexual arousal associated with urine or urination

u-ro-pyg-i-um (yuur-ŏ-PIJ-ee-ŭm) *n.*, the rear part of a bird's body to which the tail feathers attach

ur-si-form (ŬR-sĭ-fohrm) *adj.*, bear-shaped

ur-ti-cate (ŬRD-ĭ-kayt) *v.*, to produce a temporary, itching rash

ur-ti-ca-tion (ŭrd-ĭ-KAY-shŏn) *n.*, an itchy, prickly sensation

u-ru-bu (UU-rŭ-boo) *n.*, an American black vulture

u-shab-ti (yoo-SHAB-tee) *n.*, a small statue with inscriptions from the Egyptian Book of the Dead that is entombed with a mummy

us-que-baugh or **us-que-bagh** (ŬS-kwĕ-bah) or (ŬS-kwĕ-baw) *n.*, an Irish and Scottish term for distilled liquor

us-tion (ŬS(H)-chŏn) *n.*, the action of burning

us-tu-late (ŬS-chŭ-lit) or (ŬS-chŭ-layt) *adj.*, stained or charred as if scorched

u-su-fruct (YOO-zŭ-frŭkt) or (YOO-sŭ-frŭkt) *n.*, the right to make use of and benefit from something

---

\a\ bat \ā\ about \e\ or \ĕ\ check \ē\ letter
\é\ cafe \i\fish \ī\ tie \ĭ\ limit \o\ boat
\ŏ\ bacon \u\ sun \ŭ\ helpful \ü\ fool

u-vu-la (YOO-vyŭ-lă) *n.*, the small piece of flesh at the back of the mouth that hangs from the soft palate

ux-or-i-cide (ŭk-SOHR-ĭ-sīd) or (ŭg-ZAWR-ĭ-sīd) *n.*, a man who murders his wife

ux-o-ri-lo-cal (ŭk-sohr-ĭ-LOH-kăl) *adj.*, located or centered around the residence of the wife's family or tribe

ux-o-ri-ous (ŭk-SOHR-ee-ŭs) *adj.*, excessively fond of one's wife

vac-ca-ry (VA-kă-ree) *n.*, an area for keeping cows

va-de me-cum (vay-dee-MEE-kum) or (vah-dee-MEE-kum) *n.*, a handy reference guide

va-dose (VAY-dohs) *adj.*, found or located above the water table

va-keel or **va-kil** (vă-KEE(Ĕ)L) *n.*, a legal representative of a politically prominent Indian

val-e-tu-di-nar-i-an (val-i-too-dĭn-ER-ee-ăn) *n.*, a sickly person, especially one mainly concerned with his or her own ill health

val-gus (VAL-gŭs) *n.*, a bodily joint abnormally positioned outward, such as a bowleg or knock-knee

val-late (VA-layt) *adj.*, bordered by a ridge around a depression

vam-brace (VAM-brays) *n.*, a piece of medieval armor that shielded the forearm

van-cou-ri-er (van-KUU-ree-ĕ(r)) *n.*, an early messenger or scout

va-nil-lism (vă-NI-lĭzĕm) *n.*, an itching skin inflammation; also called grocer's itch

va-que-ro (vah-KE-roh) *n.*, a cattle driver

var-i-a (VA(A)-ree-ă) *n.*, miscellaneous things

var-i-o-late (VER-ee-ŏ-layt) or (VER-ee-ŏ-lit) *adj.*, having lesions like those of smallpox

var-i-or-um (ver-ee-OHR-ŭm) *n.*, a classic text with notes written by various scholars

var-so-vi-enne (vahr-soh-VY-en) *n.*, a graceful Polish dance in moderate waltz time

vat-ic (VAD-ik) *adj.*, relating to the ability to predict, as a prophet

vat-i-cide (VAD-ĭ-sīd) *n.*, a person who slays a prophet

va-tic-i-nal (vă-TIS-ĭ-năl) or (va-TIS-ĭ-năl) *adj.*, oracular

vaunt-lay (VAWNT-lay) or (VAHNT-lay) *n.*, in hunting, the release of a new set of hounds before other, pursuing hounds have arrived

vav (VAHV) or (VAWV) *n.*, the sixth letter of the Hebrew alphabet

vel-i-ta-tion (vel-ĭ-TAY-shŏn) *n.*, a minor conflict

ve-li-tes (VEE-li-teez) *n.*, the light infantry of ancient Rome

vel-le-i-ty (vĕ-LEE-ĭd-ee) *n.*, a vague desire

vel-li-cate (VEL-ĭ-kayt) *v.*, to cause a pleasurable physical sensation

ve-lu-ti-nous (vĕ-LOOT-ĭ-nŭs) *adj.*, having a soft, velvety surface

ve-nat-ic (vĕ-NAD-ik) or (vee-NAD-ik) *adj.*, relating to hunting

ven-di-tion (ven-DISH-ŏn) *n.*, the act of exchanging goods for money

ven-e-nif-er-ous (ven-ĕ-NIF-ĕr-ŭs) *adj.*, poisonous, especially by transmitting natural venom

ve-ni-re-man (vĕ-NĪ-ree-măn) *n.*, a member of a jury

ven-tail (VEN-tayl) *n.*, the lower, movable front piece of an armor helmet

ven-tose (VEN-tohs) or (ven-TOHS) *adj.*, an archaic term meaning prone to vain, empty talk

ven-trip-o-tent (ven-TRIP-ŏd-ĕnt) *adj.*, taking a greedy delight in eating

ve-nust (vĕ-NŬST) *adj.*, an archaic term for lovely

ver-bi-cide (VĔR-bĭ-sīd) *n.*, a person who intentionally twists the meaning of a word

ver-big-er-a-tion (vĕr-bij-ĕ-RAY-shŏn) *n.*, the meaningless, verbatim repetition of a phrase, as in schizophrenia

ver-di-gris (VĔR-dĭ-grees) or (VĔR-dĭ-gris) *n.*, a rustlike green or bluish substance that forms on copper, brass, or bronze

ver-e-cund (VER-ĕ-kŭnd) *adj.*, an archaic term meaning coy

ve-rid-i-cal (vĕ-RID-ĭ-kăl) or (vĕ-rid-EEK-ăl) *adj.*, actual and existing

ver-juice (VĔR-joos) *n.*, a general sourness of attitude, expression, or mood

ver-mi-form (VĔR-mĭ-fohrm) *adj.*, worm-shaped

ver-nix (VĔR-niks) *n.*, a protective covering of dead cells and fatty secretions on the skin of a fetus

ver-vel (VĔR-vĕl) or **var-vel** (VAHR-vĕl) *n.*, a ring that attaches a bird's leg to its perch

ver-vet (VĔR-vĕt) *n.*, a long-tailed monkey of southern and eastern Africa

ves-i-cate (VES-ĭ-kayt) *v.*, to blister

ves-per-til-i-an (ves-pĕ(r)-TIL-ee-ăn) *adj.*, batlike

ves-per-tine (VES-pĕ(r)-tīn) or (VES-pĕr-teen) *adj.*, happening in the evening

ves-pine (VE-spīn) or (VE-spĭn) *adj.*, wasplike

vetch (VECH) *n.*, a twining herb grown for soil improvement or livestock feed

vi-at-i-cum (vī-AD-ĭ-kŭm) *n.*, 1. Holy Communion given to a dying person 2. money or supplies for travel

vi-a-tor (vī-AYD-ĕ(r)) *n.*, a person who travels, especially on foot

vib-ri-o (VIB-ree-oh) *n.*, a comma- or S-shaped bacterium that causes disease in humans and animals

vic-e-nar-y (VIS-ĕ-ner-ee) *adj.*, pertaining to or consisting of 20

\a\ bat \ă\ about \e\ or \ĕ\ check \ē\ letter
\ê\ cafe \i\ fish \ī\ tie \ĭ\ limit \o\ boat
\ō\ bacon \u\ sun \ŭ\ helpful \ü\ fool

vic-i-nage (VIS-ĭ-nij) *n.*, 1. the area near to a place 2. the inhabitants of a particular neighborhood

vic-i-nal (VIS-ĭ-năl) *adj.*, relating to or belonging to a neighborhood

vi-de-li-cet (vĭ-DE-lĭ-set) *adv.*, the full spelling of the abbreviation "viz.," meaning namely

vi-du-i-ty (vĭ-D(Y)OO-ĭd-ee) or (vi-DYOO-i-tee) *n.*, the state or period of being a widow

vi-ges-i-mal (vĭ-JES-ĭ-măl) *adj.*, having a counting base of the number 20

vi-gi-a (vĭ-JEE-ă) or (vee-HEE-ă) *n.*, a mark on Spanish nautical charts that indicates a hazardous spot

vi-la-yet (vee-lah-YET) *n.*, a province in Turkey

vil-i-pend (VIL-ĭ-pend) *v.*, to treat as if worthless or trivial

vil-li-form (VIL-ĭ-fohrm) *adj.*, like the nap of velvet

vi-min-e-ous (vi-MIN-ee-ŭs) *adj.*, an obsolete term meaning made of flexible woven twigs

vi-na-ceous (vī-NAY-shŭs) *adj.*, wine-colored

vin-e-gar-roon (vin-ĭ-gă-ROON) *n.*, a nonstinging scorpion of the southern U.S. and Mexico that sprays a vinegary-smelling fluid when bothered

vir-ga (VĬR-gă) *n.*, a meteorological term for rain drops or ice particles that fall from the clouds, but evaporate before reaching the ground

vir-gate (VĬR-găt) or (VĬR-gayt) *n.*, an old English land measurement

vir-gu-late (VĬR-gyŭ-lit) or (VĬR-gyŭ-layt) *adj.*, rod-shaped

vir-tu or **ver-tu** (vĭr-TOO) or (VIR-too) *n.*, a fondness for unusual pieces of art

vis-ca-cha (vi-SKAH-chă) *n.*, a burrowing rodent, similar in size to a ground hog, that is found in parts of Paraguay and Argentina

vi-tel-lus (vī-TEL-ŭs) or (vi-TEL-ŭs) *n.*, an egg yolk

vit-u-line (VICH-ŭ-līn) or (VICH-ŭ-līn) *adj.*, calflike or veal-like

vi-var-i-um (vī-VER-ee-ŭm) *n.*, a place where animals are maintained in an environment like their natural habitat

vi-vip-a-rous (vī-VIP-(ă)-rŭs) *adj.*, 1. a zoological term meaning giving birth to live young; not laying eggs 2. a botanical term meaning sprouting while still on the plant

vi-vi-sep-ul-ture (vi-vĭ-SEP-ŭl-chŭr) *n.*, the act or practice of burying a creature alive

v-lei or **v-laie** (FLAY) or (VLAY) *n.*, a southern African term for a low-lying area that collects water in the wet season

vo-lage (voh-LAZH) *adj.*, inattentive; changeable

vo-la-pük (voh-lă-POOĔK) *n.*, a complicated artificial language based on English and some German, French, and Latin roots, once intended for international use

vol-i-ta-tion (vahl-ĭ-TAY-shŏn) *n.*, flight

vol-ti-geur (vahl-tĭ-ZHĔR) *n.*, a skilled marksman in the the French army

vol-u-crine (VAHL-yŭ-krīn) or (VAHL-yĭ-krĭn) *adj.*, birdlike

vol-vu-lus (VAWL-vyŭ-lŭs) *n.*, a twisted bowel that causes an intestinal obstruction

vom-i-to-ri-um (vahm-ĭ-TOH-ree-úm) *n.*, an opening through the bleachers in a stadium or theater that allows large numbers of people to enter or exit

vous-soir (voo-SWAHR) *n.*, an architectural term for the wedge-shaped piece of an arch or vault

vrille (VRIL) *n.*, the spinning nose dive taken by a plane in a flight maneuver

vr-ow or **vr-ouw** (VR-aw) or (FR-aw) or (FR-oh) *n.*, a form of address for a married Dutch or South African woman

vug (VŬG) or (VUUG) *n.*, a small, hollow, crystal-lined space in a rock or vein of ore

vulned (VŬLND) *adj.*, a term in heraldry meaning injured

vul-pec-u-lar (vŭl-PEK-yŭ-lăr) *adj.*, foxlike

W

wad-dy (WAHD-ee) *n.*, a straight, tapering stick thrown by Australian aborigines on a hunt or in a fight

wad-mal or **wad-mol** (WAHD-măl) *n.*, a heavy, piled woolen fabric used for warm winter clothing in Britain and Scandinavia

wad-set (WAD-set) or (WAHD-set) *v.*, a Scottish legal term meaning a real-estate mortgage that transferred land possession, not title, to the lender

wae-suck (WA-sŭk) *interj.*, a Scottish term used as an expression of sorrow or sympathy

wald-grave (WAWLD-grayv) *n.*, an officer of the Holy Roman Empire who superintended a royal forest

wal-lah (WAH-lă) *n.*, a person connected with a particular line of work

wal-la-roo (wahl-ă-ROO) *n.*, a large, reddish gray kangaroo

walla-walla (WAH-lă-WAH-lă) *n.*, the unintelligible noise made by a crowd

wal-ly-drai-gle (WAY-lee-dray-gĕl) *n.*, a Scottish term for a weak, stunted animal or person

walm (WAHM) *n.*, an obsolete term meaning the sight and sound of a boiling substance

wa-ma-ra (WAH-mă-ră) *n.*, the difficult-to-work-with hardwood of a tree of British Guiana

wam-ble (WAHM-bĕl) *n.*, a stomach grumbling

wame-fou (WAYM-foo) *n.*, a Scottish or English term for a stomach stuffed with food

---

\a\ bat \ă\ about \e\ or \ĕ\ check \ē\ letter
\é\ cafe \i\fish \ī\ tie \ĭ\ limit \o\ boat
\ŏ\ bacon \u\ sun \ŭ\ helpful \ü\ fool

wam-pus (WAHM-pŭs) *n.*, an odd, unnatural person or thing

wan-der-oo (WAHN-dĕ-roo) *n.*, an Asian monkey with purplish brown skin on its face

wan-dle (WAN-dĕl) *adj.*, a Scottish term meaning lithe or nimble

wan-i-gan (WAH-nĭ-găn) *n.*, a transportable shelter mounted on wheels, tracks, or floats for easy towing

wan-ion (WAHN-yŏn) *n.*, an archaic term for a scourge

wap-pen-schaw (WAP-pĕn-shaw) *n.*, a military parade of arms once regularly held in each Scottish district

war-a-tah or **war-ra-tau** (WAWR-ă-taw) or (WAWR-ă-tah) *n.*, an Australian shrub with clusters of crimson or scarlet flowers

wark (WAWRK) *n.*, a British term for an ache or pain

war-mouth (WAWR-mowth) *n.*, a freshwater sunfish found in the eastern U.S.

war-ple (WAWR-pĕl) *v.*, a Scottish term meaning to squirm

war-ri-gal or **war-ra-gal** (WAWR-ĭ-găl) *n.*, an Australian term for a wild dog; also called a dingo

war-saw (WAWR-saw) *n.*, a grouper of the western Pacific that is among the largest of fish; also called spotted jewfish

wash-brew (WASH-broo) or (WAHSH-broo) *n.*, English dialect for oatmeal boiled to a stiff jelly

watch-et (WAWCH-ĕt) or (WAHCH-ĕt) *n.*, a light blue color

waught (WAHKT) *v.*, a Scottish term meaning to drink freely and enthusiastically

wave-son (WAYV-sŏn) *n.*, items that float on the water following a shipwreck

wayz-goose (WAYZ-goos) *n.*, an annual picnic or party for a group of printers

web-ster (WEB-ztĕ(r)) *n.*, an archaic term for a person who makes cloth by weaving

ween (WEEN) *v.*, an archaic term meaning to guess; to think

wel-kin (WEL-kĭn) *n.*, the celestial sphere

wem (WEM) *n.*, an archaic term for a blemish

wen (WEN) *n.*, a cyst resulting from an obstructed gland below the skin surface

werf (VERF) *n.*, a southern African term for the area adjoining the farm house and barns

wer-gild (WĔR-gild) *n.*, an Anglo-Saxon legal term for the cash value of a man's life

weth-er (WETH-ĕ(r)) *n.*, a male sheep neutered as a lamb

whal-ly ((H)WAW-lee) *adj.*, having a light-colored area surrounding the pupil of the eye

whang-doo-dle ((h)wang-DOO-dĕl) *n.*, a person who eagerly attacks things he or she dislikes

wharf-in-ger ((H)WAW(R)F-ĭn-jĕ(r)) *n.*, a person or company that operates a marine facility for accommodating freighters and their goods

whaup ((H)WAHP) *n.*, British dialect for a European migratory bird with long legs and a downward-curving bill

whee-ple ((H)WEE-pĕl) *v.*, British dialect meaning to make a long, shrill cry

whelk (HWELK) *n.*, a large sea snail valued as food in Europe

whem-mel or **whem-mle** ((H)WEM-ĕl) *v.*, a Scottish term meaning to tip over or upend

whew-er ((H)WOO-ĕr) or (HYOO-ĕr) *n.*, English dialect for a freshwater duck; also called a widgeon

whick-er (HWIK-ĕ(r)) *v.*, to make the low, prolonged call of a horse

whif-fet (HWIF-ĕt) *n.*, 1. a lap-sized dog 2. a small, insignificant person

whig-ma-lee-ry (hwig-mă-LI-ree) *n.*, a spontaneous idea or wish

whil-ly-whas or **whil-ly-whaws** ((H)WIL-i-(h)waws) *n.*, a Scottish term for a persuasive, misleading speech

whi-lom (HWĪ-lŏm) *adv.*, an archaic term for a while ago

whit-tret ((H)WIT-trĕt) *n.*, a Scottish term for a weasel

whort (HWĔRT) *n.*, a sweet European blueberry

whyd-ah (HWID-ă) *n.*, a canary-sized African weaverbird with long, drooping tail feathers

wick-i-up (WIK-ee-ŭp) *n.*, a hut in the shape of a teepee built of grass or brushwood mats by nomadic Indians of the arid west and southwestern United States

wic-o-py (WIK-ŏ-pee) *n.*, a small tree with hardy, flexible stems; also called leatherwood

wid-di-fow (WID-i-foo) *n.*, a Scottish term for a person evil enough to swing from the gallows

wid-dy (WID-i) *n.*, a Scottish term for a rope made of willow branches

wid-geon (WI-jĕn) *n.*, an obsolete term for a silly person

wig-an (WIG-ăn) *n.*, a stiff, canvaslike cotton fabric used as interlining

wight (WĪT) *n.*, a living creature

wink-le-hawk (WING-kĕl-hawk) *n.*, a fabric tear in the shape of an L

winze (WINZ) *n.*, a nearly vertical channel between one mine area and another at a lower level

wir-ra (WI-ră) *interj.*, an Irish term used as an expression of sorrow or sympathy

with-er-shins (WITH-ĕ(r)-shinz) *adv.*, in a direction different from or contrary to the natural one

with-er-nam (WITH-ĕ(r)-NAHM) *n.*, the act of seizing as a means of reprisal

with-y (WITH-ee) *n.*, a pliant, supple branch

wit-tol (WID-ŏl) *n.*, an archaic term for a man who knowingly tolerates his wife's infidelities

woad (WOHD) *n.*, a dark blue color

\a\ bat \ă\ **a**bout \e\ or \ĕ\ check \ĕ\ letter
\ē\ caf**e** \i\fish \ĭ\ tie \ī\ limit \o\ b**o**at
\ŏ\ bac**on** \u\ s**u**n \ŭ\ help**fu**l \ū\ f**oo**l

woad-wax-en (WOHD-waks-ĕn) *n.*, a yellow-flowered shrub from Europe and Asia that is considered a weed in England

woald (WOHLD) *n.*, a European herb cultivated for its yellow dye; also called dyer's rocket

wob-be-gong (WAHB-ee-gahng) *n.*, an Australian term for the flat-bodied, mottle-skinned carpet shark

wom-me-ra (WAHM-ĕ-rä) *n.*, a device for throwing a dart or stick used by Australian aborigines

wong (WAHNG) *n.*, an obsolete term for a grassland

wong-a-wong-a (WAHNG-ă-WAHNG-ă) *n.*, a large, pale-fleshed Australian pigeon

won-ky (WAHN-kee) *adj.*, a British term meaning amiss; faulty

woon or **wun** (WOON) *n.*, a regional administrator in Burma

woo-ra-li (woo-RAH-lee) *n.*, the poisonous substance curare that is used by some Indians as a coating for the tips of their arrows

wootz (WOOTS) *n.*, a steel made in ancient India by the oldest known steel-making process

wor-mil (WAWR-mil) *n.*, a lump containing warble-fly larva that is found on the skin of an animal's back

wor-ri-cow (WŎR-i-koo) *n.*, a Scottish term for a dreaded, malicious, and imaginary being like the devil

woun-dy (WOON-dee) *adj.*, English dialect meaning in the highest degree; to the greatest extent

wowf (WOWF) *adj.*, a Scottish term meaning frenzied

wow-ser (WOW-zĕ(r)) *n.*, an Australian term for a puritanical person who strongly opposes minor vices

wrap-ras-cal (RAP-ras-kăl) *n.*, a long, loose overcoat popular in the 18th century

wud (WUUD) *adj.*, a Scottish term meaning mentally ill

wy-lie-coat (WĪ-li-koht) *n.*, a Scottish term for a woman's or a child's nightshirt

wyte (WĪT) *n.*, a Scottish term for the moral obligation for a mistake or injury

wy-vern (WĪ-vĕ(r)n) *n.*, an imaginary creature in the shape of a two-winged dragon

xan-the-las-ma (zan(t)-the*-LAZ-mä) *n.*, a flat, yellowish tumor appearing on the upper and lower eyelids

xan-tho-chroid (ZAN-thŏ-kroid) *adj.*, relating to light-haired, fair-skinned persons

xan-tho-derm (ZAN-thŏ-dĕrm) *n.*, a person of a yellow-skinned race

xan-tho-mel-a-nous (XAN(T)-thoh-mel-ă-nŭs) *adj.*, characterized by yellow- or olive-toned skin and black hair

xat (KAHT) *n.*, a carved-pole memorial to the dead erected by some western North American Indians

xe-bec (ZEE-bek) *n.*, a Mediterranean sailing ship with an overhanging bow and stern

xe-ni-um (ZEE-nee-ŭm) *n.*, a gift presented to a guest or stranger by the ancient Greeks and Romans

xen-o-do-che-um (zen-ŏ-dŏ-KEE-ŭm) *n.*, an inn or hostel for travelers in ancient Greece

xe-ric (SI-rik) *adj.*, an environmental term meaning too dry to support plant life

xe-roph-a-gy (zĕ-RAHF-ă-jee) *n.*, a strict Lenten fast observed in the Eastern Church

xe-roph-o-bous (ze-RAHF-ŏ-bŭs) *adj.*, a botanical term meaning almost incapable of resisting drought

xi (ZĪ) *n.*, the 14th letter in the Greek alphabet

xi-phoid (ZĪ-foid) *adj.*, sword-shaped

xi-phop-a-gus (zĕ-FAHP-ă-gŭs) *n.*, an abnormal animal twinning in which the individuals are joined at the bottom of the breastbone

xiph-os-u-ran (zif-ŏ-SUU-răn) *adj.*, a horseshoe or king crab

xy-log-ly-phy (zī-LAHG-lĕ-fee) *n.*, artistic wood carving

xy-log-ra-phy (zī-LAHG-ră-fee) *n.*, the process of cutting a pattern on the end grain of wood for use on a letterpress surface

xy-lo-man-cy (ZĪ-lŏ-man(t)-see) *n.*, predicting the future by using wood

xys-ter (ZIS-tĕr) *n.*, a surgical tool used for scraping bones

xys-tus (ZIS-tŭs) *n.*, a long, open, porchlike area used by ancient Greek and Roman athletes for winter exercise

Y

yaff (YAF) *v.*, a Scottish term meaning to make the loud, sharp sounds of a dog

yaf-fin-gale (YAF-ĭn-gayl) *n.*, English dialect for a large European woodpecker with green plumage and a red head

yaf-fle (YAF-ĕl) *n.*, U.S. dialect for a load that the arm can carry

yair (YA(A)(Ē)R) *n.*, a Scottish term for a trap for salmon catching at low tide

---

\a\ **bat** \ă\ **about** \e\ or \è\ **check** \ē\ **letter**
\ê\ **cafe** \i\ **fish** \ī\ **tie** \ĭ\ **limit** \o\ **boat**
\ŏ\ **bacon** \u\ **sun** \ŭ\ **helpful** \ü\ **fool**

yak-a-mik (YAK-ă-mik) *n.*, a large, easily domesticated South American bird similar to the crane, often kept to protect poultry

ya-pok (yă-PAHK) *n.*, a South American aquatic opossum

yar-ak (YAR-ak) *n.*, a falconry term for a physical state suitable for strong and steady flight

yar-dang (YAHR-dahng) *n.*, a sharp ridge formed by wind erosion

yash-mak (yahsh-MAHK) *n.*, a veil worn by Muslim women that covers their faces, leaving only their eyes exposed

yat-a-ghan (YAD-ă-gan) *n.*, a long knife or short sword with a double-curved edge common among Muslims

yat-ter (YAD-ĕ(r)) *n.*, small talk

yaud (YAWD) *n.*, a Scottish term for a female horse of breeding age

yauld (YAWL(D)) *adj.*, a Scottish term meaning robust

yau-pon (YOO-pahn) *n.*, a southern U.S. holly whose leaves can be substituted for tea

ya-ya (yah-YAH) *n.*, a gum-producing tree of Panama

yean (YEEN) *v.*, to give birth to lambs or kids

yegg (YEG) *n.*, a person who breaks into a safe to steal its contents

yeld (YELD) *n.*, a cow not giving milk because of age or calfing

yelm (YELM) *n.*, English dialect for a quantity of bound, combed straw used for thatching

yes-treen (ye-STREEN) *n.*, a Scottish term for yesterday evening

yet-ling (YET-lĭng) *n.*, a Scottish term for an alloy of iron, carbon, and silicon shaped in a mold; also called cast iron

yett (YET) *n.*, a Scottish term for a movable, hinged entrance through a fence

yeuk (YOOK) *n.*, a Scottish term for a prickling sensation or itch

yirr (YER) *v.*, a Scottish term meaning to make the snarling sound of a dog

ylang-ylang (EE-lahng-EE-lahng) *n.*, an aromatic tree from the Philippines whose fragrant flowers and oils are used in making perfume

ylem (Ī-lĕm) *n.*, the first substance from which all other elements were formed

y-nam-bu (ee-nahm-BOO) *n.*, a very large bird of southern Brazil and Argentina

yod (YAWD) *n.*, the 10th letter of the Hebrew alphabet that corresponds to Y

yoicks (YOIKS) *interj.*, an archaic term used to encourage the hounds in a hunt

yo-ni (YOH-nee) *n.*, a symbolic figure that represents the female genitals

youn-ker (YŎNG-kĕ(r)) *n.*, a youth

y-per-ite (EE-pĕ-rīt) *n.*, a blistering poison gas used in warfare; also called mustard gas

yu-an (YOO-ăn) *n.*, the unit of currency in China

yuft (YUUFT) *n.*, a Russian leather naturally protected from insects by the odd-smelling birch-tar oil used in curing

Z

za-ba-glio-ne ((d)zah-bĕl-YOH-nee) *n.*, a custardlike dessert of eggs, sugar, and wine or fruit juice

za-bra (ZAH-brǎ) or (SAH-brǎ) *n.*, a small sailing ship used by Spain in the 16th and 17th centuries

zac-a-ton (ZAK-ǎ-tohn) *n.*, a tough, wiry grass found in dry regions of the United States

zad-dik (TSAHD-ik) *n.*, a just and virtuous person

zaf-fer (ZAF-ĕ(r)) *n.*, a chemical compound used to produce a blue color in glass and enamel

za-kus-ka (ze-KUUS-kǎ) *n.*, an appetizer or canape

za-mar-ra (zǎ-MAHR-ǎ) *n.*, a coat made of sheepskin and worn by Spanish shepherds

za-min-dar (zǎ-MEEN-dahr) *n.*, an Indian revenue collector during Muslim rule

zan-der (ZAN-dĕ(r)) *n.*, a fish of central Europe related to the pike

zan-za (ZAN-zǎ) *n.*, an African musical instrument played by plucking metal bars that resonate into a wooden box

za-pa-teo (zah-pǎ-TAY-oh) *n.*, a Spanish dance that incorporates a rhythmic stamping or tapping step

zap-ti-ah (zǎp-TEE-ah) *n.*, a Turkish police officer

za-re-ba (zǎ-REE-bǎ) *n.*, a stockade improvised from thorn bushes for defense in parts of Africa

zarf (ZAHRF) *n.*, an ornamental metal holder for a handleless coffee cup

zar-zue-la (zahrz-WAY-lǎ) *n.*, a comic Spanish opera with spoken dialogue

zax (ZAKS) *n.*, a hatchetlike tool that cuts and punches holes in roofing slate

za-yin (ZAH-yǐn) *n.*, the seventh letter of the Hebrew alphabet

ze-brass (ZEE-bras) *n.*, the hybrid offspring of an ass and a zebra

ze-bru-la (ZEE-brŭ-lǎ) *n.*, the docile, disease-resistant offspring of a zebra and a female horse

ze-bu (ZEE-byoo) *n.*, a domesticated Asian ox used as a draft animal and food source

ze-bub (ZEE-bŭb) *n.*, a large, two-winged fly of Ethiopia

zec-chi-no (ze-KEE-noh) *n.*, an old gold coin of Italy and Turkey

zem-mi (ZEM-ee) *n.*, a large mole rat of eastern Europe

\a\ bat \ă\ about \e\ or \è\ check \ĕ\ letter
\é\ cafe \i\ fish \ī\ tie \ĭ\ limit \o\ boat
\ŏ\ bacon \u\ sun \ŭ\ helpful \ü\ fool

zem-stvo (ZEMST-voh) *n.*, a Russian local council founded in 1864 to replace the authority of the nobles

zeug-ma (ZOOG-mă) *n.*, a figure of speech in which a modifying word is applied in different senses to two or more words

zib-el-ine (ZIB-ĕ-leen) *n.*, a decorative clothes trimming made from the fur of a sable

zib-et (ZIB-ĕt) *n.*, the civet cat of Asia

zig-gu-rat (ZIG-ŭ-rat) *n.*, an ancient, pyramidal temple of Babylon built in stepped tiers with a shrine at the top

zil-lah (ZIL-ă) *n.*, an Indian administrative division

zin-co-graphy (ZING-kah-gră-fee) *n.*, the art of engraving on zinc plates for printing

zin-diq (zin-DEEK) *n.*, a heretic in opposition to Islam

zin-ga-ro (TSEENG-gah-roh) *n.*, an old Italian term for a gypsy man

zin-ke (ZING-kĕ) or **zink** (ZINK) *n.*, a Renaissance woodwind of wood or ivory that accompanied choral music

zo-an-thro-py (zoh-AN(T)-thrŏ-pee) *n.*, a hysterical obsession in which a person imagines himself a beast

zo-et-ic (zoh-ED-ik) *adj.*, having life; alive

zo-e-a (zoh-EE-a) *n.*, an early stage in the life cycle of some crabs

zo-lot-nik (zah-lŏt-NEEK) or (zah-lŏt-NIK) *n.*, a Russian weight

zon-da (ZON-dă) *n.*, a hot, oppressive north wind of South America

zoo-mor-phism (zoh-ŏ-MOHR-fizĕm) *n.*, a conceptualization of god or the gods that uses animal forms or characteristics

zo-on (ZOH-ahn) *n.*, the offspring produced from a single, fertilized egg

zo-o-pho-bi-a (ZOH-ŏ-foh-bee-ă) *n.*, an abnormal fear of animals

zo-o-prax-i-scope (zoh-ŏ-PRAKS-ĭ-skohp) *n.*, an early motion-picture projector

zo-o-tech-ny (ZOH-ŏ-tek-nee) *n.*, the science of maintaining and improving the desirable qualities of domesticated animals

zo-ot-o-my (zoh-AHD-ŏ-mee) *n.*, animal dissection

zoo-zoo (ZOO-zoo) *n.*, English dialect for a common European pigeon

zo-pho-rus (ZOH-fŏr-ŭs) *n.*, an ornamental band with carved or painted representations of men or animals

zop-pa (TSAH-pă) *adj.*, a musical term meaning having a shifting, accented beat

zo-ri (ZAWR-ee) *n.*, a low, flat Japanese sandal kept on the foot by a thong between toes

zor-il (ZAWR-il) *n.*, an easily tamed, weasel-like African animal about the size of a ferret

zo-ril-lo (zŏ-RI-loh) *n.*, a foul-smelling tropical American shrub that provides a headache remedy

zor-tzi-co (zaw(r)-SEE-koh) *n.*, a Basque melody in 5/8 time

zos-ter (ZOS-tĕr) *n.*, an acute inflammation of the spinal and cranial nerves in which painful blisters form on the skin

zuc-chet-to (zoo-KED-oh) *n.*, a small, close-fitting cap worn by Roman Catholic clergymen

zug-zwang (TSOOK-tsfahng) *n.*, a chess situation in which only damaging moves are left to a player

zum-boo-ruk (zem-BOO-rŭk) *n.*, a small cannon mounted on a swivel and fired from a stand on a camel's back

zy-go-mor-phic (ZĪ-gŏ-mawr-fik) *adj.*, symmetrical on each side

zy-mol-o-gy (zi-MAHL-ŏ-jee) *n.*, the study of fermentation and enzyme action

zy-mot-ic (zi-MAHD-ik) *adj.*, infectious; contagious

zy-mur-gy (ZĪ-mŭr-jee) *n.*, the applied chemistry of fermentation processes such as wine making

zy-thum (ZĪ-thŭm) *n.*, a fermented beverage brewed in ancient times

\a\ bat \ä\ about \e\ or \è\ check \ĕ\ letter
\é\ cafe \i\fish \ī\ tie \i̇\ limit \o\ boat
\ŏ\ bacon \u\ sun \ŭ\ helpful \ü\ fool

Score Card

Player	Word																				Total
	1	2	3	4	5	6	7	8	9	10	11	12	13	14	15	16	17	18	19	20	

Points: For detailed information on scoring, see p. 3.

Initials: _____ # Definitions **Number:** _____

Word: _____

Definition: _____

_____

_____

_____

_____

_____

_____

_____

Initials: _____ # Ballot

Word: _____

Definitions: (key phrases) check one

☐ 1 _____

☐ 2 _____

☐ 3 _____

☐ 4 _____

☐ 5 _____

☐ 6 _____

☐ 7 _____

☐ 8 _____

☐ 9 _____

☐ 10 _____

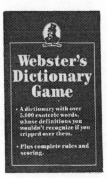

Webster's Dictionary Game
by Wilbur Webster

Dictionary Game fans will love this wacky word game invented by the black sheep of the famous dictionary family. Includes a special dictionary of over 5,000 esoteric words. **$5.95**

Ordering #: 6030

The Best Baby Shower Book
by Courtney Cooke

Who says baby showers have to be dull? Finally, a contemporary guide for planning baby showers that's chock-full of helpful hints, recipes, decorating ideas and activities that are fun without being juvenile. **$4.95**

Ordering #: 1239

The Best Wedding Shower Book
by Courtney Cooke

The contemporary guide for planning wedding showers. Contains time- and money-saving ideas for decorating and food; innovative gifts; and fun creative games! **$4.95**

Ordering #: 6059

Mother Murphy's Law
by Bruce Lansky

The wit of Bombeck and the wisdom of Murphy are combined in this collection of 325 laws that detail the perils and pitfalls of parenthood. Cartoon illustrations by Christine Tripp. **$2.95**

Ordering #: 1149

Mother Murphy's 2nd Law
by Bruce Lansky

A ribald collection of laws about love, sex, marriage and other skirmishes in the battle of the sexes. Mother Murphy offers rib-tickling advice to singles, marrieds and the divorced that they won't find in marriage and sex manuals. **$2.95**

Ordering #: 4010

Grandma Knows Best
by Mary McBride

Mary McBride instructs grandmas who have been stuck with baby-sitting how to "scheme, lie, cheat, and threaten so you'll be thought of as a sweet, darling grandma." **$4.95**

Ordering #· 4009

David, We're Pregnant!
by Lynn Johnston
101 laughing-out-loud cartoons about the humorous side of having a baby by the creator of the "For Better or Worse" comic strip. $3.95
Ordering #: 1049

Hi Mom! Hi Dad!
by Lynn Johnston
101 cartoons about the funny things that happen to parents of infants. $3.95
Ordering #: 1139

Do They Ever Grow Up?
by Lynn Johnston
A hilarious, 101-cartoon survival guide for parents of the tantrum and pre-school set. **$3.95**
Ordering #: 1089

Wordplay
by Charles Thiesen and
Deanna King

A stimulating alternative to
run-of-the-mill activity books
that turns kids 8-14 into
budding writers by: making
up plots and secret codes,
inventing tongue twisters,
creating cartoons, and
more. **$4.95**

Ordering #: 2200

Successful Dieting Tips
by Bruce Lansky

Over 1,000 proven ideas in an
easy-to-read format that helps die-
ters stick to any diet. **$2.95(was
$4.95)**

Ordering #: 6010

The Traveler's Guide to
European Customs and
Manners
by Nancy Braganti and Elizabeth
Devine

How to get along with Europeans;
how to converse, live, tip, drive, make
friends and conduct business while in
Europe. The best-selling book of its
kind. **$6.95**

Ordering #: 5080

ORDER FORM

Qty.	Book Title	Author	Price
_____	**Best Baby Shower Book, The**	Cooke, C.	$ 4.95
_____	**David, We're Pregnant!**	Johnston, L.	$ 3.95
_____	**Do They Ever Grow Up?**	Johnston, L.	$ 3.95
_____	**European Customs and Manners**	Braganti/Devine ...	$ 6.95
_____	**Grandma Knows Best**	McBride, M.	$ 4.95
_____	**Hi Mom! Hi Dad!**	Johnston, L.	$ 3.95
_____	**Mother Murphy's Law**	Lansky, B.	$ 2.95
_____	**Mother Murphy's 2nd Law**	Lansky, B.	$ 2.95
_____	**Successful Dieting Tips**	Lansky, B.	$ 2.95
_____	**Webster's Dictionary Game**	Webster, W.	$ 5.95
_____	**Wedding Shower**	Cooke, C.	$ 4.95
_____	**Wordplay**	Thiesen, C.	$ 4.95

Please send me copies of the books checked above. I am enclosing $ _____ which covers the full amount per book shown above plus $1.00 for postage and handling for the first book and $.50 for each additional book. (Add $2.00 to total for postage and handling for books shipped to Canada. Overseas postage and handling will be billed. MN residents add 6% sales tax.) Allow up to four weeks for delivery. Quantity discounts available upon request.

Send check or money order to Meadowbrook, Inc. No cash or C.O.D.s, please.

For purchases over $10.00, you may use VISA or MasterCard (order by mail or phone). For these orders we need information below.

Charge to: ☐ VISA ☐ MasterCard

Account # _____

Expiration Date _____

Card Signature _____

Send Book(s) to:

Name _____

Address _____

City _____ State _____ Zip _____

Mail order to: Book Orders, Meadowbrook, Inc., 18318 Minnetonka Blvd., Deephaven, MN 55391, Phone orders: Toll Free (800) 338-2232.